6th Workshop on Challenges and Applications of Automated Extraction of Socio-political Events from Text (CASE 2023)

Varna, Bulgaria
7 September 2023

ISBN: 978-1-7138-9047-8

Printed from e-media with permission by:

Curran Associates, Inc.
57 Morehouse Lane
Red Hook, NY 12571

Some format issues inherent in the e-media version may also appear in this print version.

Association for Computational Linguistics
209 N. Eighth Street
Stroudsburg, Pennsylvania 18360

Phone: 1-570-476-8006
Fax: 1-570-476-0860

acl@aclweb.org

Additional copies of this publication are available from:

Curran Associates, Inc.
57 Morehouse Lane
Red Hook, NY 12571 USA
Phone: 845-758-0400
Fax: 845-758-2633
Email: curran@proceedings.com
Web: www.proceedings.com

CASE 2023

Proceedings of the 6th Workshop on Challenges and Applications of Automated Extraction of Socio-political Events from Text

associated with

The 14th International Conference on Recent Advances in Natural Language Processing RANLP'2023

7 September, 2023
Varna, Bulgaria

WORKSHOP ON CHALLENGES AND APPLICATIONS OF AUTOMATED EXTRACTION OF SOCIO-POLITICAL EVENTS FROM TEXT
ASSOCIATED WITH THE INTERNATIONAL CONFERENCE
RECENT ADVANCES IN
NATURAL LANGUAGE PROCESSING'2023

PROCEEDINGS

7 September 2023
Varna, Bulgaria

Designed by INCOMA Ltd.
Shoumen, BULGARIA

Preface

The CASE 2023 workshop consists of regular papers, three keynotes (one social science and two computer science oriented), working papers of shared task participants, and shared task overview papers. This workshop series has brought together all aspects of event information collection across technical and social science fields. In addition to contributing to the progress in text-based event extraction, the workshop provides a space for organizing a multimodal event information collection task. Many aspects of event information modeling and collection are reported in the scope of CASE 2023. Hosting a shared task that is on multimodal problem and having submissions in minority languages such as in Bulgarian are distinguishing aspects of this edition. The shared tasks advance the field in terms comparing manually and automatically created event datasets, multimodal hate event detection, and event causality detection.

The CASE 2023 Organisers

Organization committee:

Ali Hürriyetoğlu (KNAW Humanities Cluster DHLab)
Hristo Tanev (European Commission, Joint Research Centre)
Erdem Yörük (Koc University)
Fiona Anting Tan (University of Singapore)
Benjamin Radford (University of North Carolina at Charlotte)
Peratham Wiriyathammabhum (no institution)
Tadashi Nomoto (National Institute of Japanese Literature)
Surendrabikram Thapa (Virginia Tech)
Jaap Kamps (University of Amsterdam)
Sneha Mehta (Virginia Tech)
Stoehr Niklas (ETH Zurich)
Kumari Neha (IIIT Delhi)
Milena Slavcheva (IICT, Bulgarian Academy of Sciences)
Pasquale Lisena (EURECOM)
Guneet Singh Kohli (Thapar Institute of Engineering and Technology)
Guneet Singh Kohli (International Institute of Information Technology Hyderabad (IIIT-H))
Onur Uca (Mersin University)
Nelleke Oostdijk (Radboud University)
Hansi Hettiarachchi (Birmingham City University)
Francielle Vargas (University of São Paulo)
Brendan O'connor (University of Massachusetts Amherst)
Farhana Ferdousi Liza (University of East Anglia)

Programme Committee:

Andrew Halterman (Michigan State University)
Giuseppe Tirone (European Commission, Joint Research Centre)
Osman Mutlu (Koc University)
Tadashi Nomoto (National Institute of Japanese Literature)
Hristo Tanev (European Commission, Joint Research Centre)
Onur Uca (Mersin University)
Peratham Wiriyathammabhum (no institution)
Marijn Schraagen (Utrecht University)
Gaurav Singh (S&P Global)
Fiona Anting Tan (University of Singapore)
Surendrabikram Thapa (Virginia Tech)
Alexandra DeLucia (Johns Hopkins University)
Kumari Neha (Indraprastha Institute of Information Technology Delhi)
Maria Eskevich (Huygens Institute)
Guanqun Yang (Stevens Institute of Technology)
Cagri Toraman (Aselsan, Turkey)
Debanjana Kar (IBM)
Man Luo (Arizona State University)

Nelleke Oostdijk (Radboud University)
Hansi Hettiarachchi (Birmingham City University)

Table of Contents

Classifying Organized Criminal Violence in Mexico using ML and LLMs

Javier Osorio
School of Government and Public Policy
University of Arizona
josorio1@arizona.edu

Juan Vásquez
Department of Computer Science
University of Colorado Boulder
juan.vasquez-1@colorado.edu

Abstract

Natural Language Processing (NLP) tools have been rapidly adopted in political science for the study of conflict and violence. In this paper, we present an application to analyze various lethal and non-lethal events conducted by organized criminal groups and state forces in Mexico. Based on a large corpus of news articles in Spanish and a set of high-quality annotations, the application evaluates different Machine Learning (ML) algorithms and Large Language Models (LLMs) to classify documents and individual sentences, and to identify specific behaviors related to organized criminal violence and law enforcement efforts. Our experiments support the growing evidence that BERT-like models achieve outstanding classification performance for the study of organized crime. This application amplifies the capacity of conflict scholars to provide valuable information related to important security challenges in the developing world.

1 Introduction

Recent advancements in Natural Language Processing (NLP) have revolutionized political science analyses by enabling efficient and accurate analysis of large volumes of text. These tools have demonstrated impressive capabilities in tackling complex text analysis tasks, leading to their increasing adoption by political scientists including conflict scholars specialized in the study of violence and crime (Hu et al., 2022; Halterman et al., 2023b,a; Hürriyetoğlu et al., 2022; Motlicek, 2023). In this paper, we present an application of various Machine Learning (ML) algorithms and Large Language Models (LLMs) to analyze a variety of behaviors by organized criminal groups in Mexico by processing text written in Spanish.

By leveraging these state-of-the-art NLP techniques, we aim to make significant contributions to the study of organized criminal violence and law enforcement efforts in developing countries. Based on a set of high-quality annotations, we train and evaluate different ML algorithms and LLMs to determine their effectiveness in detecting and categorizing organized crime violence and law enforcement. Furthermore, we extend our analysis beyond simple document-level classification by analyzing the relevance of specific sentences within documents and then analyzing the specific types of events described in the narratives. In this way, we move beyond the identification of organized criminal groups as named entities (Osorio and Beltrán, 2020; Coscia and Rios, 2012; Signoret et al., 2021), and focus on analyzing criminal behaviors.

Results show the high levels of performance of BERT-like models to effectively classify relevant news articles, as well as relevant sentences within them. The models also have remarkable results for classifying a variety of violent and non-violent actions perpetrated by criminal groups or conducted by law enforcement forces.

Overall, our research emphasizes the advantages of leveraging NLP tools in political science research, particularly in the domain of political violence and organized crime analysis. By exploiting their remarkable capabilities for document, sentence, and class classification, researchers can extract valuable insights from vast corpora in local languages, thus enabling a more comprehensive understanding of complex social behaviors. The elements advanced in this research can pave the way toward the development of a fully integrated ML crime analysis system in Spanish.

2 Recent Developments

NLP researchers have advanced various supervised learning and deep-learning architectures to address a variety of text analysis challenges (Thangaraj and Sivakami, 2018; Minaee et al., 2021). Due to the complexities of analyzing unstructured text, rule-based developments showed limited performance when tackling complex NLP tasks until the emer-

Proceedings of the 6th Workshop on Challenges and Applications of Automated Extraction of Socio-political Events from Text, pages 1–10, Varna, Bulgaria, Sep 7, 2023.
https://doi.org/10.26615/978-954-452-089-2_001

gence of pre-trained language models. In particular, Google's Bidirectional Encoder Representations from Transformers (BERT) language model (Devlin et al., 2019) became a game-changer in a variety of NLP tasks. After BERT's initial development in English, Google released multilingual BERT (mBERT). Political scientists quickly noted these NLP tools and applied them to a variety of tasks relevant to political analysis (Kowsari et al., 2019; Rodriguez and Spirling, 2022; Terechshenko et al., 2020; Lowe and Benoit, 2013; Rudkowsky et al., 2018; Häffner et al., 2023).

Computerized text analysis has a long trajectory in the study of international conflict, but recent ML developments are just gaining traction among conflict scholars. Early efforts to identify incidents of political conflict or cooperation using text analysis relied on complex systems of rules (Schrodt et al., 2010; Schrodt and Van Brackel, 2013; Boschee et al., 2016; Ward et al., 2013; Osorio and Reyes, 2017; Osorio et al., 2019). Unfortunately, these rule-based systems are too rigid and expensive to update, and the algorithms showed limited performance when tackling even basic NLP tasks.

Due to the limitations of rule-based approaches, recent NLP developments such as ConfliBERT (Hu et al., 2022) and POLECAT (Halterman et al., 2023b,a) bring more flexibility and effectiveness in analyzing political violence. Unfortunately, those tools are focused exclusively on the English language. To address this challenge, scholars such as Hürriyetoğlu et al. (2022), Caselli et al. (2021), and Yang et al. (2023) have been advancing multilingual ML tools and LLM to study conflict.

Within this constellation of research, scholars have been using NLP tools to study organized crime in Mexico by processing text written in Spanish. Early efforts relied on rule-based approaches to track the territorial presence of organized criminal groups (Osorio and Reyes, 2017; Osorio, 2015; Coscia and Rios, 2012; Signoret et al., 2021). A common limitation of these studies is their exclusive focus on tracking the location of criminal groups. Unfortunately, this only provides information about "who" is present but does not say much about their behavior. Although (Osorio and Beltrán, 2020) and (Parolin et al., 2021) have been incorporating ML approaches to study organized crime, these ML applications have only focused on a narrow set of behaviors. To address these limitations, this study provides a fully integrated ML application to identify a broad range of behavioral trends of criminal groups and state authorities from news stories written in Spanish.

3 Training Data

Computational social scientists have paid increasing attention to the quality of training data annotations (Grimmer and Stewart, 2013; Hsueh et al., 2009; Erlich et al., 2022; Krommyda et al., 2021). Due to the need for high-quality annotations to maximize ML performance, this study implements a rigorous annotation protocol. To generate the training data, the study relied on a group of three human annotators supervised by the Principal Investigator (PI). The meticulous training, supervision, and validation protocols implemented in this project allowed generating high-quality annotations. The protocol consisted of human annotators classifying information from high a level of aggregation to progressively fine-grained annotations in three stages: document classification (task 1), sentence relevance (task 2), and event type (task 3).

Task 1: Document relevance. To ensure the validity of the data at the highest level of aggregation, the first task consists of identifying news articles conveying information on organized criminal violence and law enforcement efforts against criminal groups. Failing to discriminate the domain-specificity of the documents increases the risk of including false positives which are likely to undermine the ML performance and the output validity. This study relies on the document classification originally conducted by Osorio and Beltrán (2020), who used a team of human annotators to classify news articles as "relevant" or "not relevant". The first step consisted of using a query to gather news articles from 110 national and local newspapers in Mexico. Then, annotators classified as "relevant" news reports that provide descriptions of factual incidents of criminal violence or law enforcement against criminal groups. These incidents include armed confrontations between criminals; armed clashes between criminals and government authorities; arrests of members of criminal groups; drug seizures; seizures of assets (e.g. vehicles, money, real state); seizures of weapons; or the capture of high-profile targets. The team of annotators classified as "not relevant" news stories that do not make direct reference to organized criminal violence events; editorial opinions about criminal violence; statements or claims from victims, civil

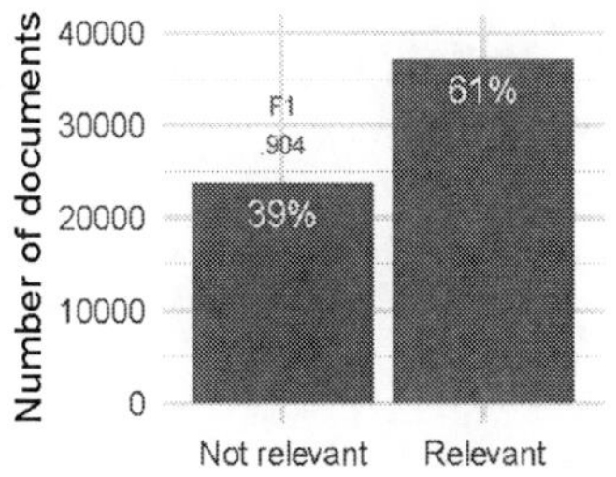

Figure 1: Annotations of relevant news articles (task 1)

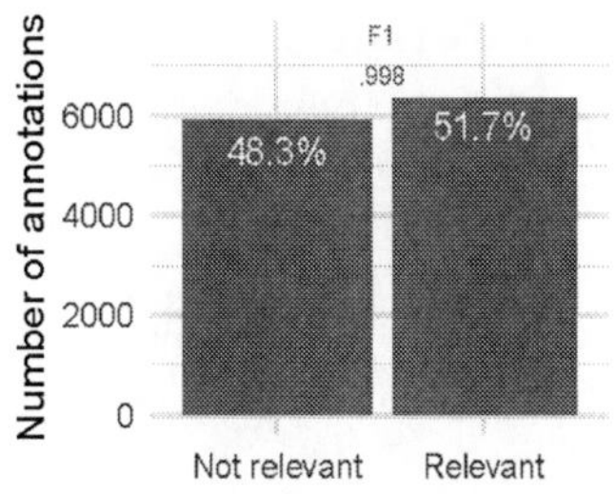

Figure 2: Annotations of relevant sentences (task 2)

society organizations, or government officials; or summaries from government authorities providing a cumulative report of law enforcement activities.

The training data at the document level consists of 60,837 news articles in Spanish, out of which 61% are "relevant" and the other 39% are "not relevant" (see Figure 1). This large training data was produced with high inter-annotator reliability (F1=0.904), reported by Osorio and Beltrán (2020).

Task 2: Sentence relevance. This study goes beyond the document-level classification initially implemented by Osorio and Beltrán (2020) and analyzes the relevance of specific sentences. To do so, we selected a random sample of relevant documents from task 1 and disaggregated them into individual sentences. A team of human annotators classified sentences as "relevant" or "not relevant" following the criteria proposed by Osorio and Beltrán (2020). An initial group of six annotators underwent a three-week training program to gain familiarity with the ontology. In this process, the annotators labeled the same corpus in several rounds. Then, the PI selected the three annotators with the highest inter-annotator reliability score (F1>0.8) to work on task 2.

We used `www.tagtog.com`, a web-based annotation platform, to annotate a collection of 12,252 sentences. Under the PI's supervision, the team of annotators independently classified each sentence and implemented a cross-validation process consisting of several rounds of revision to ensure the consistency of their labeling decisions. After each sentence received three validated classifications, the team generated the gold standard record (GSR). To do so, the PI randomly assigned a set of sentences to each annotator, who evaluated the set of anonymous annotations from the previous round and determined the most accurate one as the GSR. Figure 2 shows the binary annotation that produced a balanced collection of 51.7% of the sentences as "relevant" and the other 48.3% as "not relevant", with a high inter-annotator agreement of F1=0.9982.

Task 3: Event type. The next step consists of annotating the type of event in the relevant paragraphs derived from the previous step. To do so, the annotators relied on a detailed codebook to classify 11 different types of events: (i) Criminal violence vs. criminals, (ii) Criminal violence vs. state, (iii) Criminal violence vs. civilians, (iv) Drug trafficking or production, (v) State violence vs. criminals, (vi) State arrest of criminals, (vii) State seizure of drugs, (viii) State seizure of guns, (ix) State seizure of assets, (x) State violence vs. civilians, and (xi) Civilian violence vs. criminals.

Classifying unstructured text using a large number of categories can be challenging, particularly when the narrative conveys information about multiple events. Identifying multiple actors conducting different actions in the same sentence can generate intractable annotation schemes. To address this challenge, the PI modified the annotation space to enable multiple-actor-action classification. Figure 3 shows the interface using the same sentence to classify three different actions: an arrest (event 1), an attack on the police (event 2), and violence against civilians (event 3). The interface allows coding up to four distinct types of actions from the same sentence.[1]

According to the annotation output in Figure 4, about 51.7% of the sentences contain a single event, 12.2% sentences have two events, 3.9% include three events, and 1.3% contain four events. The inter-annotator reliability assessment also indicates a high level of agreement between annotators with an F1=0.998 in event 1, F1=0.997 in event 2, and F1=1 in both events 3 and 4.

The team of annotators classified a total of 8,466

[1] Note that the interface in Figure 3 also allows annotating the span of text, a task that will be explored in future work for fine-grained text extraction and Named Entity Recognition.

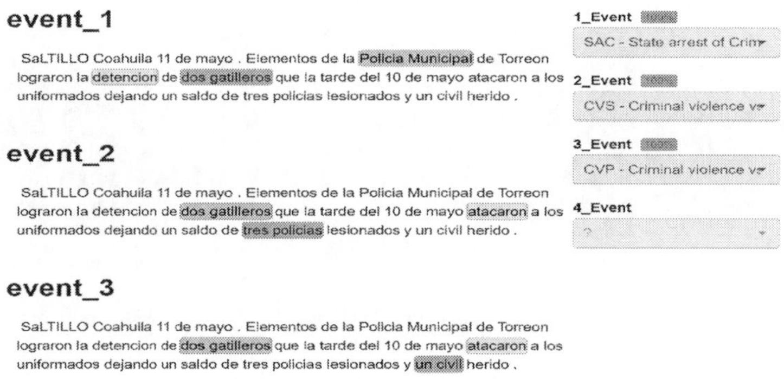

Figure 3: Annotation interface

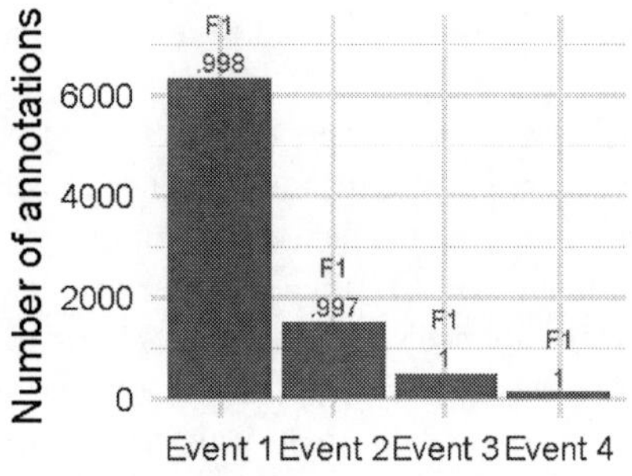

Figure 4: Event annotations

events. Figure 5 presents the distribution of annotations by different event categories and their perpetrators. Among the actions carried out by the state, the most frequent types of events are arrests (8.9%), followed by drug seizures (8.5%), gun seizures (7%), and seizures of assets (4%). Violence perpetrated by the state is rare. Annotators only identified state violence vs. criminals in 3.3% of the cases and violence vs. civilians in 0.2%.

Among the events initiated by criminal groups, criminal violence against civilians stands out as the most common category with 20.9% of the cases. In contrast, violence between criminal groups is less frequent (3.2%). In practice, it is difficult to distinguish between criminal violence against the population and against rival criminals using news articles. The reason is that news reports tend to provide a generic description of the incident without giving details about the victims. For example, an article may just indicate that "a group of hitmen conducted an attack and killed three men." In this case, the criminal character of the perpetrators is clear, but there is no information about the victims. The annotation protocol used in this research classifies this type of event as violence against the population.[2] Following the codebook, annotators classified events of violence between criminals when the news reports explicitly mention the criminal character of the perpetrator as well as the victim (e.g. name of the criminal group or the person's role such as hitman or lieutenant).

Criminal violence against the state constitutes the second most frequent annotation of criminal behavior (9.4%). In addition, annotators detected instances of criminal violence against the state in 3.3% of the sentences. Finally, the annotation output indicates that violence from the population against criminals is very rare, with only 0.2%.

Overall, as Figure 5 shows, the distribution of annotations in the training data is not balanced. There are some categories with a substantial number of annotations (particularly, criminal violence against civilians), while others do not have many annotations. This could affect the performance of ML algorithms and it is not plausible to expect good performance in categories with scarce annotations. Section 6.1 below discusses future research to address this challenge.

4 Experiment Setting

This study analyzes organized criminal violence in Mexico using a set of experiments to progressively process finer-grained information. The first stage focuses on classifying relevant documents. The second stage consists of classifying relevant sentences extracted from the relevant documents identified in the previous step. The final stage classifies the

[2]This coding decision rests on methodological and ethical grounds. Methodologically, annotators only classify information based on explicit evidence in the news report and make no assumptions about the victims. Ethically, the annotating procedure is based on the victim's presumption of innocence, which helps to reduce double victimization and stigmatization (Moon and Treviño-Rangel, 2020).

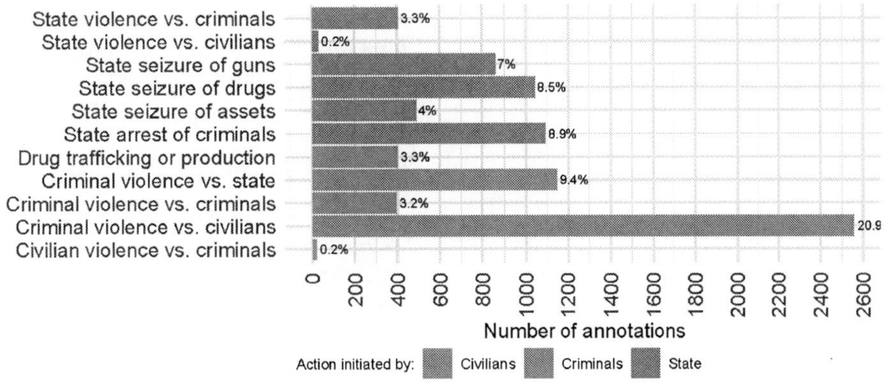

Figure 5: Annotations of event types (task 3)

specific type of organized criminal violence or law enforcement actions contained in the relevant sentences. This sequential approach helps to ensure the validity of the output data based on the concatenated focus on documents, sentences, and events. The large number and high quality of the annotations included in the training data provide a strong empirical foundation to assess the performance of the different ML algorithms and LLM considered.

Task 1: Document relevance. To address the challenge of determining which news articles are relevant to the topic of organized criminal violence, the study approaches this problem as a binary classification task at the document level. Based on the annotations provided in the training data, a positive outcome is operationalized as "relevant" and a negative outcome as "not relevant." In line with standards in computer science research, the experiment setup takes an agnostic approach and puts a variety of algorithms to compete in this binary classification task. This experiment considers a set of five traditional ML algorithms and three LLMs: Multinomial Naive Bayes (NB), Logistic Regression (LR), Random Forest Classifier (RF) (Breiman, 2001), Support Vector Machine (SVM) (Cortes and Vapnik, 1995), Extreme Gradient Boosting (XGB) (Chen and Guestrin, 2016), BETO (José et al., 2020), and Multilingual BERT (mBERT) (Devlin et al., 2018). The experimental setting uses this whole set of ML algorithms and LLM to assess the performance of tasks 2 and 3.

First, we pre-processed the data. We lemmatized the text in the corpus using the `es_core_news_sm` model from spaCy. Then, we removed Latin diacritics and stop-words. Next, we trained the traditional ML algorithms using their default settings in scikit-learn, and fine-tuned the LLMs using the Hugging Face library. We split the corpus into 90% for training and 10% for evaluation. To test the performance of our classifiers, we used the metrics implemented in scikit-learn.

Task 2: Sentence relevance. Based on the selection of relevant news stories derived from the previous stage, the experiment setup then focuses on classifying relevant sentences within the relevant documents. To do so, the study approaches this task as a binary classification at the sentence level. Based on the annotations, a positive outcome is operationalized as a "relevant" sentence, while a negative outcome indicates "not relevant" sentences. For the automatic classification, we follow the pipeline described for Task 1 and the experiments evaluate the full set of ML and LLM.

Task 3: Event type. The final set of experiments use a variety ML algorithms and LLM to classify different types of events at the sentence level. To do so, the study considers the 11 types of actions discussed in section 3 as a multi-class classification task. For each type of event, the algorithms classify as a "positive" outcome a specific type of event mentioned in the sentence, and "negative" otherwise. This phase applies the same pre-processing steps as in Tasks 1 and 2. To perform the classification, we generated individual binary subsets for each event label, enabling a binary classification for every label. This means that, from the 11 available classes, we created 11 subsets, each one with only two classes: positive and negative. This allows us to evaluate the performance of the learning algorithms with respect to each event type.

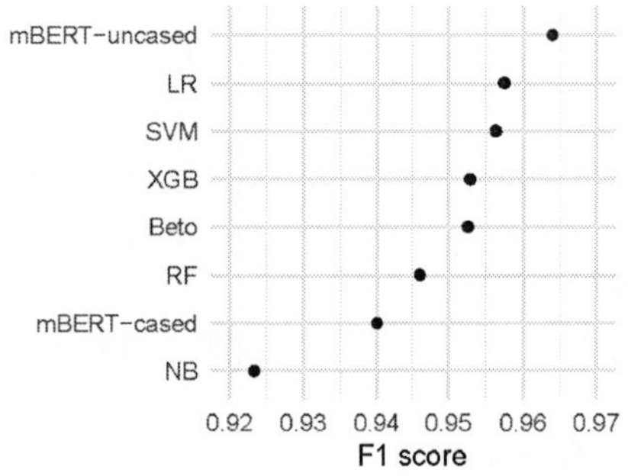

Figure 6: Document binary classification (task 1)

5 Results

5.1 Task 1: Document relevance

Figure 6 presents the results of the binary document classification using a diverse set of ML algorithms and LLM. According to the results, the model with the best performance in classifying relevant and not relevant news articles associated with criminal violence and law enforcement efforts in Spanish is mBERT-uncased with an F1=0.9630.

All other models in the binary document classification task report lower performance than mBERT-uncased. The Logistic Regression (LR) model reports the second-best results with an F1=0.9574, closely followed by the Support Vector Machine (SVM) with an F1=0.9563; the Extreme Gradient Boosting (XGB) model performs with an F1=0.9529; BETO reports an F1=0.9526; the Random Forest (RF) Classifier indicates an F1=0.9461; the cased version of Multilingual BERT (mBERT-cased) model reports an F1=0.94; and finally, the Multinomial Naive Bayes (NB) has the lowest performance with an F1=0.9233.

The result of the mBERT-uncased application in this study considerably outperforms the performance of the Logistic Regression model originally implemented by Osorio and Beltrán (2020) for document classification, which reached an F1=0.949. The high F1 performance of the mBERT-uncased model in this application also stands out with respect to the performance of other binary document classification efforts on similar domains. For example, the highest score of binary document classification of protest data reported in the CASE 2022 joint task reached an F1=0.7496 (Hürriyetoğlu et al., 2022), which is considerably lower than the performance reported in this study. The results of the mBERT-uncased pre-trained language model in Spanish also puts into perspective the results of other studies showing that other models outperform mBERT in Spanish on similar conflict-related domains such as hate speech (Castillo-lópez et al., 2023) and sexism detection (Schütz et al., 2022).

5.2 Task 2: Sentence relevance

As indicated in the experiment setting in section 4, we proceed in an agnostic way with respect to the different ML algorithms and LLM considered in this study and put them all to compete in classifying relevant sentences. The first row of Table 1 reports the results of the different models on the classification of relevant sentences. The performance metric used to assess the models is the average macro-F1 derived from running five iterations of each model. In this way, the results provide evidence of the average performance of each model, rather than arbitrarily picking the top performance from any random seed. The model reporting the highest macro-F1 is marked in bold font to indicate the algorithm that has the best performance in each classification category.

The results of Table 1 show that BETO has the best performance for sentence relevance classification with an F1=0.8588. The model with the second best performance is mBERT-uncased (F1=0.8553), followed by mBERT-cased (F1=0.8506). All other models have slightly lower performance for classifying the relevance of specific sentences.

In general, BERT-like models stand out for their high performance in identifying relevant sentences related to organized criminal violence and law enforcement efforts from text in Spanish. The excellent performance of this model is consistent with the findings of Hürriyetoğlu et al. (2022) for classifying protest data, which reached a maximum F1=0.8245 in its top-performing model.

5.3 Task 3: Event type

Finally, the rest of the rows in Table 1 show the results of the different ML algorithms and LLM on the multi-class classification of specific event types in relevant sentences. In general, the performance of event classification reflects the expectations of unbalanced annotations discussed in the Training Data section 3. As expected, the models generally perform better for event types that have a large number of annotations, while they tend to show lower performance for rare event types.

The second section of Table 1 reports the results of the different ML and LLM tools for actions initiated by organized criminals. The BETO model

			Traditional ML					LLM		
	Task	Positive cases	NB	SVM	LR	RF	XGB	mBERT uncased	mBERT cased	BETO
1	Relevant	6,327	0.8179	0.8443	0.8449	0.8512	0.8368	0.8553	0.8506	**0.8588**
2	Criminal violence vs. criminals	396	0.0000	0.2799	0.0379	0.0805	0.2614	0.6630	0.8412	**0.8550**
	Criminal violence vs. state	1,148	0.0522	0.5836	0.4211	0.3120	0.5874	**0.8423**	0.8170	0.8380
	Criminal violence vs. civilians	2,556	0.6840	0.7397	0.7147	0.6563	0.6959	0.8558	0.8536	**0.8699**
	Drug trafficking or production	402	0.0103	0.3908	0.1333	0.1640	0.3865	0.6817	**0.8440**	0.4994
3	State violence vs. criminals	405	0.0000	0.6483	0.4547	0.2234	0.6815	0.8312	0.8457	**0.8505**
	State violence vs. civilians	30	0.0000	0.2133	0.0000	0.2133	0.2133	0.4992	0.8382	**0.8558**
	State arrest of criminal	1,093	0.0569	0.6255	0.4177	0.3727	0.6246	0.8305	0.8441	**0.8550**
	State seizure of assets	490	0.2355	0.5896	0.3204	0.5289	0.5546	0.7757	0.7450	**0.8451**
	State seizure of guns	859	0.7296	0.8268	0.7519	0.7519	0.8497	**0.9191**	0.8421	0.8567
	State seizure of drugs	1,041	0.6444	0.8086	0.7088	0.8133	0.8131	**0.9259**	0.8367	0.8596
4	Civilian violence vs. criminals	19	0.0000	0.0000	0.0000	0.0000	0.0000	0.4997	**0.8440**	0.4994

Table 1: Relevance and multi-class classification at the sentence level (tasks 2 and 3).

has the best performance for classifying criminal violence against criminals with an F1=0.8550. This performance is remarkable given the small number of positive cases in this category. The mBERT-uncased model reports the top performance for classifying incidents of criminal violence against the state with an F1=0.8423. Given the variety of potential targets among state authorities (e.g. soldiers, marines, police, and state officials), it may be difficult for the algorithm to accurately identify incidents of criminal violence against the state. Yet, the substantial number of annotations in this category likely contributes to the model's good performance. For the category related to criminal violence against civilians, BETO reports the best performance with an F1=0.8699. Given the broad range of crime victims and the different types of violent tactics used by criminal groups, it is difficult to accurately classify this category. Finally, the algorithm achieving the best performance when classifying drug trafficking or production is mBERT-cased with an F1=0.8440. This level of performance is remarkable given the limited observations in this category and the broad variety of narcotics (e.g. cocaine, heroin, fentanyl) that make their classification a challenging task.

The third section of Table 1 reports the performance for events initiated by the state. Despite the limited number of annotations of state violence against criminals and civilians, the best-performing model, BETO, reports an F1=0.8505 and F1=0.8558, respectively. BETO is also the top-performing model for classifying arrests of criminals, with an F1=0.8550. According to the results, the algorithm with the best performance at identifying seizures of assets (e.g. vehicles, real estate) is again BETO with an F1=0.8451. Results show an outstanding performance of mBERT-uncased to identify gun and drug seizures with an F1=0.9191 and F1=.0.9259, respectively.

Finally, the bottom section of Table 1 reports the results of identifying incidents of civilian violence against criminals. Due to the extremely low number of annotations in this event-type category, most models struggle with effectively classifying this type of event. However, mBERT-cased reports a strong performance with an F=0.8440.

In general, the results of Table 1 show that traditional ML algorithms have a sub-optimal performance. In contrast, the family of BERT models consistently reports higher levels of performance. This is consistent with the well-documented high-performance of BERT models in a variety of NLP tasks (Devlin et al., 2019).

6 Conclusions

This study presents an application to classify information related to organized criminal violence from unstructured text written in Spanish using ML and LLM. The results from this study enable researchers and government authorities to track the violent behavior of organized criminal groups in Mexico and assess the effects of law enforcement activities. This research allows for the generation of data on a large scale, in a timely manner, and with an unprecedented degree of granularity and accuracy. By analyzing criminal and state behaviors, the study goes beyond previous efforts exclusively focusing on tracking the territorial presence of criminal groups using rule-based approaches (Osorio and Beltrán, 2020; Signoret et al., 2021; Coscia and Rios, 2012). Tracking the territorial presence of criminal groups only provides information about *who* is present, but does not say anything about *what are they doing*. Thus, this study provides valuable tools to identify behavioral trends of criminal groups and state authorities from news stories with unprecedented accuracy.

The methodological approach in this research focuses on a sequence of classification tasks of increasing levels of detail. Based on a large collection of documents and a robust set of high-quality annotations in the training data, the first task focuses on classifying the relevance of entire news articles related to organized criminal violence and law enforcement. To do so, the experimental setting puts a variety of ML algorithms to compete in the binary classification task. The algorithm reporting the best performance is Multilingual BERT - uncased, with an F1 score of 0.9630. This high level of performance provides a strong indicator of the effectiveness of this ML algorithm.

The second stage evaluates the different algorithms for the identification of relevant sentences. Results show that BETO presents the highest level of performance for the binary sentence classification task with an F1 score of 0.8588.

Finally, the study focuses on classifying the specific types of events of organized criminal violence and law enforcement contained in the data. This application considers 11 different types of events of lethal and non-lethal violence initiated by criminal groups, government authorities, and the civilian population. Given the variations in the distribution of annotations across event categories, results show varying degrees of performance in the multi-class classification of event types. In general, the family of BERT-like models shows a strong performance when classifying different types of organized criminal violence and law enforcement efforts. Results of these NLP tasks report F1 scores ranging from 0.8440 to 0.9259. In particular, BETO consistently presents high performance in many categories.

Beyond the technical performance evaluated in this application, results provide great confidence about the use of NLP tools to accurately extract and classify a broad range of behavioral information related to organized criminal violence from text written in Spanish. These results offer valuable contributions to researchers, security analysts, and government agencies in Spanish-speaking countries in their efforts to understand organized criminal behavior using high-quality data.

6.1 Future Work

A key limitation in this study is the combination of imbalanced training data and the low number of annotations in some event categories that undermine performance. In order to overcome this limitation, future research will explore different data augmentation techniques (Şahin, 2022; Yang et al., 2022). In particular, the Confli-T5 method (Parolin et al., 2022) is a promising one as it specializes in political violence and conflict. However, Confli-T5 was developed in English and requires multi-lingual extensions.

Future research should also consider recent developments in pre-training language models relevant to crime, violence, and politics. Recently, Parolin et al. (2021) proposed the 3M-Transformers (Multilingual, Multi-label, Multitask) method to classify and extract information related to crime and conflict in English, Spanish, and Portuguese. Most importantly, future research should consider using ConfliBERT (Hu et al., 2022) and the ConfliBERT variation in Spanish (Yang et al., 2023), a domain-specific language model specialized in conflict and violence. Independent research has shown that ConfliBERT is the state-of-the-art model for NLP tasks on political violence and conflict (Häffner et al., 2023). Unfortunately, the current ConfliBERT version is only capable of processing text in English.

6.2 Ethical considerations

This study was conducted in compliance with the ACL ethical research guidelines and operated under the supervision of the University of Arizona IRB (protocol 2012326746A001). This project only used secondary data and did not involve human research subjects. Also, as discussed in section 3, the coding protocol took extra measures to avoid further stigmatizing crime victims.

Acknowledgments

This research was possible thanks to the support of the Technology and Research Initiative Fund of the University of Arizona, the National Science Foundation [SES-2116406, OAC-2311142], and the U.S. Department of Defense [W911NF-20-1-0303]. Thanks to Mariana Marín, Rubén Oliva, and Íñigo Casares for their research support. The replication files of this study are available at `https://github.com/javierosorio/classifying_criminal_violence_mx`

References

Elizabeth Boschee, Jennifer Lautenschlager, Sean O'Brien, Steve Shellman, James Starz, and Michael Ward. 2016. ICEWS Coded Event Data. Publication Title: Harvard Dataverse.

Leo Breiman. 2001. Random Forests. *Machine Learning*, 45(1):5–32.

Tommaso Caselli, Osman Mutlu, Angelo Basile, and Ali Hürriyetoğlu. 2021. PROTEST-ER: Retraining BERT for Protest Event Extraction. In *Proceedings of the 4th Workshop on Challenges and Applications of Automated Extraction of Socio-political Events from Text (CASE 2021)*, pages 12–19, Online. Association for Computational Linguistics.

Galo Castillo-lópez, Arij Riabi, and Djamé Seddah. 2023. Analyzing Zero-Shot transfer Scenarios across Spanish variants for Hate Speech Detection. In *Tenth Workshop on NLP for Similar Languages, Varieties and Dialects (VarDial 2023)*, pages 1–13, Dubrovnik, Croatia. Association for Computational Linguistics.

Tianqi Chen and Carlos Guestrin. 2016. XGBoost: A Scalable Tree Boosting System. In *Proceedings of the 22nd ACM SIGKDD International Conference on Knowledge Discovery and Data Mining*, pages 785–794. ArXiv:1603.02754 [cs].

Corinna Cortes and Vladimir Vapnik. 1995. Support-vector networks. *Machine Learning*, 20(3):273–297.

Michelle Coscia and Viridiana Rios. 2012. Knowing Where and How Criminal Organizations Operate Using Web Content. In *CIKM'12. ACM international conference on Information and knowledge management*, volume October, Maui, HI.

Jacob Devlin, Ming-Wei Chang, Kenton Lee, and Kristina Toutanova. 2018. BERT: Pre-training of Deep Bidirectional Transformers for Language Understanding.

Jacob Devlin, Ming-Wei Chang, Kenton Lee, and Kristina Toutanova. 2019. BERT: Pre-training of Deep Bidirectional Transformers for Language Understanding. In *Proceedings of the 2019 Conference of the North American Chapter of the Association for Computational Linguistics: Human Language Technologies, Volume 1 (Long and Short Papers)*, pages 4171–4186, Minneapolis, Minnesota. Association for Computational Linguistics.

Aaron Erlich, Stefano G. Dantas, Benjamin E. Bagozzi, Daniel Berliner, and Brian Palmer-Rubin. 2022. Multi-Label Prediction for Political Text-as-Data. *Political Analysis*, 30(4):463–480. Publisher: Cambridge University Press.

Justin Grimmer and Brandon M. Stewart. 2013. Text as Data: The Promise and Pitfalls of Automatic Content Analysis Methods for Political Texts. *Political Analysis*, 21(3):267–297.

Andy Halterman, Philip A Schrodt, Andreas Beger, Benjamin E. Bagozzi, and Grace Scarborough. 2023a. Creating Custom Event Data Without Dictionaries: A Bag-of-Tricks.

Andy Halterman, Philip A Schrodt, Andreas Beger, Benjamin E. Bagozzi, and Grace Scarborough. 2023b. PLOVER and POLECAT: A New Political Event Ontology and Dataset.

Pei-Yun Hsueh, Prem Melville, and Vikas Sindhwani. 2009. Data quality from crowdsourcing: a study of annotation selection criteria. In *Proceedings of the NAACL HLT 2009 Workshop on Active Learning for Natural Language Processing*, HLT '09, pages 27–35, USA. Association for Computational Linguistics.

Yibo Hu, MohammadSaleh Hosseini, Erick Skorupa Parolin, Javier Osorio, Latifur Khan, Patrick Brandt, and Vito D'Orazio. 2022. ConfliBERT: A Pre-trained Language Model for Political Conflict and Violence. In *Proceedings of the 2022 Conference of the North American Chapter of the Association for Computational Linguistics: Human Language Technologies*, pages 5469–5482.

Sonja Häffner, Martin Hofer, Maximilian Nagl, and Julian Walterskirchen. 2023. Introducing an Interpretable Deep Learning Approach to Domain-Specific Dictionary Creation: A Use Case for Conflict Prediction. *Political Analysis*, pages 1–19. Publisher: Cambridge University Press.

Ali Hürriyetoğlu, Osman Mutlu, Fırat Duruşan, Onur Uca, Alaeddin Gürel, Benjamin J. Radford, Yaoyao Dai, Hansi Hettiarachchi, Niklas Stoehr, Tadashi Nomoto, Milena Slavcheva, Francielle Vargas, Aaqib Javid, Fatih Beyhan, and Erdem Yörük. 2022. Extended Multilingual Protest News Detection - Shared Task 1, CASE 2021 and 2022. In *Proceedings of the 5th Workshop on Challenges and Applications of Automated Extraction of Socio-political Events from Text (CASE)*, pages 223–228, Abu Dhabi, United Arab Emirates (Hybrid). Association for Computational Linguistics.

Canete José, Chaperon Gabriel, Fuentes Rodrigo, and Pérez Jorge. 2020. Spanish pre-trained BERT model and evaluation data. *PML4DC at ICLR*, 2020.

Kamran Kowsari, Kiana Jafari Meimandi, Mojtaba Heidarysafa, Sanjana Mendu, Laura Barnes, and Donald Brown. 2019. Text classification algorithms: A survey. *Information*, 10(4):150.

Maria Krommyda, Anastasios Rigos, Kostas Bouklas, and Angelos Amditis. 2021. An Experimental Analysis of Data Annotation Methodologies for Emotion Detection in Short Text Posted on Social Media. *Informatics*, 8(1):19. Number: 1 Publisher: Multidisciplinary Digital Publishing Institute.

Will Lowe and Kenneth Benoit. 2013. Validating estimates of latent traits from textual data using human judgment as a benchmark. *Political analysis*, 21(3):298–313.

Shervin Minaee, Nal Kalchbrenner, Erik Cambria, Narjes Nikzad, Meysam Chenaghlu, and Jianfeng Gao. 2021. Deep learning–based text classification: a comprehensive review. *ACM computing surveys (CSUR)*, 54(3):1–40.

Claire Moon and Javier Treviño-Rangel. 2020. "Involved in something (involucrado en algo)": Denial and stigmatization in Mexico's "war on drugs". *The British Journal of Sociology*, 71(4):722–740. _eprint: https://onlinelibrary.wiley.com/doi/pdf/10.1111/1468-4446.12761.

Petr Motlicek. 2023. ROXANNE - Real time network, text, and speaker analytics for combating organized crime.

Javier Osorio. 2015. The Contagion of Drug Violence: Spatiotemporal Dynamics of the Mexican War on Drugs. *Journal of Conflict Resolution*, 59(8):1403–1432.

Javier Osorio and Alejandro Beltrán. 2020. Enhancing the Detection of Criminal Organizations in Mexico using ML and NLP. *2020 International Joint Conference on Neural Networks (IJCNN)*, pages 1–7. Glasgow, Scottland.

Javier Osorio, Mohamed Mohamed, Viveca Pavon, and Brewer-Osorio Susan. 2019. Mapping Violent Presence of Armed Actors. *Advances in Cartography in GIScience of the International Cartographic Association*, pages 1–16.

Javier Osorio and Alejandro Reyes. 2017. Supervised Event Coding From Text Written in Spanish: Introducing Eventus ID. *Social Science Computer Review*, 35(3):406–416.

Erick Skorupa Parolin, Yibo Hu, Latifur Khan, Patrick T. Brandt, Javier Osorio, and Vito D'Orazio. 2022. Confli-T5: An AutoPrompt Pipeline for Conflict Related Text Augmentation. In *2022 IEEE International Conference on Big Data (Big Data)*, pages 1906–1913.

Erick Skorupa Parolin, Latifur Khan, Javier Osorio, Patrick Brandt, Vito D'Orazio, and Jennifer Holmes. 2021. 3M-Transformers for Event Coding on Organized Crime Domain. *IEEE International Conference on Data Science and Advanced Analytics (DSAA)*. Publisher: IEEE.

Pedro L Rodriguez and Arthur Spirling. 2022. Word embeddings: What works, what doesn't, and how to tell the difference for applied research. *The Journal of Politics*, 84(1):101–115.

Elena Rudkowsky, Martin Haselmayer, Matthias Wastian, Marcelo Jenny, Štefan Emrich, and Michael Sedlmair. 2018. More than bags of words: Sentiment analysis with word embeddings. *Communication Methods and Measures*, 12(2-3):140–157.

Philip A. Schrodt, Brandon Stewart, Jennifer Lautenschlager, Andrew Shilliday, David Van Brackel, and Will Lowe. 2010. Automated Production of High-Volume, Near-Real-Time Political Event Data. Technical report. Publication Title: Event (London).

Philip A. Schrodt and David Van Brackel. 2013. Automated Coding of Political Event Data. In Devika Subramanian, editor, *Handbook of Computational Approaches to Counterterrorism*, pages 23–50. Springer, New York.

Mina Schütz, Jaqueline Boeck, Daria Liakhovets, Djordje Slijepčević, Armin Kirchknopf, Manuel Hecht, Johannes Bogensperger, Sven Schlarb, Alexander Schindler, and Matthias Zeppelzauer. 2022. Automatic Sexism Detection with Multilingual Transformer Models. ArXiv:2106.04908 [cs].

Patrick Signoret, Marco Alcocer, Cecilia Farfan-Mendez, and Fernanda Sobrino. 2021. Mapping Criminal Organizations.

Zhanna Terechshenko, Fridolin Linder, Vishakh Padmakumar, Michael Liu, Jonathan Nagler, Joshua A Tucker, and Richard Bonneau. 2020. A comparison of methods in political science text classification: Transfer learning language models for politics. *Available at SSRN 3724644*.

Muthuraman Thangaraj and Muthusamy Sivakami. 2018. Text classification techniques: A literature review. *Interdisciplinary journal of information, knowledge, and management*, 13:117.

Michael Ward, Andreas Beger, Josh Cutler, Matthew Dickenson, Cassy Dorff, and Ben Radford. 2013. Comparing GDELT and ICEWS Event Data.

Guanqun Yang, Mirazul Haque, Qiaochu Song, Wei Yang, and Xueqing Liu. 2022. TestAug: A Framework for Augmenting Capability-based NLP Tests. In *Proceedings of the 29th International Conference on Computational Linguistics*, pages 3480–3495, Gyeongju, Republic of Korea. International Committee on Computational Linguistics.

Wooseong Yang, Sultan Alsarra, Lujay Abdeljaber, Niamat Zawad, Zeinab Delaram, Javier Osorio, Latifur Khan, Patrick T. Brandt, and Vito D'Orazio. 2023. ConfliBERT-Spanish: A Pre-trained Spanish Language Model for Political Conflict and Violence. In *Proceedings of the 2023 Recent Advances in Natural Language Processing conference*, Varna, Bulgaria.

Gözde Gül Şahin. 2022. To Augment or Not to Augment? A Comparative Study on Text Augmentation Techniques for Low-Resource NLP. *Computational Linguistics*, 48(1):5–42.

Where "where" Matters : Event Location Identification with a BERT Language Model

Hristo Tanev and **Bertrand De Longueville**
Joint Research Centre, European Commission
Ispra, Italy
hristo.tanev@ec.europa.eu
bertrand.de-longueville@ec.europa.eu

Abstract

Detecting event location is a key aspect of event extraction from news and social media. However, this task has not received strong attention recently in comparison to event classification or identifying the event time and the semantic arguments of the event, such as victims, perpetrators, means of action, affected infrastructure, etc. Nevertheless, the location as an event argument plays a crucial role in all event detection applications: conflict detection, health threat monitoring, disaster impact assessment, etc. The method presented in this paper uses a BERT model for classifying location mentions in event reporting news texts into two classes: a place of an event, called *main location*, or another location mention, called here *secondary location* . Our evaluation on articles, reporting protests, shows promising results and demonstrates the feasibility of our approach and the event geolocation task in general.

1 Introduction

Detecting event location from online text sources is a key area of research since the advent of social networks (Intagorn et al., 2010) , (De Longueville et al., 2010). Applications have been developed in fields as diverse as disaster management (De Longueville et al., 2009), (Kongthon et al., 2014), tracking disease outbreaks (Grishman et al., 2002b), or fight against crime (Kounadi et al., 2015). Detecting socio-political events (and in particular, protests) emerged as an important use case (Zhang et al., 2017), which relies on comprehensive, timely and high-quality data that is sometimes not available or it is difficult to be obtained.

Recently, the CASE (Challenges and Application of Automatic Extraction of Socio-political Events from News) series of workshops (Hürriyetoğlu et al., 2021a) have introduced a set of event detection shared tasks and an annotated corpora of protest events, which contains annotations of event places among the other arguments. The CASE initiative significantly boosted the work in the area of socio-political event analysis and gave birth to shared tasks and research works with focus on event location identification, (Giorgi et al., 2021) and (Zavarella et al., 2022).

Formally, geographical place recognition is a sub-category of named entity recognition (NER) (Densham and Reid, 2003). However, it has many particular features: First, geographic names are in the range of millions and unlike names of people and organizations, there are no reliable rules for recognizing these entities by their textual form. Therefore, the first level in recognizing geographic entities is by searching for them in big geographical dictionaries, called *gazetteers*. Second, geographic names can be mismatched with names of people: as an example, let's consider place names like *Washington*, *Georgia*, *Alexandria* and many others. Third, identifying the place names in text is just the first step in recognizing them: disambiguating locations (i.e. which of the many *Paris* is it) and identifying their precise coordinates is even more challenging task (Overell, 2009).

The fourth problem, related to location analysis is recognizing the semantic role of the location mentions. Currently, very little work is dedicated to this important problem: Our paper aims at filling this gap, by applying the latest advances in Natural Language Processing (Devlin et al., 2018), leveraging large language models and the knowledge encoded in them, to recognize locations, where events happen, distinguishing them from other location mentions.

Our approach is designed to be used as an integral part of an automated process for Event Extraction: In particular, we aim at linking protest events from news articles to the locations where they took place. A classical problem of such location identification is the fact that apart from the locations of the main events reported in the news, here called *main locations*, many more places are usually referred

Proceedings of the 6th Workshop on Challenges and Applications of Automated Extraction of Socio-political Events from Text, pages 11–17, Varna, Bulgaria, Sep 7, 2023.
https://doi.org/10.26615/978-954-452-089-2_002

to in the text, called here *secondary locations*. Typically, a news article focuses on one main event, which however is related to various reported real or possible happenings, which took place before or after the main one. Each event also has an elaborated structure and may feature different semantic arguments, among them places, as well as sub-events and larger events, which encompass it. Conversely, locations may be used to define the places of the events, as well as to address the origins and affiliations of people and organizations ("refugees from Syria", "the mayor of Brussels"),

To answer the event location detection challenge, we proposed an approach which uses a BERT (Devlin et al., 2018) model for text classification; it classifies each location as the place of an event on which the news article is focused (main location) or as a secondary location mention (places of secondary events or location mentions, which are not event places). Our model uses only lexical context and the position of the sentence in the article. However, our approach makes use of the implicit semantic knowledge about the similarities of the words and their relations, encoded in the BERT model. In this way, we avoid using semantic features and other text pre-processing, relying entirely on the semantic knowledge, encoded in BERT. Moreover, recent research (Muller et al., 2022) aims at transferring BERT models across languages , potentially bringing making our our approach multilingual.

2 Related work

Earlier work on event extraction, such as (Humphreys et al., 1997) and the REES system (Aone and Ramos-Santacruz, 2000) use syntactic patterns for detecting locations and other event arguments. Similarly, one of the first disease outbreak systems, PULSE (Grishman et al., 2002a), makes use of syntactic clues and proximity to essential event arguments, such as disease names, to select the outbreak locations. Some recent approaches for event location detection like (Giorgi et al., 2021) also makes use of proximity of the location to specific event arguments.

These linguistic approaches, although having a reasonable precision, are limited in their application, since syntactic patterns and clues require a significant amount of expert knowledge and efforts and strongly depend on the event classes, which are being considered in the event extraction system. Moreover, linguistic approaches cannot efficiently exploit big data repositories, i.e. corpora and public event data bases, such as ACLED (Raleigh et al., 2010), Global Terrorism Database (LaFree and Dugan, 2007), and others, which has recently emerged.

In contrast, Machine Learning (ML) models can significantly benefit from such data: A recent ML work on event geolocation, based on an existing event data set (ICEWS (Ward et al., 2013)) is presented in (Lee et al., 2019). Their work is similar to the approach presented in this paper. However, they use semantic pre-processing of the text by annotating each event-specific keyword and expression: event trigger verbs and nouns (e,g, *breaking into*), actors (e,g, *Ukraininan soldiers*), temporal expressions and others. This work reports 75% accuracy for detecting the main event location in a protest event data set. They use Support Vector Machines (SVM), Neural Network and Random Forests, all methods delivering similar results.

Another work which relies on training a classifier for event location detection is presented in (Imani et al., 2017). They use SVM classifier and word embeddings for identifying the sentences likely to contain the main event location. Then they extract from them the most frequent location.

Similartly, (Halterman, 2019) proposes a Convolutional Neural Network, which finds the main event location. They have manually created a data set of 8'000 sentences, containing information about military offensives in the Syrian war. The event geolocation accuracy they achieve is around 84%.

3 Protest events and their locations

Protest are socio-political events, which include rallies, protests, marches, strikes, riots, violent disorders and civil unrest. Each socio-political event assumes action by a large group of people. In particular, the protest events express disapproval and oppose to concrete actions or policies of governments, administrators, parties, institutions or companies. The definition of protest event, given in (Makarov et al., 2015) is:

A protest event is open to the public, politically motivated and not institutionalised as opposed to e.g. elections.

In some cases protest actions pose concrete demands, e.g. lowering taxes or raising wages. On certain occasions, these events attempt to focus the public attention on causes, such as minority rights, peace in war zones, environmental problems, etc. These events may include spontaneous violent actions, mass violence against people, vehicles and infrastructure. Such actions may manifest characteristics of crime or event small-scale armed conflicts, when armed opposition to the police takes place.

In order to better understand the dynamics of the protest events and their relation with various geographic locations, we have manually analyzed a small set of news, identifying the main and the secondary events and their related locations.

Our analysis found four basic types of location mentions:

- The place of the reported protest, *the main location*, "Farmers staged a protest in *Santa Fe* province on Tuesday ", "they hacked Sabata Petros Chale to death in *Marikana West* , allegedly over the allocation of low cost houses". Main locations can be reported using several levels of accuracy, for example mentioning the country, the district, the city and the place inside the city, e.g. "Clashes erupted in *Dalian, Liaoning*" , resulting in several location mentions, referring to a single event. Also, in some cases, more than one main event can be reported, causing mentioning of more than one main location.

- The place of the event which is the cause for the protest - "The incident came about as protests and riots formed in cities across the country following the killing of George Floyd in *Minneapolis* "; "A demonstration against supplying *Ukraine* with weapons for war with *Russia* attracted 10,000 people on Saturday" Such locations we consider *secondary*.

- Another source of secondary location mentions are the populated places from where the protesters come, also their national origin - "Farmers from the nearby states of *Punjab, Haryana* and *Uttar Pradesh* began arriving by tractors and on foot at the outskirts of New Delhi last week, where they blocked roads and set up makeshift camps"

- Locations related to response actions and consequences: places of police block, places of blocked traffic, countries reacting towards the event, and places where politicians or organizers make statement about the main event ("press conference with the French Prime Minister in Paris about the protests across the country"). Although these locations may be important for the dynamics of the event reported, they are still considered *secondary locations*.

Let's consider as an example, a news article fragment describing a protest in Oslo:

"Dozens of activists, including Greta Thunberg of neighboring *Sweden*, blocked the entrance to the energy ministry in *Oslo* Monday to protest a wind farm they say hinders the rights of the Sami Indigenous people to raise reindeer in *Arctic Norway*"

In this fragment three locations are mentioned, while only one, i.e. *Oslo*, is the main location. The other locations mentions , (*Sweden* and *Arctic Norway*), are secondary ones. The first relates to the origin of one of the prominent protesters (Greta Thunberg) and the second is the place, where the cause for the protest is located: a wind farm in *Arctic Norway*.

Our analysis shows that the complexity of the events, described in the news, not only the sociopolitical ones, has its impact on the location references: one happening can trigger mentions of multiple related events and people, and the corresponding locations, related to them. In the case of protest actions, the event which is a cause for them is frequently mentioned along with its place. Moreover, the effects of the protest on the people and the urban environment: blocked traffic, police actions and similar, bring in the text additional locations.

In some sense, this is in agreement with Davidson's view on the event semantics (Davidson, 1969), for whom the cause and effect constitute important characteristics of the event phenomena.

4 Approach

The approach we propose for geolocating events belongs to the class of Machine Learning approaches, it is similar in spirit to the work of (Halterman, 2019). We, however, chose to use a BERT classification model, since it provides the necessary level of abstraction by encoding the texts into a semantic space, trained on millions of documents. In this way, we avoided the feature abstraction phase, which is part of all the other ML approaches for geocoding, cited so far.

In order to train and evaluate our approach, we used a corpus of protest news, reporting various types of protests in India and China. (Hürriyetoğlu et al., 2021b). In this corpus the annotated event locations are main locations. Moreover, we have additionally annotated the secondary location mentions, which were not annotated in the corpus, using the Mordecai open source software (Halterman, 2017). In this way, we obtained a corpus with main and secondary locations.

A sample annotated sentence from the corpus is shown below:

"$India_{[main]}$: $NewDelhi_{[main]}$, Thu May 30 2013 , 22:07 hrs Activists of Youth Indian National Trade Union Congress (INTUC) protest against recent Naxal attack on Congress leaders , in $Raipur_{[secondary]}$ on Thursday . "

4.1 Generating location windows

We used the following procedure to extract location-specific data from the annotated corpus:

1. We found each main or secondary location mention.

2. We masked each location mention with a placeholder token *EVENT_PLACE* (both for main or secondary locations) and extracted a *location window* of maximum of twenty one tokens from the same sentence: maximum of ten tokens before and after the placeholder without crossing the sentence boundaries.

3. After several experiments, we have found out that the BERT model is sensitive to the exact position of the location place holder, therefore, for the shorter windows we have artificially inserted before and after a series of filler tokes (BEGIN before the window or END after it), so that the length of the window is always twenty one tokens and EVENT_PLACE is in the center of the window.

4. In order to account for the position of the sentence inside the article, we inserted the position of the sentence in front of every location window. Some smaller scaled experiments, not reported here, showed to us that the number of the sentence slightly contributes to the accuracy of the model.

5. Finally, we assigned a label to each of the location windows which shows if it was a *main location* (the place of the event annotated manually) or a *secondary location* (any other location mention, annotated by the Mordecai tool).

Table 1 shows several samples of location windows with the sentence position and the EVENT_PLACE placeholder. For clarity, we do not show the BEGIN and END filler tokens. Each window is labeled as a main location or a secondary one.

4.2 Fine-tuning the BERT model

Location windows were used to fine-tune a FastBERT model (Liu et al., 2020), thus obtaining a large language model which classifies a geolocation as a main or a secondary location mention, using only its location window.

The FastBERT was chosen because of its speed of performance, which allowed us to experiment with multiple data splits in reasonable time. Moreover, the speed of the model is crucial, when applying it in real-world settings: The FastBERT speed can be flexibly adjusted in the classification phase. Moreover, this model adopts a unique "self distillation mechanism" at fine-tuning, further enabling a greater computational efficacy with minimal loss in performance.

5 Experimental set up

In our experiments we used the corpus of protest events with already annotated locations, enriched with automatic location identification from Mordecai, as explained in the previous section.

Following the procedure for extraction of location windows (Table 1) from the annotated corpus, we have obtained an experimental data set of 829 main location windows, considered here as positive instances, and 472 secondary location ones, considered as negative ones.

From this data we have performed a cross-validation, generating 10 random train/test data splits, each containing 66% location windows for training and 34% for test.

We fine-tuned the FastBert model on the training set of each data split and evaluated the performance of the model on the test set.

In order to evaluate the difficulty of the location classification task, we introduced also a simple baseline *First sentence*, which considers a location

Table 1: Data sample. Main and secondary location text windows.

Location window	Main or second.
1 The house of a PDP MP was torched in south EVENT_PLACE .	Main
0 AM The clash between police and the local people in EVENT_PLACE .	Main
6 In EVENT_PLACE district, about 25-30 Maoists attacked the premises of	Main
5 midnight , they set fire to the tower in EVENT_PLACE police station area .	Main
2 The agitation was organized by the EVENT_PLACE district unit of the BJP .	Main
5 Passengers to the EVENT_PLACE airport did not have much of a problem .	Secondary
3 The march was intercepted at the EVENT_PLACE .	Secondary
7 thanks to the providential arrest of a terrorist in EVENT_PLACE	Secondary
0 Seers protest arrest at EVENT_PLACE police station 17th January	Secondary

mention to be a main location (positive), only if it appears in the first sentence of the news article. We also compared the performance of our BERT model to the performance of an SVM, classifier, which uses the Radial Base Kernel Function (RBF) with C parameter set to 1.

We performed 2 runs of the SVM model: In the first run we used bag-of-word vectors, where each dimension corresponds to a word and its value is the number of the word appearance in the text window. In the second run of the SVM model we used Word2Vec Google News vectors (Church, 2017), which are Word Embeddings with 300 dimensions, pretrained on 3 billion Google News Texts.

6 Evaluation

We have calculated precision, recall, the F1 measure and the accuracy of the FastBERT, the two SVM models, bag-of-words (BoW) and Google News Word2Vec (W2V), and the First sentence baseline on the test set of each of the 10 data splits.

In Table 2 we report the average FastBERT performance across the 10 splits, as well as the average performance of the SVM models and the baseline First sentence.

Clearly, FastBERT significantly outperforms the baseline First sentence, especially as a recall, F1 measure and accuracy. Notably, the recall of FastBERT is more than twice the recall of the baseline: This shows the importance of the model for identifying main event locations, which can frequently be mentioned after the first sentence.

Compared to the SVM BoW and SVM W2V, our method showed significantly better accuracy with respect to the two SVM models: 0.73 vs 0.64 for SVM BoW and 0.65 for SVM W2V. The $F1$ measure of BERT and the SVM models are comparable, still BERT outperforms the two SVM models with 0.02 and 0.03.

The standard deviation of the F1 of FastBERT across all the 10 splits is $s = 0.03$. This shows that our evaluation was reliable and the results do not depend strongly on the data split.

Our evaluation shows that BERT outperforms two state-of-the-art machine learning models and a baseline for detecting event locations.

Although not directly comparable, the results we achieved are similar in terms of accuracy to the results reported by (Lee et al., 2019) on a different data set of protest events: The best accuracy they achieve is 0.75, using SVM. Their approach, however, uses a significant amount of semantic and morphological pre-processing. In contrast, we entirely relied on the semantic knowledge encoded in the BERT model. This is a clue that the BERT models could decrease the need of extensive feature engineering and provide a basis for non complex identification of event arguments.

7 Conclusions

The objective of this paper was to validate an approach, based on the use of a large language model (FastBERT) to leverage context and semantics in the task of detecting primary (main) event locations. In this process we completely avoided complex feature engineering and linguistic pre-processing. We achieved encouraging results, outperforming an heuristic baseline and SVM classifiers based on bag of words and word embedding vectors.

In this work we focused on protest events, since they are important measure for the level of political discontent in the society and provide a basis for conflict prediction. Other socio-political events, such as armed conflicts, manifest similar problems when analysing their spacial dynamics. In this line of thought, locations are important parameters

Table 2: Evaluation and comparison of BERT with SVM and a baseline

Model	Precision	Recall	F1 measure	Accuracy
FastBERT	0.75	0.86	0.80	0.73
SVM BoW	0.64	0.99	0.78	0.64
SVM W2V	0.65	0.95	0.77	0.65
Baseline First sentence	0.68	0.34	0.46	0.40

for each news report. Moreover, distinguishing main location mentions from secondary ones is an important and challenging task. Therefore, our work has larger scope and applicability which goes beyond the protest events.

The question of performance of such approach for less resourced languages should be tackled. Being multilingual by design is of paramount importance for many Automatic Event Detection applications. The promise of last generation models to transpose learning efficiently from one language to another is in this view a strong incentive to further invest in their use. In this perspective training, testing and evaluating the latest large language models with multi-lingual annotated event location corpora is a relevant research direction in the context of automated location analysis in news and social media streams.

References

Chinatsu Aone and Mila Ramos-Santacruz. 2000. Rees: a large-scale relation and event extraction system. In *Sixth applied natural language processing conference*, pages 76–83.

Kenneth Ward Church. 2017. Word2vec. *Natural Language Engineering*, 23(1):155–162.

Donald Davidson. 1969. *The Individuation of Events*, pages 216–234. Springer Netherlands, Dordrecht.

Bertrand De Longueville, Gianluca Luraschi, Paul Smits, Stephen Peedell, and Tom De Groeve. 2010. Citizens as sensors for natural hazards: A vgi integration workflow. *Geomatica*, 64(1):41–59.

Bertrand De Longueville, Robin S Smith, and Gianluca Luraschi. 2009. " omg, from here, i can see the flames!" a use case of mining location based social networks to acquire spatio-temporal data on forest fires. In *Proceedings of the 2009 international workshop on location based social networks*, pages 73–80.

Ian Densham and James Reid. 2003. System demo: A geo-coding service encompassing a geo-parsing tool and integrated digital gazetteer service. In *Proceedings of the HLT-NAACL 2003 workshop on Analysis of geographic references*, pages 79–80.

Jacob Devlin, Ming-Wei Chang, Kenton Lee, and Kristina Toutanova. 2018. Bert: Pre-training of deep bidirectional transformers for language understanding. *arXiv preprint arXiv:1810.04805*.

Salvatore Giorgi, Vanni Zavarella, Hristo Tanev, Nicolas Stefanovitch, Sy Hwang, Hansi Hettiarachchi, Tharindu Ranasinghe, Vivek Kalyan, Paul Tan, Shaun Tan, et al. 2021. Discovering black lives matter events in the united states: Shared task 3, case 2021. In *Proceedings of the 4th Workshop on Challenges and Applications of Automated Extraction of Socio-political Events from Text (CASE 2021)*, pages 218–227.

Ralph Grishman, Silja Huttunen, and Roman Yangarber. 2002a. Information extraction for enhanced access to disease outbreak reports. *Journal of biomedical informatics*, 35(4):236–246.

Ralph Grishman, Silja Huttunen, and Roman Yangarber. 2002b. Real-time event extraction for infectious disease outbreaks. In *Proceedings of Human Language Technology Conference (HLT)*, pages 366–369.

Andrew Halterman. 2017. Mordecai: Full text geoparsing and event geocoding. *The Journal of Open Source Software*, 2(9):91.

Andrew Halterman. 2019. Geolocating political events in text. In *Proceedings of the Third Workshop on Natural Language Processing and Computational Social Science*, pages 29–39.

Kevin Humphreys, Robert Gaizauskas, and Saliha Azzam. 1997. Event coreference for information extraction. In *Operational Factors in Practical, Robust Anaphora Resolution for Unrestricted Texts*.

Ali Hürriyetoğlu, Hristo Tanev, Vanni Zavarella, Jakub Piskorski, Reyyan Yeniterzi, and Erdem Yörük. 2021a. Challenges and applications of automated extraction of socio-political events from text (case 2021): Workshop and shared task report. *arXiv preprint arXiv:2108.07865*.

Ali Hürriyetoğlu, Erdem Yörük, Osman Mutlu, Fırat Duruşan, Çağrı Yoltar, Deniz Yüret, and Burak Gürel. 2021b. Cross-context news corpus for protest event-related knowledge base construction. *Data Intelligence*, 3(2):308–335.

Maryam Bahojb Imani, Swarup Chandra, Samuel Ma, Latifur Khan, and Bhavani Thuraisingham. 2017. Focus location extraction from political news reports with bias correction. In *2017 IEEE International Conference on Big Data (Big Data)*, pages 1956–1964. IEEE.

Suradej Intagorn, Anon Plangprasopchok, and Kristina Lerman. 2010. Harvesting geospatial knowledge from social metadata. In *ISCRAM*.

Alisa Kongthon, Choochart Haruechaiyasak, Jaruwat Pailai, and Sarawoot Kongyoung. 2014. The role of social media during a natural disaster: A case study of the 2011 thai flood. *International Journal of Innovation and Technology Management*, 11(03):1440012.

Ourania Kounadi, Thomas J Lampoltshammer, Elizabeth Groff, Izabela Sitko, and Michael Leitner. 2015. Exploring twitter to analyze the public's reaction patterns to recently reported homicides in london. *PloS one*, 10(3):e0121848.

Gary LaFree and Laura Dugan. 2007. Introducing the global terrorism database. *Terrorism and political violence*, 19(2):181–204.

Sophie J. Lee, Howard Liu, and Michael D. Ward. 2019. Lost in space: Geolocation in event data. *Political Science Research and Methods*, 7(4):871–888.

Weijie Liu, Peng Zhou, Zhiruo Wang, Zhe Zhao, Haotang Deng, and Qi Ju. 2020. FastBERT: a self-distilling BERT with adaptive inference time. In *Proceedings of the 58th Annual Meeting of the Association for Computational Linguistics*, pages 6035–6044, Online. Association for Computational Linguistics.

Peter Makarov, Jasmine Lorenzini, Klaus Rothenhäusler, and Bruno Wüest. 2015. Towards automated protest event analysis. *New Frontiers of Automated Content Analysis in the Social Sciences*.

Benjamin Muller, Antonios Anastasopoulos, Benoît Sagot, and Djamé Seddah. 2022. When being unseen from mbert is just the beginning: Handling new languages with multilingual language models. In *TALN 2022-29° conférence sur le Traitement Automatique des Langues Naturelles*, pages 450–451. ATALA.

Simon E Overell. 2009. *Geographic information retrieval: Classification, disambiguation and modelling*. Ph.D. thesis, Imperial College London (University of London).

Clionadh Raleigh, Andrew Linke, Håvard Hegre, and Joakim Karlsen. 2010. Introducing acled: an armed conflict location and event dataset: special data feature. *Journal of peace research*, 47(5):651–660.

Michael D Ward, Andreas Beger, Josh Cutler, Matthew Dickenson, Cassy Dorff, and Ben Radford. 2013. Comparing gdelt and icews event data. *Analysis*, 21(1):267–297.

Vanni Zavarella, Hristo Tanev, Ali Hürriyetoğlu, Peratham Wiriyathammabhum, and Bertrand De Longueville. 2022. Tracking covid-19 protest events in the united states. shared task 2: Event database replication, case 2022. In *Proceedings of the 5th Workshop on Challenges and Applications of Automated Extraction of Socio-political Events from Text (CASE)*, pages 209–216.

Chao Zhang, Liyuan Liu, Dongming Lei, Quan Yuan, Honglei Zhuang, Tim Hanratty, and Jiawei Han. 2017. Triovecevent: Embedding-based online local event detection in geo-tagged tweet streams. In *Proceedings of the 23rd ACM SIGKDD International Conference on Knowledge Discovery and Data Mining*, pages 595–604.

A Multi-instance Learning Approach to Civil Unrest Event Detection using Twitter

Alexandra DeLucia*, **Mark Dredze***, **Anna L Buczak**†
*Center for Language and Speech Processing, Johns Hopkins University
†Johns Hopkins University Applied Physics Laboratory
{aadelucia, mdredze}@jhu.edu, Anna.Buczak@jhuapl.edu

Abstract

Social media has become an established platform for people to organize and take offline actions, often in the form of *civil unrest*. Understanding these events can help support pro-democratic movements. The primary method to detect these events on Twitter relies on aggregating many tweets, but this includes many that are not relevant to the task. We propose a multi-instance learning (MIL) approach, which jointly identifies relevant tweets and detects civil unrest events. We demonstrate that MIL improves civil unrest detection over methods based on simple aggregation. Our best model achieves a 0.73 F1 on the Global Civil Unrest on Twitter (G-CUT) dataset.

https://github.com/AADeLucia/MIL-civil-unrest

1 Introduction

Social media has become an established platform for people around the world to share opinions and react to socio-political events. Platforms enable communication between like-minded individuals and can facilitate offline action. These actions can take the form of democratic expression, such as protests or other types of *civil unrest*. In the right situation, these events can lead to pro-democracy actions and lead to political changes towards more free and open governments and societies. Researchers who study these political movements often turn to social media platforms, especially the globally used Twitter,[1] to facilitate an understanding of how these events develop (Smidi and Shahin, 2017; Soengas-Pérez, 2013; Steinert-Threlkeld, 2017), which in turn may be used to study pro-democratic movements.

As part of that research program, different efforts have considered how to detect or forecast the start of the spread of these movements, including answering what will happen when. Detection and forecasting models identify civil unrest either at the macro- (global or country) (Muthiah et al., 2015; Islam et al., 2020) or micro- (city) level (Alsaedi et al., 2017; Giorgi et al., 2021) using one or multiple data sources, like social media, news, or economic indicators. Others study event extraction, whose goal is to extract information about an ongoing or recent event, such as where it happened and who was involved.

One of the challenges of developing models for detecting civil unrest events – is there an ongoing event? – is developing models responsive to rapid on the ground changes. Social media provides a mechanism for rapid detection; messages can be collected and analyzed as the event unfolds. Several studies have examined how Twitter can be utilized in a civil unrest detection model (Chinta et al., 2021; Islam et al., 2020; Muthiah et al., 2015). While there are a wealth of tweets from all over the world at any given time, not all tweets from a given location are relevant to an event. Filtering and identifying relevant tweets remains a challenging problem (Sech et al., 2020; Mishler et al., 2017; Rogers et al., 2019; Zhang and Pan, 2019).[2] Given the goal of detecting *any* event, it is important for a detection method to work even without knowing which tweets are necessarily relevant.

We follow Wang et al. (2016) and propose a multi-instance learning (MIL) approach to detecting civil unrest events at the country-level using Twitter data. In MIL, examples are grouped and labeled as a group instead of individually (i.e., weak supervision). Instead of aggregating all tweets from a given country within a specified time period, we utilize the MIL formulation where at least one tweet is relevant while most are not to predict

[1] We discuss recent access changes to Twitter API in Section 8.

[2] Rogers et al. (2019) used data from a Russian social media site (VKontakte) and Zhang and Pan (2019) used data from a Chinese site (Sina Weibo).

Proceedings of the 6th Workshop on Challenges and Applications of Automated Extraction of Socio-political Events from Text, pages 18–33, Varna, Bulgaria, Sep 7, 2023.
https://doi.org/10.26615/978-954-452-089-2_003

an event. We learn a tweet-level representation using a BERT-style model and then group these representations (i.e., *instances*) into a single *bag* (country/time period, in our case a single day).

We apply this method to the Global Civil Unrest on Twitter (G-CUT) dataset (Chinta et al., 2021),[3] which contains 200 million English tweets from 2014–2019 from 42 countries in Africa, the Middle East, and Southeast Asia. We focus on English tweets to take advantage of this large dataset and for easier analysis without the need for translation. Following Chinta et al. (2021), we use the Riots and Protests labels at the day level for a country from the Armed Conflict Location & Event Data Project (ACLED) (Raleigh et al., 2010) as ground truth, where a bag is positive if at least one event occurred in that country on that day.

We show that providing the model with all tweets (i.e., not filtering for civil unrest) and allowing it to choose relevant information leads to improved performance on detecting that an event occurred on a specific day in a country, as measured by F1. We support these results with an analysis showing the key tweets identified by the model during prediction.

In summary, we contribute the following:

- A trained MIL model for civil unrest detection on Twitter that achieves 0.73 F1 on G-CUT.
- Variations of the MIL model with varying levels of bag- and instance-level information.
- Analysis of example tweets identified as important for the model prediction.

2 Related Work

Work in civil unrest analysis, also referred to as socio-political event analysis, focuses on event characterization (Scharf et al., 2021), protest detection and forecasting (Hürriyetoğlu, 2021; Hürriyetoğlu et al., 2022), and event extraction (You et al., 2022; Mehta et al., 2022). Prior work on protest detection on the macro level (global or country) is most relevant to our task of country-level civil unrest detection. Existing work differs with regard to source data, event ground truth, and methods.

Most prior work uses news, social media, or economic indicators as features, or sometimes, a combination for a fuller picture. For news data, the goal is often to identify whether an article is discussing a protest or event, as opposed to identifying whether an event is occurring at a location of interest. Wang et al. (2016) use an MIL framework to predict whether a news article is discussing a protest, with sentences considered as *instances* and news articles as *bags*. They use the sentences that were most informative for the article prediction for further analysis in event extraction. Our approach is inspired by this work; we describe it in Section 3.2. This setup of classifying the overall articles and the sentences within them was a part of the Multilingual Protest News Detection CASE 2021 shared task (Hürriyetoğlu et al., 2021).

Similar to sentence-level event identification, prior work has trained models for social media post-level identification of civil unrest discussion (Sech et al., 2020). While not their final goal, Islam et al. (2020) and Alsaedi et al. (2017) incorporate tweet-level models as filters for whether to include a tweet in future steps. Their tweet labels were gathered from manual annotation. We omit this filtration step since the proposed MIL approach can handle irrelevant tweets. This is an important note since our dataset was not collected with event-specific tweets as in Alsaedi et al. (2017).[4]

Alsaedi et al. (2017) leverage tweets discussing the London Riots (2011) to predict micro (small-scale) events like fires, car accidents, and assaults identified by police records through tweet filtering, clustering, and then automatically selecting a tweet as an event summary. Our model allows for a flexible number of posts to be provided as an explanation for each prediction. They also evaluate their system on larger-scale events across the Middle East in 2015, clustering with a variety of features like hashtags, sentiment, time, and location, if provided. Thus, predictions are on an event-level and not exactly a country-level as ours is (i.e., using only information from a single country).

Zheng and Sun (2019) also extract event-related keywords from clustered tweets, but cluster tweets in an online active-learning MIL setting. This MIL formulation differs from ours because their "bags" are clusters of similar tweets that are hand-labeled, whereas our bags represent a day in a country. They use a strict formulation where a cluster is predicted as positive (i.e., event) if it has at least one positive tweet (i.e., discussing event/unrest), and negative if there are no positive tweets. This assumption

[3] https://zenodo.org/record/5816218

[4] The London Riots dataset was collected with a list of event-related hashtags such as #tottenhamshooting and #UKRiots.

does not work for our setting, where we expect unrest-related tweets even on days where no event occurred.

Similar to our goal of detecting unrest on the country-level while maintaining tweets individuality, Islam et al. (2020) learn weights on individual tweets for a location that are updated in a temporally streaming fashion. Their tweet weights are based on a civil unrest dictionary of terms that correspond to different unrest "stages" (observe, agitation, mobilization, organization, occurrence), along with other temporal and spatial information. Our method does not rely on keyword dictionaries and instead, we update embeddings to obtain tweet weights for a given country-day. They also include a spatial component that incorporates information of nearby events. For ground truth they used the Global Data on Events, Location, and Tone (GDELT) database (Leetaru and Schrodt, 2013) and restricted to events with high coverage. In this work we follow other work and use labels from ACLED (Chinta et al., 2021; Zavarella et al., 2022).

Other systems combine multiple streams of information, such as news and Twitter data (Muthiah et al., 2015; Ramakrishnan et al., 2014; Giorgi et al., 2021) and news and macro-socio political indicators like GDELT and Worldwide Governance Indicators (WGI) (Buczak et al., 2022). We focus on Twitter because prior work has shown strong civil unrest indicators in past events such as the Arab Spring (Smidi and Shahin, 2017; Soengas-Pérez, 2013).

There is also work on civil unrest prediction in the fields of social and political science. Goldstone et al. (2010) built a model that incorporates a variety of socioeconomic and political indicators (e.g., infant mortality rate, stability of neighboring countries, and type of government) to predict whether a country in a given year would experience a large-scale event like a regime change or genocide. Similarly, Chenoweth and Ulfelder (2015) use structural condition theories (e.g., political opportunity) to predict large-scale non-violent events in a country-year. While Goldstone et al. (2010) and Chenoweth and Ulfelder (2015) achieved impressive 80% accuracy and 0.75 AUC, respectively, curating their rich political and socioeconomic country profiles requires a large amount of domain knowledge compared to our Twitter-centric approach.

3 Multi-Instance Learning for Detecting Civil Unrest

Our task is to identify days on which, in a given country, there is a civil unrest event based on Twitter data. For each country and day, we acquire a large number of tweets potentially relevant to an event. A model examines this data and predicts whether or not an event is taking place. Instead of aggregating the tweets, we propose a multi-instance learning approach that considers whether or not tweets are relevant. Specifically, the model assumes that on a day in which an event occurs, only a subset of the provided tweets are relevant to the event. This framing supports explainable predictions, where the tweets deemed relevant by the model can be examined for further context.

3.1 Multi-instance Learning

Multi-instance learning (MIL) is a form of weak supervision wherein individual examples, or *instances*, are grouped in a *bag* and are labeled at the bag level. MIL can be useful for large datasets where labeling individual instances is time-consuming, or for problems where a single label is associated with a set of samples. For example, a task may be to identify if a newspaper contains a fashion section. A newspaper would be represented as a bag, and individual articles as instances. If a newspaper has a fashion section, we assume at least one instance (article) is about fashion; otherwise, no articles are about fashion. Alternatively, in content-based image retrieval, images are segmented and each segment is analyzed individually, and the image is classified based on the contained objects in the instances (segments) (Carbonneau et al., 2018).

In the case of civil unrest detection from tweets, we assume that if an event takes place, then at least one tweet (and likely many) will discuss that event, while many will not. If no event takes place, no tweets discuss an event. In our work, each tweet is an instance, and all tweets from a single country on one day constitute a bag. A positive instance is a tweet that discusses civil unrest (e.g., expressing dissatisfaction or describing a protest in real-time) and a *positive bag* is a day and country where a protest occurred.

There are two different assumptions in MIL. The *standard assumption* assumes that every positive bag contains at least one positive instance and for a negative bag to only contain negative instances.

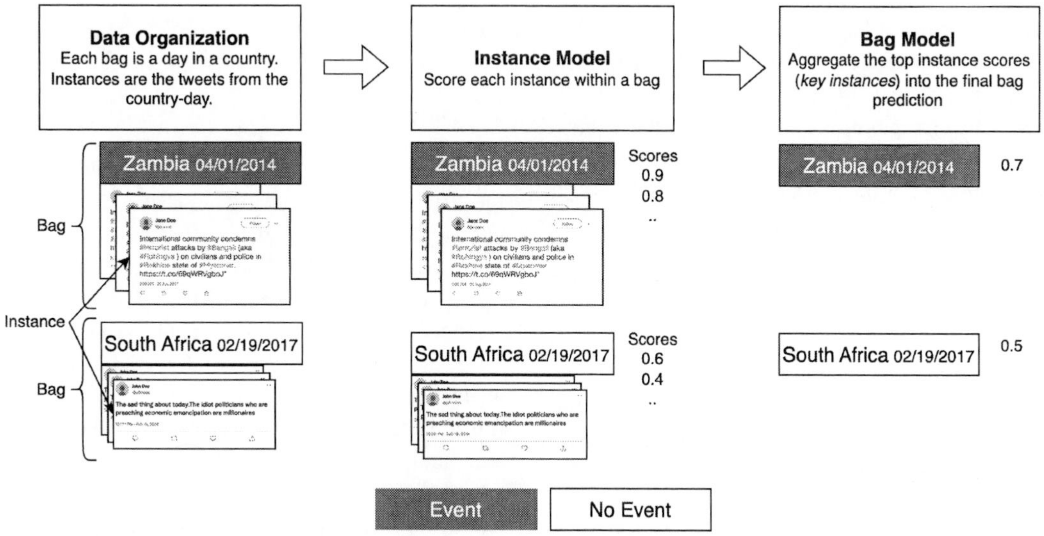

Figure 1: Overview of the proposed multi-instance learning (MIL) approach for civil unrest detection. We follow the country-day groupings and labels from the Global Civil Unrest on Twitter (G-CUT) dataset (Chinta et al., 2021).

This assumption is overly strict for our purposes, so we follow the relaxed *collective assumption*, where bags can contain some level of instances from the other class (Carbonneau et al., 2018). This assumption is a better fit since there can be tweets expressing dissatisfaction or discussing protests on non-event days.

There are multiple ways to combine instance-level features and scores at the bag level, such as averaging the instance-level scores, considering only the top-k instances, or using the max score. In our task, this flexibility can help overcome a weak signal of positive instances in positive bags. Furthermore, MIL identifies instances that were most influential in the final bag prediction, known as "key" instances. While there is a trade-off between optimizing a model for bag classification and instance classification (Vanwinckelen et al., 2016), there is work that uses identified key instances for downstream tasks, such as bag summarization (Wang et al., 2016).

3.2 MIL for Twitter

Our MIL-based model for Twitter data is based on Wang et al. (2016), but we replace sentences and news articles with tweets and sets of tweets. Consider a collection of tweets $\mathcal{D} = \{(x_1, y_1), \ldots, (x_i, y_i), \ldots\}$, where a bag $x_i = \{(x_i^1, y_i^1), \ldots, (x_i^j, y_i^j), \ldots\}$ contains all tweets (indexed by j) from a single day in a country (country-day for brevity). We aim to find informative key instances that predict the bag-level class of civil unrest (protest for brevity): no protest or protest, $y_i \in \{0, 1\}$. Figure 1 shows an overview of our model.

Instance Model We represent individual tweets with BERTweet (Nguyen et al., 2020), a BERT model pretrained on English tweets. In order to better represent civil-unrest related tweets, we fine-tuned BERTweet on the Civil Unrest on Twitter (CUT) dataset (Sech et al., 2020) with the HuggingFace Trainer. The model has a macro-F1 score of 0.82. More training details are in Appendix B.1. This trained model is the **instance classification model**, where the score (probability) of an instance is $p(y_i^j = 1) = \sigma(\theta x_i^j)$. The instance-level scores are not incorporated in the standard MIL model, but the representations are fine-tuned starting from the instance model representations.

Bag Model The score of bag x_i is determined by aggregating the instance scores. We use the average of the top K_i instances in the bag:

$$p(y_i = 1) = \frac{1}{K_i} \sum_{j<K_i} \sigma(\theta x_i^j) \qquad (1)$$

The number of top instances for bag x_i (K_i) is chosen by hyperparameter $0 \leq \eta \leq 1$ so that $K_i \triangleq \max(1, \lfloor |x_i| \times \eta \rfloor)$. This dynamic average was used in Wang et al. (2016) and handles bags with differing volumes of instances. For example, with $\eta = 0.2$, the score of bags with 100 and 87 instances would be based on the top 20 and 17 instances, respectively. We train using the binary cross entropy loss (BCE) for bag-level event prediction. The loss is propagated through to the instance model so that instance representations are adjusted to better predict the overall bag label. We refer to this model as the **MIL** model.

Instance-level Supervision Vanwinckelen et al. (2015) showed that a good bag classifier does not imply a good instance classifier. Since we want a model to identify useful key instances for downstream tasks, a model that performs well on both bag and instance classification would be useful. Unlike most MIL tasks, we have instance-level knowledge in the form of tweet-level civil unrest prediction probabilities from our trained instance classification model.[5]

We modify our MIL formulation by incorporating these instance-level scores in addition to the bag labels. Our new loss function is

$$\underbrace{-\frac{1}{|X|}\sum_{x_i \in X} \text{BCELoss}(y_i, p(y_i))}_{\text{bag-level loss}} \quad (2)$$
$$\underbrace{-\beta\frac{1}{|X|}\sum_{x_i \in X}\frac{1}{|x_i|}\sum_{x_i^j \in x_i} \text{BCELoss}(y_i^j, p(y_i^j))}_{\text{instance-level loss}}$$

see Appendix B.2 for the unabridged loss function and a comparison of our function to the one from Wang et al. (2016).

To encourage correct bag-level classification we used the typical binary cross entropy loss (BCE) for logistic regression. Note that $p(y_i = 1)$ is the same as in eq. (1) and is only calculated using the key instances (controlled by η). The second portion of the loss function, the instance level loss, is also a BCE loss to minimize the difference between the MIL instance prediction score and the true score from the trained instance model. β is a hyperparameter to control the impact of instance-level loss on training. We call this model the MIL with Bag and Instance Supervision (**MIL-BI**).

Observe that the MIL model is a special case of MIL-BI. When $\beta = 0$, no instance-level information is incorporated and it is a standard MIL model with only bag loss. Also, when $\eta = 0$, the top-k average is simply the max operation, another commonly used MIL aggregation function (albeit rather noisy and prone to false positives).

4 Data

We use existing datasets for general civil unrest: the Armed Conflict Location & Event Data Project (ACLED) (Raleigh et al., 2010), Global Civil Unrest on Twitter (G-CUT) (Chinta et al., 2021), and Civil Unrest on Twitter (CUT) (Sech et al., 2020).

Together G-CUT and ACLED provide the tweets for each day in a country and the label of whether an event occurred on that day. G-CUT contains 200 million English tweets from 2014–2019 covering 42 countries in Africa, the Middle East, and Southeast Asia. Due to the large variety of amount of tweets for each day, we randomly sampled a maximum of 1000 tweets from each country from each day to represent the "bag". We also pruned the dataset further than Chinta et al. (2021) to remove spam-like tweets; see Appendix A for details.

Following Chinta et al. (2021), we use the Riots and Protests labels at the day label for a country from ACLED. We consider a day in a country as "positive" for a civil unrest event if ACLED identified a protest or riot on that day in that country.[6] Even if multiple events are identified on the same day, that still only counts as one positive example. All other days are negative (i.e., no event).

As mentioned in Section 3.2, we used CUT to train our instance model.

5 Experiments

We evaluate the proposed MIL models along with baselines for the civil unrest detection task. We follow prior work and evaluate model performance on F1, precision, and recall (Chinta et al., 2021; Alsaedi et al., 2017). The model's prediction is marked as correct if it predicts a civil unrest event occurred on a country-day (i.e., bag) that is also identified by the ACLED ground truth. We use the weighted F1 score due to the class imbalance (roughly 30% positive in the training set).

5.1 MIL Models

We evaluate the MIL and MIL-BI models described in Section 3.2 across key instance ratios, $\eta \in \{0.1, 0.2, 0.3, 0.4, 0.5, 0.6, 0.7, 0.8, 0.9\}$, and instance supervision, $\beta \in \{0.0, 0.25, 0.5, 0.75, 1.0\}$.

[5] This differs from other MIL tasks where no instance labels are available to train an instance classification model.

[6] ACLED includes six main event types: battles, explosions/remote violence, violence against civilians, protests, riots, and strategic development

All models had a batch size of 20, a maximum of 100 instances per bag (depending on the number of tweets per country-day), and were trained for 50 epochs (patience of 20 epochs) with AdamW optimizer and 1×10^{-5} learning rate with 100 warmup steps. These models were implemented in PyTorch and trained with the HuggingFace Trainer on 4 NVIDIA A100 80GB GPUs. To ensure the model sees a variety of instances for each bag, the 100 instances were sampled from the maximum of 1000 instances in each bag for each iteration (see Section 4).

5.2 Comparison Models

We compare our MIL models against other aggregation-based representations.[7] See Appendix C for training details.

MIL (max) We also include MIL with $\eta = 0$ ($|K_i| = 1$) to evaluate max aggregation instead of top-k average.

MIL-Instance only (MIL-I) Average only the tweet-level scores and do not include any bag information. This model does not require any training as the instance model is already trained. Instead, the top instance scores are averaged as-is.

AVG Bag This model is the most direct comparison to our MIL approach since it tests whether the instance-level representation is useful or if only the bag representation is useful. To represent each day in a country, we use the average instance representation, or average instance model embedding across all tweets for that country for the day. The classifier is a random forest model.

AVG Bag (BERTweet) This model is the same as AVG Bag except instead of using the instance representations, we use BERTweet representations. These embeddings were trained on general, non-civil unrest tweets. We include this model to evaluate if the AVG Bag model benefits from the civil unrest-aware embeddings provided by the instance model.

5.3 Baselines

The following baselines were re-run from (Chinta et al., 2021). The random baselines were also used in Wu and Gerber (2018) and Qiao and Wang (2015). The train/dev/test split is the same as for the MIL models (2014–2016/2017/2018–2019). See Appendix C for details.

N-gram A random forest classifier with unigrams from all the tweets for each bag as features. We did not remove location-specific words as in Chinta et al. (2021). We preprocess the tweets with the MIL model tokenizer for a consistent vocabulary (i.e., the BERTweet tokenizer).

Random baseline Model that uses the rate of events (i.e., positive class) from the train set to predict whether an event will occur. For example, since the train set has 30% positive examples, this model predicts an event occurs for 30% of the test data. This baseline is included purely for comparison and will not be analyzed in-depth along with the other models.

Country-Random baseline This model a country-specific version of the random baseline. It predicts an event for a country based on the rate of events for that country in the training set (2014-2016). For example, the prediction for a bag from Zambia would be based on the positive rate specifically for Zambia in the training set as opposed to the overall positive rate.

Model	F1	Precision	Recall
MIL-max	0.71	**0.73**	**0.74**
MIL (η=0.4)	**0.73**	**0.73**	**0.74**
MIL-BI ($\beta = 1$)	0.67	**0.73**	0.72
MIL-I-max	0.52	0.37	0.90
AVG-Bag	0.48	0.33	0.88
AVG-Bag BERTweet	0.38	0.58	0.29
Ngram	0.48	0.64	0.38
Random	0.31	0.33	0.28
Country-random	0.50	0.54	0.46

Table 1: Model performance on civil unrest event detection task. The scores shown are from the test set (years 2018-2019). Reported F1 is weighted-F1.

6 Results

The notable findings are as follows:

The MIL models outperformed all the baselines. All variations of the MIL models outperformed the other aggregation models and baselines. The strongest baseline was one of the more simple, the Country-Random model, as shown in Table 1. Personalizing the model from the overall positive

[7] The code from Wang et al. (2016) was not available for reproduction.

η	MIL			MIL-I		
	F1	Precision	Recall	F1	Precision	Recall
0.0	0.71	0.73	0.74	**0.52**	**0.37**	**0.9**
0.1	0.73	0.73	0.74	0.34	0.43	0.29
0.2	0.73	0.73	0.74	0.17	0.55	0.1
0.3	0.72	0.74	0.74	0.042	0.44	0.022
0.4	**0.73**	**0.73**	**0.74**	0.0073	0.29	0.0037
0.5	0.73	0.73	0.74	0.0024	0.27	0.0012
0.6	0.72	0.73	0.74	0.0016	0.32	0.00078
0.7	0.72	0.74	0.74	0.00089	0.36	0.00045
0.8	0.72	0.73	0.74	0.0	0.0	0.0
0.9	0.72	0.73	0.74	0.0	0.0	0.0
1.0	0.72	0.72	0.73	0.0	0.0	0.0

Table 2: Ablation over the key instance ratio, η for the MIL and MIL instance-only (MIL-I) models. The results are on the test set. $\eta = 0$ refers to the *max* aggregation. Reported F1 is weighted-F1.

class rate to the positive class rate for each country helped significantly, with an increase of 0.2 F1 from the Random model. The Ngram model outperformed the Random and AVG-Bag BERTweet models by roughly 0.2 and 0.1 F1, respectively. AVG-Bag BERTweet performed worse than the AVG-Bag model, indicating that the civil unrest pre-training from the instance model was helpful.

Number of key instances does not have an effect on MIL performance. The effect of adjusting the key instance ratio for the top-k average had little to no impact on the performance, with all models achieving within ± 0.1 F1 of 0.73 on the test set (Table 2). This low impact might be due to the high variance in the number of tweets per bag (see Appendix Figure 4). However, all models with $\eta > 0$ outperformed $\eta = 0$, or the MIL-max model, indicating an advantage in basing the prediction for a country-day on more than one tweet. While very close, a key instance ratio of 0.4 had the highest performance and we refer to it as **MIL (best)**.

Incorporating instance supervision hurts model performance. We use the best η from the MIL sweep (0.4) to experiment with instance-level supervision, β. Similar to the key instance ratio sweep, the instance loss weight also does not have a large impact on model performance, with only a difference of a few F1 points. Table 3 shows the tested β values on the validation set. While the difference is not great, it is still more apparent than with the η sweep, indicating incorporating instance loss is more impactful on the model than the number of key instances. As β increases, performance

β	F1	Precision	Recall
0.0	**0.73**	0.73	0.74
0.25	0.72	**0.74**	**0.74**
0.5	0.71	0.73	**0.74**
0.75	0.70	0.73	0.73
1.0	0.67	0.73	0.72

Table 3: Instance loss parameter sweep (β) for the MIL-BI model. As β increases, F1 decreases. All other settings are the same as for the best MIL model. Scores are on the test set.

decreases, confirming the conflict of optimizing for both instance and bag-level classification. While all models with $\beta > 0$ do not perform as well as MIL (best), the best MIL-BI model ($\beta = 0.25$) achieves an F1 of 0.77 on the validation set and 0.72 on the test set. While $\beta = 0.25$ has the best performance, we analyze $\beta = 1.0$ further in Section 7.1 to evaluate whether the decline in civil unrest prediction performance is offset by more informative key instances.

Bag information is needed alongside instances for accurate bag prediction. Finally, we do not incorporate the bag labels at all and evaluate the MIL instance-only model. In Table 2 we see the drastic change in model performance, with the lack of training with bag labels leading to a performance worse than MIL and the baselines. The exception is with $\eta = 0$ which outperformed most of the baselines at 0.52 F1, 0.37 precision, and 0.90 recall. However, this high F1 is skewed by the very high recall as opposed to precision, indicating the model over-predicts positive bags. This use of only the single highest-scoring instance for bag label prediction confirms the presence of positive instances in negative bags, or the *collective assumption* (see Section 3).

Performance varies across countries Following prior work that uses tweets from multiple countries, we check our model's performance across all 42 countries in the dataset (Zhang et al., 2022; Chinta et al., 2021). The per-country F1, precision, and recall scores from MIL (best) on the test set are shown in Appendix Figure 5. Roughly half of the countries (22) have an F1 score below the aggregated score, and there is a clear gap in performance between countries with the highest (Pakistan, 1.0 F1) and lowest (Morocco, 0.28 F1) scores. This performance discrepancy can in part be explained by unequal country presence in the training set as well as differing rates of events. As shown in Figure 2, Pakistan (PAK) is not only very prevalent in the data, it also has a very high rate of events, indicating a very simple task if the model associates Pakistani tweets with civil unrest. Countries with either very high or very low levels of civil unrest in the train set generally perform better than those in the middle (40-60% positive events). The relationship is not as clear with Morocco (MAR), which appears to be an outlier, since other countries with similar size and rate of events perform better, such as Thailand (THA).

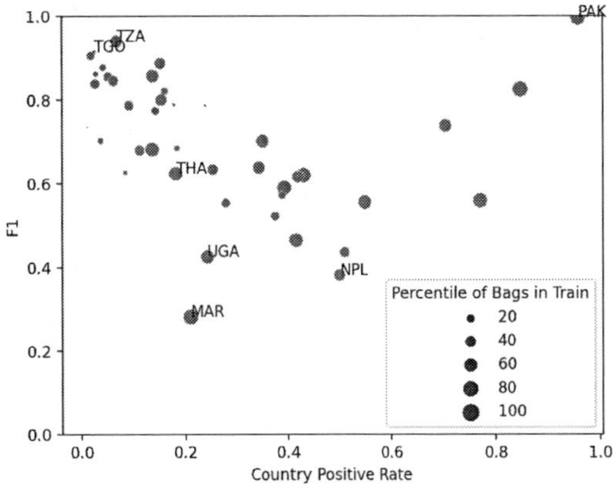

Figure 2: The test F1 scores from the MIL (best) across all countries present in the data. The countries with the highest and lowest F1 scores are annotated. The size of each point is relative to the number of bags each country has in the training data. The model performs best on countries with either very low or very high rates of civil unrest. The included countries are Togo (TGO), Tanzania (TZA), Thailand (THA), Uganda (UGA), Morocco (MAR), Nepal (NPL), and Pakistan (PAK).

7 Discussion

While performance is important, a strength of the MIL approach is the identification of which tweets contribute the most to the final prediction, i.e. those with the highest probabilities. These top tweets can be used to *explain* the model's prediction. We examine the top tweets for a single event below. Also, we revisit the MIL *collective assumption* in an analysis of civil-unrest related tweet distributions on days with and without events.

7.1 Key Instance Analysis: Case Study

In Table 4 we compare top tweets from MIL models of interest: the best-performing MIL-$\eta = 0.4$, MIL-BI-($\beta = 1$), and MIL-max. We focus on a single event identified by ACLED, a protest in Sri Lanka on September 5, 2018, shown in Table 4.

The selected event was a large protest concerning a political demonstration demanding the government to step down and was organized by the Joint Opposition, a political alliance. The MIL model predicted a protest with probability 0.53 and identified informative tweets, with specific mentions of the Joint Opposition as well as police presence for riot control. There is also a noisy, irrelevant tweet directed at the then-president of the US. While the MIL-max model is typically easily skewed by its top tweets, in this specific example it was distracted by an irrelevant tweet about the weather and did not predict that a protest occurred on this day, with a too-low probability of 0.49. Oddly, while identifying tweets of interest discussing unrest, the MIL-BI model had the lowest prediction of all, with a probability of 0.38. These tweets are indicative of unrest and one even tags the president of Sri Lanka, but are not as informative as those from the MIL model. From this example, the MIL model identified mostly informative tweets while MIL-max was distracted by irrelevant noise. The MIL and MIL-BI models had low overall prediction confidence due to a skewed positive instance distribution, i.e. while the top tweets had very high scores, most of the tweets were not identified as civil-unrest related and brought down the average.

This is a single qualitative example and more quantitative analyses are needed for evaluating the usefulness of identified key tweets in downstream tasks like event extraction and summarization.

Event description: On 5-6 Sept, in Fort (Colombo, Colombo), thousands gathered at Lake House roundabout in a JO-organized protest demanding the government to step down. Protesters marched from different locations in Colombo city - including Galleface and Kurunduwatta - to Colombo Fort to join a JO-organized protest. Despite peaceful protest, 1 protester died due to cardiac arrest and several hospitalized due to food poisoning, minor injuries, and excessive drinking.

Model	Bag Score	Tweet Score	Tweet
MIL ($\eta = 0.4$)	0.53	0.99	@realDonaldTrump What about Saudi attacks ?
		0.99	The Joint Opposition (JO) is planning to carry out a huge mass protest called "Janabalaya Kolabata" against the Government targeting Colombo on the 5th September 2018 from 1400 Hrs.
		0.98	Over 5,000 policemen from various units armed with all riot controlling mechanisms will remain standby to face the...
MIL-max	0.49	0.49	current weather in Colombo: scattered clouds, 24°C 88% humidity, wind 3kmh, pressure 1010mb
MIL-BI ($\beta = 1.0$)	0.38	0.99	Dear Mr. Ranjan, the salve of @RW_UNP, majority is suffering your mismanagement...
		1.0	@USER @UN Yes UN, world Bank and other international organizations must be responsible for poverty because...
		0.97	@vijaytelevision @Vivo_India This cheater; poi Kari deserves ah

Table 4: Top key tweets identified by MIL models with different parameters for September 5, 2018 in Sri Lanka. The event description is from ACLED. The tweet scores are from the instance model and the bag score is the aggregated score. The bag score differs from the tweet scores for the MIL and MIL-BI models because not all the top η tweets are shown.

7.2 Distribution of Tweet Scores

An important part of the MIL formulation that we chose was to embrace the noisy Twitter data with the *collective assumption*. In this assumption, a country-day where an event did not occur can still contain civil-unrest related tweets, as identified by the instance model. Appendix Figure 6 shows the distribution of instance scores grouped by country across days with and without an event. The majority of tweets are not unrest-related (i.e., instance score below 0.5), but there is a long tail toward high-scoring instances. The most important note is that for most countries there is little to no visible difference in civil-unrest related tweets on days with and without events. This is a strong indication of why this task of civil unrest prediction on the country-day level is difficult. We discuss potential model improvements in Section 8. Examples of protest-related tweets on a day without civil unrest are shown in Appendix Table 6.

8 Conclusion

Our goal was to evaluate how well a multi-instance learning (MIL) approach to civil unrest detection on Twitter performed to other, aggregated methods. We modeled tweets that occurred on the same day in a country as a *bag* where each tweet is an *instance*. We showed that this formulation worked well, achieving an F1 score of 0.73 on detecting events identified by ACLED. The number of instances that contributed to the final prediction for each bag had little effect, but incorporating instance-level supervision in the form of a loss penalty for misclassifying unrest-related tweets did negatively impact overall event prediction performance.

Since we only evaluated on the civil unrest task, it is unclear if these results are task or data-specific. The remaining challenges are to quantitatively test whether the identified key instances (1) contain event information from the ACLED event(s) (bag labels) and (2) can be used in a full event extraction or summarization pipeline, as in Wang et al. (2016).

We showed that this approach is promising for civil unrest detection, but it can easily be adapted for a new task by substituting new tweets and bag labels, such as the detection of other types of events or even stance classification. The common thread between these problems is that tweets are commonly analyzed in aggregate and all are assumed to be directly related to the topic in question, however since Twitter data is noisy, this is a potentially incorrect assumption.

Acknowledgments

We thank Suzanna Sia, Arya McCarthy, Justin Sech, and the anonymous reviewers for their invaluable feedback. This work relates to Department of Navy award N00014-19-1-2316 issued by the Office of Naval Research. The United States Government has a royalty-free license throughout the world in all copyrightable material contained herein. Any opinions, findings, and conclusions or recommendations expressed in this material are those of the author(s) and do not necessarily reflect the views of the Office of Naval Research.

Ethical Considerations

The main ethical considerations of this work lie in demographic representation, user privacy, and dual use.

We chose Twitter to gain direct access to the "voice" of the people, but through our filtration of non-English and non-geotagged tweets, the data is not a representative sample of the population. Also, some countries do not have a large number of Twitter users in general. The result is that some countries are vastly over-represented in the dataset than others (e.g. South Africa vs Ethiopia). See the G-CUT paper for details on Twitter coverage of the ACLED-identified civil unrest events.

All of the above culminates in a dataset not representative of the population of a country. In future work we will use a multi-lingual approach to mitigate the bias of using English-only tweets. For the chosen regions of Africa, Middle East, and Southeast Asia, we would incorporate Arabic and French at a minimum.

A way to better represent the population would be to use Twitter Geolocation tools, such as the recently introduced Geo-Seq2seq Carmen (Zhang et al., 2023). This data expansion potentially comes at the expense of user privacy.

And finally, the dual use of a tool which identifies tweets discussing civil unrest is a very real possibility. For the purposes of this work, we focus solely on observing and modeling civil unrest and not instigating or curtailing it.

Limitations

The limitations in this work are mostly from not fully exploring the model space with respect to training parameters and architecture and the discontinued access to Twitter going forward.

While we ablated over multi-instance learning-specific parameters such as key instance ratio and instance-level loss, there is always more to be done for hyperparameter tuning of the learning rate and other optimizer parameters. Also, to address limitations of commonly used aggregation functions, one could automatically learn an aggregation, such as through an attention layer (Ilse et al., 2018).

Further, the effect of instance model performance on instance model loss inclusion was not included, i.e., as the instance model becomes more accurate, do the bag predictions become more accurate as well? Also, the effects of instance selection was not explored beyond random sampling.

Also of note is the focus on English tweets, which as discussed in Section 8, limits the population represented in the data. If moving to a multilingual setting, we would use Bernice, a multilingual BERT model trained from-scratch on tweets (DeLucia et al., 2022), for the instance representation instead of BERTweet.

We leave these areas to be addressed in future work.

Regarding data access, in March 2023, Twitter changed its API pricing and effectively closed off its public API stream with undetermined plans for an academic pricing tier.[8] This means while no new tweets can be collected, but past tweets already collected can still be modeled. Our MIL approach can be applied to past tweets for historical events, or other social media platforms like Reddit or Facebook.

References

Nasser Alsaedi, Pete Burnap, and Omer Rana. 2017. Can We Predict a Riot? Disruptive Event Detection Using Twitter. *ACM Transactions on Internet Technology*, 17(2):1–26.

Anna L. Buczak, Benjamin D. Baugher, Adam J. Berlier, Kayla E. Scharfstein, and Christine S. Martin. 2022. Explainable forecasts of disruptive events using recurrent neural networks. In *2022 IEEE International Conference on Assured Autonomy (ICAA)*, pages 64–73.

Lars Buitinck, Gilles Louppe, Mathieu Blondel, Fabian Pedregosa, Andreas Mueller, Olivier Grisel, Vlad Niculae, Peter Prettenhofer, Alexandre Gramfort, Jaques Grobler, Robert Layton, Jake VanderPlas, Arnaud Joly, Brian Holt, and Gaël Varoquaux. 2013. API design for machine learning software: experiences from the scikit-learn project. In *ECML PKDD Workshop: Languages for Data Mining and Machine Learning*, pages 108–122.

Marc-André Carbonneau, Veronika Cheplygina, Eric Granger, and Ghyslain Gagnon. 2018. Multiple in-

[8] https://twitter.com/TwitterDev/status/1641222782594990080

stance learning: A survey of problem characteristics and applications. *Pattern Recognition*, 77:329–353.

Erica Chenoweth and Jay Ulfelder. 2015. Can structural conditions explain the onset of nonviolent uprisings? *Journal of Conflict Resolution*, page 0022002715576574.

Abhinav Chinta, Jingyu Zhang, Alexandra DeLucia, Mark Dredze, and Anna L. Buczak. 2021. Study of manifestation of civil unrest on Twitter. In *Proceedings of the Seventh Workshop on Noisy User-generated Text (W-NUT 2021)*, pages 396–409, Online. Association for Computational Linguistics.

Alexandra DeLucia, Shijie Wu, Aaron Mueller, Carlos Aguirre, Philip Resnik, and Mark Dredze. 2022. Bernice: A multilingual pre-trained encoder for Twitter. In *Proceedings of the 2022 Conference on Empirical Methods in Natural Language Processing*, pages 6191–6205, Abu Dhabi, United Arab Emirates. Association for Computational Linguistics.

Salvatore Giorgi, Vanni Zavarella, Hristo Tanev, Nicolas Stefanovitch, Sy Hwang, Hansi Hettiarachchi, Tharindu Ranasinghe, Vivek Kalyan, Paul Tan, Shaun Tan, Martin Andrews, Tiancheng Hu, Niklas Stoehr, Francesco Ignazio Re, Daniel Vegh, Dennis Atzenhofer, Brenda Curtis, and Ali Hürriyetoğlu. 2021. Discovering black lives matter events in the United States: Shared task 3, CASE 2021. In *Proceedings of the 4th Workshop on Challenges and Applications of Automated Extraction of Socio-political Events from Text (CASE 2021)*, pages 218–227, Online. Association for Computational Linguistics.

Jack A Goldstone, Robert H Bates, David L Epstein, Ted Robert Gurr, Michael B Lustik, Monty G Marshall, Jay Ulfelder, and Mark Woodward. 2010. A global model for forecasting political instability. *American Journal of Political Science*, 54(1):190–208.

Ali Hürriyetoğlu, editor. 2021. *Proceedings of the 4th Workshop on Challenges and Applications of Automated Extraction of Socio-political Events from Text (CASE 2021)*. Association for Computational Linguistics, Online.

Ali Hürriyetoğlu, Osman Mutlu, Erdem Yörük, Farhana Ferdousi Liza, Ritesh Kumar, and Shyam Ratan. 2021. Multilingual protest news detection - shared task 1, CASE 2021. In *Proceedings of the 4th Workshop on Challenges and Applications of Automated Extraction of Socio-political Events from Text (CASE 2021)*, pages 79–91, Online. Association for Computational Linguistics.

Ali Hürriyetoğlu, Hristo Tanev, Vanni Zavarella, and Erdem Yörük, editors. 2022. *Proceedings of the 5th Workshop on Challenges and Applications of Automated Extraction of Socio-political Events from Text (CASE)*. Association for Computational Linguistics, Abu Dhabi, United Arab Emirates (Hybrid).

Maximilian Ilse, Jakub M. Tomczak, and Max Welling. 2018. Attention-based Deep Multiple Instance Learning. *arXiv:1802.04712 [cs, stat]*. ArXiv: 1802.04712.

Kamrul Islam, Manjur Ahmed, Kamal Z. Zamli, and Salman Mehbub. 2020. An online framework for civil unrest prediction using tweet stream based on tweet weight and event diffusion.

Kalev Leetaru and Philip A Schrodt. 2013. GDELT: Global Data on Events, Location and Tone,. page 51.

Sneha Mehta, Huzefa Rangwala, and Naren Ramakrishnan. 2022. Improving zero-shot event extraction via sentence simplification. In *Proceedings of the 5th Workshop on Challenges and Applications of Automated Extraction of Socio-political Events from Text (CASE)*, pages 32–43, Abu Dhabi, United Arab Emirates (Hybrid). Association for Computational Linguistics.

Alan Mishler, Kevin Wonus, Wendy Chambers, and Michael Bloodgood. 2017. Filtering Tweets for Social Unrest. In *2017 IEEE 11th International Conference on Semantic Computing (ICSC)*, pages 17–23.

Sathappan Muthiah, Bert Huang, Jaime Arredondo, David Mares, Lise Getoor, Graham Katz, and Naren Ramakrishnan. 2015. Planned Protest Modeling in News and Social Media. In *Twenty-Seventh IAAI Conference*.

Dat Quoc Nguyen, Thanh Vu, and Anh Tuan Nguyen. 2020. BERTweet: A pre-trained language model for English Tweets. *arXiv:2005.10200 [cs]*. ArXiv: 2005.10200.

Fengcai Qiao and Hui Wang. 2015. Computational Approach to Detecting and Predicting Occupy Protest Events. In *2015 International Conference on Identification, Information, and Knowledge in the Internet of Things (IIKI)*, pages 94–97.

Clionadh Raleigh, Andrew Linke, Håvard Hegre, and Joakim Karlsen. 2010. Introducing ACLED: An Armed Conflict Location and Event Dataset: Special Data Feature. *Journal of Peace Research*. Publisher: SAGE PublicationsSage UK: London, England.

Naren Ramakrishnan, Gizem Korkmaz, Chris Kuhlman, Achla Marathe, Liang Zhao, Ting Hua, Feng Chen, Chang Tien Lu, Bert Huang, Aravind Srinivasan, Khoa Trinh, Patrick Butler, Lise Getoor, Graham Katz, Andy Doyle, Chris Ackermann, Ilya Zavorin, Jim Ford, Kristen Summers, Youssef Fayed, Jaime Arredondo, Dipak Gupta, Sathappan Muthiah, David Mares, Nathan Self, Rupinder Khandpur, Parang Saraf, Wei Wang, Jose Cadena, and Anil Vullikanti. 2014. 'Beating the news' with EMBERS: forecasting civil unrest using open source indicators. In *Proceedings of the 20th ACM SIGKDD international conference on Knowledge discovery and data mining - KDD '14*, pages 1799–1808, New York, New York, USA. ACM Press.

Anna Rogers, Olga Kovaleva, and Anna Rumshisky. 2019. Calls to action on social media: Detection, social impact, and censorship potential. In *Proceedings of the Second Workshop on Natural Language Processing for Internet Freedom: Censorship, Disinformation, and Propaganda*, pages 36–44, Hong Kong, China. Association for Computational Linguistics.

James Scharf, Arya D. McCarthy, and Giovanna Maria Dora Dore. 2021. Characterizing news portrayal of civil unrest in Hong Kong, 1998–2020. In *Proceedings of the 4th Workshop on Challenges and Applications of Automated Extraction of Socio-political Events from Text (CASE 2021)*, pages 43–52, Online. Association for Computational Linguistics.

Justin Sech, Alexandra DeLucia, Anna L. Buczak, and Mark Dredze. 2020. Civil unrest on Twitter (CUT): A dataset of tweets to support research on civil unrest. In *Proceedings of the Sixth Workshop on Noisy User-generated Text (W-NUT 2020)*, pages 215–221, Online. Association for Computational Linguistics.

Adam Smidi and Saif Shahin. 2017. Social Media and Social Mobilisation in the Middle East: A Survey of Research on the Arab Spring:. *India Quarterly*. Publisher: SAGE PublicationsSage India: New Delhi, India.

Xosé Soengas-Pérez. 2013. The role of the Internet and social networks in the arab uprisings an alternative to official press censorship. *Comunicar*, 21(41):147–155.

Zachary C Steinert-Threlkeld. 2017. Spontaneous collective action: peripheral mobilization during the arab spring. *American Political Science Review*, 111(2):379–403.

Gitte Vanwinckelen, Vinicius Tragante do O, Daan Fierens, and Hendrik Blockeel. 2016. Instance-level accuracy versus bag-level accuracy in multi-instance learning. *Data Mining and Knowledge Discovery*, 30(2):313–341.

Gitte Vanwinckelen, Ó ViniciusTragantedo, Daan Fierens, and Hendrik Blockeel. 2015. Instance-level accuracy versus bag-level accuracy in multi-instance learning. *Data Mining and Knowledge Discovery*.

Wei Wang, Yue Ning, Huzefa Rangwala, and Naren Ramakrishnan. 2016. A Multiple Instance Learning Framework for Identifying Key Sentences and Detecting Events. In *Proceedings of the 25th ACM International on Conference on Information and Knowledge Management*, CIKM '16, pages 509–518, Indianapolis, Indiana, USA. Association for Computing Machinery.

Congyu Wu and Matthew S. Gerber. 2018. Forecasting Civil Unrest Using Social Media and Protest Participation Theory. *IEEE Transactions on Computational Social Systems*, 5(1):82–94. Conference Name: IEEE Transactions on Computational Social Systems.

Huiling You, David Samuel, Samia Touileb, and Lilja Øvrelid. 2022. EventGraph: Event extraction as semantic graph parsing. In *Proceedings of the 5th Workshop on Challenges and Applications of Automated Extraction of Socio-political Events from Text (CASE)*, pages 7–15, Abu Dhabi, United Arab Emirates (Hybrid). Association for Computational Linguistics.

Vanni Zavarella, Hristo Tanev, Ali Hürriyetoğlu, Peratham Wiriyathammabhum, and Bertrand De Longueville. 2022. Tracking COVID-19 protest events in the United States. shared task 2: Event database replication, CASE 2022. In *Proceedings of the 5th Workshop on Challenges and Applications of Automated Extraction of Socio-political Events from Text (CASE)*, pages 209–216, Abu Dhabi, United Arab Emirates (Hybrid). Association for Computational Linguistics.

Han Zhang and Jennifer Pan. 2019. CASM: A deep-learning approach for identifying collective action events with text and image data from social media. *Sociological Methodology*, 49(1):1–57.

Jingyu Zhang, Alexandra DeLucia, and Mark Dredze. 2022. Changes in tweet geolocation over time: A study with carmen 2.0. In *Proceedings of the Eighth Workshop on Noisy User-generated Text (W-NUT 2022)*, pages 1–14, Gyeongju, Republic of Korea. Association for Computational Linguistics.

Jingyu Zhang, Alexandra DeLucia, and Mark Dredze. 2023. Geo-seq2seq: Twitter user geolocation on noisy data through sequence to sequence learning. In *Findings of the Association for Computational Linguistics: ACL 2023*, Toronto, CA. Association for Computational Linguistics.

Xin Zheng and Aixin Sun. 2019. Collecting event-related tweets from twitter stream. *Journal of the Association for Information Science and Technology*, 70(2):176–186.

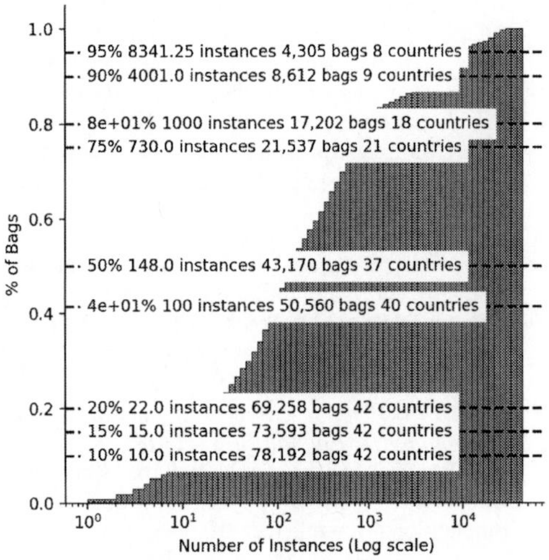

Figure 3: Plot is cumulative and normalized to show the percentage of bags that remain after raising the minimum number of instances threshold. Note the log scale for number of instances.

A Data Preparation

As discussed in Section 4, we use the Global Civil Unrest on Twitter (G-CUT) dataset introduced by (Chinta et al., 2021). In this work, we perform further data cleaning:

- Removed retweets and quote tweets
- Removed tweets identified as spam (tweets with more than three hashtags or user mentions or less than three non-URL, hashtag, or user mention tokens)
- Removed exact text duplicates

After cleaning 86,096 bags out of 86,270 (99.80%) remained.

Another change is we removed samples, or bags, that did not have at least 10 tweets, or instances. This threshold was based on dropping the bottom 10% of bags, which still retained 78,192 samples (91% of the original dataset) from all 42 countries (see Figure 3).

B Model Training Details

Parameters not detailed in the main paper are discussed here.

B.1 Civil Unrest Filtration Model

For the Civil Unrest Filtration model, or instance model in the context of multi-instance learning,

Metric	Validation	Test
Accuracy	0.85	0.82
Loss	1.5	1.9
F1 (Positive)	0.65	0.6
F1 (Macro)	0.86	0.82
Precision	0.89	0.84
Recall	0.85	0.82

Table 5: Results for the validation and test set of the best performing civil unrest filtration model.

we fine-tuned a BERTweet model on the Civil Unrest of Twitter (CUT) dataset (Sech et al., 2020). After removing samples identified as non-English, the dataset consists of 2761 samples, 553 of which discuss general unrest (20%). We split the dataset into train, validation, and test sets of sizes 2235/249/277, respectively.[9] To encourage equal class prevalence we used stratified sampling for the splits. We chose the general unrest label instead of specific protests or events since our overall model aims to predict civil unrest.

The BERTweet model was fine-tuned with a HuggingFace classification head for 100 epochs, AdamW optimizer, linear schedular warmup of 50 steps, binary cross-entropy loss, 0.00006815 learning rate, 0 weight decay, betas (0.9, 0.999), epsilon $1.000e-8$, 128 batch size, and early stopping with a patience of 10. These parameters were chosen after performing a hyperparameter sweep for best positive F1 score on the validation set of 100 trials, selecting randomly from weight decay values $\{1e-10, 1e-09, 1e-08, 1e-07, 1e-06, 1e-05, 0.0001, 0.001, 0.01, 0\}$ and a learning rate uniformly sampled from $[1e-6, 1e-2]$. To address the large class imbalance we included a weight for the positive class calculated as

$$\text{positive weight} = \frac{n_{samples}}{n_{classes} \times n_{positivesamples}}$$

where the sample stats are based on the train split. Choosing a model based on best positive F1 score was important because we found that best validation loss did not necessarily correlate with accurate predictions of the positive class, most likely due to the large class imbalance. Performance details of the final model are in Table 5.

[9]This is 10% of the dataset set aside for test and then 10% of the remaining data set aside for evaluation.

B.2 MIL Loss

The full loss function is in Equation (3). While similar to the loss function from Wang et al. (2016), ours is simpler and does not use the instance-ratio control loss or the instance-level manifold propagation. Since the overall model is initialized with meaningful representations from the BERT-based instance model, we omitted the other instance losses. The losses were more necessary in Wang et al. (2016) since the instance/bag representations were learned from averaged word2vec embeddings, which are not as powerful as BERT embeddings. Further, unlike Wang et al. (2016), we have "ground-truth" labels for the instances, allowing us to use a BCE loss instead of their instance hinge loss. A future iteration of this work could incorporate these other losses.

C Baseline Training Details

Parameters not detailed in the main paper are discussed here.

C.1 N-gram Baseline

Inspired by the simple baselines from Chinta et al. (2021), we included a similar baseline in this work.

For a more direct comparison to the MIL and MIL-AVG models we used the BERTweet tokenizer to normalize and tokenize the tweets. We used the random forest classifier implementation from sklearn (Buitinck et al., 2013) with the following settings: 10 estimators, max depth of 32, minimum samples split of 32, and a balanced class weight. These settings were copied from Chinta et al. (2021). We used the same train, validation, and test splits as for the MIL model.

C.2 AVG-Bag Baseline

The AVG-Bag model is a direct comparison to the standard method of using all tweets to represent each bag as opposed to the MIL approach. With the same instance model discussed in Appendix B.1 and Section 3.2, we represent each bag as the average instance representation ([CLS] token). These representations are then used as features for a random forest model, with the same settings as for the N-gram model. We used the same train, validation, and test splits as for the MIL model.

$$L(x,y;\theta) = \underbrace{-\frac{1}{|X|}\sum_{x_i \in X} y_i \log(p(y_i)) + (1-y_i)\log(1-p(y_i))}_{\text{bag-level loss (BCE)}} \quad (3)$$

$$\underbrace{-\beta \frac{1}{|X|}\sum_{x_i \in X} \frac{1}{|x_i|}\sum_{x_i^j \in x_i} y_i^j \log(p(y_i^j)) + (1-y_i^j)\log(1-p(y_i^j))}_{\text{instance-level loss (BCE)}}$$

Date	Country	Tweet Score	Tweet
2017-01-11	UGA	1.0	Somalia's militant Islamist group al-Shabab has shot dead two people it accused of being gay.
2017-02-19	ZAF	1.0	The sad thing about today.The idiot politicians who are preaching economic emancipation are millionaires
2017-04-08	UGA	1.0	Some of issues we need Govt to address:non prioritisation of National Health insurance scheme. #Ugbudget17 @USER @HealthVoice_UG

Table 6: Example positive tweets (i.e., civil-unrest related) in negative bags (i.e., a country-day with no event) from the validation set (2017). The tweet scores are from the instance classification model (see Section 3.2). UGA and ZAF refer to Uganda and Zambia, respectively.

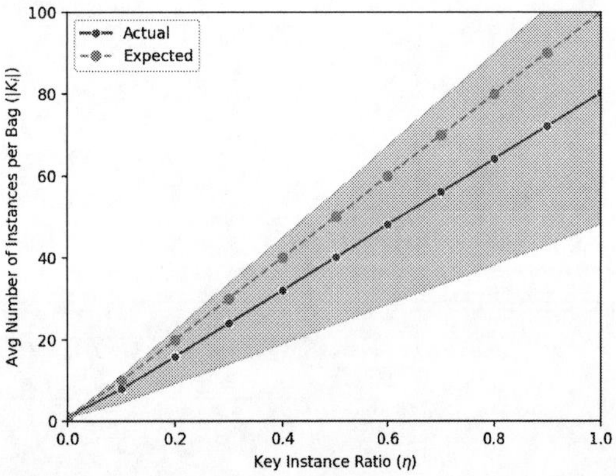

Figure 4: The expected number of key instances for each bag and the average from the train set. The shaded region is the standard deviation.

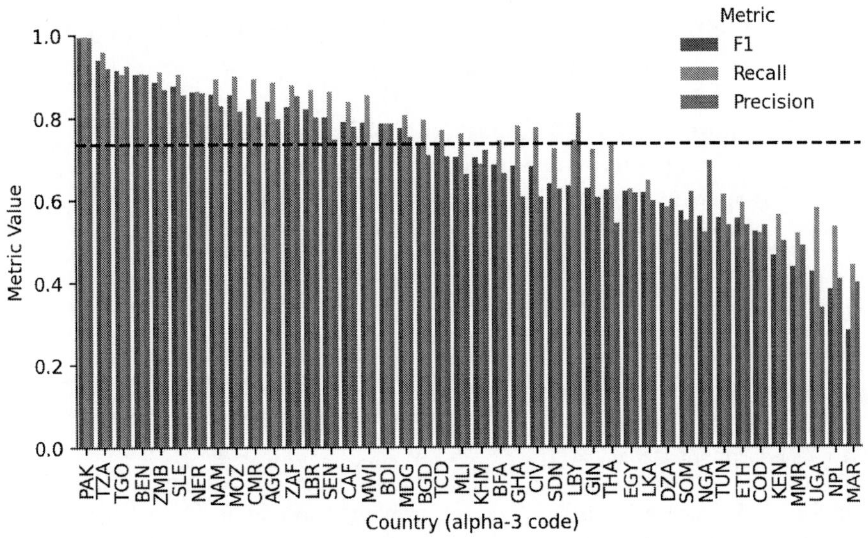

Figure 5: Per-country F1 results of top MIL model on the test set.

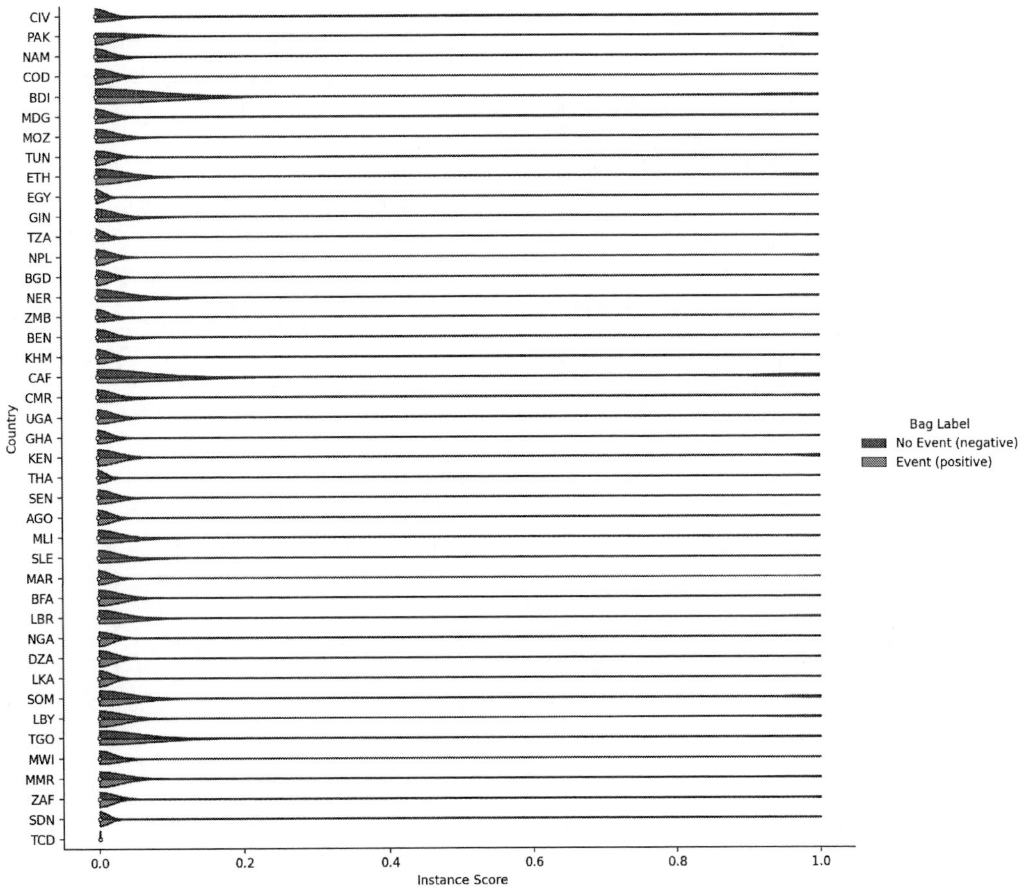

Figure 6: Distribution of instance scores for each country. Scores are from the instance model (see Section 3.2) on the validation set (year 2017). Countries are identified by their ISO 3166-1 alpha-3 codes.

MLModeler5 @ Causal News Corpus 2023: Using RoBERTa for Casual Event Classification

Amrita Bhatia, Ananya Thomas, Nitansh Jain, Jatin Bedi
Computer Science and Engineering Department
Thapar Institute of Engineering and Technology
nonie.bhatia@gmail.com, ananyathomas10@gmail.com
njain_be20@thapar.edu, jatin.bedi@thapar.edu

Abstract

Identifying cause-effect relations plays an integral role in the understanding and interpretation of natural languages. Furthermore, automated mining of causal relations from news and text about socio-political events is a stepping stone in gaining critical insights, including analyzing the scale, frequency and trends across timelines of events, as well as anticipating future ones. The Shared Task 3, part of the 6th Workshop on Challenges and Applications of Automated Extraction of Socio-political Events from Text (CASE @ RANLP 2023), involved the task of Event Causality Identification with Causal News Corpus. We describe our approach to Subtask 1, dealing with causal event classification, a supervised binary classification problem to annotate given event sentences with whether they contained any cause-effect relations. To help achieve this task, a BERT based architecture - RoBERTa was implemented on four different datasets with the main difference being the inclusion and exclusion of both stopwords and various abbreiviations/acronyms present in the dataset. The results of this model are validated on the dataset provided by the organizers of this task. We achieved a rank of 8 with an F1 Score of 0.7475 on Dataset 1 (Removed Stop Words and Replaced Abbreviations).

1 Introduction

The ability to comprehend underlying cause-and-effect associations holds paramount significance across a multitude of disciplines. This knowledge facilitates informed decision making processes. Hence, the investigation of causal relationships assumes a pivotal position in the study of understanding the underlying mechanisms that govern the correlation between actions and their consequences.

With the uncertainty and complexity that characterizes various domains of inquiry, predictive capabilities empower individuals and organizations to navigate the intricate interplay of variables, facilitating better planning, risk management, and mitigation strategies.

The primary objective of this task is to develop a method to classify casual relations and in turn help identify the variable that acts as a reason for another. This will help in anticipating contingencies. The impact of casual analysis is not only seen in the extrapolation of likelihood of events under static conditions but also in events observed in continuously altering conditions, for example, changes induced by treatments or external interventions. [3]

This paper presents our use of the BERT based architecture RoBERTa, in **Subtask 1 Casual Event Classification of CASE 2023 Shared Task 3**.

2 Task Description

The **CASE 2023 Shared Task 3, Event Causality Identification with Causal News Corpus** [4] [5], focuses on the problem of detecting and extracting causal relations in protest event news. A causal relation is defined as a semantic relation between the cause and effect arguments, such that the occurrence of the latter is the subsequent result of the occurrence of the former. For an example to be considered a causal sentence, it has to include at least one cause-effect attribute pair where one argument provides the reason, explanation or justification for the situation described by the other.[1][7]

Subtask 1 - Causal Event Classification [6] is an event detection task which focuses on the automatic identification of the presence of causality in event sentences, i.e, a supervised classification task to detect causality in a given text. The aim is to develop a model to annotate event sentences with binary labels indicating whether

Proceedings of the 6th Workshop on Challenges and Applications of Automated Extraction of Socio-political Events from Text, pages 34–37, Varna, Bulgaria, Sep 7, 2023.
https://doi.org/10.26615/978-954-452-089-2_004

they contained any cause-effect relations.

3 Dataset Description

The subtask used the second version of the Causal News Corpus (CNC), an annotated news corpus comprising 3,767 event sentences extracted from randomly sampled protest event news from varying sources. For the first subtask, the data consisted of event sentences annotated with binary labels indicating the absence or presence of causality within the span of each text, represented by 0 and 1 respectively.

The training and development dataset consisted of 3075 and 340 annotated text samples respectively. In the testing phase, the development dataset could be incorporated into the training of the model, and an additional test set of 352 un-annotated event sentences was provided.

4 Methodology

4.1 Data Pre-processing

This process entails cleaning of data through numerous methods like removing noise, handling missing data, normalising skewed data, etc. When it comes to text data, removing noise can include the removal of stop words, links, abbreviated words, punctuation and numbers or the conversion of numbers to words and abbreviations to their respective full forms or translating text from one language to another.

For Subtask 1, the training data consisted of 3075 samples with gold labels, the development data consisted of 340 samples with gold labels and the testing data consisted of 352 samples without gold labels.

The training, development and test data was pre-processed using the same methods. Data pre-processing involved removal of links using 'urllib', contractions handling using the 'contractions' library, replaced abbreviations and acronyms, removed punctuations, stop words and words with a length less than 3. Numbers were also converted to words using the library 'num2words'.

A dictionary was created with the most common abbreviations and acronyms present in the dataset. This dictionary was used to replace the respective abbreviations and acronyms from the text.

Libraries like 'nltk' and 'spacy' were also used for further pre-processing.
Four different datasets were created to compare results :

- Dataset 1 - Removed Stop Words and Replaced Abbreviations
- Dataset 2 - Included Stop Words and Replaced Abbreviations
- Dataset 3 - Removed Stop Words and didn't Replace Abbreviations
- Dataset 4 - Included Stop Words and didn't Replace Abbreviations

4.2 Model Building & Experimental Setup

RoBERTa [2] - a BERT based architecture was used for **Casual Event Classification**. The model was initialised using pre-trained RoBERTa weights "roberta-base" [1]. The text data was encoded using RoBERTa Tokenizer. The text was encoded to a length of 100 to generate embeddings that were passed through the model. The architecture included the RoBERTa Transformer layer followed by a Dropout layer, Flatten layer and two Dense Layers.

Since, the task calls for a binary classification, sigmoid activation function was used for the final dense layer. The model was compiled with **Adam** optimizer that had a learning rate of 0.00001, binary_crossentropy loss function and F1 score as metric. The model was run for 20 epochs.

5 Results

The final leaderboard for Subtask 1 was based on **Binary F1 Score**. The **baseline Binary F1 Score** was **0.8191**. Our submission using RoBERTa and Dataset 1 achieved a Binary F1 score of **0.7475**. The organisers also measured Precision, Recall, Accuracy and MCC(Matthews Correlation Coefficient).

It is clear from Table 1 that, Dataset 1 had the highest Recall value as compared to the other datasets. Dataset 2 and Dataset 4 had lower Recall values as compared to Dataset 1 but outperformed

[1] https://huggingface.co/docs/transformers/model_doc/roberta

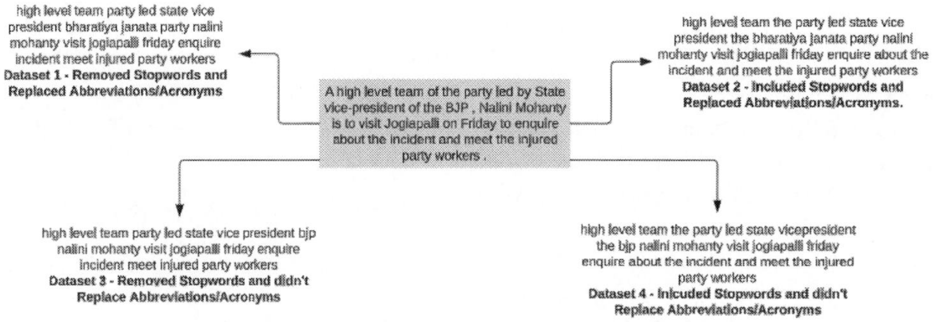

Figure 1: *Datasets Examples*

Models	RoBERTa				
Metrics	Recall	Precision	F1	Accuracy	MCC
Dataset 1	0.87283	0.65367	0.74752	0.71022	0.44829
Dataset 2	0.82081	0.71357	0.76344	0.75	0.50664
Dataset 3	0.73988	0.73142	0.73563	0.73863	0.47725
Dataset 4	0.80346	0.74731	0.77437	0.76988	0.54169

Table 1: *Test Results obtained for Subtask 1 using RoBERTa*

it in all the other metrics.

The only difference between Dataset 2 and 4 was the replacement of abbreviations/acronyms; Dataset 4 had outperformed Dataset 2 on F1 Score by a small margin. This shows that abbreviations/acronyms did not affect the model as massively as the presence or lack of stopwords. Transformers are able to understand context better than other deep learning models like RNN, LSTM, etc and in Casual Event Classification, the presence of the stopwords are generally the way to differentiate between cause and effect.

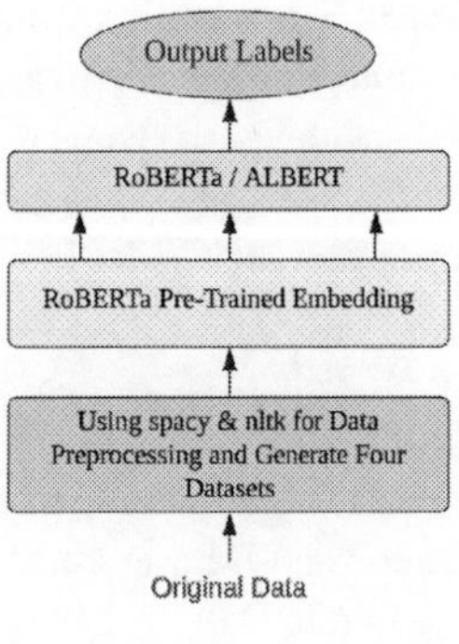

Figure 2: *Overall Methodology*

6 Conclusion

This paper addresses Subtask 1 - Casual Event Classification, which is a binary classification task, with the aim to annotate samples to indicate the presence of causality in a given text.

Our method includes basic data pre-processing techniques to generate four different datasets, which are used as inputs for the RoBERTa model and to the compare the results across five metrics - F1 Score, Recall, Precision, Accuracy and MCC(Matthews Correlation Coefficient).

Our system achieved a rank of eight based on Binary F1 Score i.e., 0.74752 achieved using Dataset 1. The best Binary F1 score value obtained was 0.77347 for Dataset 4, post competition.

Results may be improved by increasing the embedding size to a max length of 500 for RoBERTa. Hyperparameter tuning of the RoBERTa model should also be considered for better results.

References

[1] Biswanath Barik, Erwin Marsi, and Pinar Ozturk. Event causality extraction from natural science lit-

erature. *Research in Computing Science*, 117, 12 2016.

[2] Yinhan Liu, Myle Ott, Naman Goyal, Jingfei Du, Mandar Joshi, Danqi Chen, Omer Levy, Mike Lewis, Luke Zettlemoyer, and Veselin Stoyanov. Roberta: A robustly optimized BERT pretraining approach. *CoRR*, abs/1907.11692, 2019.

[3] Judea Pearl. Causal inference. In Isabelle Guyon, Dominik Janzing, and Bernhard Schölkopf, editors, *Proceedings of Workshop on Causality: Objectives and Assessment at NIPS 2008*, volume 6 of *Proceedings of Machine Learning Research*, pages 39–58, Whistler, Canada, 12 Dec 2010. PMLR.

[4] Fiona Anting Tan, Hansi Hettiarachchi, Ali Hürriyetoğlu, Tommaso Caselli, Onur Uca, Farhana Ferdousi Liza, and Nelleke Oostdijk. Event causality identification with causal news corpus - shared task 3, CASE 2022. In *Proceedings of the 5th Workshop on Challenges and Applications of Automated Extraction of Socio-political Events from Text (CASE)*, pages 195–208, Abu Dhabi, United Arab Emirates (Hybrid), December 2022. Association for Computational Linguistics.

[5] Fiona Anting Tan, Hansi Hettiarachchi, Ali Hürriyetoğlu, Nelleke Oostdijk, Onur Uca, Surendrabikram Thapa, and Farhana Ferdousi Liza. Event causality identification with causal news corpus - shared task 3, CASE 2023. In *Proceedings of the 6th Workshop on Challenges and Applications of Automated Extraction of Socio-political Events from Text (CASE)*, Varna, Bulgaria (Hybrid), September 2023. Association for Computational Linguistics.

[6] Fiona Anting Tan, Ali Hürriyetoğlu, Tommaso Caselli, Nelleke Oostdijk, Tadashi Nomoto, Hansi Hettiarachchi, Iqra Ameer, Onur Uca, Farhana Ferdousi Liza, and Tiancheng Hu. The causal news corpus: Annotating causal relations in event sentences from news. In *Proceedings of the Thirteenth Language Resources and Evaluation Conference*, pages 2298–2310, Marseille, France, June 2022. European Language Resources Association.

[7] Bonnie Webber, Rashmi Prasad, Alan Lee, and Aravind Joshi. The penn discourse treebank 3.0 annotation manual. *Philadelphia, University of Pennsylvania*, 35:108, 2019.

BoschAI @ Causal News Corpus 2023: Robust Cause-Effect Span Extraction using Multi-Layer Sequence Tagging and Data Augmentation

Timo Pierre Schrader[1,2] **Simon Razniewski**[1] **Lukas Lange**[1] **Annemarie Friedrich**[2]
[1]Bosch Center for Artificial Intelligence, Renningen, Germany
[2]University of Augsburg, Germany
timo.schrader|simon.razniewski|lukas.lange@de.bosch.com
annemarie.friedrich@informatik.uni-augsburg.de

Abstract

Understanding causality is a core aspect of intelligence. The Event Causality Identification with Causal News Corpus Shared Task addresses two aspects of this challenge: Subtask 1 aims at detecting causal relationships in texts, and Subtask 2 requires identifying signal words and the spans that refer to the cause or effect, respectively. Our system, which is based on pre-trained transformers, stacked sequence tagging, and synthetic data augmentation, ranks third in Subtask 1 and wins Subtask 2 with an F1 score of 72.8, corresponding to a margin of 13 pp. to the second-best system.

1 Introduction

In this paper, we describe our approach to the Event Causality Identification with Causal News Corpus shared task (Tan et al., 2023), which took place at The 6th Workshop on Challenges and Applications of Automated Extraction of Socio-political Events from Text (CASE 2023). The task, which builds on the 2022 iteration of the same shared task (Tan et al., 2022a), but including more labeled data, targets the detection and extraction of causal relationships. In Subtask 1, participating systems need to decide whether a sentence contains any causal relationship. Subtask 2 requires extracting the spans that denote cause, effect, and trigger words (if any).

Our system leverages pre-trained transformer encoders and synthetic data augmentation methods, and ranks third in Subtask 1. We address Subtask 2 using a supervised sequence labeling model, which wins by a margin of 13 percentage points in terms of F1 over the second-best system. We model multiple causal chains per sentence via stacked labels and find that synthetic data augmentation consistently improves performance. Our code is publicly available.[1]

[1] https://github.com/boschresearch/boschai-cnc-shared-task-ranlp2023

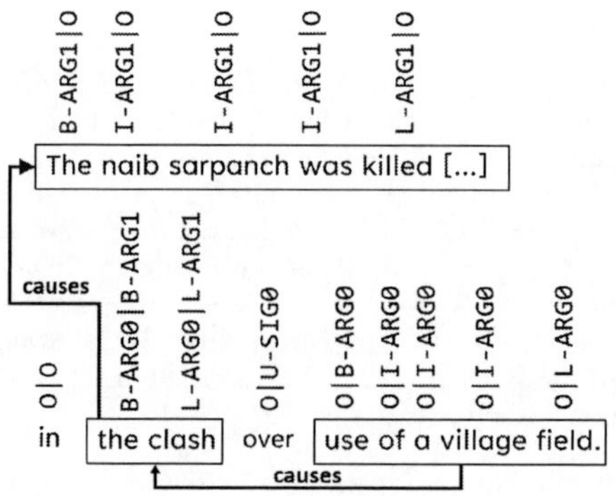

Figure 1: Our proposed modeling technique for extracting causal relationships (Subtask 2) using stacked BILOU labels. `ARG0` = cause, `ARG1` = effect.

2 Dataset and Task

The Causal News Corpus (CNC, Tan et al., 2022b) consists of 3767 sentences extracted from news articles. CNC provides annotations of semantic relations of the form "*X* causes *Y*" that indicate a *causal* relationship between arguments *X* and *Y*. The definition of causality follows that of the CONTINGENCY label in the PDTB-3 corpus (Webber et al., 2019), which is used when a statement provides the reason, explanation, or justification for another event. Following TimeML (Pustejovsky et al., 2003), the definition of events includes both actions that happen or occur and states. As illustrated by the example in Figure 1, one event is the immediate effect of another, e.g., the event expressed by "the use of a village field" is the cause of that expressed by "the clash."

While following the definition of causal relations of PDTB-3, which focuses on causal relations between sentences or clauses, CNC provides span annotations for causes (`ARG0`), effects (`ARG1`) and signals (`SIG0`) within sentences. Spans may comprise one to several words. Their boundaries are

Proceedings of the 6th Workshop on Challenges and Applications of Automated Extraction of Socio-political Events from Text, pages 38–43, Varna, Bulgaria, Sep 7, 2023.
https://doi.org/10.26615/978-954-452-089-2_005

not restricted to clause or constituent boundaries. Signals are expressions such as "has led to" or "causing," but not every causal relation annotation requires a signal. Of all annotated relations, 30% do not contain a signal, for example: "[Dissatisfied with the package$_{\text{Cause}}$], [workers staged an all-night sit-in$_{\text{Effect}}$]." The average signal length is 1.46 words. Tan et al. (2022b) describe the annotation guidelines in detail.

The shared task is divided into two subtasks: Subtask 1 is a binary classification problem, deciding whether a sentence contains a cause-effect chain or not. Subtask 2 deals with the more challenging problem of extracting the correct spans of cause, effect, and signal, where a sentence may contain more than one causal relation. In CNC, the maximum number of causal relations per sentence is four. Spans are annotated using XML-like tags: ⟨ARG0⟩ refers to causes, ⟨ARG1⟩ to effects, and ⟨SIG0⟩ to signals.

3 Modeling and Augmentation

In this section, we describe the neural architectures that we use to solve the two subtasks. To produce contextualized embeddings of the input sentences, we use BERT-Large (Devlin et al., 2019) and RoBERTa-Large (Liu et al., 2019).

3.1 Subtask 1

We implement a binary classifier to detect whether a sentence contains a cause-effect relation. The sentence-level `[CLS]` embedding is fed into a linear output layer that outputs a prediction on whether a sentence contains a cause-effect meaning or not. We design the output layer to yield two prediction scores, one for each class. During our experiments, we observe that the classifier has shown prediction bias towards negative samples. Hence, we apply a weighted cross entropy loss that upweights the positive samples.

3.2 Subtask 2

We model the problem of detecting cause, effect, and signal spans, potentially with multiple causal relations within a single sentence, as sequence tagging task using the BILOU labeling scheme (Alex et al., 2007). The BILOU scheme extends the commonly used BIO scheme by introducing two additional markers, where "L" denotes the end of a multi-token sequence and "U" refers to a single-token entity. For example, the argument span "Beijing launched a campaign" has the label sequence `[B-ARG1 I-ARG1 I-ARG1 L-ARG1]` (ignoring BERT-specific subword tokens here). A linear layer on top of the embedding model produces the logits for all BILOU tags for each token individually. These logits are fed into a conditional random field (CRF, Lafferty et al., 2001) output layer, which computes the most likely consistent tag sequence.

However, this approach can only predict a single output sequence per sample, i.e., is not able to detect multiple causal chains in an instance. Consider the example shown in Figure 1. The expression "the clash" can be either the cause of one killing and 17 injuries or the effect of not being able to agree about the usage of a village field. As a result, there are two causal relations within this instance. To address this, we "stack" the BILOU labels by concatenating them using a pipe ("|") operator, similar to Straková et al. (2019), who also use a label stacking approach. As shown in Figure 1, this means that the word "clash" is tagged with `L-ARG0|L-ARG1|O`, which decodes to being the end of a cause in the first layer, being the end of an effect in the second one and not being part of any span in the third one.

To keep the label space manageable, we model three layers. There are only nine samples in the training set with four possible sequences. Without filtering, we would end up with about 39,000 labels. We only add stacked labels that occur in the training and validation data, resulting in roughly 300 three-layer BILOU labels. During evaluation, these stacked labels are split into their three distinct layers and each instance is evaluated separately. As a result, the model is able to predict up to three different causal relations per sentence.

3.3 Data Augmentation and Resampling

As for both subtasks, there is only limited training data available, we incorporate additional synthetic data into the training. In the 2022 edition of the shared task, several teams also experimented with data augmentation methods. Chen et al. (2022) trained BART (Lewis et al., 2020) to rephrase instances in the dataset. Kim et al. (2022) create additional data by adding the SemEval-2010 dataset (Hendrickx et al., 2010) and replacing words by their POS tag.

Augmenting using EDA Our first augmentation approach makes use of the Easy Data Augmenta-

Original Sentence	EDA Augmented Sentence
His arrest has sparked widespread protests by students, teachers as well as opposition parties.	His arrest has sparked widespread resist by student, teacher as advantageously as confrontation parties.
Month-long escalating protests to mark 4th anniversary of Mullivaikkal pogrom.	Month-long step up protests to mark off quaternary day of remembrance of Mullivaikkal pogrom.
They also rubbished suggestions that the student protests were losing steam [...]	They besides rubbish suggestions that the scholar protests were lose steam [...]

Table 1: Comparison between original sentences and their EDA-augmented counterparts. Differences are underlined.

tion (EDA, Wei and Zou, 2019) tool to generate additional training data for both subtasks. EDA offers different augmentation techniques: synonym replacement (*sr*), random word insertion (*ri*), random word deletion (*rd*), and random word swaps (*rs*). The percentage of words on which these techniques are applied are defined by hyperparameters α_{sr}, α_{ri}, α_{rd}, and α_{rs}.

For Subtask 1, we employ synonym replacement, random word insertion, and random swaps and generate four synthetic samples per original instance in the training set. This results in a training set five times as large as the original dataset with a total sample count of over 15.000 samples.[2] In Subtask 2, keeping the ordering of ⟨ARG0⟩, ⟨ARG1⟩ and ⟨SIG0⟩ consistent is of high importance. To avoid adding destructive noise to the training data, we only use synonym replacement and random insertion for this subtask. We add one augmented sample per single-relation instance, i.e., we do not augment data based on samples with more than one causal relation. We discard augmented samples that are invalid w.r.t. the annotation scheme. Data augmentation for the challenging multi-relation cases is an interesting direction for future research. The augmented training set contains 4.611 instances, i.e., about 1.500 more than the original set.

Table 1 shows three instances and their augmented counterparts. The first example shows a replacement of *opposition* by *confrontation*, which is not fully synonymous, but still related. In the second one, there is a synonym replacement of *4th* by *quaternary*. In the third example, noise is added by replacing "losing" with "lose", illustrating that the data augmentation method does not control for grammatical correctness.

[2]We noticed that the tool also clones each original sample in our implementation.

Oversampling of Multi-Relation Samples About 32% of all instances with at least one causal relation in the training set are labeled with more than one causal relation. Out of these, we sample 400 instances (with replacement) and add them to the training dataset. In contrast to EDA, we only use this setting only for Subtask 2.

Generating Samples using ChatGPT We experiment with GPT-3.5-turbo and prompt it to generate 100 novel samples containing causal relations that are similar to those of the CNC corpus. We prompt ChatGPT with multiple samples of the CNC train set, and the rules of placing ⟨ARG0⟩, ⟨ARG1⟩, and ⟨SIG0⟩, and let it generate novel samples. This additional data is only used for Subtask 2.

The ChatGPT-based data augmentation approach generates relatively simple examples by always sticking to a Cause-Signal-Effect or Effect-Signal-Cause structure without overlapping spans. Examples include "[The lack of rain$_{\text{Cause}}$] [caused$_{\text{Signal}}$] [the crops to fail and farmers to suffer losses$_{\text{Effect}}$]." and "[A decrease in greenhouse gas emissions$_{\text{Effect}}$] [was a result of$_{\text{Signal}}$] [the decrease in demand for fossil fuels$_{\text{Cause}}$]".

4 Experimental Evaluation

This section describes our experimental results for both subtasks. Evaluation of Subtask 2 is performed using FairEval[3], which implements a relaxation of traditional hard-matching span evaluation metrics on sentences marked as containing a causal relation in the gold standard only. We train our on all samples of the train split, including those without causal relations.

4.1 Hyperparameters

To find the best learning rates and augmentation parameter combinations, we employ a grid search

[3]https://huggingface.co/spaces/hpi-dhc/FairEval/tree/main

	Team	Precision	Recall	F1
1	DeepBlueAI	**83.2**	86.1	**84.7**
2	InterosML	81.6	87.3	84.4
3	BoschAI	80.0	87.9	83.8
	baseline	75.9	**89.2**	81.9

Table 2: Subtask 1: results on **test** of the best three systems and the baseline provided by Tan et al. (2023). Scores are based on the public leaderboard.

LM	Precision	Recall	F1	Accuracy
BERT	86.9	**89.7**	**88.3**	87.1
RoBERTa	**88.6**	88.1	**88.3**	**87.4**

Table 3: Subtask 1: results on **dev** (large model variants).

and refine the learning rates after an initial coarse-grained search ranging from $1e^{-7}$ to $9e^{-4}$ for the pre-trained language model. The binary classifier for Subtask 1 is trained with a learning rate of 8e-6, using the EDA augmented training data and a batch size of 32. For Subtask 1, we use the following parameter values for the different EDA techniques: $\alpha_{sr} = 0.4$, $\alpha_{ri} = 0.1$, and $\alpha_{rs} = 0.6$. We use a weighted cross entropy loss for this subtask, using a weight of 1.5 for class *causal*. For Subtask 2, we apply the following settings: $\alpha_{sr} = 0.4$ and $\alpha_{ri} = 0.5$.

The CRF-based tagger for Subtask 2 uses a learning rate of $7e^{-5}$ for the language model and the linear layer, whereas a learning rate of $3e^{-4}$ is applied on the CRF. During fine-tuning, EDA-augmentated data is included in the training set. Training the models is performed on Nvidia A100 GPUs using one GPU per run, which takes several hours per model. Early stopping is applied using the F1 score on the dev set and a patience of three epochs to select the best model. The models are optimized using AdamW (Loshchilov and Hutter, 2019) and an inverse square-root learning rate scheduler taken from Grünewald et al. (2021).

4.2 Results

In the following, we refer to the public leaderboard of the Event Causality Identification with Causal News Corpus shared task.[4] We report results on test as provided by the leaderboard evaluation script.

Subtask 1 Our RoBERTa-based binary classifier ranks third of 10 participants. Results are shown

[4]https://codalab.lisn.upsaclay.fr/competitions/11784#results

		All relations			Multi-relation		
		P	R	F1	P	R	F1
1	BoschAI	**84.4**	**64.0**	**72.8**	82.6	53.5	64.9
	- Cause	85.3	59.7	70.2	82.5	47.4	60.2
	- Effect	82.8	62.9	71.5	80.3	50.4	61.9
	- Signal	85.4	70.4	77.2	82.6	53.5	64.9
2	tanfiona*	60.3	59.2	59.7	-	-	-
3	CSECU-DSG	40.0	36.1	38.0	-	-	-

Table 4: Per-class scores on the **test** for Subtask 2 of our best scoring model using RoBERTa-Large and EDA. The last two rows show the results of the second- and third-best system. *System of Chen et al. (2022).

in Table 2, including the best two systems and the baseline by Tan et al. (2023). Among the top three, we achieve the best recall score. Qualitatively, we find that neither sentence length nor the presence of signal words are strongly correlated with misclassifications.

We report the results of our classifier that uses BERT-Large in comparison to RoBERTa-Large in Table 3 on the dev set (since we do not have access to the gold standard of test). Both models perform almost equally on this task, with RoBERTa outperforming BERT by a slight margin in terms of accuracy with a difference 0.3% pp.

Subtask 2 On this task, we compare our models against the baseline provided by Tan et al. (2023), which is the best performing system from the previous iteration of the shared task by team "1Cademy" (Chen et al., 2022). They also build upon a BERT-based embedding model, but output prediction scores for begin and end tokens of the respective spans. In order to produce consistent output, i.e., non-overlapping cause and effect spans and correctly ordered spans, they implement a beam-search algorithm on top that aims to find the top m most likely spans for each of the three types.

Per-label scores of our best-performing model and those of the other two competitors are shown in Table 4. Our best system is based on RoBERTa-Large with a CRF layer on top and trained on EDA-augmented data. Our system clearly outperforms the last year's winning system by more than 13 percentage points in terms of F1 on the latest CNC data, exceeding precision by 24 percentage points. Our system performs best on the signal label, which could be explained by two factors: signals are much more repetitive in the corpus (with "to" occurring 293 times in the train data) and the average length

LM	Cause P	Cause R	Cause F1	Effect P	Effect R	Effect F1	Signal P	Signal R	Signal F1	*avg* P	*avg* R	*avg* F1
BERT-Large	82.4	59.9	69.4	83.2	58.7	68.9	86.3	72.0	78.5	83.8	62.6	71.6
RoBERTa-Large	86.8	66.1	75.1	85.2	**68.5**	76.0	82.8	75.4	78.9	85.1	69.3	76.4
+ EDA*	86.4	**67.9**	76.1	**88.5**	67.9	**76.8**	85.0	**77.5**	**81.1**	86.8	**70.3**	**77.7**
+ Oversampling	87.5	67.7	**76.3**	86.8	66.2	75.1	**85.1**	74.3	79.3	86.6	68.8	76.7
+ ChatGPT	**88.4**	65.7	75.4	87.5	66.8	75.8	84.3	75.2	79.5	**86.9**	68.5	76.6

Table 5: Subtask 2 results on **dev**: precision, recall and F1 scores for cause, effect and signal span predictions. *Our system used to produce leaderboard scores.

Relations/Sentence	Cause	Effect	Signal
1	85.5	80.9	84.7
2	67.7	76.1	84.0
3	52.8	61.8	57.9

Table 6: Per-class F1 scores by the numbers of causal relations per sentence on **dev** for Subtask 2.

of 1.46 words is much smaller than those of causes (11.74) and effects (10.74). Table 4 also lists the results for multi-relation instances only, showing that recall drops for those instances.

Table 5 compares several settings, including various data augmentation techniques, by label on the dev set. We evaluate on the dev set because we do not have access to the gold standard of the test set.

First of all, using RoBERTa over BERT improves the average F1 score by 4.8 points in terms of F1. Next, all three data augmentation methods contribute performance improvements over the RoBERTa baseline with the recall of **Effect** being the only exception. Best overall results are achieved using EDA augmentation. However, ChatGPT-augmented significantly improves precision of **Cause** (1.6 points F1 over baseline) and also yields the best average precision. Tan et al. (2022b) also experiment with using two additional corpora, however, they do not get significant improvements, likely due to more different foci of the datasets. The synthetic data augmentation methods that we used have the advantage of producing training data very similar to CNC.

Finally, Table 6 breaks down results on dev split by single-relation, two-relation and three-relation instances. While scores for Effect and Signal remain high for two-relation instances, performance is much smaller (yet still strong) for three-relation instances.

5 Conclusion and Outlook

In this paper, we have described our modeling approach to the "Event Causality Identification with Causal News Corpus" shared task (CASE 2023). We have proposed a multi-layer sequence tagging model that aims at identifying causal relations within news-related sentences. Our approach significantly outperforms all participating systems in Subtask 2. Furthermore, we have shown that synthetic data augmentation methods are beneficial for this task. Our results indicate that careful modeling, more advanced data augmentation, and leveraging larger language models may be fruitful directions for further improvements.

References

Beatrice Alex, Barry Haddow, and Claire Grover. 2007. Recognising nested named entities in biomedical text. In *Biological, translational, and clinical language processing*, pages 65–72, Prague, Czech Republic. Association for Computational Linguistics.

Xingran Chen, Ge Zhang, Adam Nik, Mingyu Li, and Jie Fu. 2022. 1Cademy @ causal news corpus 2022: Enhance causal span detection via beam-search-based position selector. In *Proceedings of the 5th Workshop on Challenges and Applications of Automated Extraction of Socio-political Events from Text (CASE)*, pages 100–105, Abu Dhabi, United Arab Emirates (Hybrid). Association for Computational Linguistics.

Jacob Devlin, Ming-Wei Chang, Kenton Lee, and Kristina Toutanova. 2019. BERT: Pre-training of deep bidirectional transformers for language understanding. In *Proceedings of the 2019 Conference of the North American Chapter of the Association for Computational Linguistics: Human Language Technologies, Volume 1 (Long and Short Papers)*, pages 4171–4186, Minneapolis, Minnesota. Association for Computational Linguistics.

Stefan Grünewald, Annemarie Friedrich, and Jonas Kuhn. 2021. Applying occam's razor to transformer-based dependency parsing: What works, what doesn't, and what is really necessary. In *Proceedings of the 17th International Conference on Parsing Technologies and the IWPT 2021 Shared Task on Parsing into Enhanced Universal Dependencies (IWPT 2021)*, pages 131–144, Online. Association for Computational Linguistics.

Iris Hendrickx, Su Nam Kim, Zornitsa Kozareva, Preslav Nakov, Diarmuid Ó Séaghdha, Sebastian Padó, Marco Pennacchiotti, Lorenza Romano, and Stan Szpakowicz. 2010. SemEval-2010 task 8: Multi-way classification of semantic relations between pairs of nominals. In *Proceedings of the 5th International Workshop on Semantic Evaluation*, pages 33–38, Uppsala, Sweden. Association for Computational Linguistics.

Juhyeon Kim, Yesong Choe, and Sanghack Lee. 2022. SNU-causality lab @ causal news corpus 2022: Detecting causality by data augmentation via part-of-speech tagging. In *Proceedings of the 5th Workshop on Challenges and Applications of Automated Extraction of Socio-political Events from Text (CASE)*, pages 44–49, Abu Dhabi, United Arab Emirates (Hybrid). Association for Computational Linguistics.

John D. Lafferty, Andrew McCallum, and Fernando C. N. Pereira. 2001. Conditional random fields: Probabilistic models for segmenting and labeling sequence data. In *Proceedings of the Eighteenth International Conference on Machine Learning (ICML 2001), Williams College, Williamstown, MA, USA, June 28 - July 1, 2001*, pages 282–289. Morgan Kaufmann.

Mike Lewis, Yinhan Liu, Naman Goyal, Marjan Ghazvininejad, Abdelrahman Mohamed, Omer Levy, Veselin Stoyanov, and Luke Zettlemoyer. 2020. BART: Denoising sequence-to-sequence pre-training for natural language generation, translation, and comprehension. In *Proceedings of the 58th Annual Meeting of the Association for Computational Linguistics*, pages 7871–7880, Online. Association for Computational Linguistics.

Yinhan Liu, Myle Ott, Naman Goyal, Jingfei Du, Mandar Joshi, Danqi Chen, Omer Levy, Mike Lewis, Luke Zettlemoyer, and Veselin Stoyanov. 2019. Roberta: A robustly optimized bert pretraining approach.

Ilya Loshchilov and Frank Hutter. 2019. Decoupled weight decay regularization.

James Pustejovsky, José Castaño, Robert Ingria, Roser Saurí, Rob Gaizauskas, Andrea Setzer, and Graham Katz. 2003. Timeml: A specification language for temporal and event expressions.

Jana Straková, Milan Straka, and Jan Hajic. 2019. Neural architectures for nested NER through linearization. In *Proceedings of the 57th Annual Meeting of the Association for Computational Linguistics*, pages 5326–5331, Florence, Italy. Association for Computational Linguistics.

Fiona Anting Tan, Hansi Hettiarachchi, Ali Hürriyetoğlu, Tommaso Caselli, Onur Uca, Farhana Ferdousi Liza, and Nelleke Oostdijk. 2022a. Event causality identification with causal news corpus - shared task 3, CASE 2022. In *Proceedings of the 5th Workshop on Challenges and Applications of Automated Extraction of Socio-political Events from Text (CASE)*, pages 195–208, Abu Dhabi, United Arab Emirates (Hybrid). Association for Computational Linguistics.

Fiona Anting Tan, Hansi Hettiarachchi, Ali Hürriyetoğlu, Onur Uca, Farhana Ferdousi Liza, and Nelleke Oostdijk. 2023. Event causality identification with causal news corpus - shared task 3, CASE 2023. In *Proceedings of the 6th Workshop on Challenges and Applications of Automated Extraction of Socio-political Events from Text (CASE)*. Association for Computational Linguistics.

Fiona Anting Tan, Ali Hürriyetoğlu, Tommaso Caselli, Nelleke Oostdijk, Tadashi Nomoto, Hansi Hettiarachchi, Iqra Ameer, Onur Uca, Farhana Ferdousi Liza, and Tiancheng Hu. 2022b. The causal news corpus: Annotating causal relations in event sentences from news. In *Proceedings of the Thirteenth Language Resources and Evaluation Conference*, pages 2298–2310, Marseille, France. European Language Resources Association.

Bonnie Webber, Rashmi Prasad, Alan Lee, and Aravind Joshi. 2019. The penn discourse treebank 3.0 annotation manual. *Philadelphia, University of Pennsylvania*, 35:108.

Jason Wei and Kai Zou. 2019. EDA: Easy data augmentation techniques for boosting performance on text classification tasks. In *Proceedings of the 2019 Conference on Empirical Methods in Natural Language Processing and the 9th International Joint Conference on Natural Language Processing (EMNLP-IJCNLP)*, pages 6382–6388, Hong Kong, China. Association for Computational Linguistics.

An Evaluation Framework for Mapping News Headlines to Event Classes in a Knowledge Graph

Steve Fonin Mbouadeu
St. John's University
steve.mbouadeu19@stjohns.edu

Martin Lorenzo
IBM Research
mlorenzo@ibm.com

Ken Barker
IBM Research
kjbarker@us.ibm.com

Oktie Hassanzadeh
IBM Research
hassanzadeh@us.ibm.com

Abstract

Mapping ongoing news headlines to event-related classes in a rich knowledge base can be an important component in a knowledge-based event analysis and forecasting solution. In this paper, we present a methodology for creating a benchmark dataset of news headlines mapped to event classes in Wikidata, and resources for the evaluation of methods that perform the mapping. We use the dataset to study two classes of unsupervised methods for this task: 1) adaptations of classic entity linking methods, and 2) methods that treat the problem as a zero-shot text classification problem. For the first approach, we evaluate off-the-shelf entity linking systems. For the second approach, we explore a) pre-trained natural language inference (NLI) models, and b) pre-trained large generative language models. We present the results of our evaluation, lessons learned, and directions for future work. The dataset and scripts for evaluation are made publicly available.

1 Introduction

Businesses and organizations can benefit from seeking knowledge of new events that may have an impact on their business. To assist in this task, there are several media monitoring solutions with features that can provide alerts and real-time analysis for ongoing events. The majority of existing solutions are centered around entities and/or topics. For example, they identify mentions of key companies or people, group texts by topics, and analyze contents for sentiment. On the other hand, there is great value in an event-centric solution that identifies ongoing events and analyzes the characteristics of the identified events to enable event-based reasoning. In particular, such a solution would enable causal reasoning to determine the causes and consequences of ongoing events and identify potential risks and opportunities (Hassanzadeh et al., 2022).

To enable a knowledge-driven event-centric news analysis and monitoring solution, a key requirement is the ability to accurately map ongoing news to event-related classes in a knowledge base. One way to perform this mapping is to treat event-related classes as a set of categories (or topics) and classify news headlines into these categories. Prior work has studied classification methods for news headlines (e.g., see Awasthy et al. (2021); Rana et al. (2014) and references therein). The majority of existing methods rely on supervised learning and therefore require a training corpus. For a generic solution that can adapt to changing event classes or one that can be tuned easily for different domains, it is not feasible to rely on the availability of training corpora large enough for accurate classification.

In the absence of training data, the alternative solution is to apply unsupervised or weakly supervised classification methods that rely on little or no training data. Such methods often rely on rules and pre-trained generic models. More recently, pre-trained language models, and in particular large language models, have shown superior performance in such settings. As a result, we have seen a surge in the number of available models, each using different architectures, parameters, pre-training corpora, and fine-tuning strategies. Choosing the right model for a given task requires an evaluation framework to measure the accuracy of the models on the end task.

In this paper, we present an evaluation framework for unsupervised mapping of news headlines to event classes in a knowledge graph. To the best of our knowledge, this is the first benchmark dataset and evaluation framework for this task. In what follows, we first present the task definition and use cases we envision for the task. We then describe our methodology for creating the benchmark dataset. Next, we present the results of our evaluation of a number of methods belonging to two different kinds of unsupervised techniques. We discuss key lessons learned and a number of avenues for future work. The datasets used in our

Proceedings of the 6th Workshop on Challenges and Applications of Automated Extraction of Socio-political Events from Text, pages 44–52, Varna, Bulgaria, Sep 7, 2023.
https://doi.org/10.26615/978-954-452-089-2_006

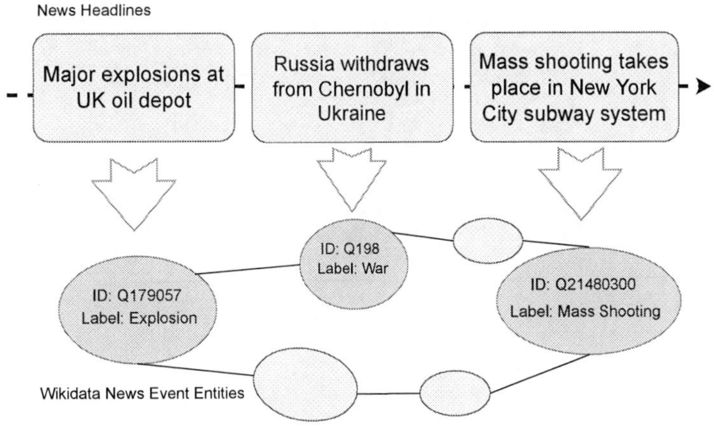

Figure 1: Example of News Headlines and Event Classes in Our Benchmark

experiments as well as the evaluation framework are publicly available (Mbouadeu et al., 2023).

2 Task Definition and Use Cases

Our target task in this paper is as follows: Given a news headline and a set of event classes from a knowledge graph, find the most relevant event class to the news headline. The news headline is a short text (typically a sentence) that indicates the content of a news article by providing a concise summary of the article's contents. The knowledge graph contains event-related classes. Each class comes with one or more labels, a description of the class, and possibly a class hierarchy and other attributes. Figure 1 shows examples of news headlines, event classes, and their mappings. We refer to this task as *News Headline Event Mapping*. Note that this task is different from the event linking task defined by Yu et al. (2023) which takes an event mention (a phrase) and a context as input, and finds a specific Wikipedia article as output. Nevertheless, as described in Section 4.1, such methods can be used for our task.

Figure 2 shows example use cases for news headline event mapping in the context of a knowledge-based news event analysis solution (Hassanzadeh et al., 2022). In this context, news headlines from a variety of sources or a news content aggregation service (e.g., EventRegistry (Leban et al., 2014)) are monitored in order to identify major news that could have an impact on a users' organization, on a certain region, or more generally on society. This domain of interest is defined through a knowledge graph of events that contains a rich source of knowledge about past events and event classes. Such a source of knowledge can be gathered through automated knowledge extraction methods (Hassanzadeh et al., 2020; Heindorf et al., 2020) or be derived from domain-specific or general-domain knowledge sources such as Wikidata (Vrandečić and Krötzsch, 2014). The knowledge graph provides event classes along with labels and descriptions to be used for news headline event mapping. The output of headline event mapping is then used for an analysis of the potential causes and effects of the identified event. The outcome can be used as a part of a news monitoring solution to create alerts for the identified event or its consequences so that it can assist with managing a potential risk or opportunity. It can also provide the required knowledge for an analyst looking at the implications of ongoing news for a business or organization. Finally, it can be used as an input for scenario planning (Sohrabi et al., 2019) or event forecasting (Muthiah et al., 2016; Radinsky et al., 2012).

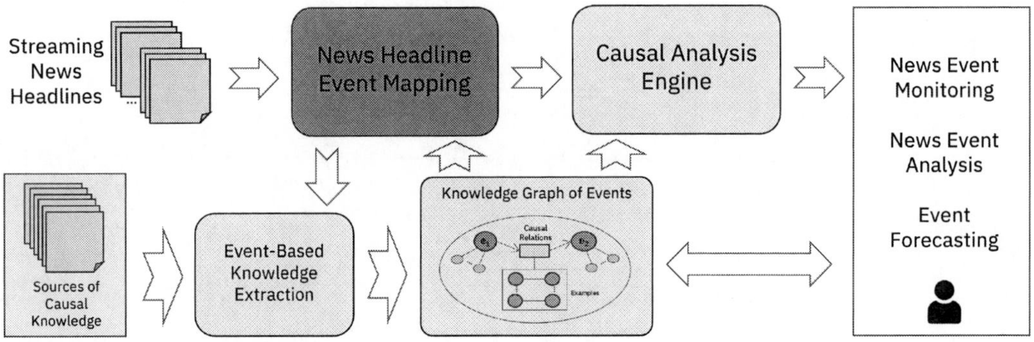

Figure 2: News Headline Event Mapping in a Knowledge-Based Event Analysis Solution (Hassanzadeh et al., 2022)

3 Benchmark Dataset

To the best of our knowledge, there is no benchmark dataset for the task of news headline event mapping. There are benchmarks on related tasks such as entity linking (van Erp et al., 2016) that include news headlines. However, none of these benchmarks provide ground truth event class annotations. We have, therefore, curated a new dataset designed for the news headline event mapping task using Wikidata and Wikinews. First, we leveraged the links to Wikinews articles in Wikidata to gather a collection of event-related instances. To focus on event classes, we then filtered out instances that are not subclasses of `occurrence` `(Q1190554)` as well as classes with very short labels, as some non-event related entities are also linked to Wikinews. Finally, these articles were reviewed manually to check whether they related to news headlines and news events. This yielded 105 Wikinews headlines mapped to Wikidata event classes. We manually added five headlines from other sources for a final dataset of 110 mappings of headlines to Wikidata event classes. The labels of all of the Wikidata classes included in our benchmark are shown in Figure 3. The examples of Figure 1 were taken from the dataset.

There are a number of other benchmark datasets in the literature for related tasks. Closest to our task is that of zero-shot sentence classification. Yin et al. (2019) present an excellent review of benchmarks for this task. Many benchmarks for news headline classification and for zero-shot sentence classification target binary classification (e.g., for emotions or sentiment or clickbait detection), or a small number of topics. The closest to our benchmark is the Yahoo! dataset (Zhang et al., 2015), which consists of 10 topics. To our knowledge, there is no benchmark that targets the task of assigning news headlines to event classes in a knowledge graph or a large number of well-defined topics.

4 Evaluation

We use our benchmark and evaluation framework to evaluate the effectiveness of a number of different kinds of methods in news headline event mapping. We first describe the approaches and implementation details for each method. We then present the results of the evaluation and a detailed discussion on key lessons learned and directions for future work.

4.1 Methods

We experiment with news headline event mapping methods ranging from a simple similarity-based baseline to adaptations of classic entity linking tools and large generative language models.

4.1.1 Zero-Shot Classifiers

We evaluate two zero-shot text classification methods. One is a simple baseline based on textual similarity, while another uses state-of-the-art pre-trained language models for classification.

Similarity-Based Baseline (`Fuzzy`) This method identifies a substring of a headline that is suggestive of an event occurrence, and finds the most similar event class label in the knowledge graph to that substring. The substring is found through a sliding window of bigrams and trigrams of word tokens in the input, and matching them using Levenshtein distance (Chandrasekar et al., 2017) to our target event class labels. The event class with the lowest distance is returned as the most similar class to the headline.

aircraft_crash attack aviation_accident bomb_attack climate_change
coup_d'état crime cyberattack death disease_outbreak earthquake espionage
explosion fire flood impeachment_in_the_United_States infectious_disease
killing mass_murder mass_shooting massacre murder natural_disaster
procession scandal school_shooting social_issue stabbing_attack
terrorist_attack transport_accident volcanic_eruption war work_accident

Figure 3: News Event Classes in Our Benchmark

Zero-Shot Text Classifier using Natrual Language Inference (ZSTC) This classifier is a standard "MNLI" model: a pre-trained language model fine-tuned on the multi-genre textual entailment corpus for the Natural Language Inference (NLI) task from the RepEval workshop (Williams et al., 2018). Instances in the MNLI corpus are pairs of sentences with a label indicating whether the first sentence Entails the second sentence, is Contradicted by it, or is independent of it ("Neutral"). MNLI models can be used for zero-shot text classification by supplying the text to be classified as sentence1, and a textual representation of a target class as sentence2. For our experiments, the textual representation of a class (sentence2) is simply the English label of the class in Wikidata. Sentence1 is the headline to be classified. The target class whose textual representation (label) has the highest Entailment score is the predicted class for the text. Our zero-shot text classifier uses the RoBERTa-large (Liu et al., 2019) language model fine-tuned on MNLI.

4.1.2 Classic Entity Linkers & Adaptations

We considered a number of state-of-the-art open-source entity linking (EL) systems to adapt to include in our experiments. Most entity linking solutions are trained to work only on named entities (e.g., people, locations, organizations) and fail when it comes to events. We considered EL systems that are more easily adaptable for mapping to event classes. The systems we considered include BLINK (Wu et al., 2020), OpenTapioca (Delpeuch, 2019), Falcon (Sakor et al., 2020), and Wikifier (Brank et al., 2017). Out of these, our adaptation of BLINK failed to perform well, and OpenTapioca required a training corpus. Although training OpenTapioca using our dataset provided promising results (another potential use case for our dataset), we excluded the results in this paper to focus on fully unsupervised (zero-shot) methods.

Falcon 2.0 (Falcon EM) Falcon 2.0 (Sakor et al., 2020) leverages NLP techniques to achieve state-of-the-art entity linking performance on a number of EL datasets, notably on question-structured prompts (Sakor et al., 2020). Given a prompt, it generates a list of entity surface forms, similar to event mentions. After generating these surface forms or tokens, it selects candidate entities for each of them by searching them in an information retrieval (IR) index (powered by Elasticsearch) of a Wikidata data dump. We only included Wikidata concepts that were recursively instances or subclasses of event classes in the dump to tailor it to our task. In our evaluation, we used Falcon to match headlines to Wikidata concept labels. If Falcon did not generate at least one candidate concept, we successively stripped tokens from the right of the headline, approximating more general phrases. we repeated the process until either a candidate concept was found or the phrase became empty. The resulting candidate concepts were then ranked using SPARQL ASK queries, measuring the taxonomic distance between the candidate concepts and our chosen news event classes. The class from our set of target event classes that was the shortest distance from a Falcon-generated candidate concept was chosen as the predicted class for the headline.

Wikifier (`Wikifier`) Wikifier (Brank et al., 2017) is a service for the task of "wikification" – taking an input text and annotating phrases in the text with Wikipedia URLs. Wikifier employs surface forms of hyperlinks in Wikipedia to perform linking to Wikipedia entities. For example, the Wikipedia page for earthquakes contains a link to the tsunami page. This suggests that earthquake is related to tsunami. For any surface form throughout Wikipedia that is present in the given text, Wikifier makes a candidate entity of the underlying entity. A directed mention-concept graph is created, linking surface forms to these candidate entities. Wikifier performs a global disambiguation based on the distance between entities. Distance represents the number of hyperlink hops required to get from one page to another. The smaller the distance, the more related the entities are considered. The relatedness metrics are used to score the candidate entities. Wikifier returns these candidate entities as predictions along with their scores. We converted the Wikipedia hyperlinks to Wikidata concepts with a simple lookup query. For our evaluation, we picked the top prediction that was among one of our target event classes.

4.1.3 Large Generative Language Models

Another way to perform zero-shot classification is through the use of generative large language models (LLMs) and prompts. There are a number of LLMs available with different architectures, parameter sizes, and resource requirements. For the results in this paper, we decided to pick just one of the popular LLMs with reasonable resource requirements, namely GPT-J 6B (Wang and Komatsuzaki, 2021), so that our experiments are reproducible without requiring access to commercial APIs or expensive GPUs. We include two different prompting strategies for the results in this paper. Experiments with a wider variety of LLMs and more extensive prompt engineering are a subject for future work.

GPT-J Event Mapping (`GPT-J EM`) Our goal here is to form a prompt that yields the generation of the relevant event class by the LLM. One way to create a prompt is to provide a few examples (a "few-shot" strategy) of headline + delimiter + known event class label, followed by the headline to be classified and the same delimiter, and ask the model to generate completion text. Having experimented with a number of prompting strategies, we decided to use a co-training approach (Lang et al., 2022).

Co-training works similarly to cross-validation, where each individual headline is mapped with zero shots using GPT-J and then the best-performing headlines are used to generate a few-shot prompt. The output of this method is an event label that we then mapped to Wikidata.

GPT-J Event Mapping with Types (`GPT-J EMT`) We continued our experiments with GPT-J by including all the event classes in the prompt along with the pre-training. The set of labels from our news event classes were listed separately and prefixed with "types:". We then added this list to the beginning of the prompt to signal the categories to be picked from. We also prefixed each annotation in the pre-training examples with "type:" to establish that association. Additionally, we implemented a catch-all for non-event classifications. If a prediction didn't match an event class label, we performed textual similarity matching with our target event labels to find the most similar event class to return as output.

Table 1: Accuracy Results

	Fuzzy	ZSTC	Falcon EM	Wikifier	GPT-J EM	GPT-J EMT
Correct @1	22	23	33	49	65	74
Accuracy	0.2	0.209	0.3	0.445	0.591	0.673

4.2 Results

For our evaluation we ran each system from Section 4.1 on the headlines from our news event corpus to generate the systems' best predicted event classes. We calculated accuracy of each system as the percentage of top-ranked predictions matching the gold event class.

The results are shown in Table 1. In addition to the benchmark datasets, all of our outputs as well as our evaluation script are available on our GitHub repository (Mbouadeu et al., 2023).

The zero-shot classifier methods (`Fuzzy` and `ZSTC`) performed comparably. They both did well on headlines that have linguistic overlap with a target class label. `Fuzzy` works when there is surface/lexical overlap, whereas `ZSTC` takes advantage of semantic overlap. Examples of headlines having linguistic overlap with target classes are: "*Major explosions at UK oil depot*", "*Mass shooting takes place in New York City subway system*", and "*Myanmar military vows to abide by constitution amid coup fears*". The first two, for example, have *explosion* and *mass shooting* target event classes, and labels for those classes appear verbatim in the headlines.

Linguistic overlap can result in frequent false positives, particularly for very general target classes. For example, for the headline "*More than 80 people killed in Nice, France attack on Bastille Day*", both methods associated "killed" with the `killing` event class and "attack" with the `attack` class. Ideally, both classes would be included among the gold classes and a ranking metric used to give credit to multiple (ranked) system predictions. For simplicity, and for even comparison to systems without ranked/scored output, we only report accuracy (correct @1).

Among the classic entity linking methods, `Wikifier` performed better than `Falcon EM`. In general, it was able to map more challenging headlines having no obvious linguistic overlap with class labels. For example, it was able to map the headline "*Russia withdraws from Chernobyl in Ukraine*" to the `war` event class.

The LLM-based methods also showed the ability to map news headlines to event classes whose labels do not appear in the headline. Examples of such headlines are: "*Nine firefighters killed in South Carolina blaze*" (event class `fire`), and "*Attack at Texas elementary school kills at least 19, including 18 children*". (event class `school shooting`). The second example is particularly interesting because the LLM-based methods preferred the more specific `school shooting` event class in spite of the headline's overlap with the label of the `killing` class. The LLM-based methods (`GPT-J EM` and `GPT-J EMT`) also showed a more consistent ability to map news headlines to events with labels that are generalizations of text appearing in headlines, such as `violence` and `natural disasters`.

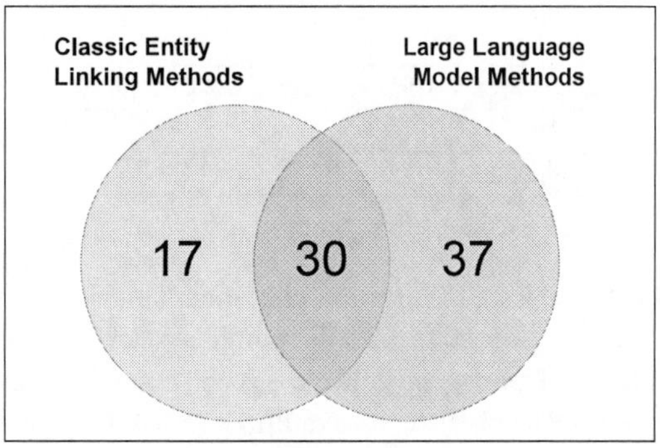

Figure 4: Overlap of Accurate Prediction Coverage of Entity Linking Adaptations and LLM-based Methods

4.3 Lessons Learned and Future Work

An Ensemble Approach Although the classifier and entity linking based methods did not perform as well as the LLM-based methods, they complement each other. Combining their coverage of successfully mapping headlines in the dataset yields 95% accuracy. When comparing their coverage of the dataset, they generally succeed and fail on different types of headlines. The classic entity linker adaptations do well with headlines with single-worded event mentions that match directly to event classes. LLM-based mappers do well with multi-worded event mentions that are not necessarily substrings of the event class labels and those without any clear event mentions as well. They are still able to make the association between these more ambiguous mentions and the event entities, presumably from their learning from large amounts of text. This is further supported by the fact that of the 33% of headlines that the LLM-based mappers failed to correctly map, 87% have a clear event mention that closely matches the labels of their event classes. Nevertheless, there is still a noticeable amount of overlap between the two types of methods, as shown in Figure 4. However, these results do suggest that an ensemble approach that combines techniques used in classic entity linking and leverages large language models, intentionally deciding how and when to apply them, would improve performance on this task.

A Larger Dataset Despite the relatively small size of the current version of our dataset, we believe our results are informative, and highlight the strengths and weaknesses of different classes of methods. We also believe the small size of the data reflects well the real-world use case of building a generic and adaptable event monitoring solution, where gathering ground truth data for supervised solutions could be prohibitively expensive. Still, the methodology we outlined in Section 3 can be extended to gather a larger and more diverse collection of news headlines mapped to event classes. At the time of writing this manuscript, we are applying a similar strategy to news headlines that are referenced from within Wikipedia-related event articles to curate a second, much larger version of our dataset.

More Experiments on LLMs With the ever-growing number of publicly-available LLMs as well as commercial APIs enabling access to such models and allowing a more extensive prompt engineering effort, our dataset and its larger extensions can be used for a study on various LLM-based news headline event mapping methods.

5 Conclusion

In this paper, we defined the task of news headline event mapping and outlined a few use cases for the task in event monitoring, analysis, and forecasting solutions. We presented an approach for creating a benchmark dataset, and used it to create the first benchmark dataset for the evaluation of news headline event mapping methods. We used the benchmark to evaluate different classes of mapping methods, including a) zero-short classification based methods, b) adaptations of classic entity linking methods, and c) methods based on large generative language models. Our results provide interesting insights on the strengths and weaknesses of each of the methods. We outlined several avenues for future work, including our plan to extend the dataset, work on an ensemble method, and further experiments on LLM-based methods. Our dataset, as well as our evaluation script and outputs of the models, are publicly available on our GitHub repository.

References

Parul Awasthy, Jian Ni, Ken Barker, and Radu Florian. 2021. IBM MNLP IE at CASE 2021 task 1: Multi-granular and multilingual event detection on protest news. In *Proceedings of the 4th Workshop on Challenges and Applications of Automated Extraction of Socio-political Events from Text (CASE 2021)*, pages 138–146, Online. Association for Computational Linguistics.

Janez Brank, Gregor Leban, and Marko Grobelnik. 2017. Annotating documents with relevant wikipedia concepts. *Proceedings of the Slovenian Conference on Data Mining and Data Warehouses (SiKDD 2017)*, 472.

B. Chandrasekar, Bharath Ramesh, Vishalakshi Prabhu, S. Sajeev, Pratik K. Mohanty, and G. Shobha. 2017. Development of intelligent digital certificate fuzzer tool. In *Proceedings of the 2017 International Conference on Cryptography, Security and Privacy*, ICCSP '17, page 126–130, New York, NY, USA. Association for Computing Machinery.

Antonin Delpeuch. 2019. OpenTapioca: Lightweight entity linking for Wikidata. *CoRR*, abs/1904.09131.

Oktie Hassanzadeh, Parul Awasthy, Ken Barker, Onkar Bhardwaj, Debarun Bhattacharjya, Mark Feblowitz, Lee Martie, Jian Ni, Kavitha Srinivas, and Lucy Yip. 2022. Knowledge-based news event analysis and forecasting toolkit. In *Proceedings of the Thirty-First International Joint Conference on Artificial Intelligence, IJCAI 2022, Vienna, Austria, 23-29 July 2022*, pages 5904–5907. ijcai.org.

Oktie Hassanzadeh, Debarun Bhattacharjya, Mark Feblowitz, Kavitha Srinivas, Michael Perrone, Shirin Sohrabi, and Michael Katz. 2020. Causal knowledge extraction through large-scale text mining. In *The Thirty-Fourth AAAI Conference on Artificial Intelligence, AAAI 2020, The Thirty-Second Innovative Applications of Artificial Intelligence Conference, IAAI 2020, The Tenth AAAI Symposium on Educational Advances in Artificial Intelligence, EAAI 2020, New York, NY, USA, February 7-12, 2020*, pages 13610–13611. AAAI Press.

Stefan Heindorf, Yan Scholten, Henning Wachsmuth, Axel-Cyrille Ngonga Ngomo, and Martin Potthast. 2020. CauseNet: Towards a Causality Graph Extracted from the Web. In *Proceedings of the 29th ACM International Conference on Information & Knowledge Management*, pages 3023–3030, Virtual Event Ireland. ACM.

Hunter Lang, Monica N Agrawal, Yoon Kim, and David Sontag. 2022. Co-training improves prompt-based learning for large language models. In *Proceedings of the 39th International Conference on Machine Learning*, volume 162 of *Proceedings of Machine Learning Research*, pages 11985–12003. PMLR.

Gregor Leban, Blaz Fortuna, Janez Brank, and Marko Grobelnik. 2014. Event registry: Learning about world events from news. In *Proceedings of the 23rd International Conference on World Wide Web*, WWW '14 Companion, page 107–110, New York, NY, USA. Association for Computing Machinery.

Yinhan Liu, Myle Ott, Naman Goyal, Jingfei Du, Mandar Joshi, Danqi Chen, Omer Levy, Mike Lewis, Luke Zettlemoyer, and Veselin Stoyanov. 2019. Roberta: A robustly optimized bert pretraining approach.

Steve Mbouadeu, Ken Barker, and Oktie Hassanzadeh. 2023. An Evaluation Framework for Mapping News Headlines to Event Classes in a Knowledge Graph. `https://github.com/mbouadeus/news-headline-event-linking`.

Sathappan Muthiah, Patrick Butler, Rupinder Paul Khandpur, Parang Saraf, Nathan Self, Alla Rozovskaya, Liang Zhao, Jose Cadena, Chang-Tien Lu, Anil Vullikanti, Achla Marathe, Kristen Summers, Graham Katz, Andy Doyle, Jaime Arredondo, Dipak K. Gupta, David Mares, and Naren Ramakrishnan. 2016. EMBERS at 4 years: Experiences operating an open source indicators forecasting system. In *Proceedings of the 22nd ACM SIGKDD International Conference on Knowledge Discovery and Data Mining*, KDD '16, page 205–214, New York, NY, USA. Association for Computing Machinery.

Kira Radinsky, Sagie Davidovich, and Shaul Markovitch. 2012. Learning causality for news events prediction. In *Proceedings of the 21st International Conference on World Wide Web*, WWW '12, page 909–918, New York, NY, USA. Association for Computing Machinery.

Mazhar Iqbal Rana, Shehzad Khalid, and Muhammad Usman Akbar. 2014. News classification based on their headlines: A review. In *17th IEEE International Multi Topic Conference 2014*, pages 211–216.

Ahmad Sakor, Kuldeep Singh, Anery Patel, and Maria-Esther Vidal. 2020. Falcon 2.0: An entity and relation linking tool over wikidata. In *Proceedings of the 29th ACM International Conference on Information & Knowledge Management*, CIKM '20, page 3141–3148, New York, NY, USA. Association for Computing Machinery.

S. Sohrabi, M. Katz, O. Hassanzadeh, O. Udrea, M. D. Feblowitz, and A. Riabov. 2019. IBM scenario planning advisor: Plan recognition as AI planning in practice. *AI Commun.*, 32(1):1–13.

Marieke van Erp, Pablo Mendes, Heiko Paulheim, Filip Ilievski, Julien Plu, Giuseppe Rizzo, and Joerg Waitelonis. 2016. Evaluating entity linking: An analysis of current benchmark datasets and a roadmap for doing a better job. In *Proceedings of the Tenth International Conference on Language Resources and Evaluation (LREC'16)*, pages 4373–4379, Portorož, Slovenia. European Language Resources Association (ELRA).

Denny Vrandečić and Markus Krötzsch. 2014. Wikidata: A free collaborative knowledgebase. *Commun. ACM*, 57(10):78–85.

Ben Wang and Aran Komatsuzaki. 2021. GPT-J-6B: A 6 Billion Parameter Autoregressive Language Model. `https://github.com/kingoflolz/mesh-transformer-jax`.

Adina Williams, Nikita Nangia, and Samuel Bowman. 2018. A broad-coverage challenge corpus for sentence understanding through inference. In *Proceedings of the 2018 Conference of the North American Chapter of the Association for Computational Linguistics: Human Language Technologies, Volume 1 (Long Papers)*, pages 1112–1122, New Orleans, Louisiana. Association for Computational Linguistics.

Ledell Wu, Fabio Petroni, Martin Josifoski, Sebastian Riedel, and Luke Zettlemoyer. 2020. Scalable zero-shot entity linking with dense entity retrieval. In *Proceedings of the 2020 Conference on Empirical Methods in Natural Language Processing (EMNLP)*, pages 6397–6407, Online. Association for Computational Linguistics.

Wenpeng Yin, Jamaal Hay, and Dan Roth. 2019. Benchmarking zero-shot text classification: Datasets, evaluation and entailment approach. In *Proceedings of the 2019 Conference on Empirical Methods in Natural Language Processing and the 9th International Joint Conference on Natural Language Processing (EMNLP-IJCNLP)*, pages 3914–3923, Hong Kong, China. Association for Computational Linguistics.

Xiaodong Yu, Wenpeng Yin, Nitish Gupta, and Dan Roth. 2023. Event linking: Grounding event mentions to Wikipedia. In *Proceedings of the 17th Conference of the European Chapter of the Association for Computational Linguistics*, pages 2679–2688, Dubrovnik, Croatia. Association for Computational Linguistics.

Xiang Zhang, Junbo Zhao, and Yann LeCun. 2015. Character-level convolutional networks for text classification. In *Advances in Neural Information Processing Systems*, volume 28. Curran Associates, Inc.

Ometeotl@Multimodal Hate Speech Event Detection 2023: Hate Speech and Text-Image Correlation Detection in Real Life Memes Using Pre-Trained BERT Models over Text

Jesús Armenta-Segura and **César-Jesús Núñez-Prado** and **Grigori Sidorov** and **Alexander Gelbukh** and **Rodrigo Román-Godínez**
Instituto Politécnico Nacional,
Centro de Investigación en Computación,
Mexico City, Mexico
{jarmentas2022, sidorov, gelbukh, rromang2019}@cic.ipn.mx,
cnunezp@ipn.mx

Abstract

Hate speech detection during times of war has become crucial in recent years, as evident with the recent Russo-Ukrainian war. In this paper, we present our submissions for both subtasks from the Multimodal Hate Speech Event Detection contest at CASE 2023, RANLP 2023. We used pre-trained BERT models in both submission, achieving a F1 score of 0.809 in subtask A, and F1 score of 0.567 in subtask B. In the first subtask, our result was not far from the first place, which led us to realize the lower impact of images in real-life memes about feelings, when compared with the impact of text. However, we observed a higher importance of images when targeting hateful feelings towards a specific entity. The source code to reproduce our results can be found at the github repository https://github.com/JesusASmx/OmeteotlAtCASE2023

1 Introduction

In recent decades, online platforms have gained increasing relevance in the worldwide sociopolitical scenario, to the extent that they have become significant representations of the so-called *soft power* (Mavrodieva et al., 2019). This growing importance has also led to an alarming spread of offensive, discriminatory, and harmful content, particularly during periods of significant political changes such as elections (Ezeibe, 2021) or wars (Aslan, 2017; Thapa et al., 2022).

Detecting hate speech, both in text and images, is crucial in order to mitigate its negative impact on digital platforms and safeguarding individuals from its harmful effects (Parihar et al., 2021). As an example of this need, in 2022, social networks witnessed a surge in activity following the outbreak of the Russo-Ukrainian war; numerous content, full of hate speech from both sides, went viral, and the need for a specific focus to that particular conflict became evident.

For this reason, the Multimodal Hate Speech Event Detection contest was proposed during the CASE 2023 workshop (Thapa et al., 2023) to tackle this problem with a dataset of manually annotated text-image memes (Bhandari et al., 2023). This shared task was divided into two subtasks A and B. In subtask A, participants were required to determine whether a meme related to the Russo-Ukrainian war constituted hate speech or not. In subtask B, participants were tasked with identifying the target of a hate speech meme, classifying it as directed against an individual (such as Volodymyr Zelensky or Vladimir Putin), an organization (such as the Ukrainian army), or a community (such as the Russian speakers in the Donbass region).

In this paper, we present out participation in both subtasks, under the name of *Team Ometeotl*. Our proposal consists on a fine-tunning of the pre-trained BERT model (Devlin et al., 2018), trained solely on the text extracted from the memes, without incorporating any image feature. Surprisingly, those experiments outperformed models that considered image features, such as ResNet152, and even multimodal ensemble learning approaches, such as ResNet152+BERT. These approaches achieved the sixth position in Subtask A, with an $F1$ score of 0.809, and the seventh position in Subtask B, with an $F1$ score of 0.567.

The structure of the paper is as follows: in Section 2, we describe the updated research on automatic hate speech detection. In Section 3, we describe the database. In Section 4, we detail the methodology used. In Section 5, we show the results of our experiments. In Section 5, we discuss the results. Finally, in Section 6 we present the conclusions.

Proceedings of the 6th Workshop on Challenges and Applications of Automated Extraction of Socio-political Events from Text, pages 53–59, Varna, Bulgaria, Sep 7, 2023.
https://doi.org/10.26615/978-954-452-089-2_007

2 Related Work

Hate speech detection in social media are one of the most prominent classification tasks in recent years (Schmidt and Wiegand, 2017). One of the earliest known approaches is the General Inquirer (Stone and Hunt, 1963), an IBM system developed in 1961 that enabled content analysis for behavioral sciences. It focused on pattern detection in text to categorize words based on their semantics, particularly positive or negative sentiments. In 1997, a more targeted approach was proposed with the system Smokey (Spertus, 1997), designed to detect abusive messages. Smokey utilized a rule-based approach to identify offensive language and contexts.

From there, several new approaches were proposed to address the task and its variations. In (Warner and Hirschberg, 2012), the authors proposed a lexicon-based approach for hate speech detection, starting from the hypothesis that the task can be related with word sense disambiguation. However, such approach was vulnerable in front of incomplete datasets, as they discovered when every method learnt *jew* as a inherent word for antisemitism speech. In order to deal to this sort of datasets, several methods and further methodologies has been developed: one of the most recent machine learning techniques who had brought promising results are the transformers (Vaswani et al., 2017), including BERT models (Devlin et al., 2018). In a nutshell, BERT models are is a family of language models composed of Transformer encoder layers. Such architectures has been successfully used in transphobic-homophobic speech detection, as can be seen in the LT-EDI-ACL2022 homophobia/transphobia speech detection contest in English, Tamil and Tamil-English (Chakravarthi et al., 2022). Team Sammaan (Upadhyay et al., 2022) employed ensemble transformers and obtained the second place in English; team Nozza (Nozza, 2022) obtained the third position in English and used ensemble learning over fine-tunned models of BERT (Devlin et al., 2018), RoBERTa (Liu et al., 2019), and HateBERT (Caselli et al., 2021).

Another hate speech detection contest in which transformers were used was in the IberLEF2023 shared task of HOMO-MEX: Hate Speech Detection towards the Mexican Spanish-Speaking LGBT+ (Bel-Enguix et al., 2023). Contrary to the previous contest, in which only the first places used transformers (the last place used TF-IDF with traditional classifiers such as Support Vector Machine (Swaminathan et al., 2022)), here team LIDOMA, the last place of the competition, employed a BERT model (Shahiki-Tash et al., 2023). However, in their paper, the authors explained how the lack of a preprocessing highly affected the efficiency of the attention mechanisms. To dive further, in this work we find a counterexample to their hypothesis in the shared task A, where preprocessing actually brought worse results.

All the related works discussed so far have focused solely on text-based hate speech detection. This is because text has historically been the most prevalent format for hate speech across the internet, especially during the early days of the worldwide web. However, it is crucial to recognize that there exists a wealth of historical data on hate speech in images, such as visual propaganda (Margolin, 1979), extensive datasets from the Second World War (Kallis, 2005; Basilio, 2014) and the Cold War (Snyder, 1995). Nevertheless, it is worth noting that these works were handcrafted by artists, hence impossible to get mass-produced during the early stages of the worldwide web, unlike the solely text-based propaganda. This landscape has since changed with the advent of text-image memes, which are pre-designed images that can have accompanying text, making possible the mass-production of visual propaganda and hence attracting the attention of researchers all across the world. For instance, Meta AI initiated the paid contest titled "Hateful Memes Challenge and Dataset for Research on Harmful Multimodal Contest" (Kiela et al., 2020), in which they provided a dataset of memes and the task to detect hate speech on them. One of the most interesting aspects of the challenge was that the dataset considered the significant phenomena of text-image interaction through phrase-sense disambiguation. For instance, a meme featuring the text *I love the way you smell today* could be classified as hate speech if accompanied by an image of a skunk (Mephitidae), but as non-hate speech if accompanied by a picture of a rose.

Another relatable example of multimodal hate speech text-image detection is (Perifanos and Goutsos, 2021). In this work, the authors combined natural language processing techniques with computer vision models to analyze both text and images in greek social media. For text processing they fine-tuned a pre-trained BERT model (Devlin et al., 2018). For image processing, the authors fine-tuned a pre-trained ResNet118 (He et al., 2015) in the ImageNet dataset (Deng et al., 2009). Their best result was an F1 score of 0.947.

In (Yang et al., 2022), the authors proposed a multimodal hate speech detection approach that uses cross-domain knowledge transfer to improve hate speech detection accuracy. To address the semantic inconsistency between hate speech and sarcasm, the authors combined the contrastive attention mechanism with representational dissociation to design a semantic adaptive module. In addition, they applied curricular learning to accelerate the training process. Experimental results showed that the proposed approach outperformed existing multimodal hate speech detection methods in terms of accuracy and F1-score on two public datasets: the Facebook Hateful Memes dataset from the Meta AI's contest, mentioned before, and the Twitter sarcasm detection dataset (Cai et al., 2019).

3 Dataset

The dataset for both subtasks consists in $6,913$ text-image memes concerning the Ukraine-Russia conflict. These samples were collected from social media platforms such as Twitter, Reddit and Facebook with keywords for specialized searches. The labeling was done manually, and they used Cohen's Kappa statistical measure (Matthijs, 2015) to assess the agreement between two or more annotators which ranges from -1 to 1, where the value 1 indicates perfect agreement, 0 indicates casual agreement and -1 total disagreement (Bhandari et al., 2023).

3.1 Sub-task A

The main goal is to identify whether or not a text-image meme contains hate speech or not. The training set for this sub-task contains $3,600$ images in jpg format, where $1,942$ are hate speech and $1,658$ are no hate speech. There is also a evaluation set with samples, where 243 are hate speech and 200 are no hate speech. Finally, the test set consists in 443 images. Table 1 shows the statistics for this subtask.

Label	Amount	Data
Hate Speech	1,942	Training
No Hate Speech	1,658	Training
Hate speech	243	Evaluation
No Hate speech	200	Evaluation
–	443	Test

Table 1: Subtask A Dataset Statistics.

3.1.1 Sub-task B

In this task, the goal is to identify to whom the hate speech of a given meme is directed. Possible targets to be identified are community, individual and organization. For this task, the training dataset consists of $1,942$ images in jpg format, where 335 are hate speech against a community, 823 are directed towards an individual and 728 are aimed to an organization. There is also an evaluation set with 244, where 102 are community, 40 are individual and 101 are organization. Finally, the test set has 242 images. Table 2 shows the statistics for this subtask.

Label	Amount	Data
Community	335	Training
Individual	823	Training
Organization	784	Training
Community	102	Evaluation
Individual	40	Evaluation
Organization	101	Evaluation
–	242	Test

Table 2: Subtask B Dataset Statistics.

In addition to the text-image memes, the organizers also provided the texts, extracted with the Google vision API[1]. Table 3 shows examples of these extracted texts.

Label	Example
Hate	Death of Russian
No Hate	Putin recognises Ukraine rebel region
Community	Russian troop pronuons are were was
Individual	Zelenskyys massiv balls Putins balls
Organization	Love is sitting together and watching Russian tanks burn

Table 3: Example of texts extracted from the memes.

4 Methodology

The first step was to encode each labeling into a numerical value. In the case of subtask A, 0 was

[1]https://cloud.google.com/vision/

used to represent no hate speech and 1 to indicate hate speech. In subtask B, we utilized 0 for hateful messages towards a community, 1 for individual, and 2 for organization. All these labelings were chosen following the indications of the organizers.

The next step involved an optional preprocessing outside the BERT processing of the text. It consisted of a function that removed special characters, converted to lowercase, and removed the stopwords using the spacy python library[2]. The main idea behind this function was to enhance the efficiency of the attention mechanisms as mentioned in (Shahiki-Tash et al., 2023). However, as anticipated in Section 2, it only worked for subtask B.

Regarding the model specifications, we utilized the *BertForSequenceClassification* model with the *bert-base-uncased* architecture, which was pre-trained on the English corpus. The employed parameters for the preparation of the data were:

- add_special_tokens = True,
- max_length = 256,
- padding = max_length,
- return_attention_mask = True,
- Truncation = True,
- return_tensors = pt.

The input tokens and attention masks were concatenated into separate tensors using the *torch.cat* and *torch.tensor* libraries.

The parameter for training the *bert-base-uncased* model were:

- number of labels = 2 (for Sub-task B number of labels = 3),
- optimizer = AdamW, with a learning rate of 2e-5,
- batch size = 16,
- with training inputs, training masks and training labels is created a *TensorDataset*,
- epochs = 4.

The system infraestructure consisted in a CPU with a AMD Rysen 2 5600x processor with six kernels, along with 46gb of RAM. With this system, the run for the subtask A spent around ten hours while the run for the subtask B spent around eight.

[2]https://spacy.io/

5 Results and Discussion

In subtask A, we did not utilized preprocessing and achieved an F1 score of 0.809. The first-place score was 0.856, which is only 0.047 points higher than ours. This difference is relatively low, especially when considering that we did not employ image features in our predictions. See Table 4 to check the full leaderboard of subtask A, with F1 score and Accuracy.

Team	F1	Accuracy
arc-nlp	0.856	0.858
bayesiano98	0.853	0.853
karanpreet_singh	0.846	0.846
DeepBlueAI	0.834	0.835
csecudgs	0.825	0.826
Ometeotl	**0.810**	**0.810**
Avanthika	0.788	0.790
Sarika11	0.782	0.759
rabindra.nath	0.780	0.783
md_kashif_20	0.729	0.736
Sathvika.V.S	0.429	0.578
lueluelue	0.522	0.526
pakapro	0.494	0.497

Table 4: Sub-task A Results. Numbers were rounded up from 6, starting on the fourth digit. (Team Ometeotl achieved a $F1$ score of 0.8099)

In subtask B, we employed preprocessing and achieved an F1 score of 0.567. This time, the difference with the first-place score was more substantial (of 0.195 points), leading us to hypothesize that visual features may have a stronger correlation when determining the target of a hateful meme. The leaderboard of this subtask can be found in Table 5.

5.1 Image features in subtask A

To incorporate visual features and improve the results, we experimented with ResNet152 on the image data alone. Initially, without data augmentation, the best F1 score achieved in subtask A was 0.55, but the model exhibited significant overfitting. To address this issue, we augmented the data ten times by performing rotations, expansion, and narrowing, which resulted in an enhanced F1 score of 0.71. However, this performance was still far below that of BERT. We attempted Voting Ensemble, but it only led to a marginal improvement, reaching an F1 score of 0.76, so we discarded it for the last submission.

Team	F1	Accuracy
arc-nlp	0.763	0.793
bayesiano98	0.741	0.773
karanpreet singh	0.697	0.723
Sarika22	0.680	0.715
csecudgs	0.653	0.690
DeepBlueAI	0.652	0.698
Ometeotl	**0.568**	**0.640**
Avanthika	0.526	0.640
Sathvika.V.S	0.433	0.529
pakapro	0.334	0.351

Table 5: Sub-task B Results. Numbers were rounded up from 6, starting on the fourth digit.

Figure 1: On top, sample $10,465$ labelled as no hate speech. On bottom, sample $11,381$ labelled as hate speech.

We hypothesize that the reason for the low correlation between visual features and hate speech in subtask A is that images in memes are primarily used as conceptual support for the message rather than pragmatic support. For instance, consider Figure 1. In this figure, sample $11,381$ is labeled as hate speech due to its text, but its visual features consist entirely of the well-known *The-What* meme[3], which solely portrays a woman with a funny smile, and no further information about whether the messages is hateful or not. On the other hand, sample $10,465$ consists in a frame from the movie *Star Wars I: The Phantom Menace*[4], in which an old man (Governor Sio Bibble) is sitting in a wide chamber while speaking, once again, withouth further visual information about the emotion of the message.

6 Conclusions

In this paper, we presented our approach to address both subtasks from the Multimodal Hate Speech Event Detection at CASE 2023, which consists in A) Detect hate speech in text-image memes spread during the Russo-Ukranian war, and B) given a hateful meme about that conflict, determine if the target is a community, an individual or an organization. We utilized text-based transformers, specifically fine-tunned pre-trained BERT models, and achieved high results in subtask A using only text features.

Our methodology involved the numerical encoding of the labels, and a preprocessing step for subtask B consisting in lowercase conversion and the removal of stopwords and special characters. Afterward, we conducted a four-epoch training of the fine-tunned pre-trained BERT model *bert-base-uncased*.

We discovered that visual features played a more significant role in determining the target of hate speech rather than determining whether the meme itself was hateful or not, at least in this particular database. As a result, further research and analysis are needed to explore this phenomenon comprehensively. Exploring other datasets could provide valuable insights into the dynamics between visual features and hate speech, offering a more comprehensive understanding of the varying impact these elements have across different contexts and social settings. Such investigations can shed light on the broader implications of visual cues and how they interact with textual content in influencing the perception and spread of hateful memes.

Acknowledgments

This work was done with partial support from the Mexican Government through the grant A1-S-47854 of CONACYT, Mexico, grants 20232138, 20232080, 20231567 of the Secretaría de Inves-

[3]https://knowyourmeme.com/memes/the-what-rug-doctor-woman-ad

[4]https://knowyourmeme.com/photos/1810076-prequel-memes

tigación y Posgrado of the Instituto Politécnico Nacional, Mexico. The authors thank the CONACYT for the computing resources brought to them through the Plataforma de Aprendizaje Profundo para Tecnologías del Lenguaje of the Laboratorio de Supercómputo of the INAOE, Mexico and acknowledge the support of Microsoft through the Microsoft Latin America PhD Award.

References

Alev Aslan. 2017. Online hate discourse: A study on hatred speech directed against syrian refugees on youtube.

Miriam Basilio. 2014. *Visual Propaganda, Exhibitions, and the Spanish Civil War*. Ashgate Publishing, Ltd.

Gemma Bel-Enguix, Helena Gómez-Adorno, Gerardo Sierra, Juan Vásquez, Scott-Thomas Andersen, and Sergio Ojeda-Trueba. 2023. Overview of HOMO-MEX at Iberlef 2023: HOMO-MEX: Hate Speech Detection in Online Messages Directed Towards the MEXican Spanish Speaking LGBTQ+ Population. *Procesamiento del lenguaje natural*, 71.

Aashish Bhandari, Siddhant Bikram Shah, Surendrabikram Thapa, Usman Naseem, and Mehwish Nasim. 2023. Crisishatemm: Multimodal analysis of directed and undirected hate speech in text-embedded images from Russia-Ukraine conflict. In *Proceedings of the IEEE/CVF Conference on Computer Vision and Pattern Recognition*.

Yitao Cai, Huiyu Cai, and Xiaojun Wan. 2019. Multi-modal sarcasm detection in Twitter with hierarchical fusion model. In *Proceedings of the 57th Annual Meeting of the Association for Computational Linguistics*, pages 2506–2515, Florence, Italy. Association for Computational Linguistics.

Tommaso Caselli, Valerio Basile, Jelena Mitrović, and Michael Granitzer. 2021. HateBERT: Retraining BERT for abusive language detection in English. In *Proceedings of the 5th Workshop on Online Abuse and Harms (WOAH 2021)*, pages 17–25, Online. Association for Computational Linguistics.

Bharathi Raja Chakravarthi, Ruba Priyadharshini, Thenmozhi Durairaj, John McCrae, Paul Buitelaar, Prasanna Kumaresan, and Rahul Ponnusamy. 2022. Overview of the shared task on homophobia and transphobia detection in social media comments. In *Proceedings of the Second Workshop on Language Technology for Equality, Diversity and Inclusion*, pages 369–377, Dublin, Ireland. Association for Computational Linguistics.

Jia Deng, Wei Dong, Richard Socher, Li-Jia Li, Kai Li, and Li Fei-Fei. 2009. Imagenet: A large-scale hierarchical image database. In *2009 IEEE Conference on Computer Vision and Pattern Recognition*, pages 248–255.

Jacob Devlin, Ming-Wei Chang, Kenton Lee, and Kristina Toutanova. 2018. Bert: Pre-training of deep bidirectional transformers for language understanding. *CoRR*.

Chidiebere Ezeibe. 2021. Hate Speech and Election Violence in Nigeria. *Journal of Asian and African Studies*, 56(4):919–935.

Kaiming He, X. Zhang, Shaoqing Ren, and Jian Sun. 2015. Deep residual learning for image recognition. *2016 IEEE Conference on Computer Vision and Pattern Recognition (CVPR)*, pages 770–778.

Aristotle Kallis. 2005. *Nazi propaganda and the second world war*. Springer.

Douwe Kiela, Hamed Firooz, Aravind Mohan, Vedanuj Goswami, Amanpreet Singh, Pratik Ringshia, and Davide Testuggine. 2020. The hateful memes challenge: Detecting hate speech in multimodal memes. *ArXiv*, abs/2005.04790.

Yinhan Liu, Myle Ott, Naman Goyal, Jingfei Du, Mandar Joshi, Danqi Chen, Omer Levy, Mike Lewis, Luke Zettlemoyer, and Veselin Stoyanov. 2019. Roberta: A robustly optimized BERT pretraining approach. *CoRR*, abs/1907.11692.

Victor Margolin. 1979. The visual rhetoric of propaganda. *Information design journal*, 1(2):107–122.

J Warrens Matthijs. 2015. Five ways to look at Cohen's Kappa. *Journal of Psychology Psychotherapy*, 5(4).

Aleksandrina V Mavrodieva, Okky K Rachman, Vito B Harahap, and Rajib Shaw. 2019. Role of social media as a soft power tool in raising public awareness and engagement in addressing climate change. *Climate*, 7(10):122.

Debora Nozza. 2022. Nozza@LT-EDI-ACL2022: Ensemble modeling for homophobia and transphobia detection. In *Proceedings of the Second Workshop on Language Technology for Equality, Diversity and Inclusion*, pages 258–264, Dublin, Ireland. Association for Computational Linguistics.

Anil Singh Parihar, Surendrabikram Thapa, and Sushruti Mishra. 2021. Hate speech detection using natural language processing: Applications and challenges. In *2021 5th International Conference on Trends in Electronics and Informatics (ICOEI)*, pages 1302–1308. IEEE.

Konstantinos Perifanos and Dionysis Goutsos. 2021. Multimodal hate speech detection in greek social media. *Multimodal Technologies and Interaction*.

Anna Schmidt and Michael Wiegand. 2017. A survey on hate speech detection using natural language processing. In *Proceedings of the Fifth International Workshop on Natural Language Processing for Social Media*.

Moein Shahiki-Tash, Jesús Armenta-Segura, Zahra Ahani, Olga Kolesnikova, Grigori Sidorov, and Alexander Gelbukh. 2023. Lidoma at homomex2023@iberlef: Hate speech detection towards the mexican spanish-speaking lgbt+ population. the importance of preprocessing before using bert-based models. In *CEUR Workshop Proceedings*.

Alvin A Snyder. 1995. *Warriors of disinformation: American propaganda, Soviet lies, and the Winning of the Cold War: an insider's account*. Arcade Publishing.

Ellen Spertus. 1997. Smokey: Automatic recognition of hostile messages. In *AAAI/IAAI*.

Philip J. Stone and Earl B. Hunt. 1963. A computer approach to content analysis: Studies using the general inquirer system. *Proceedings of the May 21-23, 1963, spring joint computer conference*.

Krithika Swaminathan, Bharathi B, Gayathri G L, and Hrishik Sampath. 2022. SSNCSE_NLP@LT-EDI-ACL2022: Homophobia/transphobia detection in multiple languages using SVM classifiers and BERT-based transformers. In *Proceedings of the Second Workshop on Language Technology for Equality, Diversity and Inclusion*, pages 239–244, Dublin, Ireland. Association for Computational Linguistics.

Surendrabikram Thapa, Farhan Ahmad Jafri, Ali Hürriyetoğlu, Francielle Vargas, Roy Ka-Wei Lee, and Usman Naseem. 2023. Multimodal hate speech event detection - shared task 4, case 2023. In *Proceedings of the 6th Workshop on Challenges and Applications of Automated Extraction of Socio-political Events from Text (CASE)*.

Surendrabikram Thapa, Aditya Shah, Farhan Jafri, Usman Naseem, and Imran Razzak. 2022. A multimodal dataset for hate speech detection on social media: Case-study of Russia-Ukraine conflict. In *Proceedings of the 5th Workshop on Challenges and Applications of Automated Extraction of Socio-political Events from Text (CASE)*, pages 1–6, Abu Dhabi, United Arab Emirates (Hybrid). Association for Computational Linguistics.

Ishan Sanjeev Upadhyay, Kv Aditya Srivatsa, and Radhika Mamidi. 2022. Sammaan@LT-EDI-ACL2022: Ensembled transformers against homophobia and transphobia. In *Proceedings of the Second Workshop on Language Technology for Equality, Diversity and Inclusion*, pages 270–275, Dublin, Ireland. Association for Computational Linguistics.

Ashish Vaswani, Noam M. Shazeer, Niki Parmar, Jakob Uszkoreit, Llion Jones, Aidan N. Gomez, Lukasz Kaiser, and Illia Polosukhin. 2017. Attention is all you need. In *NIPS*.

William Warner and Julia Hirschberg. 2012. Detecting hate speech on the world wide web. In *Proceedings of the Second Workshop on Language in Social Media*, pages 19–26, Montréal, Canada. Association for Computational Linguistics.

Chuanpeng Yang, Fuqing Zhu, Guihua Liu, Jizhong Han, and Songlin Hu. 2022. Multimodal hate speech detection via cross-domain knowledge transfer. In *MM'22: Proceedings of the 30th ACM International Conference on Multimedia*.

InterosML @ Causal News Corpus 2023: Understanding Causal Relationships: Supervised Contrastive Learning for Event Classification

Rajat Patel
Interos Inc. Arlington VA 22203, USA
rpatel@interos.ai

Abstract

Causal events play a crucial role in explaining the intricate relationships between the causes and effects of events. However, comprehending causal events within discourse, text, or speech poses significant semantic challenges. We propose a contrastive learning-based method in this submission to the Causal News Corpus - Event Causality Shared Task 2023, with a specific focus on Subtask 1 centered on causal event classification. In our approach we pre-train our base model using Supervised Contrastive (SuperCon) learning. Subsequently, we fine-tune the pre-trained model for the specific task of causal event classification. Our experimentation demonstrates the effectiveness of our method, achieving a competitive performance, and securing the 2nd position on the leaderboard with an F1-Score of 84.36.

1 Introduction

Understanding the intricate relationships between cause and effect within events is a fundamental aspect of language comprehension. Causal events, which provide insights into these connections, present semantic challenges when it comes to their classification and analysis in discourse, text, or speech.

We tackle the specific problem of causal event classification in Subtask 1 of the Causal News Corpus -Event Causality Shared Task 2023 (Tan et al., 2023) in our submission. This task involves accurately identifying and categorizing causal events, which plays a vital role in unraveling the underlying mechanisms behind real-world phenomena. Successful classification enables a wide range of applications, such as information extraction, summarization, and knowledge graph construction. To address this challenge, we propose an innovative approach that leverages SuperCon learning and source-aware sampling.

Contrastive learning has shown promising results in computer vision to learn a better and robust visual representations (Chen et al., 2020) and various natural language processing task like knowledge graph embeddings (Luo et al., 2021), text classification (Chen et al., 2022), entity linking (Yuan et al., 2022) and entity resolution (Brinkmann et al., 2023) etc. It allows the models to learn by contrasting positive and negative pairs, capturing informative representations.

The use of contrastive learning in text classification has been investigated in various contexts. For instance, the study by (Zuo et al., 2021) employed self-supervised learning techniques to address event causality identification in scenarios with limited annotated datasets. Similarly, (Chen et al., 2022) took an approach to incorporate contrastive learning with synthesized counterfactuals for data augmentation, demonstrating notable improvements in aspects such as counterfactual robustness, cross-domain generalization.

In this paper we apply the idea of SuperCon learning introduced by (Khosla et al., 2020) to the causal event classification task. Further, we loosely connect to the idea of source-aware sampling strategy introduced by (Peeters and Bizer, 2022) and modify it to suite the classification SubTask for pre-training the base encoder architecture.

Our methodology involves pre-training a transformer based encoder model using SuperCon Loss with naive source-aware sampling, followed by fine-tuning the pre-trained model on the causal event classification task. Through extensive experimentation and evaluation on the Causal News Corpus dataset, we demonstrate the effectiveness of our approach.

This paper's contributions can be summarized as follows: (1) Introducing contrastive learning as a method for causal event classification. (2) Achieving competitive performance in the Causal News Corpus - Event Causality Shared Task 2023,

Proceedings of the 6th Workshop on Challenges and Applications of Automated Extraction of Socio-political Events from Text, pages 60–65, Varna, Bulgaria, Sep 7, 2023.
https://doi.org/10.26615/978-954-452-089-2_008

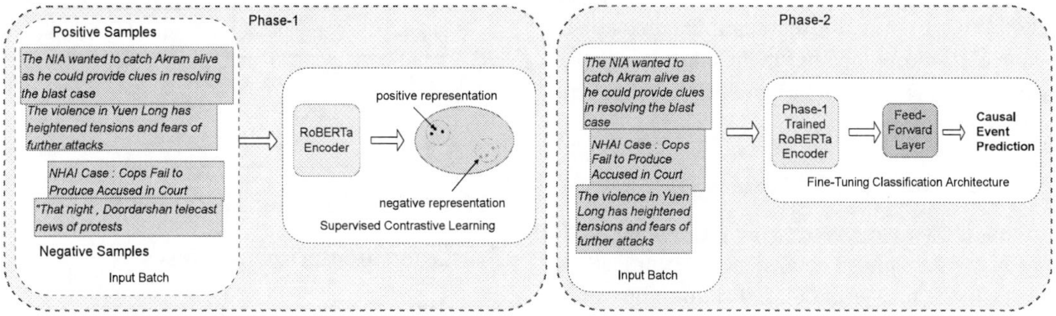

Figure 1: **Learning Phases for Causal Event Classification**: Phase-1: Pre-training with SuperCon I Phase-2: Fine-tuning for Causal Events

with the F1 Score of 84.36.[1]

2 Methodology

In this section, we present the methodology employed to address the causal event classification task. Our approach utilizes contrastive learning and consists of two main phases (Figure 1): (1) Pre-training the baseline transformer architecture with SuperCon, and (2) Fine-tuning the pre-trained model on the downstream classification task. For the encoder architecture, we adopt the RoBERTa base model[2] which has been shown to achieve strong results across different benchmark tasks (Liu et al., 2019).

2.1 Contrastive Pre-training

During the pre-training phase, we employ a batch creation process similar to the work of (Khosla et al., 2020) and augment it with the' naive source-aware sampling strategy introduced by (Peeters and Bizer, 2022). To train the encoder model, we create two copies of the input dataset. From the first dataset, we randomly select N records of input text x and subsequently sample another set of N records of input text x' from the second dataset, where we record in the batch (of size $2N$) has at least one corresponding record with the same label (even if it is a duplicate record only)

The RoBERTa encoder maps each input causal text record x to an embedding z as

$$z = \text{RoBERTa}(x). \quad (1)$$

To enhance the robustness and generalization of the record embeddings, we perform mean pooling on the encoder's output embeddings

$$z = \frac{1}{n}\sum_{i=1}^{n} z_i \quad (2)$$

and normalize them using the L^2-norm

$$z \to \frac{z}{\|z\|} \quad (3)$$

— a strategy effectively employed by (Brinkmann et al., 2023) for entity resolution tasks. To train the parameter of the encoder RoBERTa architecture we apply SupCon Loss to to cluster or position records with the same label more densely within the embedding space.

The SuperCon Loss employs the principle of contrastive learning, leveraging the label information of the input text records. It maximizes the agreements between causal text records belonging to the same class while minimizing agreements for causal text records from different classes. The formulation of the SuperCon loss is given as follows: Given a batch of $2N$ embedded records, z,

$$L = \sum_{i \epsilon I} L_i = \sum_{i \epsilon I} \frac{1}{|P_i|} \sum_{p \epsilon P(i)} \log \frac{\exp(z_i \cdot z_p/\tau)}{\sum_{a \epsilon A} \exp(z \cdot z_a/\tau)} \quad (4)$$

where i belongs to $I = 1, ..., N$ and represents the index of the anchor embedding z_i. The set of positive indices distinct from the anchor index i is denoted by $P_i \equiv p_i \in A(i) : y_p = y_i$, and $|P_i|$ is its cardinality. Here, y_p and y_i indicate the labels of the corresponding records. The scalar temperature parameter τ is used to scale the similarity measure.

In the loss calculation for a given batch, each record embedding z_i acts as an anchor embedding,

[1] Our code is available at https://github.com/rajathpatel23/causal-events.

[2] We use *roberta-base* model from Hugging Face model hub - https://huggingface.co/roberta-base

attempting to bring all record embeddings of the same class closer together in the embedding space while pushing away the record embeddings from different classes.

2.2 Fine-Tuning For Classification Task

In this phase, we leverage the pre-trained model from the first phase and adapt it specifically to the task of causal event classification.Fine-tuning is employed to optimize the model's parameters for this specific task, effectively utilizing its prior knowledge to enhance its ability to discern and categorize causal relationships within textual data.

To accommodate the classification task, we introduce a *Classification Head* atop the RoBERTa encoder

$$z = \text{RoBERTa}(x) \quad (5)$$

$$z = W_{ch}^{T} \cdot z + b_{ch} \quad (6)$$

where W_{ch} and b_{ch} are feed-forward layer specific weights and x is the input causal text. This is a simple single-layer feed-forward architecture. The primary purpose of this additional layer is to process the extracted embeddings and make predictions for the causal event classification. We employ the sigmoid activation function on the feed-forward output to derive the final probability

$$z_{out} = \sigma(z). \quad (7)$$

For training the model's parameters, we use binary cross-entropy loss, defined as follows:

$$J(\theta) = -\frac{1}{N}\sum_{i=0}^{N} \cdot y_i \cdot \log(z_{out}) + (1 - y_i) \cdot \log(1 - z_{out}) \quad (8)$$

where θ represents the parameters optimized during the fine-tuning phase, and y_i denotes the original labels for the causal input text records. The binary cross-entropy loss minimizes the difference between predicted and actual class assignments by comparing probabilities and true labels.

During fine-tuning, the encoder layer parameters are not frozen and fine-tuned end-to-end along with *Classification Head* parameters. This allows the model to specialize its learned representations for the causal event classification task without losing the valuable knowledge gained from pre-training.

Dataset	Causal	Non-Causal	Total
train	1624	1421	3075
dev	185	155	340
test	173	179	352

Table 1: Dataset distribution of Causal New Corpus

3 Experimentation Settings

3.1 Dataset

We utilize the Causal News Corpus, which is derived from the work of (Tan et al., 2022) for our experiments. This corpus is specifically prepared for the Shared Task on CASE 2023 Workshop on Event Causality Identification (Tan et al., 2023), focusing on Subtask 1 for causal event classification. This version contains more data than previous version of the dataset (Tan et al., 2022) while some previous annotations have been revised. The dataset comprises 869 news documents and 3767 English sentences that have been annotated with causal information. The corpus is partitioned into three sets: *train*, *dev*, and *test* splits to facilitate fair evaluation. A detailed distribution of the dataset can be found in Table 1.

3.2 Model Training

In the pre-training phase, we train the encoder architecture using the SuperCon Loss, with a batch size of 128. To guide the training process, we set the learning rate to 5e-5 and use a scalar temperature parameter, denoted as τ, which is set to 0.07. The pre-training runs for five epochs and involves both the *train* and *dev* splits from the causal news corpus dataset. To efficiently handle the data, we limit the maximum number of tokens for the encoder tokenizer to 256.

During the fine-tuning phase, we extend the pre-trained encoder architecture by adding a feed-forward network on top, known as the *Classification Head*. This additional network allows us to perform the specific task of causal event classification. We employ the binary cross-entropy loss (Eq. (8)) for training the model. Throughout fine-tuning, we solely use the *train* dataset and use the *dev* dataset to evaluate the model's performance. Finally, we submit the trained model's predictions on the *test* dataset to Codalab for evaluation on the hold-out test set. The parameters used for fine-tuning include - batch size of 16, the learning rate of 2e-5, and the number of training epochs set to 3, with an early stopping criterion.

User	Recall	Precision	F1-score	Accuracy	MCC
DeepBlueAI	0.8613 (5)	0.8324 (2)	0.8466 (1)	0.8466 (1)	0.6937 (1)
rpatel12	**0.8728 (4)**	**0.8162 (3)**	**0.8436 (2)**	**0.8409 (2)**	**0.6837 (2)**
timos	0.8786 (3)	0.8000 (4)	0.8375 (3)	0.8324 (3)	0.6683 (3)
csecudsg	0.8555 (6)	0.8000 (4)	0.8268 (4)	0.8239 (4)	0.6495 (4)
elhammohammadi	0.8960 (1)	0.7635 (6)	0.8245 (5)	0.8125 (5)	0.6352 (5)
tanfiona	0.8902 (2)	0.7586 (7)	0.8191 (6)	0.8068 (6)	0.6237 (7)
sgopala4	0.8613 (5)	0.7801 (5)	0.8187 (7)	0.8125 (5)	0.6288 (6)
nitanshjain	0.8728 (4)	0.6537 (8)	0.7475 (8)	0.7102 (8)	0.4483 (9)
kunwarv4	0.5260 (7)	0.8585 (1)	0.6523 (9)	0.7244 (7)	0.4819 (8)
pakapro	0.4740 (8)	0.4409 (9)	0.4568 (10)	0.4460 (9)	-0.1072 (10)

Table 2: The performance of the our model compared to all the other submission made to Codalab to CASE 2023 Shared Task 3 - Subtask 1 (Tan et al., 2023) on causal event classification

We manually select the hyper-parameters for the model during training. This approach ensures that the model's configuration aligns with the specific task requirements and contributes to its overall performance.

3.3 Evaluation Metrics

We employ various metrics, including Precision, Recall, F1-scores, Accuracy, and Matthew's correlation coefficient (MCC) to assess the performance of our binary classification model. Among these metrics, our model is optimized for the F1-score, which provides a balanced evaluation of both precision and recall.

4 Results and Analysis

This section presents the outcomes of our model architecture in the context of the causal event classification task. We conducted the model training on an A10 GPU with 24GB RAM, utilizing the available computational resources effectively.

4.1 Performance on Classification Task

Our contrastive learning based architecture is tailored for binary classification, determining if a given input text record x exhibits a semantic causal relationship. We compare its performance against other submissions in the event causality shared task 1 (Tan et al., 2023), summarized in Table 2. The results reveal our model's highly competitive performance in the classification task. It secures the 2nd position in three key metrics - F1-Score, Accuracy, and MCC. Additionally, it ranks 3rd in Precision and 4th in Recall among all submissions. Compared to the baseline model presented by (Tan et al., 2023), a fine-tuned BERT model with hyper-parameter tuning, our model shows significant improvements. Specifically, it achieves a remarkable 6-point increase in precision, a 3-point boost in F1-Score, and a substantial 6-point improvement in MCC score. These results provide strong evidence supporting the effectiveness of applying SuperCon learning to this specific classification problem.

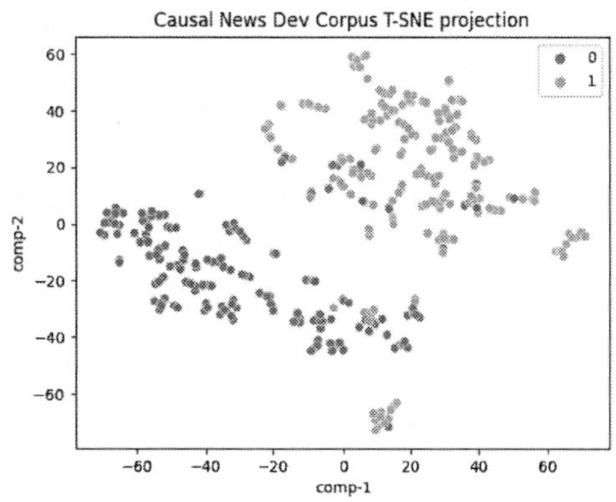

Figure 2: TSNE visualization of the representations from the pre-training phase

4.2 Analyzing Pre-trained Feature Spaces via t-SNE

To deepen our understanding of the impact of contrastive pre-training, we examine the feature representation generated from the *dev* dataset. The representation are visualized using the t-SNE technique (van der Maaten and Hinton, 2008). As depicted in Figure 2, the t-SNE plot reveals two clusters among the text records in the dataset. This clustering underscores the efficacy of our SuperCon-based pre-training approach. The visualization validates that the pre-training phase successfully imbues the model with meaningful representations, which, in turn, bolsters the model's performance in the causal event classification task. Interestingly, we observe

Model	Recall	Precision	F1-Score	Accuracy	MCC
BERT Baseline Model (Tan et al., 2023)	**0.887**	0.841	0.863	0.8471	0.6913
RoBERTa Non-Pre-trained Model	**0.9180**	0.8212	0.8181	0.8470	0.6941
Pre-trained OnlyModel	0.8756	0.7677	0.8673	0.7882	0.5755
Proposed SuperCon Model	0.8617	**0.8556**	**0.8972**	**0.8617**	**0.7210**

Table 3: Comparative study on the effectiveness of contrastive pretraining

some data point overlaps within the clusters, suggesting that these could be further refined through downstream tasks.

4.3 Effectiveness of Contrastive Pre-training

To comprehensively investigate the role of contrastive pre-training, we designed and executed experiments involving various model architectures. Specifically, we tested four different configurations:

BERT Baseline Model: This version uses the BERT architecture trained by (Tan et al., 2023) and serves as our foundational comparison point for the causal event classification task.

RoBERTa Non-Pre-trained Model: In this setup, we circumvent the pre-training phase altogether and train a RoBERTa encoder model with a classification head for the same combined number of epochs as our proposed model.

Pre-trained Only Model: In this scenario, the RoBERTa encoder model undergoes initial pre-training. During the fine-tuning stage, the feature-extracting layers are frozen, leaving only the classification head to be updated.

Proposed SuperCon Model: Our proposed architecture leverages the benefits of SuperCon Loss during the RoBERTa encoder model's pre-training phase, followed by a fine-tuning stage on the causal event classification task.

For a balanced comparative analysis, all model training was confined to the available *train* set, while evaluations were conducted on the *dev* dataset. The outcomes are summarized in Table 3.

The data reveal that our Proposed SuperCon Model excels in four metrics: Precision, F1-Score, Accuracy, and MCC, outperforming the other configurations. We also see a drop in performance metrics on the Pre-trained Only Model configuration, underscoring the necessity of fine-tuning subsequent to pre-training for achieving optimal results. Further the RoBERTa Non-Pretrained Model shows high recall but with lower F1-Score, Precision scores over our proposed model architecture.

5 Conclusion and Future Work

In this study, we have delved into the application of SuperCon learning for the task of causal event classification. By harnessing the power of SuperCon, our model achieved competitive performance, securing the 2nd position in key evaluation metrics such as F1-Score, Accuracy, and Matthew's correlation coefficient (MCC). These competitive results provide strong evidence for the efficacy of our approach in comprehending intricate causal relationships within textual data. Additionally, our comparative analysis highlights the model's learning strength and the benefits of this learning approach.

In the future we could explore the use of a large dataset from a distinct domain during the pre-training phase. This would enable us to gauge the inductive capacity of our learning paradigm on the causal news corpus domain dataset. Such investigations hold the potential for promising implications in the realms of low-resource, few-shot, and domain-specific causality event understanding.

Acknowledgements I thank members of Machine Learning Department at Interos Inc, including Britt Torrance, Hunter Powers, Rabia Turan for the support, compute resources, and their valuable comments and suggestions. I thank Saurabh Shringarpure for his insightful feedback. I also appreciate and acknowledge reviewers for their valuable comments and suggestions.

References

Alexander Brinkmann, Roee Shraga, and Christian Bizer. 2023. Sc-block: Supervised contrastive blocking within entity resolution pipelines. *arXiv*, abs/2303.03132.

J. Chen, Richong Zhang, Yongyi Mao, and Jie Xue. 2022. Contrastnet: A contrastive learning framework for few-shot text classification. *arXiv*, abs/2305.09269.

Ting Chen, Simon Kornblith, Mohammad Norouzi, and Geoffrey E. Hinton. 2020. A simple framework for contrastive learning of visual representations. *arXiv*, abs/2002.05709.

Prannay Khosla, Piotr Teterwak, Chen Wang, Aaron Sarna, Yonglong Tian, Phillip Isola, Aaron Maschinot, Ce Liu, and Dilip Krishnan. 2020. Supervised contrastive learning. *arXiv*, abs/2004.11362.

Yinhan Liu, Myle Ott, Naman Goyal, Jingfei Du, Mandar Joshi, Danqi Chen, Omer Levy, Mike Lewis, Luke Zettlemoyer, and Veselin Stoyanov. 2019. Roberta: A robustly optimized bert pretraining approach. *arXiv*, abs/1907.11692.

Zhiping Luo, W. Xu, Weiqing Liu, J. Bian, Jian Yin, and Tie-Yan Liu. 2021. Kge-cl: Contrastive learning of tensor decomposition based knowledge graph embeddings. In *International Conference on Computational Linguistics*.

Ralph Peeters and Christian Bizer. 2022. Supervised contrastive learning for product matching. In *Companion Proceedings of the Web Conference 2022*. ACM.

Fiona Anting Tan, Hansi Hettiarachchi, Ali Hürriyetoğlu, Onur Uca, Thapa Surendrabikram, Farhana Ferdousi Liza, and Nelleke Oostdijk. 2023. Event causality identification with causal news corpus - shared task 3, CASE 2023. Association for Computational Linguistics.

Fiona Anting Tan, Ali Hürriyetoğlu, Tommaso Caselli, Nelleke Oostdijk, Tadashi Nomoto, Hansi Hettiarachchi, Iqra Ameer, Onur Uca, Farhana Ferdousi Liza, and Tiancheng Hu. 2022. The causal news corpus: Annotating causal relations in event sentences from news. In *Proceedings of the Thirteenth Language Resources and Evaluation Conference*, pages 2298–2310, Marseille, France. European Language Resources Association.

Laurens van der Maaten and Geoffrey E. Hinton. 2008. Visualizing data using t-sne. *Journal of Machine Learning Research*, 9:2579–2605.

Hongyi Yuan, Zheng Yuan, and Sheng Yu. 2022. Generative biomedical entity linking via knowledge base-guided pre-training and synonyms-aware fine-tuning. *arXiv*, abs/2204.05164.

Xinyu Zuo, Pengfei Cao, Yubo Chen, Kang Liu, Jun Zhao, Weihua Peng, and Yuguang Chen. 2021. Improving event causality identification via self-supervised representation learning on external causal statement. In *Findings of the Association for Computational Linguistics: ACL-IJCNLP 2021*, pages 2162–2172, Online. Association for Computational Linguistics.

SSN-NLP-ACE@Multimodal Hate Speech Event Detection 2023: Detection of Hate Speech and Targets using Logistic Regression and SVM

K Avanthika
SSN College of Engineering
Tamil Nadu, India
avanthika@ssn.edu.in

Mrithula KL
SSN College of Engineering
Tamil Nadu, India
mrithula2010075@ssn.edu.in

Thenmozhi D
SSN College of Engineering
Tamil Nadu, India
theni_d@ssn.edu.in

Abstract

Hate speech has become a noteworthy concern in the digital age owing to its ability to brew violence, spread discrimination, and foster a belligerent atmosphere. Identifying and distinguishing hate speech from harmless discourse on online platforms is essential to maintain a safe and inclusive digital environment.

In this research paper, we propose a multimodal approach to hate speech detection, directed towards the identification of hate speech and its related targets. Our method uses logistic regression and support vector machines (SVMs) to analyse textual content extracted from social media platforms. We exploit natural language processing techniques to preprocess and extract relevant features from textual content, capturing linguistic patterns, sentiment, and contextual information.

These features are fed into logistic regression and SVM classifiers and trained on the labelled dataset. In addition, we performed a comparative analysis to evaluate the effectiveness of the multimodal approach compared to the use of existing methods. The proposed method holds promise for automated hate speech detection systems, facilitating censorship, and proactive intervention to mitigate the harmful effects of hate speech on online platforms.

1 Introduction

Hate speech is a form of communication that expresses prejudice, hatred, or discrimination against a specific individual or group based on attributes such as race, ethnicity, religion, nationality, gender, sexual orientation, disability, or other characteristics. It is distinguished by its goal to denigrate, belittle, or encourage violence or harm against persons or groups based on perceived differences or qualities.

In this ever-expanding digital landscape, the emergence and proliferation of hate speech represent an alarming concern. This not only promotes prejudice and division, but it also endangers societal cohesion and individual well-being. As a result, it is now more important than ever to build effective methods for its identification and mitigation.

In this paper, we delve into the crucial area of hate speech detection with a specific focus on identifying not only offensive language but also the intended targets. This dual objective addresses a critical gap in the existing literature, as understanding the context and impact of hate speech requires considering both its content and the entities it targets. To this end, we explore the effectiveness of two powerful machine learning algorithms, logistic regression and support vector machines (SVM), in the field of hate speech detection. These algorithms have a rich history of success in text classification tasks and provide valuable insight into the complexity of hate speech identification.

We present a novel approach to multimodal hate speech event detection, focusing on two SubTasks: Hate Speech Detection and Target Detection. The proposed solutions for these subtasks of Multimodal Hate Speech Event Detection at CASE 2023 (Thapa et al., 2023) has been evaluated with the baseline score presented by the work (Bhandari et al., 2023). We were placed seventh on SubTask A and eighth on SubTask B. For Hate Speech Detection, we employ Support Vector Machines (SVM), while for Target Detection, we utilise Logistic Regression.

The first SubTask, Hate Speech Detection, involves distinguishing between hate speech and non-hate speech textual content. Traditional approaches have primarily relied on textual analysis techniques to identify hateful language. We leverage the SVM model on a diverse dataset comprising labelled instances of hate speech and non-hate speech, enabling the model to learn the underlying patterns and discriminatory characteristics of hate speech.

Proceedings of the 6th Workshop on Challenges and Applications of Automated Extraction of Socio-political Events from Text, pages 66–70, Varna, Bulgaria, Sep 7, 2023.
https://doi.org/10.26615/978-954-452-089-2_009

The second SubTask, Target Detection, aims to identify the specific targets of hate speech within three categories: community, individual, and organisation. This is crucial for understanding the impact and potential harm caused by hate speech instances. By training the Logistic Regression model on labelled data, we enable it to predict the target category for a given hate speech instance accurately.

While the focus of this paper is on textual content analysis using SVM for Hate Speech Detection and Logistic Regression for Target Detection, we acknowledge that visual elements, such as images or videos, can also contribute valuable information in detecting and understanding hate speech events. Future research could explore the integration of visual analysis techniques alongside textual analysis to further enhance the accuracy and robustness of hate speech event detection.

To evaluate the effectiveness of our proposed approach, we conduct comprehensive experiments on a diverse dataset comprising hate speech instances from various domains. By comparing our results with existing state-of-the-art hate speech detection techniques, we establish the competitiveness of our methodology.

Beyond academic contributions, our research holds practical implications for content moderation, social media platforms, and online communities. Appropriate measures can be taken to mitigate the spread of harmful content, protect targeted individuals and communities, and foster a more inclusive and respectful online environment.

The subsequent sections of this research paper namely Methodology and Result and Discussion, will provide detailed explanations of our methodology, including data collection and preprocessing, feature extraction techniques, model development using SVM and Logistic Regression, evaluation procedures, and the interpretation of experimental results. We will also discuss the limitations of our approach and suggest potential avenues for future research in the field of multimodal hate speech event detection.

2 Related Work

Flow of information is vital to a society, and now with the advent of social media, the need to process them faster, better and in any form is on the rise. Multimodal learning is a type of learning which uses multiple forms of data such as text, audio and images. The obstacles and challenges are clearly articulated by (Cukurova et al., 2020) and (Karan and Šnajder, 2018). The authors of (Blikstein, 2013) present their insights in learning mainly multimodal learning analytics. The works of (Ngiam et al., 2011) and (Ramachandram and Taylor, 2017) discuss deep learning related to multimodal learning. In particular, the work (Ngiam et al., 2011) deals with cross modality feature learnings.The authors of (Ramachandram and Taylor, 2017) have highlighted methods to fuse learned multimodal representations in deep-learning architectures. The authors of (Srivastava and Salakhutdinov, 2012) have presented their model which uses multimodal learning, and also shown a comparison with other deep learning models.

With the increasing amount of data, identifying hate speech has become an important task. A lot of research has taken place regarding the detection and recognition of hate speech.A survey by authors of (Schmidt and Wiegand, 2017) to recognize hate speech uses natural language processing approach. The authors of the work (Parihar et al., 2021) have explored the state-of-the-art algorithms and prospects of AI in the field of Machine Learning and Natural Language Processing. The work (Poletto et al., 2021) analyzes resources available, and discusses the issues and venues for improvement in the field of hate speech. Hate speech recognition not only concerns a single language, but research on multilingual problems have also been undertaken worldwide. For instance, the authors of (Basile et al., 2019) have taken up the problem of hate speech against immigrants and women in different languages, English and Spanish. This work is also targeted, in the sense, it deals with hate speech against a particular community. The authors of the work (Ousidhoum et al., 2019) have considered multi-aspect multilingual hate speech problem and applied state-of-the-art learning models on their dataset for evaluation.

Research has been conducted in the field of hate speech by many, among those,much lesser in number are those that relates to multimodal learning. The authors of (Kiela et al., 2020) propose a new challenge set for multimodal classification, focusing on detecting hate speech in multimodal memes. The work (Fortuna et al., 2021) also deals with hate speech using multimodal learning. This paper highlights multimodal dataset and models to recognising hate speech and the targets of the directed hate.

Problem	label	Text-embedded images
Hate	hate	2,665
Speech	no hate	2,058
	Individual	1,027
Target	Organization	984
	Community	417

Table 1: Dataset distribution.

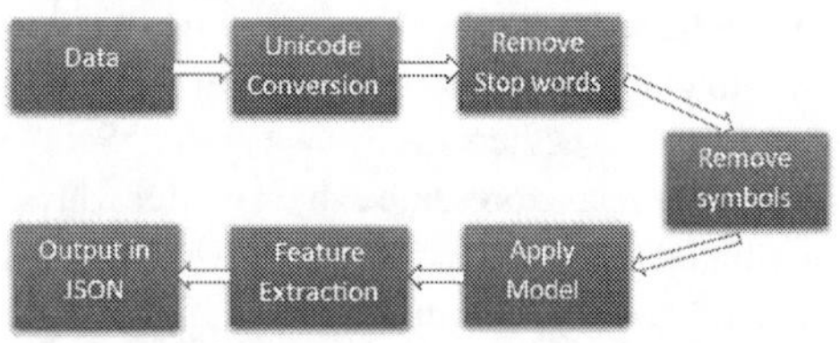

Figure 1: Flow Diagram of the building blocks of the model is shown in the figure

3 Dataset and Task

CrisisHateMM (dataset from the task), is multimodal and contains data related to Russia-Ukraine crisis. The work (Bhandari et al., 2023) presented the dataset for the task. It contains social media posts, memes and infographics in the form of text-embedded images which contains some information and context as mentioned above in it.

The first sub task, to detect hate speech, includes a total of 4,723 entries. A hate detected image entry was labelled as 1 and no hate detected entry was labelled as 0.

The second sub task, on the other hand, is to identify the target of hate, which has a total of 2,428 entries. Three different classes were identified as targets namely individual, community and organization. Hate directed towards a individual was labelled as 0, hate directed towards a community as 1 and hate directed towards an organization as 2. The dataset distribution is shown in Table 1.

4 Methodology

We present solutions based on classical machine learning models namely SVM and Logistic Regression on this paper. There are advantages to utilising classical ML rather than deep learning. When compared to deep learning models, the need for data is substantially lower, and classical models are often less computationally intensive. In short, classical ML has its own set of benefits, especially when interpretability, data availability, speed or resource constraints are significant factors. The decision to use conventional ML over deep learning was based on the unique situation, data availability, computational resources and the necessity for interpretability and simplicity. In many circumstances, hybrid techniques that include parts of both classical ML and deep learning can be powerful answers.

4.1 Preprocessing

Data available may contain noise, missing values or unusable format. Cleaning of raw data helps in the model performance. Preprocessing is an important step which transforms unstructured data to a consistent format, paving way to good working models.

The data given is in the form of text-embedded images. The information from the text-embedded images was collected using Google OCR Vision API.

Textual information obtained from OCR extraction also underwent filtering. This process removed stop words, that is, filtering out words which were considered insignificant. The preprocessing also removed non-alphabetical characters from the text. This included a removal of hyperlinks, symbols and quotes.

Feature extraction was done, to convert the raw data into numeric form. TF-IDF (Term Frequency-Inverse Document Frequency) was used to extract features from the text. It converts a collection of documents to TF-IDF features, which helps in reducing the amount of input features during model building.

4.2 SubTask A

Considering the SubTask A is to be a binary classification problem, SVM (Support Vector Machine) was employed.

SVM is a supervised learning algorithm which finds the optimal hyperplane separating the data points of different classes. The hyperplane maximizes the margin between the closest data points from different classes. These data points are the support vectors in finding the optimal hyperplane. This algorithm was chosen owing to its ability to handle both linear and non-linear relationship between the features and the target variables.

We have applied RBF (Radial Basis Function) kernel and tuned the parameters with the objective of maximising the F1-score. The output of the model was converted to JSON format for evaluation.

Problem	F1 score	Accuracy
Hate Speech	76.06	76.11
Target	64.46	64.26

Table 2: Training Performance.

Problem	F1 score	Accuracy
Hate Speech	78.6	79.8
Target	61.5	68.4

Table 3: Baseline scores.

4.3 SubTask B

The SubTask B is identified to be a classification problem with three classes. Hence we opted for a cost-sensitive logistic regression model.

Logistic Regression is yet another supervised learning technique for classification. It is a statistical analysis method which used probability estimation. Cost-sensitive logistic regression takes misclassification into consideration. This technique was used so as to improve the performance on the imbalanced dataset given. Weights for model building were considered according to the data distribution.

Again, the output generated by model was converted to JSON format for evaluation.

5 Result and Discussion

The main evaluation parameter for performance was the F1-score. The training performance parameters of different SubTasks are shown in table 2. On the training dataset, F1-scores of 76% and 64% were obtained in hate speech detection (SubTask A) and target identification (SubTask B) respectively. On the test dataset, our model achieved F1-scores of 78.80% in SubTask A and 52.58% in SubTask B. The details are shown in the table 4. The baseline score from the task paper (Bhandari et al., 2023) are F1 -scores of 78.6% for SubTask A and 61.5% for SubTask B. The table 3 presents the baseline scores.

The SubTask A used SVM for handling complex nonlinear relationships and SubTask B model used cost-sensitive logistic regression to account for misclassification and imbalanced dataset. Our model does not perform better than baseline scores in sub task B. It performed slightly better than random guess, on the other hand, our model was able to improve the score of sub task A from the baseline by a slight margin.

Problem	F1 score	Accuracy
Hate Speech	78.8	79.01
Target	52.58	64.05

Table 4: Testing Performance.

In any problem, the dataset plays a major role. The imbalance in dataset could be one of the reasons for misclassification. It could also be attributed to the fact that hate directed images themselves might not be directed explicitly, thus making it hard for models to recognise and learn them. Preprocessing the available forms of data always plays a significant role in learning. All the above factors indicate the need for better performing models in the field of multimodal data.

6 Conclusion

With the rising need to process data in different forms like opinions and perspectives in social media, identification of hate speech and its targets has become vital. In this paper, we have presented solutions to the task Multimodal Hate Speech Event Detection - CASE 2023. The paper proposes solutions to the task of detecting hate speech in multimodal dataset and identifying the target of the hate as individual,community or organization. The performance metrics includes precision, recall, accuracy with F1-score as the key parameter. Although the results presented herein are good, there remains potential for improvement. Future research can focus on fine-tuning parameters for hate speech recognition. Additional investigation may be undertaken to enhance the performance of existing models and to choose superior models.

References

Valerio Basile, Cristina Bosco, Elisabetta Fersini, Debora Nozza, Viviana Patti, Francisco Manuel Rangel Pardo, Paolo Rosso, and Manuela Sanguinetti. 2019. SemEval-2019 task 5: Multilingual detection of hate speech against immigrants and women in Twitter. In *Proceedings of the 13th International Workshop on Semantic Evaluation*, pages 54–63, Minneapolis, Minnesota, USA. Association for Computational Linguistics.

Aashish Bhandari, Siddhant B Shah, Surendrabikram Thapa, Usman Naseem, and Mehwish Nasim. 2023. Crisishatemm: Multimodal analysis of directed and undirected hate speech in text-embedded images from russia-ukraine conflict. In *Proceedings of the IEEE/CVF Conference on Computer Vision and Pat-*

tern Recognition (CVPR) Workshops, pages 1993–2002.

Paulo Blikstein. 2013. Multimodal learning analytics. In *Proceedings of the third international conference on learning analytics and knowledge*, pages 102–106.

Mutlu Cukurova, Michail Giannakos, and Roberto Martinez-Maldonado. 2020. The promise and challenges of multimodal learning analytics. *British Journal of Educational Technology*, 51(5):1441–1449.

Paula Fortuna, Juan Soler-Company, and Leo Wanner. 2021. How well do hate speech, toxicity, abusive and offensive language classification models generalize across datasets? *Information Processing Management*, 58(3):102524.

Mladen Karan and Jan Šnajder. 2018. Cross-domain detection of abusive language online. In *Proceedings of the 2nd Workshop on Abusive Language Online (ALW2)*, pages 132–137, Brussels, Belgium. Association for Computational Linguistics.

Douwe Kiela, Hamed Firooz, Aravind Mohan, Vedanuj Goswami, Amanpreet Singh, Pratik Ringshia, and Davide Testuggine. 2020. The hateful memes challenge: Detecting hate speech in multimodal memes. In *Advances in Neural Information Processing Systems*, volume 33, pages 2611–2624. Curran Associates, Inc.

Jiquan Ngiam, Aditya Khosla, Mingyu Kim, Juhan Nam, Honglak Lee, and Andrew Y Ng. 2011. Multimodal deep learning. In *Proceedings of the 28th international conference on machine learning (ICML-11)*, pages 689–696.

Nedjma Ousidhoum, Zizheng Lin, Hongming Zhang, Yangqiu Song, and Dit-Yan Yeung. 2019. Multilingual and multi-aspect hate speech analysis. *arXiv preprint arXiv:1908.11049*.

Anil Singh Parihar, Surendrabikram Thapa, and Sushruti Mishra. 2021. Hate speech detection using natural language processing: Applications and challenges. *2021 5th International Conference on Trends in Electronics and Informatics (ICOEI)*, pages 1302–1308.

Fabio Poletto, Valerio Basile, Manuela Sanguinetti, Cristina Bosco, and Viviana Patti. 2021. Resources and benchmark corpora for hate speech detection: a systematic review. *Language Resources and Evaluation*, 55:477–523.

Dhanesh Ramachandram and Graham W Taylor. 2017. Deep multimodal learning: A survey on recent advances and trends. *IEEE signal processing magazine*, 34(6):96–108.

Anna Schmidt and Michael Wiegand. 2017. A survey on hate speech detection using natural language processing. In *Proceedings of the Fifth International Workshop on Natural Language Processing for Social Media*, pages 1–10, Valencia, Spain. Association for Computational Linguistics.

Nitish Srivastava and Russ R Salakhutdinov. 2012. Multimodal learning with deep boltzmann machines. *Advances in neural information processing systems*, 25.

Surendrabikram Thapa, Farhan Ahmad Jafri, Ali Hürriyetoğlu, Francielle Vargas, Roy Ka-Wei Lee, and Usman Naseem. 2023. Multimodal hate speech event detection - shared task 4, case 2023. In *Proceedings of the 6th Workshop on Challenges and Applications of Automated Extraction of Socio-political Events from Text (CASE)*.

ARC-NLP at Multimodal Hate Speech Event Detection 2023: Multimodal Methods Boosted by Ensemble Learning, Syntactical and Entity Features

Umitcan Sahin, Izzet Emre Kucukkaya, Oguzhan Ozcelik, Cagri Toraman
Aselsan Research Center, Ankara, Turkiye
{ucsahin, ekucukkaya, ogozcelik, ctoraman}@aselsan.com.tr

Abstract

Text-embedded images can serve as a means of spreading hate speech, propaganda, and extremist beliefs. Throughout the Russia-Ukraine war, both opposing factions heavily relied on text-embedded images as a vehicle for spreading propaganda and hate speech. Ensuring the effective detection of hate speech and propaganda is of utmost importance to mitigate the negative effect of hate speech dissemination. In this paper, we outline our methodologies for two subtasks of Multimodal Hate Speech Event Detection 2023. For the first subtask, hate speech detection, we utilize multimodal deep learning models boosted by ensemble learning and syntactical text attributes. For the second subtask, target detection, we employ multimodal deep learning models boosted by named entity features. Through experimentation, we demonstrate the superior performance of our models compared to all textual, visual, and text-visual baselines employed in multimodal hate speech detection. Furthermore, our models achieve the first place in both subtasks on the final leaderboard of the shared task.

1 Introduction

The Russia-Ukraine War has been a long and bitter conflict that has caused a lot of division and tension among people. Unfortunately, hate speech has played a big role in this war, spreading negativity, fueling hatred, and making the situation even more volatile. It is important to find ways to detect and combat hate speech in order to promote unity and peace.

Deep learning models are increasingly being employed in multimodal hate speech detection (Parihar et al., 2021; Thapa et al., 2022; Boishakhi et al., 2021; Gomez et al., 2020; Yang et al., 2019; Perifanos and Goutsos, 2021; Rana and Jha, 2022; Vijayaraghavan et al., 2021; Sabat et al., 2019; Madukwe et al., 2020; Kiela et al., 2020). These models leverage the power of neural networks to process and analyze complex data consisting of text, images, and videos, allowing them to capture the nuances and context of online content. By combining various modalities, such as textual and visual contents, these models can better understand the overall meaning and intent behind the shared information. They learn from large amounts of labeled data, enabling them to identify patterns and distinguish between genuine information and harmful content, including hate speech and misinformation (Toraman et al., 2022a). With their ability to integrate multiple modalities, deep learning models are playing a vital role in combating online abuse, fostering safer digital environments, and promoting responsible information dissemination.

This study addresses the challenge of combating hate speech using multiple modalities, specifically focusing on the shared task of Multimodal Hate Speech Event Detection at CASE 2023 (Thapa et al., 2023). In the shared task, Subtask A requires determining whether a text-embedded image contains hate speech. To address this, we propose a novel ensemble model that merges predictions from a multimodal deep learning model and multiple text-based tabular models which are trained with various syntactical features. On the other hand, for Subtask B, the goal is to identify the target of hate speech in a text-embedded image and classify it into the categories of "Individual", "Community", or "Organization". To tackle this challenge, we introduce a novel multimodal deep learning model. We train a multimodal deep learning model and then combine its embeddings with named entity features, which are then used as input to train a new fusion model. Through experimentation, we show that our proposed models achieve superior classification performance compared to the multimodal hate speech detection baselines. Notably, our proposed models achieve the highest rank on

Proceedings of the 6th Workshop on Challenges and Applications of Automated Extraction of Socio-political Events from Text, pages 71–78, Varna, Bulgaria, Sep 7, 2023.
https://doi.org/10.26615/978-954-452-089-2_010

Subtask	Problem	Labels	#Text-embedded Images Train	Eval	Test
A	Hate Speech	Hate	1,942	243	443
		Non-Hate	1,658	200	
B	Target	Individual	823	102	242
		Community	335	40	
		Organization	784	102	

Table 1: Dataset for the shared task on Multimodal Hate Speech Event Detection at CASE 2023. Numbers of text-embedded images in the train, evaluation and test sets for both Subtask A and B are given. Labels of the test set examples are not shared.

the final leaderboard for both subtasks in the shared task.

2 Dataset & Task

The shared task on Multimodal Hate Speech Event Detection at CASE 2023[1] consists of two distinct subtasks: Subtask A and B. The details of each subtask are presented in Table 1 along with the number of text-embedded images in the training, evaluation and test sets. It is important to note that the labels of the test set examples are not disclosed to the participants during the shared task. These labels are reserved for calculating the final prediction performance, which determines the leaderboard rankings upon completion of the shared task. Furthermore, text within the images are extracted using OCR with Google Vision API[2].

2.1 Subtask A: Hate Speech Detection

In Subtask A, it is aimed to determine the presence or absence of hate speech within text-embedded images (Thapa et al., 2022). The dataset specifically designed for this subtask includes annotated examples that indicate the existence of hate speech (Bhandari et al., 2023). The dataset features two distinct labels: "Hate Speech" and "No Hate Speech".

2.2 Subtask B: Target Detection

Subtask B aims to identify the targets of hate speech within a given hateful text-embedded image (Thapa et al., 2022). The dataset provided for this subtask includes labels categorizing the hate speech targets into "Individual", "Community", and "Organization" (Bhandari et al., 2023).

[1]https://github.com/therealthapa/case2023_task4

[2]https://cloud.google.com/vision/docs/ocr

Feature	Count
Word counts	1
Character counts	1
Capital ratio	1
Digit ratio	1
Special character ratio	1
White space ratio	1
Symbol (!, ?, @, %, *, $, &, #, ., :, /, -, =) ratios	13
Symbol counts	13
Lowercase ratio	1

Table 2: Syntactical features used in our proposed model for Subtask A.

3 Methodology

In this section, we describe our proposed models for Subtask A and B of the shared task, respectively.

3.1 Proposed model for Subtask A: Ensemble of multimodal deep learning and text-based tabular models

The process of identifying hate speech within an image and its OCR-generated text can be approached using various methods, including relying solely on image-based or text-based models. However, in our approach, we adopt a multimodal approach to leverage the full knowledge present in the dataset. We employ both textual and visual features to train our deep learning models, aiming to capture a comprehensive understanding of the data. Additionally, we incorporate various syntactical features into our model. For this, we construct a 33-dimensional syntactical feature vector as shown in Table 2.

Furthermore, we also use the Bag-of-words (BoWs) method to extract n-grams ($n \in \{1, 2, 3\}$) from text and use them as additional features. This choice is motivated by our observation that the BoW method has competitive performance in hate speech detection and these features might possibly serve as indicators of hate speech, independent of the overall meaning conveyed by the text and image (Toraman et al., 2022b).

As illustrated in Figure 1a, our methodology begins by combining a text encoder with a vision encoder model via a multi-layer perceptron (MLP) module. This multimodal structure is initially trained on the entire training set using a linear classifier layer with the cross-entropy loss function. We select the best-performing model based on the

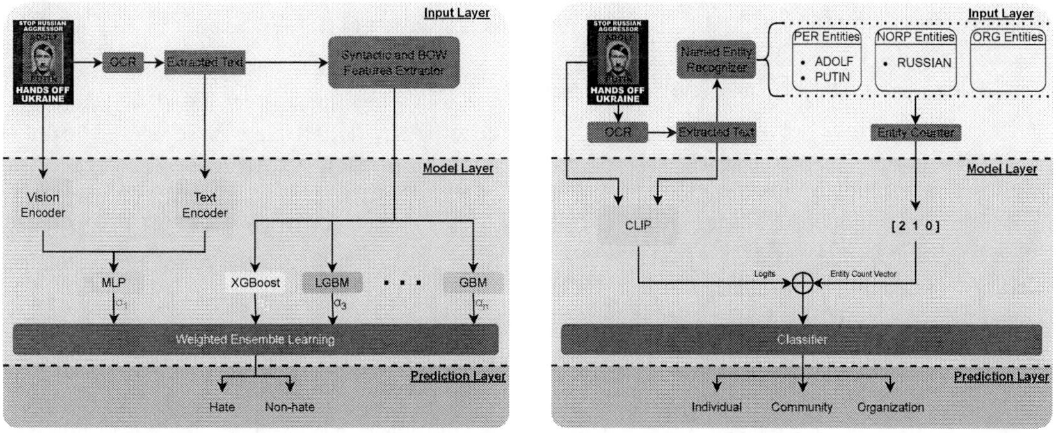

(a) (b)

Figure 1: High-level illustrations of our models for (a) Subtask A and (b) Subtask B. Each model consists of three stages, which are the Input, Model, and Prediction layers. Input layer describes the processes of text and syntactic feature extraction, and entity recognition. In Model layer, we indicate the training procedures. Furthermore, we represent the the joint learning of the models with the same colored blocks. For instance, in (a) Vision and Text encoder, and MLP is jointly trained, while XGBoost, LGBM, and GBM have independent training procedures. The last layer, i.e., Prediction, shows the classified labels for each model.

accuracy metric across multiple training epochs using the evaluation set. Subsequently, we extract the aforementioned syntactical and BoW features from the text, which are then used to train tabular learning models (i.e., classifiers), including LightGBMXT, LightGBMLarge, LightGBM (Ke et al., 2017), CatBoost (Prokhorenkova et al., 2018), and XGBoost (Chen and Guestrin, 2016). We then combine these models to maximize the utilization of available information. To accomplish this, we adopt an ensemble approach similar to our previous work in CASE2022 (Hürriyetoğlu et al., 2022; Sahin et al., 2022). However, this time we utilize a weighted ensembler which assigns adaptive weights to each model and generates final predictions based on these weights. The weight assignment is determined during the training phase and optimized with respect to the validation accuracy computed on the evaluation set of Subtask A.

3.2 Proposed model for Subtask B: Combining multimodal deep learning with named entity recognition

In our proposed model for Subtask B, instead of using syntactical features, we employ named entities which are extracted from the text. Named entity recognition (NER) aims to extract important information from unstructured text (Ozcelik and Toraman, 2022) and can be used as a supportive feature to improve the classification performance of a deep learning model. Therefore, we obtain named entities for the unstructured texts extracted from the text-embedded images using the spaCy library (Honnibal and Montani, 2017). SpaCy is an open source NLP library including several tasks such as Part-of-Speech (POS) tagging and NER. We use the English pretrained large NER model[3] as a named entity recognizer (see Figure 1b). The motivation behind using this model is that it contains individual, community, and organization named entity classes, which are directly related to the prediction classes of Subtask B. Therefore, we only extract `PER`, `NORP`, and `ORG` entities as shown in Figure 1b. The `PER` entities include people or fictional character names. The `NORP` entities represent nationalities or religious and political groups (e.g., communities). Finally, the `ORG` entities are referred to organization names, such as NATO.

In a previous study (Zhu, 2020), these identified entities are employed as additional textual inputs, demonstrating their contribution to the improvement of multimodal hateful meme detection. However in our work, after we obtain the aforementioned entities from the extracted texts of the images, we generate a feature vector, consisting of the counts of each entity. For instance, from Figure 1b, we represent the vector for the extracted text "STOP RUSSIAN AGRESSOR ADOLF PUTIN

[3] en_core_web_lg-3.6.0

HANDS OFF UKRAINE" as $\begin{bmatrix} 2 & 1 & 0 \end{bmatrix}$ since two (i.e., *Putin*, *Adolf*), one (i.e., *Russian*), and no entities are obtained for PER, NORP, and ORG classes, respectively.

Figure 1b shows the overall structure of our proposed model for Subtask B. Using the text-embedded images and the extracted OCR text from these images in the training set, we first fine-tune a Contrastive Language-Image Pre-Training (CLIP) model, which is a multimodal deep learning model that is pre-trained on a variety of (image, text) pairs (Radford et al., 2021). Following the completion of the CLIP training, we proceed to extract the embedding vector for each (image, text) pair in the training set of Subtask B. These embedding vectors and the entity count vector are then concatenated together to create a novel fusion vector. This newly formed vector serves as the input for training multiple tabular learning models (i.e., classifiers), including LightGBMLarge, LightGBM, and XGBoost. The classifier that achieves the highest validation accuracy score on the evaluation set of Subtask B is then selected to generate final predictions.

4 Results & Discussion

4.1 Baselines

We employ the AutoGluon framework (Erickson et al., 2020) for the implementation of our proposed models and the baselines for multimodal hate speech detection. AutoGluon is an AutoML toolkit and provides a comprehensive environment for multimodal training. We use the following hyperparameter setting for the training of all models: The learning rate is set to 1e-4, learning rate decay is set to 0.9, learning rate scheduler is cosine decay, maximum number of epochs is 10, warm-up step is 0.1, per GPU batch size is 8. During the training phase of our models and the baselines, we utilize four NVIDIA A4000 GPUs. We categorize the baselines into four categories: Tabular, Textual, Visual or Multimodal, which are explained below.

4.1.1 Tabular Baselines

For the tabular baseline models, we construct syntactic features derived from the textual data. These features, which are shown in Table 2, and BoW features (i.e., n-grams with $n \in \{1, 2, 3\}$) are employed to train classifiers including LightGBMXT, LightGBMLarge, LightGBM, CatBoost, and XGBoost. We use the AutoGluon implementation of the classifiers with default parameters.

4.1.2 Textual Baselines

For the text-only baseline models, we use the following transformer-based language models: BERT (BERT-base-cased[4]) (Devlin et al., 2018), RoBERTa (RoBERTa-base[5]) (Liu et al., 2019), DeBERTa-v3 (DeBERTa-v3-base[6]) (He et al., 2021), and ELECTRA (ELECTRA-base-discriminator[7]). We use the AutoGluon implementation of the models with a maximum token size of 512 and padding the rest.

4.1.3 Visual Baselines

For the image-only baseline models, we employ the following transformer-based encoders: Swin (swin-base-patch4-window7-224[8]), CoAtNet-v3 (coatnet-v3-rw-224-sw_in12k[9]) (Dai et al., 2021), DaViT (davit-base-msft-in1k[10]) (Ding et al., 2022), and ViT (vit-base-patch32-224-in21k[11]) (Dosovitskiy et al., 2020). We use the AutoGluon implementation of the models with default parameters.

4.1.4 Multimodal Baselines

For the multimodal baseline models where both text and images are used in the training process, we combine a textual and a visual baseline model together and jointly train them by using a multi-layer perceptron (MLP) on top of them with a binary cross-entropy loss function. To determine the optimal combination of the models, we select the top-performing text and vision encoders based on their individual performances in terms of the validation accuracy score computed on the evaluation set of the corresponding subtasks. For this, we employ the AutoGluon implementation of the text and vision encoders with a maximum token size of 512 and all other parameters set to their default values. For the classification layer, we use two fully connected linear layers (128 dimensional hidden layer) with a Leaky ReLU activation function between them. Furthermore, we also use the AutoGluon's implementation of the CLIP model as one of the multimodal baselines.

[4]https://huggingface.co/bert-base-cased

[5]https://huggingface.co/roberta-base

[6]https://huggingface.co/microsoft/deberta-v3-base

[7]https://huggingface.co/google/electra-base-discriminator

[8]https://huggingface.co/microsoft/swin-base-patch4-window7-224-in22k

[9]https://huggingface.co/timm/coatnet_3_rw_224.sw_in12k

[10]https://huggingface.co/timm/davit_base.msft_in1k

[11]https://huggingface.co/google/vit-base-patch32-224-in21k

	Model	Precision	Recall	F1	Accuracy
Tabular	XGBoost	82.0	82.7	80.6	80.6
	LightGBM	81.2	83.5	80.3	80.4
	LightGBMLarge	81.6	82.3	80.1	80.1
	CatBoost	79.7	82.3	78.7	78.8
	LightGBMXT	78.8	81.1	77.6	77.6
Textual	ELECTRA	82.2	89.3	83.4	83.5
	BERT	79.4	84.4	79.4	79.4
	RoBERTa	84.3	81.9	81.7	81.7
	DeBERTa-v3	83.0	86.4	82.8	82.8
Visual	Swin	74.7	84.0	75.3	75.6
	CoAtNet-v3	80.4	81.1	78.8	78.8
	DaViT	81.5	79.2	78.1	78.1
	ViT	79.0	77.7	76.0	76.1
Multimodal	ELECTRA + Swin	83.3	90.1	84.5	84.6
	DeBERTa-v3 + Swin	81.8	90.9	83.8	84.0
	ELECTRA + CoAtNet-v3	85.4	86.4	84.4	84.4
	DeBERTa-v3 + CoAtNet-v3	82.9	87.6	83.2	83.3
	CLIP	79.9	91.8	82.6	82.8
Ours	**ELECTRA + Swin + Tabular**	**84.1**	**89.0**	**84.8**	**84.9**

Table 3: **Subtask A: Hate Speech Detection** evaluation results in terms of binary precision, recall, F1-score, and accuracy metrics. Tabular, textual, visual, and multimodal baselines are implemented using the AutoGluon library (Erickson et al., 2020) and categorized into their respective categories. The model which achieves the highest test scores on the final leaderboard is indicated with a bold font.

4.1.5 Our Models

For the implementation of our proposed models for Subtask A and B in Section 3, we again employ the AutoGluon library. For Subtask A, we use ELECTRA (ELECTRA-base-discriminator) and Swin (swin-base-patch4 window7-224) as our text and vision encoders, respectively. Using the syntactical and BoW features described in Section 3, we train the tabular models LightGBMXT, LightGBMLarge, LightGBM, CatBoost, and XGBoost with default parameters. Additionally, we utilize the weighted ensembler L2, an implementation provided by AutoGluon, to combine the predictions of the individual models and generate final predictions. This weighted ensembling technique assigns weights to each model, taking into account their respective classification performance on the evaluation set of Subtask A.

Furthermore, for Subtask B, we use the the multimodal baseline CLIP model and combine its embedding vector with NER features as described in Section 3. With the combined features, we train a LightGBMlarge classifier with default parameters to produce final predictions.

4.2 Evaluation Results

Table 3 and 4 show the classification performance metrics of our models and the baselines computed on the evaluation sets of Subtask A and B, respectively. *Precision*, *Recall*, *F1*, and *Accuracy* metrics are used for measuring the classification performance on the shared task of Multimodal Hate Speech Event Detection at CASE 2023[12].

The results in Table 3 and 4 clearly show that our proposed models, along with ensemble learning and using syntactical features for Subtask A and NER features for Subtask B, perform much better than all other methods, including the tabular, textual, visual, and multimodal baselines, for detecting hate speech in a multimodal setting. These results demonstrate that including different text-based features in our models improves their performance significantly, allowing us to make better use of the information in the dataset. This emphasizes the importance of using various textual attributes to enhance the overall effectiveness of the models.

In our experiments, we observe that textual methods trained with the extracted OCR text from the text-embedded images outperform visual methods trained solely on images. Additionally, the tabular models, which are trained with syntactical and BoW features (i.e., n-grams, $n \in \{1, 2, 3\}$), achieve results comparable to the text-based methods. This once again demonstrates the effectiveness of these features in multimodal hate speech detection.

Furthermore, multimodal approaches that combine multiple modalities, such as image and text, effectively leverage both textual and visual information, resulting in significantly more powerful

[12]https://codalab.lisn.upsaclay.fr/competitions/13087#results

	Model	Precision	Recall	F1	Accuracy
Tabular	XGBoost	65.2	64.1	63.4	65.2
	LightGBM	68.0	67.3	66.6	68.0
	LightGBMLarge	68.8	68.3	67.4	68.8
Textual	ELECTRA	66.0	65.6	65.7	66.0
	BERT	66.0	64.7	64.7	66.0
	RoBERTa	71.7	71.4	71.4	71.7
	DeBERTa-v3	68.8	67.1	66.2	68.8
Visual	Swin	51.3	54.5	52.0	54.5
	CoAtNet-v3	49.5	50.8	49.9	50.8
	DaViT	47.9	51.6	48.5	51.6
	ViT	42.2	45.1	42.3	45.1
Multimodal	RoBERTa + CoAtNet-v3	68.5	69.6	68.4	69.6
	DeBERTa-v3 + CoAtNet-v3	63.8	63.6	62.6	63.6
	RoBERTa + Swin	72.7	73.8	72.6	73.8
	DeBERTa-v3 + Swin	66.2	66.0	65.0	66.0
	CLIP	74.2	76.8	75.4	76.8
Ours	**CLIP + NER**	**80.5**	**80.3**	**79.7**	**80.3**

Table 4: **Subtask B: Target Detection** evaluation results in terms of weighted precision, recall, F1-score, and multi-class accuracy metrics. Tabular, textual, visual, and multimodal baselines are implemented using the AutoGluon library (Erickson et al., 2020) and categorized into their respective categories. The model which achieves the highest test scores on the final leaderboard is indicated with a bold font.

Team Name	Recall	Precision	F1	Accuracy
ARC-NLP	**85.67**	**85.63**	**85.65**	**85.78**
bayesiano98	85.61	85.28	85.28	85.33
IIC_Team	85.08	84.76	84.63	84.65
DeepBlueAI	83.56	83.35	83.42	83.52
CSECU-DSG	82.52	82.44	82.48	82.62
Ometeotl	81.21	80.94	80.97	81.04
Avanthika	78.78	78.81	78.80	79.01
Sarika22	78.06	78.49	78.21	78.56
rabindra.nath	77.68	78.42	77.88	78.33
md_kashif_20	72.70	73.72	72.87	73.59
GT	52.19	52.19	52.19	52.60
Team +1	49.38	49.39	49.36	49.66
ML_Ensemblers	53.34	72.40	42.94	57.79

Table 5: The leaderboard results of **Subtask A: Hate Speech Detection**. Our team name is **ARC-NLP**. The teams are ranked by the F1 score. Our solution is ranked first in terms of all classification metrics.

Team Name	Recall	Precision	F1	Accuracy
ARC-NLP	**76.36**	**76.37**	**76.34**	**79.34**
bayesiano98	73.30	75.54	74.10	77.27
IIC_Team	68.94	71.05	69.73	72.31
Sarika22	67.77	68.41	68.05	71.49
CSECU-DSG	65.25	65.75	65.30	69.01
DeepBlueAI	64.62	66.48	65.25	69.83
Ometeotl	56.48	67.93	56.77	64.05
Avanthika	53.84	70.13	52.58	64.05
ML_Ensemblers	44.44	48.88	43.32	52.89
Team +1	34.42	35.59	33.42	35.12

Table 6: The leaderboard results of **Subtask B: Target Detection**. Our team name is **ARC-NLP**. The teams are ranked by the F1 score. Our solution is ranked first in terms of all classification metrics.

deep learning models. This integration of different modalities enhances the overall performance of the models in the process.

Finally, introducing a named entity recognition (NER) system capable of extracting key elements from unstructured text, like person names, organizations, and locations, proves particularly effective in identifying targets of hate speech (e.g., individuals, communities, and organizations) within a given text. By incorporating NER features into our model for Subtask B, we are able to further enhance the classification performance of the multimodal methods. This improvement is clearly demonstrated by the classification performance of our proposed model, as illustrated in Table 4.

4.3 Leaderboard Results

During the test phase of the shared task, we submitted our models to be evaluated on the test sets of both Subtask A and Subtask B. The test results have been presented in Table 5 and Table 6, respectively.

Our model, *ELECTRA+Swin+Tabular*, achieved the top rank among 13 participating teams in Subtask A, excelling in all classification metrics within the test results. Similarly, our model, *CLIP+NER*, secured the first position among 10 participating teams in Subtask B, performing exceptionally well across all classification metrics.

5 Conclusion

In conclusion, the utilization of text-embedded images on social media has become a common means of expressing opinions and emotions. However, it has also been exploited to spread hate speech, propaganda, and extremist ideologies, as witnessed during the Russia-Ukraine war. Detecting and addressing such instances are crucial, particularly in times of ongoing conflict. To tackle this challenge, we present our methodologies for the shared task of Multimodal Hate Speech Event Detection at CASE 2023 (Thapa et al., 2023). Our approach combines multimodal deep learning models with text-based tabular features, such as named entities and syntactical features, yielding superior performance compared to existing methods for multimodal hate speech detection. This is evidenced by achieving the first place in both Subtask A and B of the shared task on the final leaderboard, demonstrating the effectiveness of our models in identifying and categorizing hate speech events.

5.1 Ethical Considerations

This study discusses examples of harmful content (hate speech stereotypes). The authors do not support the use of harmful language, nor any of the harmful representations featured in this paper. Furthermore, the proposed models in this study are trained with the multimodal hate speech dataset described in Section 2, which specifically features the Russia-Ukraine War. Given the inherently subjective nature of the annotation process, it is reasonable to expect a certain bias towards specific subjects, individuals, organizations, and/or communities in our proposed models. We hereby acknowledge the fact that steps must be taken to mitigate this bias for future research.

5.2 Reproducibility

The multimodal hate speech dataset described in Section 2 can be accessed by contacting the authors of (Bhandari et al., 2023). Furthermore, for the reproducibility of our proposed models, we share all the necessary information such as network structure, parameter settings, libraries and tools utilized in Section 3 and 4.

References

Aashish Bhandari, Siddhant B Shah, Surendrabikram Thapa, Usman Naseem, and Mehwish Nasim. 2023. CrisisHateMM: Multimodal analysis of directed and undirected hate speech in text-embedded images from russia-ukraine conflict. In *Proceedings of the IEEE/CVF Conference on Computer Vision and Pattern Recognition*, pages 1993–2002.

Fariha Tahosin Boishakhi, Ponkoj Chandra Shill, and Md. Golam Rabiul Alam. 2021. Multi-modal hate speech detection using machine learning. In *2021 IEEE International Conference on Big Data (Big Data)*, pages 4496–4499.

Tianqi Chen and Carlos Guestrin. 2016. XGBoost: A scalable tree boosting system. In *Proceedings of the 22nd Acm SIGKDD International Conference on Knowledge Discovery and Data Mining*, pages 785–794.

Zihang Dai, Hanxiao Liu, Quoc V Le, and Mingxing Tan. 2021. CoAtNet: Marrying convolution and attention for all data sizes. *Advances in Neural Information Processing Systems*, 34:3965–3977.

Jacob Devlin, Ming-Wei Chang, Kenton Lee, and Kristina Toutanova. 2018. BERT: Pre-training of deep bidirectional transformers for language understanding. *arXiv preprint arXiv:1810.04805*.

Mingyu Ding, Bin Xiao, Noel Codella, Ping Luo, Jingdong Wang, and Lu Yuan. 2022. DaViT: Dual attention vision transformers. In *European Conference on Computer Vision*, pages 74–92. Springer.

Alexey Dosovitskiy, Lucas Beyer, Alexander Kolesnikov, Dirk Weissenborn, Xiaohua Zhai, Thomas Unterthiner, Mostafa Dehghani, Matthias Minderer, Georg Heigold, Sylvain Gelly, et al. 2020. An image is worth 16x16 words: Transformers for image recognition at scale. *arXiv preprint arXiv:2010.11929*.

Nick Erickson, Jonas Mueller, Alexander Shirkov, Hang Zhang, Pedro Larroy, Mu Li, and Alexander Smola. 2020. Autogluon-tabular: Robust and accurate automl for structured data. *arXiv preprint arXiv:2003.06505*.

Raul Gomez, Jaume Gibert, Lluis Gomez, and Dimosthenis Karatzas. 2020. Exploring hate speech detection in multimodal publications. In *Proceedings of the IEEE/CVF Winter Conference on Applications of Computer Vision*, pages 1470–1478.

Pengcheng He, Jianfeng Gao, and Weizhu Chen. 2021. DeBERTav3: Improving deberta using electra-style pre-training with gradient-disentangled embedding sharing. *arXiv preprint arXiv:2111.09543*.

Matthew Honnibal and Ines Montani. 2017. spaCy 2: Natural language understanding with bloom embeddings, convolutional neural networks and incremental parsing. *To appear*, 7(1):411–420.

Ali Hürriyetoğlu, Osman Mutlu, Fırat Duruşan, Onur Uca, Alaeddin Gürel, Benjamin J. Radford, Yaoyao Dai, Hansi Hettiarachchi, Niklas Stoehr, Tadashi Nomoto, Milena Slavcheva, Francielle Vargas, Aaqib Javid, Fatih Beyhan, and Erdem Yörük. 2022. Extended multilingual protest news detection - shared task 1, CASE 2021 and 2022. In *Proceedings of the 5th Workshop on Challenges and Applications of Automated Extraction of Socio-political Events from*

Text (CASE), pages 223–228, Abu Dhabi, United Arab Emirates. Association for Computational Linguistics.

Guolin Ke, Qi Meng, Thomas Finley, Taifeng Wang, Wei Chen, Weidong Ma, Qiwei Ye, and Tie-Yan Liu. 2017. LightGBM: A highly efficient gradient boosting decision tree. *Advances in Neural Information Processing Systems*, 30.

Douwe Kiela, Hamed Firooz, Aravind Mohan, Vedanuj Goswami, Amanpreet Singh, Pratik Ringshia, and Davide Testuggine. 2020. The hateful memes challenge: Detecting hate speech in multimodal memes. *Advances in Neural Information Processing Systems*, 33:2611–2624.

Yinhan Liu, Myle Ott, Naman Goyal, Jingfei Du, Mandar Joshi, Danqi Chen, Omer Levy, Mike Lewis, Luke Zettlemoyer, and Veselin Stoyanov. 2019. RoBERTa: A robustly optimized bert pretraining approach. *arXiv preprint arXiv:1907.11692*.

Kosisochukwu Madukwe, Xiaoying Gao, and Bing Xue. 2020. In data we trust: A critical analysis of hate speech detection datasets. In *Proceedings of the Fourth Workshop on Online Abuse and Harms*, pages 150–161, Online. Association for Computational Linguistics.

Oguzhan Ozcelik and Cagri Toraman. 2022. Named entity recognition in Turkish: A comparative study with detailed error analysis. *Information Processing & Management*, 59(6):103065.

Anil Singh Parihar, Surendrabikram Thapa, and Sushruti Mishra. 2021. Hate speech detection using natural language processing: Applications and challenges. In *2021 5th International Conference on Trends in Electronics and Informatics (ICOEI)*, pages 1302–1308. IEEE.

Konstantinos Perifanos and Dionysis Goutsos. 2021. Multimodal hate speech detection in greek social media. *Multimodal Technologies and Interaction*, 5(7):34.

Liudmila Prokhorenkova, Gleb Gusev, Aleksandr Vorobev, Anna Veronika Dorogush, and Andrey Gulin. 2018. CatBoost: unbiased boosting with categorical features. *Advances in Neural Information Processing Systems*, 31.

Alec Radford, Jong Wook Kim, Chris Hallacy, Aditya Ramesh, Gabriel Goh, Sandhini Agarwal, Girish Sastry, Amanda Askell, Pamela Mishkin, Jack Clark, et al. 2021. Learning transferable visual models from natural language supervision. In *International Conference on Machine Learning*, pages 8748–8763. PMLR.

Aneri Rana and Sonali Jha. 2022. Emotion based hate speech detection using multimodal learning. *arXiv preprint arXiv:2202.06218*.

Benet Oriol Sabat, Cristian Canton Ferrer, and Xavier Giro-i Nieto. 2019. Hate speech in pixels: Detection of offensive memes towards automatic moderation. *arXiv preprint arXiv:1910.02334*.

Umitcan Sahin, Oguzhan Ozcelik, Izzet Emre Kucukkaya, and Cagri Toraman. 2022. ARC-NLP at CASE 2022 task 1: Ensemble learning for multilingual protest event detection. In *Proceedings of the 5th Workshop on Challenges and Applications of Automated Extraction of Socio-political Events from Text (CASE)*, pages 175–183.

Surendrabikram Thapa, Farhan Ahmad Jafri, Ali Hürriyetoğlu, Francielle Vargas, Roy Ka-Wei Lee, and Usman Naseem. 2023. Multimodal hate speech event detection - shared task 4, CASE 2023. In *Proceedings of the 6th Workshop on Challenges and Applications of Automated Extraction of Socio-political Events from Text (CASE)*.

Surendrabikram Thapa, Aditya Shah, Farhan Jafri, Usman Naseem, and Imran Razzak. 2022. A multimodal dataset for hate speech detection on social media: Case-study of russia-Ukraine conflict. In *Proceedings of the 5th Workshop on Challenges and Applications of Automated Extraction of Socio-political Events from Text (CASE)*, pages 1–6, Abu Dhabi, United Arab Emirates. Association for Computational Linguistics.

Cagri Toraman, Oguzhan Ozcelik, Furkan Şahinuç, and Fazli Can. 2022a. Not good times for lies: Misinformation detection on the russia-ukraine war, COVID-19, and refugees. *arXiv preprint arXiv:2210.05401*.

Cagri Toraman, Furkan Şahinuç, and Eyup Yilmaz. 2022b. Large-scale hate speech detection with cross-domain transfer. In *Proceedings of the Thirteenth Language Resources and Evaluation Conference*, pages 2215–2225, Marseille, France. European Language Resources Association.

Prashanth Vijayaraghavan, Hugo Larochelle, and Deb Roy. 2021. Interpretable multi-modal hate speech detection. *arXiv preprint arXiv:2103.01616*.

Fan Yang, Xiaochang Peng, Gargi Ghosh, Reshef Shilon, Hao Ma, Eider Moore, and Goran Predovic. 2019. Exploring deep multimodal fusion of text and photo for hate speech classification. In *Proceedings of the Third Workshop on Abusive Language Online*, pages 11–18, Florence, Italy. Association for Computational Linguistics.

Ron Zhu. 2020. Enhance multimodal transformer with external label and in-domain pretrain: Hateful meme challenge winning solution. *arXiv preprint arXiv:2012.08290*.

VerbaVisor@Multimodal Hate Speech Event Detection 2023: Hate Speech Detection using Transformer Model

Sarika Esackimuthu, Prabavathy Balasundaram

Department of Computer Science and Engineering
Sri Sivasubramaniya Nadar College of Engineering
Chennai - 603110, Tamil Nadu, India
{sarika2010128, prabavathyb}@ssn.edu.in

Abstract

Thapa et al. (2023) task focuses on identifying hate speech or not from text-embedded images and also identify the targets of hate speech.Hate speech detection has emerged as a critical research area in recent years due to the rise of online social platforms and the proliferation of harmful content targeting individuals or specific groups.This task highlights the importance of detecting hate speech in text-embedded images.By leveraging deep learning models,this research aims to uncover the connection between hate speech and the entities it targets.

1 Introduction

Hate speech detection plays a crucial role in fostering a safer and more inclusive digital landscape. In today's interconnected world, where social media and online platforms dominate communication, the spread of hate speech can have far-reaching and detrimental consequences. Detecting and addressing hate speech helps protect vulnerable communities from harm, prevents the escalation of conflicts, and promotes constructive dialogue.Moreover, the integration of multimodal techniques, combining both textual and visual information, has further enhanced hate speech detection systems.

In recent years, the detection of hate speech has witnessed significant advancements, driven by the rapid progress in natural language processing (NLP) and computer vision technologies. Machine learning algorithms, particularly deep learning models, have revolutionized the field, allowing for more accurate and efficient hate speech detection. By analyzing text-embedded images and their associated textual content, algorithms can uncover hidden patterns and better identify hateful content targeted at specific entities or communities.

This research paper introduces an investigation into the detection of hate speech and identifying hate speech targets by employing NLP transformers, specifically the ALBERT base model.

2 Related works

Farooqi et al. (2021) research paper proposes an innovative method for hate speech detection in Hindi-English code-mixed conversations on Twitter. Their neural network approach leverages transformer's cross-lingual embeddings, fine-tuned for low-resource hate speech classification in transliterated Hindi text. The best-performing system, a hard voting ensemble of Indic-BERT, XLM-RoBERTa, and Multilingual BERT, achieved an impressive macro F1 score of 0.725. This highlights the method's effectiveness in accurately identifying hate speech, considering context and addressing challenges posed by code-mixing on social media platforms. The findings offer valuable insights for hate speech detection in multilingual settings.

In Jafri et al. (2023) the authors introduce a new dataset called IEHate, comprising 11,457 manually annotated Hindi tweets related to the Indian Assembly Election Campaign. They perform a comprehensive analysis of hate speech prevalence and its various forms in political discourse. The dataset is benchmarked using machine learning, deep learning, and transformer-based algorithms. Among the models, RoBERTa (multilingual) and BERT (HAM) achieved the highest F1-scores of 0.725 and 0.706, respectively. Transformer-based models outperformed machine learning and deep learning models.

Ţiţa and Zubiaga (2021) research paper focuses on hate speech detection in a cross-lingual setting, emphasizing the importance of addressing this issue on global online platforms. The study utilizes fine-tuned altered multi-lingual Transformer models (mBERT, XLM-RoBERTa) with cross-lingual training between English and French and within

Proceedings of the 6th Workshop on Challenges and Applications of Automated Extraction of Socio-political Events from Text, pages 79–83, Varna, Bulgaria, Sep 7, 2023.
https://doi.org/10.26615/978-954-452-089-2_011

each language independently. The results indicate that multi-lingual BERT outperforms XLM-RoBERTa in two out of three language pairs, showing significantly higher macro average scores for both English-only and French-only data. However, the fine-tuned altered XLM-RoBERTa performs poorly in the monolingual setting, with scores less than 0.5. The findings highlight the importance of selecting appropriate models and training strategies for effective hate speech detection in cross-lingual contexts.

3 Task and Dataset Description

3.1 Hate Speech Detection

The objective of this task is to discern the presence of hate speech in text-embedded images. These images constitute the dataset Bhandari et al. (2023) utilized for this subtask and are accompanied by annotations that denote the extent of hate speech prevalence.An example of text-embedded image used in dataset is shown in Figure 1. The features of the dataset is given in the table 1.

Figure 1: Text-embedded image

Table 1: Features of the dataset

Field	Description
filename	name of the file with index value
text	text extracted from text-embedded images

3.2 Target Detection

The objective of this subtask is to discern the specific targets of hate speech within a given text-embedded image containing hateful content. The text-embedded images in this dataset are meticulously annotated to identify the targets of hate speech, categorized into "community," "individual," and "organization" labels. To facilitate the detection process, the text within these images is extracted using sophisticated techniques, enabling the subsequent analysis for hate speech identification.The text-embedded images employed in this study were subjected to text extraction techniques to extract the textual content present within the images.Features of the dataset is given in table 1.

Label	Train
Hate	1,942
Not Hate	1,658
Total	3,600

Table 2: Data Distribution of Hate Speech Detection

Label	Train
Individual	823
Community	784
Organization	335
Total	1,942

Table 3: Data Distribution of Target Detection

4 Methodologies used

In this study, we employed the deep learning model transformers, specifically the ALBERT (A Lite BERT) Base v1 and Artificial Neural Network(ANN).

4.1 ALBERT Base v1

Albert base v1 (Lan et al., 2019) is a type of deep learning model, specifically an "ALBERT" (A Lite BERT) model, designed for natural language processing tasks, such as text classification. In this case, it is being used to detect hate speech in texts. The ALBERT model uses a technique called transfer learning to understand the underlying patterns and structures in the text data. It is pre-trained on a large corpus of text data to learn the general features of language.ALBERT tokenizes the input text, breaking it down into smaller units called tokens. Each token represents a word or subword in the text.Each token is mapped to a high-dimensional vector representation called an embedding.ALBERT utilizes a self-attention mechanism to assess token relationships in the text,thus grasping dependencies and long-range associations between words within the context.The ALBERT model is further fine-tuned on a labeled dataset of texts. During the fine-tuning process, the model adjusts its parameters to make accurate predictions based on the specific characteristics of hate speech present in the training data.The architecture is shown in figure 2

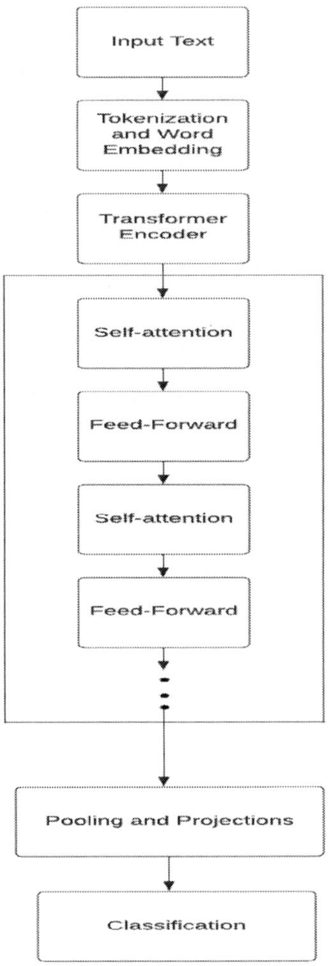

Figure 2: Architecture of Proposed System

4.2 Artificial Neural Network

Artificial Neural Networks (ANNs) have emerged as a pivotal element in the field of machine learning and artificial intelligence, owing to their ability to effectively model complex and non-linear relationships within data. Before feeding the data into the ANN, the texts are preprocessed. This includes tokenization, where each text is broken down into individual words or subwords. These words are then converted into numerical representations.The ANN is constructed using layers of interconnected artificial neurons. : The training process is where the ANN learns to detect hate speech. The training data, which consists of the numerical representations of texts and their corresponding labels, is used to adjust the internal parameters (weights and biases) of the neurons in the ANN.During training, the training data is fed into the ANN, and it performs a forward pass. This means the data flows through the layers of the network, and computations are performed to generate predictions. The predictions are then compared to the actual labels using a loss function, which measures the difference between the predicted and true labels.The architecture is shown in figure 3

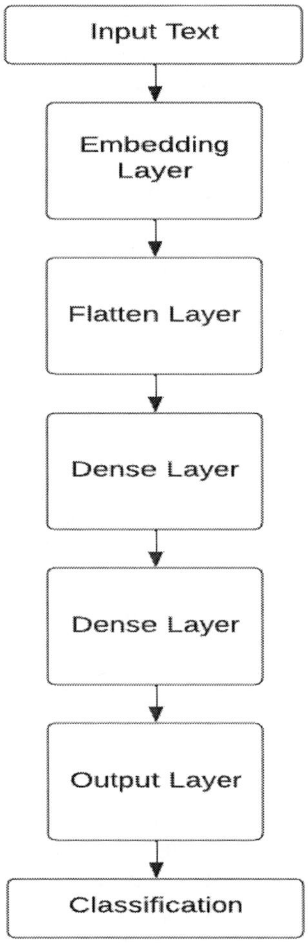

Figure 3: Architecture of Proposed System

5 Result Analysis of Hate Speech Detection Task

This section discusses about the implementation of Transformer Model and ANN with the analysis of the results using evaluation metrics.

5.1 Implementation

The implementation of the ALBERT Base v1 model for the Transformer-based classification task is achieved through the utilization of the simple-transformers library. The ClassificationModel class from the library is employed, specifying 'albert' as the model type and 'albert-base-v1' as the specific pre-trained ALBERT model variant. The model is configured to handle a binary classification and multilabel classification task. To optimize performance, several arguments are set, such as enabling input data reprocessing, disabling the use of cached evaluation features. Additionally, the model is trained for a specified number of epochs, with the option to increase this value for enhanced performance.

The ANN model is built using the Sequential API from Keras, which allows creating a sequential stack of layers.The first layer is an Embedding layer, which is used to convert the numerical tokens into dense vectors (embeddings). It maps each token to a 64-dimensional vector, which represents the meaning and context of the word in the text.The Flatten layer is used to convert the 2D tensor output from the Embedding layer into a 1D tensor, as ANN models require a 1D input.The next layer is a Dense layer with 32 units and a ReLU activation function, which introduces non-linearity and allows the model to learn complex patterns in the data.Finally, there is another Dense layer with 1 unit and a sigmoid activation function.The model is then trained on the training data for 10 epochs (iterations), with a batch size of 32.

5.2 Results

The dataset is partitioned into training and testing sets, and the evaluation results are presented in a table 4. The table contains the performance metrics and assessment outcomes for the model used in the study. The division of the dataset into training and testing sets enables to evaluate the effectiveness and generalization capabilities of their proposed hate speech detection models. The assessment table provides valuable insights into the model's performance.

Parameters	Score
Accuracy	0.7680
F1-score	0.7679
Recall	0.7681
Precision	0.7678

Table 4: Assessment of Models using Evaluation Metrics of ALBERT Base

Assessment using Artificial neural network(ANN) gave poor results as compared to ALBERT Base. The metrics are given in table 5

Parameters	Score
Accuracy	0.699
F1-score	0.733
Recall	0.729
Precision	0.738

Table 5: Assessment of Models using Evaluation Metrics of ANN

The evaluation result for the test dataset is given in table 6

Parameters	Score
Accuracy	0.7856
F1-score	0.7821
Recall	0.7806
Precision	0.7849

Table 6: Evaluation metrics of ALBERT Base for Hate Speech Detection Task

6 Result Analysis of Target Detection Task

6.1 Results

The training dataset is divided into training and testing sets to evaluate the proposed target of hate speech detection model effectively. The evaluation results, including performance metrics and assessment outcomes, are presented in a table 7 and 9.

The performance of the Artificial Neural Network (ANN) model was found to be inferior when compared to the ALBERT Base model. The evaluation metrics, presented in the table 8, clearly indicated that ALBERT Base outperformed the ANN in various aspects.

Parameters	Score
Accuracy	0.640
F1-score	0.6394
Recall	0.6401
Precision	0.6403

Table 7: Assessment of Models using Evaluation Metrics

Parameters	Score
Accuracy	0.560
F1-score	0.470
Recall	0.473
Precision	0.483

Table 8: Assessment of Models using Evaluation Metrics of ANN

7 Conclusion

We constructed an ALBERT base Model to perform hate speech detection. Preprocessing all the models with NLTK was considered essential in creating a robust model. However, accurately gauging the emotion of social media posts depends on individual perception, making it challenging for conventional models to achieve high accuracy. Another contributing factor to reduced accuracy is the imbalanced data distribution among the output class labels. To address these challenges, we plan to explore various transformer models and data augmentation techniques to enhance the performance of our hate speech detection system.

References

Aashish Bhandari, Siddhant Bikram Shah, Surendrabikram Thapa, Usman Naseem, and Mehwish Nasim. 2023. Crisishatemm: Multimodal analysis of directed and undirected hate speech in text-embedded images from russia-ukraine conflict. In *Proceedings of the IEEE/CVF Conference on Computer Vision and Pattern Recognition.*

Zaki Mustafa Farooqi, Sreyan Ghosh, and Rajiv Ratn Shah. 2021. Leveraging transformers for hate speech detection in conversational code-mixed tweets. *arXiv preprint arXiv:2112.09986.*

Farhan Ahmad Jafri, Mohammad Aman Siddiqui, Surendrabikram Thapa, Kritesh Rauniyar, Usman Naseem, and Imran Razzak. 2023. Uncovering political hate speech during indian election campaign: A new low-resource dataset and baselines. *arXiv preprint arXiv:2306.14764.*

Parameters	Score
Accuracy	0.7149
F1-score	0.6805
Recall	0.6777
Precision	0.6841

Table 9: Evaluation metrics of ALBERT Base for Target Detection Task

Zhenzhong Lan, Mingda Chen, Sebastian Goodman, Kevin Gimpel, Piyush Sharma, and Radu Soricut. 2019. Albert: A lite bert for self-supervised learning of language representations. *arXiv preprint arXiv:1909.11942.*

Surendrabikram Thapa, Farhan Ahmad Jafri, Ali Hürriyetoğlu, Francielle Vargas, Roy Ka-Wei Lee, and Usman Naseem. 2023. Multimodal hate speech event detection - shared task 4, case 2023. In *Proceedings of the 6th Workshop on Challenges and Applications of Automated Extraction of Socio-political Events from Text (CASE).*

Teodor Tiţa and Arkaitz Zubiaga. 2021. Cross-lingual hate speech detection using transformer models. *arXiv preprint arXiv:2111.00981.*

Lexical Squad@Multimodal Hate Speech Event Detection 2023: Multimodal Hate Speech Detection using Fused Ensemble Approach

Mohammad Kashif, Mohammad Zohair, Saquib Ali
Jamia Millia Islamia, New Delhi, India
iamkashif20@gmail.com, mohammadzohair2002@gmail.com
alisaquib95@gmail.com

Abstract

With a surge in the usage of social media postings to express opinions, emotions, and ideologies, there has been a significant shift towards the calibration of social media as a rapid medium of conveying viewpoints and outlooks over the globe. Concurrently, the emergence of a multitude of conflicts between two entities has given rise to a stream of social media content containing propaganda, hate speech, and inconsiderate views. Thus, the issue of monitoring social media postings is rising swiftly, attracting major attention from those willing to solve such problems. One such problem is Hate Speech detection. To mitigate this problem, we present our novel ensemble learning approach for detecting hate speech, by classifying text-embedded images into two labels, namely *"Hate Speech"* and *"No Hate Speech"*. We have incorporated state-of-art models including InceptionV3, BERT, and XLNet. Our proposed ensemble model yielded promising results with 75.21 and 74.96 as accuracy and F-1 score (respectively). We also present an empirical evaluation of the text-embedded images to elaborate on how well the model was able to predict and classify. We release our codebase here https://github.com/M0hammad-Kashif/MultiModalHateSpeech

1 Introduction

Political events have been a perpetual part of governance to date and serve as a medium of expression for those involved directly or indirectly with the process. But at times, this medium of communication might turn out to be a source of unfortunate insensitive expressions, hate speeches, etc, through verbal forms, visual representations, and physically inconsiderate actions among others. In such cases, it becomes crucial to monitor political events and other potential contributors to the circulation of hate speech and insensitive content.

According to legal publications, hate speech is defined as an expression that seeks to malign an individual for their immutable characteristics, such as their race, ethnicity, national origin, religion, gender, gender identity, sexual orientation, age or disability (Carlson, 2021). Hate speech detection is one of the most important aspects of event identification during political events like invasions (Bhandari et al., 2023; Parihar et al., 2021). As is evident in today's scenario, the incorporation of multimodal data to meet incentives is highly prevalent and is a major concern for hate speech detection and analysis.

In this paper, we elaborate on our submission for the shared task[1], for multimodal hate speech detection through text-embedded images from the Russia-Ukraine war, which is a part of the bigger picture leading to a significantly demanding issue (Thapa et al., 2023). Multimodal content being advertised through physical spaces, social media, etc, is a mode of spreading hate speech and spiteful views being used extensively in the current scenario. A significant contributor to this phenomenon is the sharing of text-embedded images, representing the views of an individual or a group of individuals, either directly or indirectly. In accordance with this fact, we aim to categorically determine if a given text-embedded image conveys hate speech in any possible form or not.

The rest of the paper is structured as follows: Section 2 illustrates the existing work which has been carried out in this field of research; Section 3 describes the dataset and task for our research study; Section 4 elaborates our proposed model architecture including the individual blocks incorporated in the same; Section 5 states the results obtained from this work along with its empirical analysis; Section 6 provides a view of the future scope in this domain besides concluding the paper.

[1] https://emw.ku.edu.tr/case-2023/

Proceedings of the 6th Workshop on Challenges and Applications of Automated Extraction of Socio-political Events from Text, pages 84–91, Varna, Bulgaria, Sep 7, 2023.
https://doi.org/10.26615/978-954-452-089-2_012

2 Literature Review

Extensive work has been carried out to survey the extent of incorporating technology for hate speech detection. For instance, in (Schmidt and Wiegand, 2017), a survey has been carried out on the scope of hate speech detection using natural language processing. Through this study, the features, terminologies, existing approaches, and techniques in this context have been highlighted.

Another similar research work (Abro et al., 2020), shows the comparison of the performance of three feature engineering techniques and eight machine learning algorithms on a publicly available dataset having three distinct classes. The results of this research work showed that the bigram features when used with the support vector machine algorithm best performed with 79% off overall accuracy.

In another study (Badjatiya et al., 2017), an experiment has been performed to emphasize the usage of deep learning for hate speech detection in tweets. A Twitter dataset containing relevant tweets has been used to classify them as being racist, sexist, or neither. As per the results obtained in this study, the deep learning methods outperform state-of-the-art char/word n-gram methods by ~18 F1 points.

In recent times, multiple attempts have been made to deal with the concern of intelligently determining the spread of hate speech and related expressions through multimodal data. For instance, as a part of the research study (Gomez et al., 2020), it was attempted to jointly analyze textual and visual information for hate speech detection, using a large-scale dataset from Twitter, MMHS150K. The researchers associated with this study have compared the implementation of models working on multimodal data with those on unimodal data.

Another research work (Das et al., 2020), featuring the detection of hate speech in multimodal memes, forms its basis for categorizing a meme as hateful or non-hateful. As a part of this, the visual modality using object detection and image captioning models to fetch the "actual caption" has been explored and combined with the multi-modal representation to perform binary classification. Along with this, an effort has been made to enhance the predictions using sentiment analysis.

Another instance of research work (Velioglu and Rose, 2020), has been carried out on a dataset containing more than 10000 examples of multimodal content, wherein VisualBERT, which is meant to be the "BERT of vision and language" was trained multimodally on images and captions and was augmented with Ensemble Learning.

3 Dataset and Task

As a part of The 6th Workshop on Challenges and Applications of Automated Extraction of Socio-political Events from Text (CASE @ RANLP 2023), the Sub-task A for this research experimentation is to identify whether the given text-embedded image contains hate speech or not (Thapa et al., 2023).

The dataset (Thapa et al., 2022) provided for this task consists of around 4700 text-embedded images, having annotations for the prevalence of hate speech. As a two-way classification task, the two classes in the given dataset correspond to "Hate Speech" and "No Hate Speech", with 2665 and 2058 samples corresponding to the respective classes. The training data consists of 1942 and 1658 samples against the "Hate Speech" and "No Hate Speech" labels (respectively). Concurrently, the evaluation and testing data consists of 443 random samples each. All the images have a unique identifier called "index".

In the training data, the classes are well-balanced, implying the occurrence of 50 text-embedded images each against the two labels, that is, "Hate Speech" as well as "No Hate Speech".

4 Model Architecture

This section describes the proposed model architecture for classifying text-embedded images as "Hate Speech" or "No Hate Speech".

As depicted in Figure 1, we hereby propose an ensemble approach for this binary classification problem. Due to the multimodal nature of the data, it is necessary to extract both visual and textual features from the provided content containing the same. To comprehend the context of a text-embedded image, it is necessary to map the textual context to its visual context. So as to have both of these contexts, we propose an ensemble model that extracts both of these characteristics from an image.

We have incorporated respective models based on convolutional neural networks (CNN), and pre-trained transformer models, which provided good results on the given dataset. InceptionV3 optimizes the neural network for better adaptation as it has a

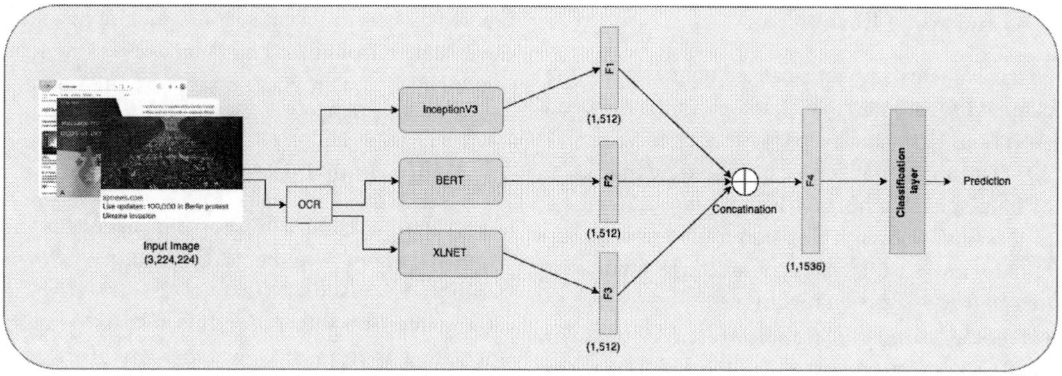

Figure 1: Proposed ensemble architecture

deeper network compared to its predecessors and uses auxiliary classifiers as regularizers. Eventually, it serves as an enhanced option for visual comprehension required for this task. Since transformer models are based on the mechanism of self-attention and differentially weigh the significance of each part of the input textual data, they serve as an ideal option for the textual comprehension of this task.

Our model is comprised of three backbones, one of which (InceptionV3) extracts visual information while the other two (BERT and XLNet) extract textual information.

4.1 InceptionV3

Inception-v3 is a convolutional neural network architecture from the Inception family that makes several improvements including using Label Smoothing, Factorized 7 x 7 convolutions, and the use of an auxiliary classifier to propagate label information lower down the network (along with the use of batch normalization for layers in the sidehead) (Szegedy et al., 2016).

The InceptionV3 architecture uses a novel "Inception module" that extracts multi-scale features using various-sized convolutional filters in the same layer (Szegedy et al., 2015). In order to improve the learning of representations, this module enables the network to capture both local and global contextual information.

Apart from that, the Inception module employs 1x1 convolutions along with dimensionality reduction strategies to lessen computational complexity. The inception block takes the input image

$$I \in R^{C*H*W}$$

and outputs a feature vector of

$$F1 \in R^{1*512}$$

4.2 BERT

BERT's model architecture is a multi-layer bidirectional Transformer encoder, designed to create state-of-the-art models for a wide range of tasks, such as question answering and language inference, without substantial task-specific architecture modifications (Devlin et al., 2018).

We have incorporated BERT into our proposed ensemble model to extract textual features. As a result of being trained on a large corpus of unlabeled text, BERT has a solid language foundation and a better understanding of general language representation. We have extracted text from the image using Google's Tesseract-OCR Engine (Smith, 2007), which is eventually tokenized and fed to the BERT model.

BERT outputs a feature vector of size 1x768 which is then provided to the linear layer to generate feature vector

$$F2 \in R^{1*512}$$

4.3 XLNet

XLNet is a pre-trained transformer model, which includes segments recurrence, introduced in Transformer-XL (Yang et al., 2019; Dai et al., 2019), allowing it to digest longer documents (Shaheen et al., 2020).

In order to pay greater attention to text features, we have incorporated a language model into our ensemble-learning model, yet again. XLNet surpasses the limitations of conventional autoregressive models by taking into account all possible permutations of words in a sentence, resulting in enhanced language representation and comprehension.

XLNet is based on the pretraining and fine-tuning paradigm and utilizes the Transformer architecture. The extracted text, from the OCR Engine (Smith, 2007), is fed to the tokenizer and XLNet, which generate a 1x768-dimensional feature vector, which is then fed to the linear layer, which generates a

$$F3 \in R^{1*512}$$

4.4 Ensemble Model

Ensemble learning or ensemble model is the combination of numerous different predictions from different models to make the final prediction (Ganaie et al., 2022). This has always been an elegant way of enhancing the performance of models.

Stacking is one of the ensemble learning integration approaches in which the meta-learning model is utilized to integrate the output of base models (Džeroski and Ženko, 2004; Zohair et al., 2022). Following this strategy, we incorporated our implemented individual models into the blueprint of a stacked ensemble model. This required the generation of individual embeddings from respective models as described in the preceding subsections.

The embeddings F1, F2, and F3 as obtained from the InceptionV3, BERT, and XLNet (respectively), are concatenated to form F4 as the final embedding for the meta-layer (Sesmero et al., 2015).

$$F4 \in R^{1*1536}$$

After the final embedding (F4), has been processed through the linear layer, a feature vector of size 128 is eventually produced. This feature vector is then forwarded to the final linear layer for classification, which eventually enhances the accuracy of the predictions. After every linear layer, a ReLU non-linearity is applied (Agarap, 2018).

4.5 Hyperparameter

Some of the hyperparameters were kept constant in all models, namely a learning rate of 3e-4, regularization factor of 3e-5, vocab size of 512, and StepLR as the learning rate scheduler.

For our training, we utilized the Adam optimizer (Zhang, 2018) and trained the model for 100 epochs. All experiments were conducted on a system equipped with an NVIDIA-A100 GPU, augmented by 64 GB of RAM, with Ubuntu 20.04 as the operating system. The implementation was carried out using the PyTorch framework.

4.6 Loss and Metric Used

We have used the weighted cross-entropy loss to penalize the ensemble model with more effectiveness during its training for multimodal classification (Phan and Yamamoto, 2020). In addition, we have used accuracy as a standard performance metric for comparing models.

5 Results and Discussion

We have mentioned the results obtained on the validation data in Table 1. The results corresponding to the submission were obtained on the test data provided for this sub-task, which have been reflected in Table 2. As it is evident from the quoted metrics in Table 1, achieved after careful experimentation for the desired task, the proposed ensemble model outperformed various individual models which have been brought into usage for classifying hate speech in the provided dataset.

Model	Accuracy	F1 Score
BERT	69.65	69.51
XLNET	71.80	71.56
InceptionV3	48.12	48.11
MobileNetV3	42.41	42.20
ResNet 152	44.47	44.38
BERT + XLNET	73.51	73.39
Ensemble Model	**75.21**	**74.96**

Table 1: Metric Comparison for proposed ensemble model with conventional models

5.1 Metric Comparison

The text-based models, including BERT and XLNet, gave an accuracy of 69.65 and 71.80 (respectively) when implemented individually with respect to the given dataset. On the other hand, the image-based models including InceptionV3, MobileNetV3, and ResNet 152, gave accuracy levels of 48.12, 42.41, and 44.47 (respectively) for the same set of data. The combination of BERT and XLNet (without the visual component) gave an accuracy of 73.51.

With regard to this, our proposed ensemble model, developed with InceptionV3, BERT, and XLNet as its individual blocks, provided promising results with an accuracy of 75.21 and an F-1 score of 74.96 on the given dataset, as quoted in Table 1.

Our model outperforms the existing works oriented towards multimodal hate speech detection, with an overall accuracy of 75.21. For instance, in

#	User	<Rank>	Recall	Precision	F1	Accuracy
1	arc-nlp	1.0000	0.8567 (1)	0.8563 (1)	0.8565 (1)	0.8578 (1)
2	bayesiano98	2.0000	0.8561 (2)	0.8528 (2)	0.8528 (2)	0.8533 (2)
3	karanpreet_singh	3.0000	0.8508 (3)	0.8476 (3)	0.8463 (3)	0.8465 (3)
4	DeepBlueAI	4.0000	0.8356 (4)	0.8335 (4)	0.8342 (4)	0.8352 (4)
5	csecudsg	5.0000	0.8252 (5)	0.8244 (5)	0.8248 (5)	0.8262 (5)
6	Jesus_Armenta	6.0000	0.8121 (6)	0.8094 (6)	0.8097 (6)	0.8104 (6)
7	Avanthika	7.0000	0.7878 (7)	0.7881 (7)	0.7880 (7)	0.7901 (7)
8	Sarika22	8.0000	0.7806 (8)	0.7849 (8)	0.7821 (8)	0.7856 (8)
9	rabindra.nath	9.0000	0.7768 (9)	0.7842 (9)	0.7788 (9)	0.7833 (9)
10	md_kashif_20	10.0000	0.7270 (10)	0.7372 (10)	0.7287 (10)	0.7359 (10)
11	lueluelue	11.7500	0.5219 (12)	0.5219 (12)	0.5219 (11)	0.5260 (12)
12	pakapro	12.7500	0.4938 (13)	0.4939 (13)	0.4936 (12)	0.4966 (13)
13	Sathvika.V.S	11.5000	0.5334 (11)	0.7240 (11)	0.4294 (13)	0.5779 (11)

Table 2: Rank Table (Sub-Task A)

(Das et al., 2020), the proposed system achieved the best accuracy of 68.4. In (Velioglu and Rose, 2020), the proposed model, VisualBERT achieved an accuracy of 70.93.

The baseline accuracy and F-1 score for the given sub-task are 79.8 and 78.6 (respectively). The proposed model's performance metrics are comparable to the median accuracy and F-1 score of 79.01 and 78.8 (respectively). The same has been mentioned in Table 3.

Model	Accuracy	F1 Score
Baseline	79.8	78.6
Median	79.01	78.8
Proposed	75.21	74.96

Table 3: Metric Comparison for proposed ensemble model with median and baseline scores

The variation of accuracy level with respect to the number of epochs taken for model training has been depicted in Figure 2. Along with this, the variation of the loss function with respect to the number of epochs taken for model training has been depicted in Figure 3.

5.2 Empirical Analysis

In this section, we provide an empirical analysis of our model's predictions for the sample instances of text-embedded images to elaborate on the precision yielded by the model as per the desired task.

Figure 4 illustrates the samples of text-embedded images corresponding to the label "Hate Speech", while Figure 5 illustrates the samples of text-

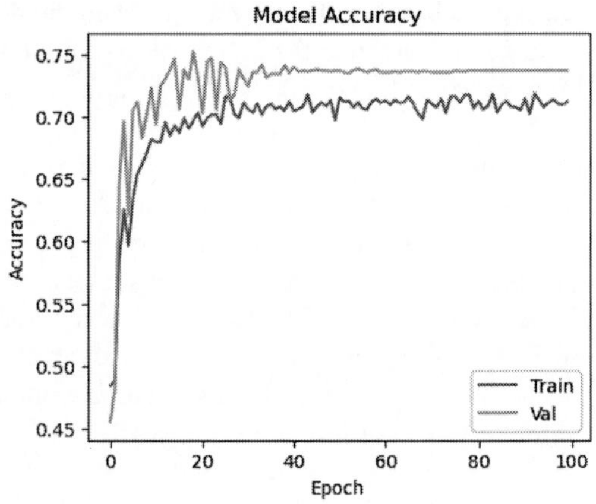

Figure 2: Variation of accuracy with respect to epochs for the **proposed ensemble model**

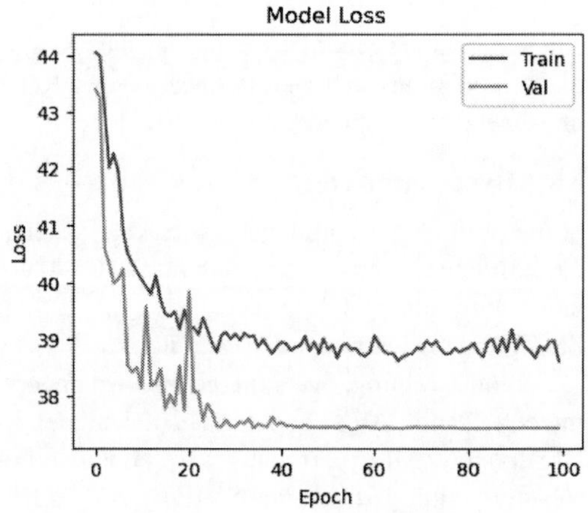

Figure 3: Variation of loss function with respect to epochs for the **proposed ensemble model**

embedded images corresponding to the label "No Hate Speech". An empirical comparison between the actual labels and the predicted labels for the respective image instances quoted in Figures 4 and 5 has been mentioned in Table 4.

With respect to the images corresponding to "Hate Speech", it has been observed for instances 4b and 4d that the labels have been predicted accurately, suggesting the correct prediction capabilities of the model. Similarly, as far as the images corresponding to "No Hate Speech" are concerned, the correct prediction of the labels for instances 5a and 5b reemphasize the correct working of the model.

On the contrary, for image instance 4a, the model fails to recognize the implicit attempt of spreading hate speech through visual sarcasm, resulting in a false prediction by the model. Along with, for image instance 4c, hate speech has been embedded in visual form, which was incorrectly detected by the model, leading to another erroneous prediction. This has been precisely due to the lack of ability of the model to decipher the historical context required to detect hate speech in the respective images.

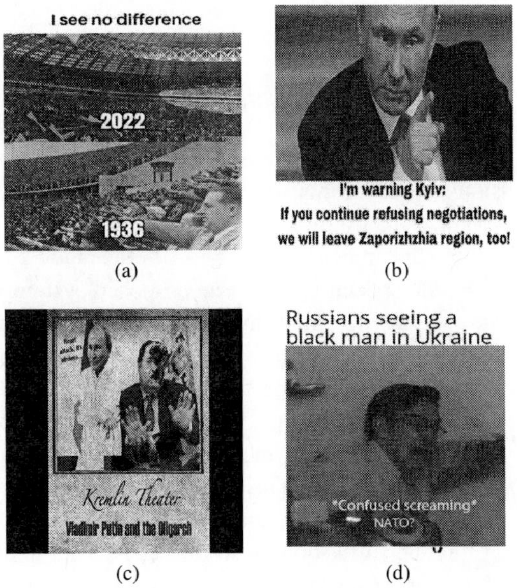

Figure 4: Sample hate speech images

Image Instance	Actual Label	Predicted Label
4a	Hate Speech	No Hate Speech
4b	Hate Speech	Hate Speech
4c	Hate Speech	No Hate Speech
4d	Hate Speech	Hate Speech
5a	No Hate Speech	No Hate Speech
5b	No Hate Speech	No Hate Speech
5c	No Hate Speech	Hate Speech
5d	No Hate Speech	Hate Speech

Table 4: Empirical Evaluation of predictions with respect to sample image instances

As far as the instances in Figure 5 are concerned, although instances 5c and 5d correspond to the label "No Hate Speech", however, the model faced difficulty in making accurate predictions when confronted with the sarcasm in the image. The prime reason for the model's inaccurate prediction of hate speech in the images is the presence of specific words and phrases that might seem to cause the same at first sight. For instance, 5c features the words "explosion" and "kills", while 5d contains the phrase "invasion of Ukraine", which is believed to have been a major cause for this erroneous prediction.

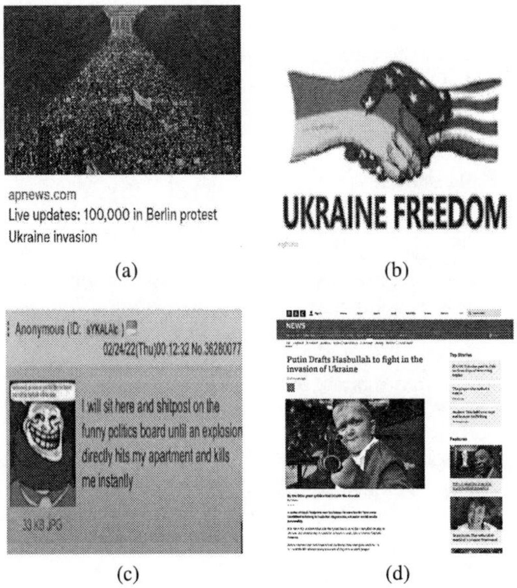

Figure 5: Sample no-hate speech images

This suggests that the model may require further training or refinement to navigate the nuances of language and accurately identify instances of hate speech more efficiently, even when presented in a lesser straightforward manner.

6 Conclusion and Future Scope

In this paper, we present our system paper submission for Lexical Squad@Multimodal Hate Speech Event Detection 2023. We aim to classify text-embedded images, indicating whether they contain hate speech or not. The proposed system is an ensemble learning model with fine-tuned InceptionV3, BERT, and XLNet serving as the individual blocks of the proposed model. Given text-embedded images and their respective extracted text through the OCR model, the submitted model classifies each image instance into one of the two labels: "Hate Speech" and "No Hate Speech". The system performs quite well to accomplish the desired task with an accuracy of 75.21%.

The proposed system can be incorporated for further applications including recommendation systems, personalized content viewing, etc. Along with, it can find usage in further research studies centered on the overlooking field of interest.

In the future, we intend to work on a multitask learning framework to handle social media postings related to other concerns pertaining to sentiment analysis, apart from Hate Speech detection. We also aim to develop models for multi-lingual postings featuring similar scenarios.

References

Sindhu Abro, Sarang Shaikh, Zahid Hussain Khand, Ali Zafar, Sajid Khan, and Ghulam Mujtaba. 2020. Automatic hate speech detection using machine learning: A comparative study. *International Journal of Advanced Computer Science and Applications*, 11(8).

Abien Fred Agarap. 2018. Deep learning using rectified linear units (relu). *arXiv preprint arXiv:1803.08375*.

Pinkesh Badjatiya, Shashank Gupta, Manish Gupta, and Vasudeva Varma. 2017. Deep learning for hate speech detection in tweets. In *Proceedings of the 26th international conference on World Wide Web companion*, pages 759–760.

Aashish Bhandari, Siddhant B Shah, Surendrabikram Thapa, Usman Naseem, and Mehwish Nasim. 2023. Crisishatemm: Multimodal analysis of directed and undirected hate speech in text-embedded images from russia-ukraine conflict. In *Proceedings of the IEEE/CVF Conference on Computer Vision and Pattern Recognition*, pages 1993–2002.

Caitlin Ring Carlson. 2021. *Hate speech*. MIT Press.

Zihang Dai, Zhilin Yang, Yiming Yang, Jaime Carbonell, Quoc V Le, and Ruslan Salakhutdinov. 2019. Transformer-xl: Attentive language models beyond a fixed-length context. *arXiv preprint arXiv:1901.02860*.

Abhishek Das, Japsimar Singh Wahi, and Siyao Li. 2020. Detecting hate speech in multi-modal memes. *arXiv preprint arXiv:2012.14891*.

Jacob Devlin, Ming-Wei Chang, Kenton Lee, and Kristina Toutanova. 2018. Bert: Pre-training of deep bidirectional transformers for language understanding. *arXiv preprint arXiv:1810.04805*.

Saso Džeroski and Bernard Ženko. 2004. Is combining classifiers with stacking better than selecting the best one? *Machine learning*, 54:255–273.

Mudasir A Ganaie, Minghui Hu, AK Malik, M Tanveer, and PN Suganthan. 2022. Ensemble deep learning: A review. *Engineering Applications of Artificial Intelligence*, 115:105151.

Raul Gomez, Jaume Gibert, Lluis Gomez, and Dimosthenis Karatzas. 2020. Exploring hate speech detection in multimodal publications. In *Proceedings of the IEEE/CVF winter conference on applications of computer vision*, pages 1470–1478.

Anil Singh Parihar, Surendrabikram Thapa, and Sushruti Mishra. 2021. Hate speech detection using natural language processing: Applications and challenges. In *2021 5th International Conference on Trends in Electronics and Informatics (ICOEI)*, pages 1302–1308. IEEE.

Trong Huy Phan and Kazuma Yamamoto. 2020. Resolving class imbalance in object detection with weighted cross entropy losses. *arXiv preprint arXiv:2006.01413*.

Anna Schmidt and Michael Wiegand. 2017. A survey on hate speech detection using natural language processing. In *Proceedings of the fifth international workshop on natural language processing for social media*, pages 1–10.

M Paz Sesmero, Agapito I Ledezma, and Araceli Sanchis. 2015. Generating ensembles of heterogeneous classifiers using stacked generalization. *Wiley interdisciplinary reviews: data mining and knowledge discovery*, 5(1):21–34.

Zein Shaheen, Gerhard Wohlgenannt, and Erwin Filtz. 2020. Large scale legal text classification using transformer models. *arXiv preprint arXiv:2010.12871*.

Ray Smith. 2007. An overview of the tesseract ocr engine. In *Ninth international conference on document analysis and recognition (ICDAR 2007)*, volume 2, pages 629–633. IEEE.

Christian Szegedy, Wei Liu, Yangqing Jia, Pierre Sermanet, Scott Reed, Dragomir Anguelov, Dumitru Erhan, Vincent Vanhoucke, and Andrew Rabinovich. 2015. Going deeper with convolutions. In *Proceedings of the IEEE conference on computer vision and pattern recognition*, pages 1–9.

Christian Szegedy, Vincent Vanhoucke, Sergey Ioffe, Jon Shlens, and Zbigniew Wojna. 2016. Rethinking the inception architecture for computer vision. In *Proceedings of the IEEE conference on computer vision and pattern recognition*, pages 2818–2826.

Surendrabikram Thapa, Farhan Ahmad Jafri, Ali Hürriyetoğlu, Francielle Vargas, Roy Ka-Wei Lee, and Usman Naseem. 2023. Multimodal hate speech event detection - shared task 4, case 2023. In *Proceedings of the 6th Workshop on Challenges and Applications of Automated Extraction of Socio-political Events from Text (CASE)*.

Surendrabikram Thapa, Aditya Shah, Farhan Jafri, Usman Naseem, and Imran Razzak. 2022. A multimodal dataset for hate speech detection on social media: Case-study of russia-Ukraine conflict. In *Proceedings of the 5th Workshop on Challenges and Applications of Automated Extraction of Socio-political Events from Text (CASE)*, pages 1–6, Abu Dhabi, United Arab Emirates (Hybrid). Association for Computational Linguistics.

Riza Velioglu and Jewgeni Rose. 2020. Detecting hate speech in memes using multimodal deep learning approaches: Prize-winning solution to hateful memes challenge. *arXiv preprint arXiv:2012.12975*.

Zhilin Yang, Zihang Dai, Yiming Yang, Jaime Carbonell, Russ R Salakhutdinov, and Quoc V Le. 2019. Xlnet: Generalized autoregressive pretraining for language understanding. *Advances in neural information processing systems*, 32.

Zijun Zhang. 2018. Improved adam optimizer for deep neural networks. In *2018 IEEE/ACM 26th international symposium on quality of service (IWQoS)*, pages 1–2. Ieee.

Mohammad Zohair, Nidhir Bhavsar, Aakash Bhatnagar, and Muskaan Singh. 2022. Innovators@ smm4h'22: An ensembles approach for self-reporting of covid-19 vaccination status tweets. In *Proceedings of The Seventh Workshop on Social Media Mining for Health Applications, Workshop & Shared Task*, pages 123–125.

On the Road to a Protest Event Ontology for Bulgarian: Conceptual Structures and Representation Design

Milena Slavcheva
Institute of Information and Communication Technologies
Bulgarian Academy of Sciences
milena@lml.bas.bg

Hristo Tanev
Joint Research Centre
European Commission
hristo.tanev@ec.europa.eu

Onur Uca
Mersin University
Sociology Department
onuruca@mersin.edu.tr

Abstract

The paper presents a semantic model of protest events, called *Semantic Interpretations of Protest Events* (SemInPE). The model is a practical application of the *Unified Eventity Representation* (UER) formalism, which is based on the *Unified Modeling Language* (UML), whose four-layer architecture (i.e., user objects, model, metamodel, and meta-metamodel) provides flexible means for building the semantic representations of the language units along a scale of generality and specificity. The analytical framework, inspired by the object-orientation paradigm in computer science and a cognitive approach to the linguistic analysis, provides suitable devices for capturing the continuously varying information in the social and political domain. The basic modeling elements of events are presented, which include modeling elements defining classes of participants in the events, types of relationship among the participants, as well as the participants behaviour. The acquisition of language objects that serve as instances of the various semantic classes contained in the model is also discussed.

1 Introduction

The paper presents a semantic model of events, which can be broadly defined as protest events. The model, which we call *Semantic Interpretations of Protest Events* (SemInPE) is a practical application of the *Unified Eventity Representation* (UER) - a cognitive theoretical approach and a graphical formalism (Schalley, 2004) based on the *Unified Modeling Language* (UML)[1] - an international standard for graphical representation and design of object-oriented systems in the field of Information Technologies (OMG, 2001).

The analytical framework used for building the semantic representations is inspired by the object-oriented paradigm in computer science and a cognitive approach to the linguistic analysis (Schalley, 2014). The application of this innovative formalism in our work is motivated by several merits of its, relevant to the task of building Language-Technologies-style ontologies utilisable in the social and political sciences.

The analytical framework we apply is based on the four-layer metamodel (i.e., user objects, model, metamodel, and meta-metamodel) of the *Unified Modeling Language* (UML). This multi-layered architecture provides flexible means for building the semantic representations of the language objects along a scale of generality and specificity. The inheritance mechanism of classes and objects provides a device for the definition of abstract, underlying semantic representations, which can be instantiated by specific descriptions corresponding to specific topics and specific languages. In our case, this particular conceptual modeling paves the way to building an ontology of protest events for Bulgarian, but it is utilisable in multilingual settings as well. The structuring devices of the applied model provide the possibility for a modular and dynamically extensible knowledge representation, which is of particular importance for capturing the continuously varying information in the social and political domain.

The cognitive approach to representing the linguistic units provides a conceptual modeling, which corresponds to the conceptualisation of the object-oriented modeling (Schalley, 2014). In this way a direct use of the handy object-orientation devices is ensured in the semantic representation of language entities. We can also point out the presence of ontological knowledge (i.e., relation to real-world knowledge) in the semantic descriptions via the reference to ontological categories (see Section 3).

The paper is structured as follows. In Section 2 we briefly refer to related work. In section 3 we present the model to be utilised in building an ontology in the domain of protest events. In section

[1] https://www.uml.org/

Proceedings of the 6th Workshop on Challenges and Applications of Automated Extraction of Socio-political Events from Text, pages 92–100, Varna, Bulgaria, Sep 7, 2023.
https://doi.org/10.26615/978-954-452-089-2_013

4 the extraction of language data necessary for our work is discussed. Section 5 provides concluding remarks and some hints on the future developments we envisage.

2 Related work

As pointed out in the Introduction, the work presented in this paper belongs to the analytical framework defined as object-oriented semantics. This relatively novel approach in linguistics so far has been demonstrated predominantly in the analysis of the meanings of verbs (e.g., (Schalley, 2004, 2014), (Benz, 2014), (Slavcheva, 2008, 2012). However, more recently, Morrissey and Schalley (2017) argue that the object-oriented approach is beneficial for the semantic representation of nominals as well, which is a useful development for large-scale conceptual modeling. The approach to the linguistic analysis in the work presented in this paper is a cognitive one. It is determined by principles relating perception, thinking and language. The basic assumption is that language reflects "patterns of thought", hence the study of language is connected to the exploration of "patterns of conceptualization" (Evans and Green, 2006). This makes it possible to relate conceptual structures of language to the conceptual base of object-oriented programming languages.

The graphical semantic formalism used in the application presented in this paper employs the *Unified Modeling Language* (UML) (OMG, 2001), which contains notation techniques for combining structural (that is, static) and behavioural (that is, dynamic) modeling. A long-term research work for developing ontological foundations for conceptual modeling has used UML in building the framework of the Unified Foundational Ontology (UFO) and especially in the development of OntoUML – "ontologically well-founded conceptual modeling version of UML" (Guizzardi et al., 2015, 2022).

The work on the conceptually grounded semantic descriptors provokes a comparison with ontologies like, for instance, the Suggested Upper Merged Ontology (SUMO)[2] (Niles and Pease, 2001), which has been mapped to WordNet (Niles and Pease, 2003). An open source knowledge engineering environment, Sigma, has been created (Pease and Benzmueller, 2013), which includes a full first order inference capability, as well as a natural language paraphrase capability for logical axioms.

[2]http://www.ontologyportal.org/

There are various taxonomies describing political events. The earliest event taxonomy for text analysis, which includes political events, is introduced in the context of the Automatic Content Extraction program (Ahn, 2006) and the following TAC initiative (Mitamura et al., 2017).

Other outstanding taxonomies in this domain include the Intrusion Detection Extensible Alert Taxonomy IDEA (Kácha, 2014), and the CAMEO taxonomy (Gerner et al., 2002). Several event data bases and systems such as GDELT and ICEWS (Ward et al., 2013) use CAMEO. Although CAMEO is sometimes referred to as ontology, the first fully fledged ontology in the domain of political events is PLOVER (Halterman et al., 2021), which includes protests and other political events as classes. An overview of the existing ontologies and taxonomies is presented in Balalia et al. (2021); they also introduce their own ontology, called COFEE.

The ontologies and taxonomies mentioned so far refer to the large domain of political event detection. In contrast, very little work is dedicated specifically to protest events: Danilova (2015) describes a model which includes arguments and classes similar to the ones we observed. Relevant to our work is also the multilingual NEXUS event detection system, which uses linguistic rules, lexicon-based event classification, and an ad-hoc taxonomy of event classes to detect protests, riots, and other conflict events (Piskorski et al., 2007).

Protest events have also been studied by the political and social sciences. Duruşan et al. (2022) defines the protest as "an action through which individuals, groups, or organizations voice their objections, oppositions, demands, or grievances to a person or institution of authority". According to Parry (2023), the value of protest consists in making a difference; the successful protest being the one that effects change in line with the protesters' goals.

Event databases, such as POLECAT (Halterman et al., 2023), the CAMEO dataset (Salam et al., 2020) and others represent a bridge between the world of ontologies and political sciences. They introduce means for qualitative political studies, trend analysis and conflict prediction.

3 The model

As pointed out above, the *Semantic Interpretations of Protest Events* (SemInPE) model we present here is based on the *Unified Eventity Representation* (UER) theoretical approach and formalism (Schalley, 2004). In the subsections that follow we present basic modeling elements and the way they will be used in the ontology construction.

3.1 Eventity frames

A central modelling element is the EVENTITY FRAME, which represents the semantics of verbs as the key lexical encoders of events (or, eventities in the UER terminology) in texts. The EVENTITY FRAMES describe the eventity PARTICIPANTS, as well as their interaction and behaviour. The EVENTITY FRAMES incorporate modelling elements, each one of which can be specified to a different degree depending on the concrete task. Figure 1 contains an EVENTITY FRAME TEMPLATE, which, after binding its parameters, can describe verbs that typically occur in texts discussing protests like, for example, bg. *protestiram* ('protest') as used in sentence (1).

(1) *Zsiteli na krivodolskoto selo Osen protestiraha sreshtu avtomobilniya trafik.*
(Eng.transl.) Inhabitants of the Osen village in the Krivodol region protested against the automobile traffic.

In the diagram in Figure 1, there is one prominent PARTICIPANT (the protester) represented by a PARTICIPANT CLASS stating that the PARTICIPANT ROLE is `Agent`, the PARTICIPANT ontological TYPE is `Individual`, and there is an ATTRIBUTE further characterising the participant as `human`. The prominent participant's behaviour is described in the dynamic core of the EVENTITY FRAME (denoted by the dashed-outline rectangle with rounded corners), which contains a STATE-machine, in this case consisting of an ACTIVE SIMPLE STATE (ASS) (depicted by the shape with straight top and bottom arcs, and convex arcs on the two sides). The ACTIVE SIMPLE STATE (ASS) denotes activities, actions performed by the prominent participant. The second participant is the reason, the motive, the stimulus[3] for the protest event.

As pointed out above, the EVENTITY FRAME in Figure 1 is a TEMPLATE, that is, it includes a parameter to be bound (indicated by the dash-outline rectangle in the upper right corner of the octagon). The parameter can be bound to names of the ACTIVE SIMPLE STATE, which refer to basic concepts like, for example:

ASS = {Protest, Strike, Demonstrate, ... }

The specification of the STATES depends on the modeling granularity determined for a given representation and ranges from underspecification to different degrees of specification with the help of clusters of PROPERTIES. The PROPERTIES, which are part of the metamodel, have values of the ENUMERATION or *Boolean* data type. For example, the STATE-machine of the verb bg. *buntuvam se* ('riot') can be represented in the way shown in Figure 2.

It should be noted that the STATE-machines can provide conceptual structuring of different complexity. They can include modeling devices like SUBMACHINE STATES or SUBCORE STATES, which can reference reusable conceptual structures (or conceptual 'macros') specified elsewhere in the model. STATE-machines can make use of COMPOSITE STATES, which model processes and can describe the sequential and concurrent steps in those processes. The granulated structure of the dynamic core is beyond the scope of the current paper. Its development will be reported in follow-up works.

3.2 Participants

The PARTICIPANT CLASSES are selectors for sets of OBJECTS, which stand for participants appropriate for a given eventity. The metamodel provides the possibility for building taxonomies of participants whose modelling elements are at a different level of abstraction.

The participants belong to different ontological categories, which are referenced by PARTICIPANT TYPES merged into a very concise participant type ontology. This small ontological type hierarchy contains generalised categories, which roughly determine the kind of modeling elements that are used to specify the PARTICIPANT CLASSES and the PARTICIPANT OBJECTS as instances of those classes. The root node of the ontological type hierarchy is `Entity` and it encompasses the two top level categories of `Eventity` and `Ineventity`[4]. There is a small number of sub-levels further down the hierarchy, but what concerns directly our work here is that: 1) one of the subdivisions of `Ineventity`

[3]One would intuitively say the cause for the protest, but the word *cause* is deliberately avoided as it is reserved to name a central modeling element, the cause-SIGNAL

[4]Currently, we follow the naming and the definition of the high-level ontological types as set in the UER (Schalley, 2004). However, the ontological type hierarchy can be adjusted and complemented by a particular ontology designer. We envisage a further development and specification of the ontological types.

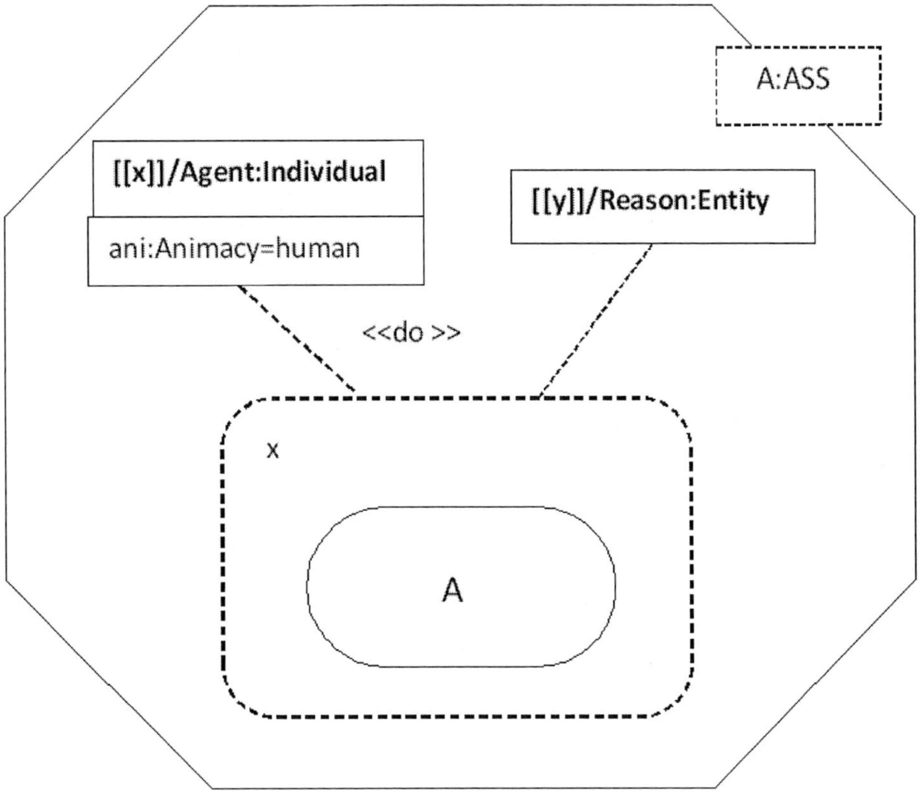

Figure 1: EVENTITY FRAME TEMPLATE modeling verbs typical for the topic of protests.

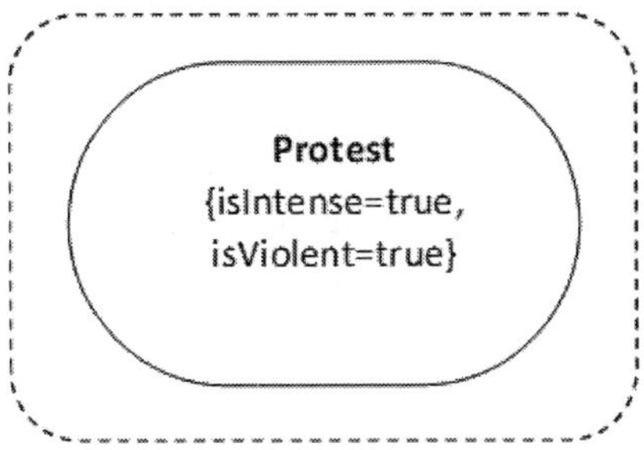

Figure 2: Dynamic core of the verb *buntuvam se* ('riot')

is the `Individual`[5] category, which is the typical category of protesters, and 2) it is possible for a participant to be of the `Eventity` category, which is a typical type for the reason, the motive for a protest.

The major discriminators of eventity PARTICIPANTS are the ATTRIBUTES that characterise them. The number and type of the ATTRIBUTES that specify a given PARTICIPANT CLASS can vary depending on the concrete task. In addition, given ATTRIBUTES can stay unspecified depending on the implementation.

For example, protesters can be characterised by clusters of ATTRIBUTES as shown in Figure 3.

The values of the ATTRIBUTES in Figure 3 are of data type ENUMERATION as exemplified in Figure 4.

Looking at the data extracted from news texts in Bulgarian (see Section 4), we can find several general semantic dimensions of reasons for protesting. Some of the protests belong to a single dimension (e.g., a political protest against a new government), others are characterised by features stemming from more than one dimension (e.g., demands for increase of the salaries of medical personnel, which concern the social, economic, and health dimensions).

The semantic dimensions are defined as follows:

[5]It should be noted that the category `Individual` does not stand for the concept of Person but for any entity that conforms to the ATTRIBUTE {inherentlyBounded = true}

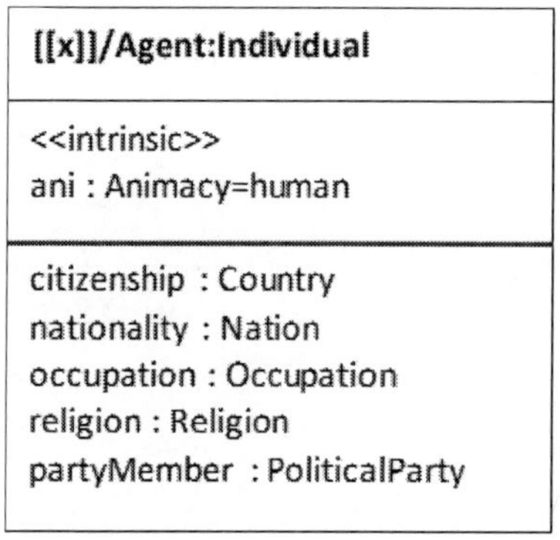

Figure 3: Attributes describing a protester participant.

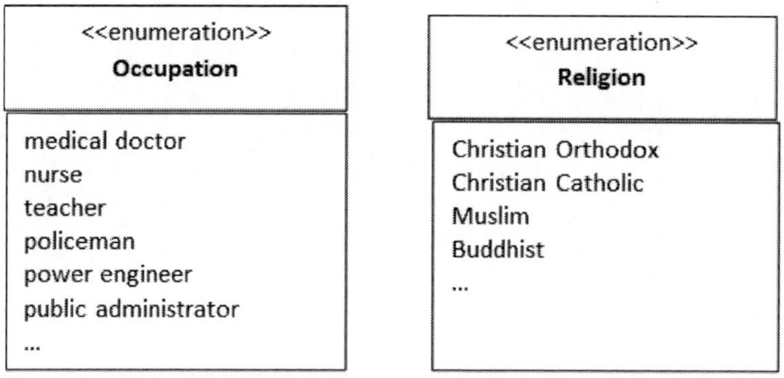

Figure 4: Enumerations of attribute values characterising protest participants.

- *Political dimension.* It is related to the political realm of the Parliament, the Presidency, the government and the governmental administration, the administration of the regions, etc.
- *Social dimension.* It concerns the rights and welfare of different social groups, for example, the status of old people, the education, etc.
- *Criminal dimension.* Criminality, mafia, corruption, and the rule of law in general are the protest triggers in this dimension.
- *Ideological dimension.* Here the concerns are related to ultra right or ultra left movements, political figures, and similar concerns of the protesting people related to various ideologies, which are not acceptable according to them.
- *Religious dimension.* It includes protests stemming from religious convictions, for example, protests for the rights of the Islamic population in China.
- *Legislation dimension.* Here the demands are directed in favour or against a new legislation or an old legislation, which is in conflict with certain social realities.
- *Health dimension.* Health is an important concern in society, especially during and after the COVID pandemic. Various protests target vaccines, health insurances, health legislation and the health system in general. This dimension is related to the social dimension.

On the basis of the above summarising, for the `Reason` participant, we can define PARTICIPANT CLASSES as exemplified in Figure 5. Examples of lexical items represented by such a participant class are: "the President", "the opposition", "the mafia", "new law", "the COVID masks", etc.

Typically, the `Reason` participant is of the ontological type `Eventity`. It can be assigned a sub-division category of `Eventity` like `Proposition` (which encompasses abstract eventities), `State`, `Process`. Except for the `Animacy` attribute, which is irrelevant for an `Eventity` type of `Reason`, the attributes in Figure 5 are valid also for the `Eventity` type of

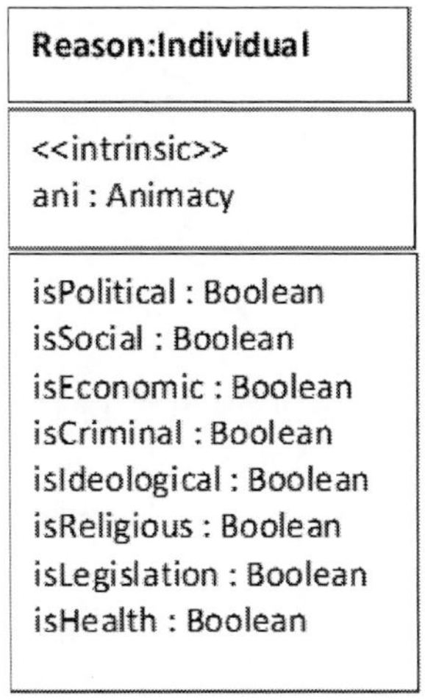

Figure 5: Participant kind of reason

`Reason`. In addition, the `Reason Eventity` can be represented, in its own right, in a structured way. Examples of `Reason` participants of the `Eventity` type are: "increase of prices", "murder", "firing of workers", "construction", "animal rights violation", "the lack of treatment of mosquitoes", etc.

Needless to say, the `Reason` ontological types are characterised by plasticity, that is, the `Individual` and the `Eventity` types are interchangeable. For example, a protest against the President, in one case, can be viewed to be against the personality of the president, in other case, against actions of the president.

The semantic representation of protest events can be enriched by modeling the relations among the participants, which is the subject of discussion of the next section.

3.3 Relationships among participants

An EVENTITY FRAME describing a protest event can incorporate different PARTICIPANTS, which are in various relationships with one another. The different aspects of those relationships can be described by the ASSOCIATION modeling element, as well as the ASSOCIATION CLASS, which displays properties of the ASSOCIATION. The modeling elements of this kind are a useful device for providing rich semantic descriptions of the relations among the different types of participants, which we illustrate by the examples below.

For a given semantic representation, it would be necessary to point out the relation of employee and employer between the participants in a protest event as displayed in Figure 6.

The ASSOCIATION CLASS connects the PARTICIPANT CLASSES and defines a set of features that describe the relationship itself as exemplified in Figure 7.

4 Data

The first step in preparing our semantic model was to acquire language objects that serve as instances of the various semantic classes contained in the model:

1. We extracted nouns in Bulgarian, whose very close equivalents in English are "protest", "demonstration", "riot", "strike", etc.

2. We identified the verbs that are morphologically and semantically related to those nouns. For example, the correlative of the noun bg.*protest* ('protest') is the verb bg.*protestiram* ('to protest'). Bulgarian is a language of very rich verb morphology, hence, specific members of the verb form paradigm are of interest, in this case, bg.*protestirat* (present tense, plural), and bg.*protestiraha* (past tense, plural). These verb forms are frequently used to denote the focus of news articles describing protest events and convey meanings related to "actions happening at the moment", "actions that happened in not distant past", and "actions performed by a number of people".

3. We searched for relevant terms in a corpus of approximately 100,000 news articles in Bul-

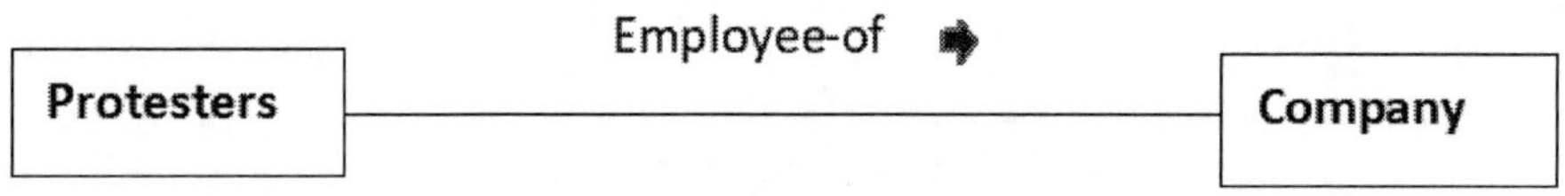

Figure 6: ASSOCIATION between two PARTICIPANTS.

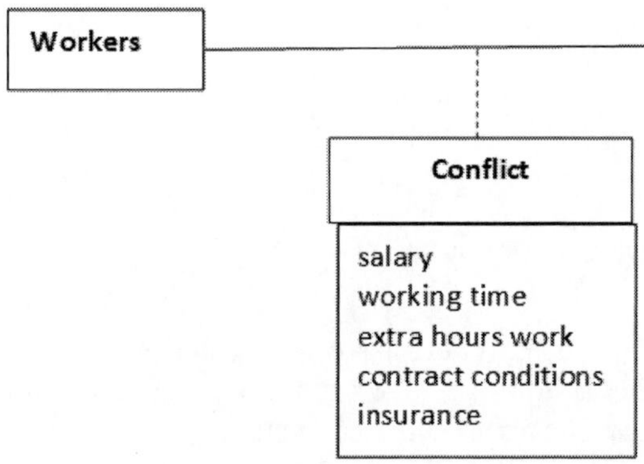

Figure 7: ASSOCIATION CLASS describing the relation of conflict between the participants.

garian gathered by scraping various Bulgarian news websites in the period 2021-2022.

4. Then we gathered all the uni- and bi-grams that appeared in immediate proximity to the search terms, where only one non-stop word was allowed between the search term and the n-gram.

5. We calculated the TF.IDF for each n-gram extracted in this way, and picked out the 500 with the highest TF.IDF.

6. Then we manually identified the terms for the respective target semantic class in this list of 500 terms adjacent to "protest", its synonyms and hyponyms in the Bulgarian language.

As an additional data source we used the Bulgarian section of Google News[6] and downloaded 100 news articles from 2022 and 2023 related to protests, riots and strikes, and manually extracted from them additional relevant terms for each semantic class under consideration.

It should be noted that all semantic classes were extracted from the aforementioned set of terms and the Google news corpus.

[6]http://news.google.com

In this way we extracted the terms for the semantic class PROTEST REASONS (here the English translations of the Bulgarian lexical items are given): "construction", "new law", "new order", "increased prices", "the President", "the opposition", "the conditions", "the mafia", "the ambassador", "the COVID masks", "murder", "working conditions", "animal rights", etc. These are protest reasons, typical for the Bulgarian society. Similarly, we can deal with the other semantic classes in the model like CONFLICT, OCCUPATION, RELIGION, etc.

5 Conclusion

We presented a semantic model, which contains flexible devices for representing the underlying conceptual structures of protest events. They include modeling elements defining classes of participants in the events, types of relationship among the participants, as well as the participants behaviour. The modeling framework of object-orientation proves to be a convenient tool for building information structures in language semantics, which can be adjusted to serve specific tasks and user demands. This assertion has been demonstrated by modeling elements of different degree of abstraction, which constitute a dynamic system of interrelated semantic classes.

The presented *Semantic Interpretations of Protest Events* (SemInPE) model underlies the construction of the protest event ontology for Bulgarian, which is the next step on the way of providing resources enhancing the text processing in the social and political domain.

References

David Ahn. 2006. The stages of event extraction. In *Proceedings of the Workshop on Annotating and Reasoning about Time and Events*, pages 1–8.

Ali Balalia, Masoud Asadpoura, and Seyed Hossein Jafaria. 2021. COfEE: A Comprehensive Ontology for Event Extraction from text, with an online annotation tool. *CoRR*.

Anton Benz. 2014. Ergativity and the object-oriented representation of verb meaning. In Klaus Robering, editor, *Events, Arguments, and Aspects – Topics in the Semantics of Verbs*, pages 65–87. John Benjamins, Amsterdam / Philadelphia.

Vera Danilova. 2015. A pipeline for multilingual protest event selection and annotation. In *2015 26th International Workshop on Database and Expert Systems Applications (DEXA)*, pages 309–313. IEEE.

Fırat Duruşan, Ali Hürriyetoğlu, Erdem Yörük, Osman Mutlu, Çağrı Yoltar, Burak Gürel, and Alvaro Comin. 2022. Global contentious politics database (GLOCON) annotation manuals.

Vyvyan Evans and Melanie Green. 2006. *Cognitive Linguistics: an Introduction*. Edinburgh University Press, UK.

Deborah J Gerner, Philip A Schrodt, Omür Yilmaz, and Rajaa Abu-Jabr. 2002. Conflict and mediation event observations (CAMEO): A new event data framework for the analysis of foreign policy interactions. *International Studies Association, New Orleans*.

Giancarlo Guizzardi, Alessander Botti Benevides, Claudenir M. Fonseca, Danielle Porello, Joao Paulo A. Almeida, and Tiago Prince Sales. 2022. UFO: Unified Foundational Ontology. *Applied Ontology*, 17(1):167–210.

Giancarlo Guizzardi, Gerd Wagner, Joao Paulo A. Almeida, and Renata S. S. Guizzardi. 2015. Towards ontological foundations for conceptual modeling: The Unified Foundational Ontology (UFO) story. *Applied Ontology*, 10(3):259–271.

Andrew Halterman, Benjamin Bagozzi, Andreas Beger, Phil Schrodt, and Grace Scraborough. 2023. PLOVER and POLECAT: A new political event ontology and dataset.

Andrew Halterman, Katherine Keith, Sheikh Sarwar, and Brendan O'Connor. 2021. Corpus-level evaluation for event QA: The IndiaPoliceEvents corpus covering the 2002 Gujarat violence. In *Findings of the Association for Computational Linguistics: ACL-IJCNLP 2021*, pages 4240–4253, Online. Association for Computational Linguistics.

Pavel Kácha. 2014. Idea: security event taxonomy mapping. In *18th International Conference on Circuits, Systems, Communications and Computers*.

Teruko Mitamura, Zhengzhong Liu, and Eduard H Hovy. 2017. Events detection, coreference and sequencing: What's next? overview of the TAC KBP 2017 event track. In *TAC*.

Lochlan Morrissey and Andrea C. Schalley. 2017. A lexical semantics for refugee, asylum seeker and boat people in Australian English. *Australian Journal of Linguistics*, 37(4):389–423.

Ian Niles and Adam Pease. 2001. Towards a Standard Upper Ontology. In *Proceedings of the 2nd international conference on Formal Ontology in Information Systems (FOIS-2001)*.

Ian Niles and Adam Pease. 2003. Linking lexicons and ontologies: Mapping WordNet to the Suggested Upper Merged Ontology. In *Proceedings of the IEEE International Conference on Information and Knowledge Engineering*.

OMG. 2001. *OMG Unified Modeling Language Specification, Version 1.4*. Object Management Group (OMG), http://www.omg.org/.

Jonathan Parry. 2023. What's the point of protest? `https://www.lse.ac.uk/philosophy/blog/2023/02/15/whats-the-point-of-protest/`.

Adam Pease and Christoph Benzmueller. 2013. Sigma: An integrated development environment for logical theories. *AI Communications*.

Jakub Piskorski, Hristo Tanev, and Pinar Oezden Wennerberg. 2007. Extracting violent events from on-line news for ontology population. In *Business Information Systems: 10th International Conference, BIS 2007, Poznan, Poland, April 25-27, 2007. Proceedings 10*, pages 287–300. Springer.

Sayeed Salam, Patrick Brandt, Vito D'Orazio, Jennifer Holmes, Javiar Osorio, and Latifur Khan. 2020. An online structured political event dataset based on CAMEO ontology.

Andrea C. Schalley. 2004. *Cognitive Modeling and Verbal Semantics. A Representational Framework Based on UML*. Trends in Linguistics. Studies and Monographs 154. Mouton de Gruyter, Berlin – New York.

Andrea C. Schalley. 2014. Object-orientation and the semantics of verbs. In Klaus Robering, editor, *Events, Arguments, and Aspects – Topics in the Semantics of Verbs*, pages 159–186. John Benjamins, Amsterdam / Philadelphia.

Milena Slavcheva. 2008. Thinking in objects: Towards an infrastructure for semantic representation of verb-centred structures. In Petr Sojka, Aleš Horák, Ivan Kopeček, and Karel Pala, editors, *Proceedings of 11th International Conference on Text, Speech and Dialogue (TSD 2008)*, Lecture Notes in Artificial Intelligence, Vol. 5246, pages 193–200. Springer-Verlag, Berlin Heidelberg.

Milena Slavcheva. 2012. Semantic descriptors of the reflexive forms of verb structures in contemporary Bulgarian, French and Hungarian. *Abstracts of Dissertations, Bulgarian Academy of Sciences, Institute of Information and Communication Technologies.*

Michael D Ward, Andreas Beger, Josh Cutler, Matthew Dickenson, Cassy Dorff, and Ben Radford. 2013. Comparing gdelt and icews event data. *Analysis*, 21(1):267–297.

CSECU-DSG@ Multimodal Hate Speech Event Detection 2023: Transformer-based Multimodal Hierarchical Fusion Model For Multimodal Hate Speech Detection

Abdul Aziz, Md. Akram Hossain, and Abu Nowshed Chy
Department of Computer Science and Engineering
University of Chittagong, Chattogram-4331, Bangladesh
{aziz.abdul.cu, akram.hossain.cse.cu}@gmail.com,
and nowshed@cu.ac.bd

Abstract

The emergence of social media and e-commerce platforms enabled the perpetrator to spread negativity and abuse individuals or organisations worldwide rapidly. It is critical to detect hate speech in both visual and textual content so that it may be moderated or excluded from online platforms to keep it sound and safe for users. However, multimodal hate speech detection is a complex and challenging task as people sarcastically present hate speech and different modalities i.e., image and text are involved in their content. This paper describes our participation in the CASE 2023 multimodal hate speech event detection task. In this task, the objective is to automatically detect hate speech and its target from the given text-embedded image. We proposed a transformer-based multimodal hierarchical fusion model to detect hate speech present in the visual content. We jointly fine-tune a language and a vision pre-trained transformer models to extract the visual-contextualized features representation of the text-embedded image. We concatenate these features and fed them to the multi-sample dropout strategy. Moreover, the contextual feature vector is fed into the BiLSTM module and the output of the BiLSTM module also passes into the multi-sample dropout. We employed arithmetic mean fusion to fuse all sample dropout outputs that predict the final label of our proposed method. Experimental results demonstrate that our proposed method obtains competitive performance and ranked 5th among the participants.

1 Introduction

Nowadays social media increasingly become popular means of information sharing because people consistently present their concepts, opinions, thoughts, and breaking news using various platforms including Twitter, Facebook, Reddit, and Instagram as their real-time behaviour and practical features. Online abuse and the spreading of negativity are common practices and important societal problem that is highly correlated with the emergence of social media platforms (Parihar et al., 2021). Analyzing and extracting social media information have various benefits as it promotes a safer online platform, reduces online harassment and cyberbullying, and reduces harmful and false information. However, detecting hate space on social media content is a complex and challenging task as people express their information sarcastically i.e., memes, the multifaceted nature of content, and multiple modalities are involved. Researchers consider hate speech detection as the text-only task at the commencement stage (Djuric et al., 2015; Badjatiya et al., 2017; Watanabe et al., 2018). However, this practice is not effective as people share text-embedded pictures or memes as well which helps to understand the real scenario of the content. Essentially, hate speech detection slowly moves to the visual-textual format named multimodal hate speech detection (Sabat et al., 2019; Thapa et al., 2022; Chhabra and Vishwakarma, 2023). Multimodal hate speech is now one of the most popular tasks and developed various methods (Cai et al., 2019; Gomez et al., 2020; Zhu et al., 2022). Facebook AI introduce hateful meme challenges (Kiela et al., 2020) and various teams proposed state-of-the-art methods (Velioglu and Rose, 2020; Lippe et al., 2020). Velioglu and Rose (2020) proposed a winning approach where they utilize VisualBERT and ensemble learning to detect hateful memes. Gomez et al. (2020) introduced a large-scale multimodal hate speech dataset of multimodal publication from Twitter and provided various unimodal and multimodal baseline methods. Yang et al. (2022) proposed a cross-domain knowledge transfer (CDKT) framework for the multimodal hate speech detection task where they used a vision-language transformer as the backbone of the proposed approach. Recently, the Russia-Ukraine issue has been a significant topic of discussion on

Proceedings of the 6th Workshop on Challenges and Applications of Automated Extraction of Socio-political Events from Text, pages 101–107, Varna, Bulgaria, Sep 7, 2023.
https://doi.org/10.26615/978-954-452-089-2_014

social media platforms and people present their opinions and thoughts on social media. Bhandari et al. (2023) proposed a multimodal hate speech detection dataset, CrisisHateMM based on the Russia-Ukraine crisis on social media. They provide a multimodal analysis of directed and undirected hate speech in text-embedded pictures from the Russia-Ukraine conflict. Thapa et al. (2023) introduce a shared task at CASE 2023 based on the CrisisHateMM dataset where the participant's system needs to detect hate speech and target from the given text-embedded image in a multimodal setting. To tackle this task we propose a transformer-based multimodal hierarchical fusion approach with the BiLSTM module and the multi-sample dropout strategy. Our system obtained competitive performance and ranked 5th in both sub-tasks.

We organize the rest of the paper as follows: In **Section 2**, we provide detailed descriptions of the task and dataset. **Section 3** describes our proposed system in the CASE 2023 task 4: multimodal hate speech event detection task to automatically detect hate speech and target. In **Section 4**, we present our proposed system design with parameter settings and conduct the results and component analysis. Finally, we conclude with some future directions in **Section 5**.

2 Task and Dataset Description

2.1 Task Description

The task aims to detect hate speech in text-embedded images on social media and the internet based on the topic of the Russia-Ukraine war. Text-embedded images were extensively used, both by the Russian and Ukrainian sides, to disseminate propaganda and hate speech during the Russia-Ukraine war. In this task, organizers featured two subtasks focusing on detecting hate speech and its target. In subtask A, the objective is to detect whether a given text-embedded image is hateful or not. Subtask B aims to detect the targets of hate speech in a given hateful text-embedded image.

2.2 Dataset Description

The organizers used a benchmark dataset CrisisHateMM (Bhandari et al., 2023) to evaluate the performance of the participants' systems at the CASE 2023 shared task 4 [1] (Thapa et al., 2023) to detect hate speech in text-embedded pictures. The dataset is collected from social media platforms including Twitter, Reddit, and Facebook based on the Russia-Ukraine conflict. The dataset comprises 4486 and 2428 text-embedded images for subtask A and subtask B, respectively. Subtask A comprised 3600 train, 443 dev, and 443 test text-embedded images and Subtask B consisted of 1942 train, 244 dev, and 242 test text-embedded images. The dataset statistics of subtask A: hate speech event detection and subtask B: target detection are presented in Table 1 based on each task's labels. For subtask B, text-embedded images are annotated for community, individual and organization targets whereas subtask A is annotated for the hate and non-hate labels. Moreover, texts are extracted from the text-embedded images using OCR with the Google Vision API [2].

3 Proposed Framework

Transformers models learn the necessary information about the relationship between words effectively. We employed the pre-trained transformers model with the BiLSTM module and a training strategy to detect the hate speech of text-embedded images in a multimodal setting. The overview of our proposed transformer-based framework is delineated in Figure 1.

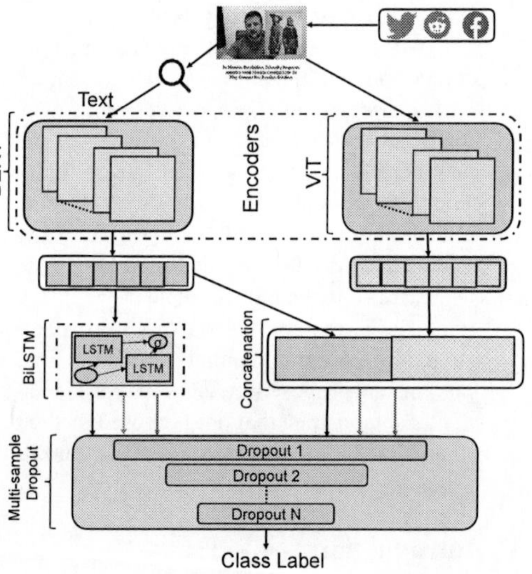

Figure 1: Overview diagram of our proposed method for multimodal hate speech detection

Given a text-embedded image, we extract the text from the image. We fed the extracted text and

[1] https://github.com/therealthapa/case2023_task4

[2] https://cloud.google.com/vision/docs/ocr

Category	Subtask A		Subtask B		
	Hate	Non-Hate	Individual	Community	Organization
Train	1,942	1,658	823	335	784
Dev	243	200	102	40	102
Test	243	200	102	42	98
Total	2,428	2,058	1,027	417	984

Table 1: The statistics of the used dataset in CASE 2023 shared task 4 across all subtasks.

text-embedded image into a language model and a vision pre-train transformer model to extract the visual-contextualized embedding features, respectively. We concatenate these feature vectors to get the multimodal unified representation of the image-text pair. Although, contextualized embedding features are fed into the BiLSTM module to learn the long-term contextual dependency that helps the model to effectively capture the hate information present in the context. A multi-sample dropout strategy is employed on top of both multimodal and BiLSTM module outputs to improve the generalization ability and robustness leading to performance enhancement. Later, we utilise an arithmetic mean fusion to get the final prediction of our proposed approach.

3.1 Transformers Model

We fine-tuned the BERT transformers model to extract the contextualized features representation of text. ViT transformers model is employed to capture the visual information in the given image.

3.1.1 BERT

BERT (Devlin et al., 2018) stands for bidirectional encoder representations from transformers, is a new method of pre-training sentence representations which achieves state-of-the-art results on many NLP tasks including question-answering, text classification, and sentence-pair regression. It is trained on a large corpus of unlabelled text which includes the entire Wikipedia (that's about 2500 million words) and a book corpus (800 million words). We take advantage of the BERT fast tokenizer and *bert-base-uncased* model with fine-tuning to learn a 768-dimensional textual feature vector of the extracted text from the text-embedded image. It is composed of 12 transformer blocks, a hidden size of 768, and 110M parameters with a vocabulary of 30K tokens in the embedding layer.

3.1.2 ViT

The vision transformer (ViT) (Dosovitskiy et al., 2020) is a transformer encoder model (BERT-like) pre-trained on a large collection of images in a self-supervised fashion. ViT split an image into patches and flatten the patches to produce lower-dimensional linear embeddings from the flattened patches. Add positional embeddings and feed the sequence as an input to a standard transformer encoder. Image patches are the sequence tokens like words. The encoder block is identical to the original transformer architecture. It is utilized ImageNet-1k, at a resolution of 224x224 pixels and fixed-size patches with a resolution of 16x16. We employ the ViT model's *facebook/dino-vitb16* checkpoint trained using the DINO method to extract the visual features of the given image.

3.2 BiLSTM Module

We employed a BiLSTM layer (Brueckner and Schulter, 2014) on top of the BERT model's textual representation that helps the model capture and enriches textual information presented in the extracted text. The BiLSTM module is strong enough in capturing long-range dependencies in sequential data that result in more informative feature representations. Multimodal hate speech detection is a text-dominant task hence BERT transformer model with BiLSTM-based effective textual representation could benefit in understanding hate information present in the text-embedded image that will lead to the improved performance of unified multimodal architecture. Here, BiLSTM can effectively learn the long-term contextual dependency from the BERT transformer model's textual representation in our approach.

3.3 Multi-sample Dropout Strategy

Different training strategies improved the performance of the transformers model. In this paper, we use a multi-sample dropout training strategy (Inoue, 2019). To improve the accuracy of the transformer-based multimodal hierarchical fusion network, we utilise the multi-sample dropout technique. Although, it improves the generalization ability and accelerates the training of base model (Inoue, 2019). We employed this technique in two stages. Firstly, we employ multi-sample dropout after the multimodal features vectors. Secondly, we fed the BiLSTM module output to the multi-sample dropout. This hierarchical fusion helps the model to learn the context effectively. In multi-sample dropouts, we duplicate the features vector of the multimodal and BiLSTM module output after the dropout layer, while sharing the weights among these duplicated fully connected layers. To obtain the final loss, we calculate the loss for each sample, and then the sample losses are leveraged using the arithmetic mean-based fusion.

Parameter	Optimal Value
Learning rate	3e-5
Max-len	128
Number of epochs	5
Batch size	8
Manual seed	42
Dropout	0.6, 0.7,0.8

Table 2: Proposed model hyperparameters settings for CASE-2023 task 4 shared task.

4 Experimentals and Evaluations

4.1 Experimental Settings

We now describe the details of our experimental settings and the hyper-parameter settings with the finetuning strategy that we have employed to design our proposed multimodal approach for the CASE 2023 shared task 4. We finetune state-of-the-art Huggingface (Wolf et al., 2019) transformer models including BERT [3] and DINO Vit [4] model for this task. We used all models as the base size in this work. We concatenate the training and development data during the model training phase. We implement our proposed method using PyTorch (Paszke et al., 2019). We used the CUDA-enabled GPU of the Google Colaboratory (Bisong and Bisong, 2019) platform and set the manual seed = 42 to generate reproducible results. We obtained the optimal parameter settings of our proposed model based on the performance of the development set which is articulated in Table 2. We use a multi-sample dropout training strategy on top of the unified representation of multimodal and multigenre tasks. To determine the optimal dropout values, we searched over the set $\{0.1, 0.2, \cdots, 0.9\}$ and found the best dropout range was 0.6 to 0.8 based on our experimental results on the development set. We used the default settings for the other parameters.

4.2 Evaluation Measures

To evaluate the performance of participants' lexical complexity prediction systems, CASE 2023 task 4 organizers used different strategies and metrics for sub-task A and sub-task B (Thapa et al., 2023). For both sub-task, standard evaluation metrics including precision, recall, F1-score and accuracy were applied to estimate the performance of a system. However, the macro-averaged F1 score is considered as the primary evaluation measure for both subtasks of this task.

4.3 Results and Analysis

In this section, we analyze the performance of our proposed CSECU-DSG system in the CASE 2023 multimodal hate speech event detection shared task. We used the full training set and validation set for training our proposed model and also the validation set for hyperparameter tuning.

The comparative performance of our proposed CSECU-DSG system on subtask A hate speech detection test data against other selected participants' systems is presented in Table 3. We have seen that our proposed method achieved a 0.8248 F1 score and 0.8262 accuracy and ranked 5th in sub-task A based on the macro-averaged F1 score. Our proposed approach surpasses the CLIP model baseline (Bhandari et al., 2023) method by 8.23% and obtains competitive performance. This validates the effectiveness of our proposed method in the multimodal hate speech detection task.

The comparative performance of our proposed CSECU-DSG system on subtask B target detection against other selected participants' systems and baseline method is presented in Table 4. In the target detection task, our method achieved a 0.6530 F1 score and a 0.6901 accuracy score. Our proposed method outperforms the baseline method by 5.82%

[3] https://huggingface.co/bert-base-uncased

[4] https://huggingface.co/facebook/dino-vitb16

Team	Recall	Precision	F1 score	Accuracy	Rank
CSECU-DSG	0.8252	0.8244	0.8248	0.8262	5th
Participants system performance on subtask A					
ARC-NLP (Sahin et al., 2023)	0.8567	0.8563	0.8565	0.8578	1st
bayesiano98 (Thapa et al., 2023)	0.8562	0.8528	0.8528	0.8233	2nd
DeepBlueAI (Thapa et al., 2023)	0.8356	0.8335	0.8342	0.8352	4th
Avanthika (Thapa et al., 2023)	0.7878	0.7881	0.7880	0.7901	7th
rabindra.nath (Thapa et al., 2023)	0.7768	0.7842	0.7788	0.7833	9th
GT (Thapa et al., 2023)	0.5219	0.5219	0.5219	0.5260	11th
Baseline (CLIP) (Bhandari et al., 2023)	-	-	0.7860	0.7980	-

Table 3: Comparative results with other selected participants and baseline on Subtask A: Hate speech detection. The teams are ranked based on the macro-averaged F1 score. Our team name is CSECU-DSG.

Team	Recall	Precision	F1 score	Accuracy	Rank
CSECU-DSG	0.6525	0.6575	0.6530	0.6901	5th
Participants system performance on subtask B					
ARC-NLP (Sahin et al., 2023)	0.7636	0.7637	0.7634	0.7934	1st
bayesiano98 (Thapa et al., 2023)	0.7330	0.7554	0.7410	0.7727	2nd
IIC_Team (Thapa et al., 2023)	0.6894	0.7105	0.6973	0.7231	3rd
DeepBlueAI (Thapa et al., 2023)	0.6462	0.6648	0.6525	0.6983	6th
Ometeotl (Thapa et al., 2023)	0.5648	0.6793	0.5677	0.6405	7th
ML_Ensemblers (Thapa et al., 2023)	0.4444	0.4888	0.4332	0.5289	9th
Baseline (CLIP) (Bhandari et al., 2023)	-	-	0.6150	0.6840	-

Table 4: Comparative results with other selected participants and baselines on Subtask B: Target detection. The teams are ranked based on the macro-averaged F1 score. Our team name is CSECU-DSG.

and is ranked 5th in this task leaderboard [5] in terms of primary evaluation measure macro-averaged F1 score. This validates the potency and applicability of our proposed method in the target detection task.

4.4 Discussion

To estimate the contribution of the BiLSTM module and multi-sample dropout training strategy in our proposed approach for multimodal hate speech event detection task, we performed the component ablation study. In this regard, we first removed the multi-sample dropout training strategy, the BiLSTM module, and both multi-sample dropout strategies at each time and repeated the experiment. The results of our ablation study are reported in Table 5. We first report our team's CSECU-DSG performance and then the other method's performance based on the macro-averaged F1 score. It shows that when removing the multi-sample dropout strategy the results decrease on average 1% and removing the BiLSTM module from the proposed method leads to a decrease in the results of 1.3% in terms

Method	Subtask A	Subtask B
CSECU-DSG	0.8248	0.6530
- MSD	0.8164	0.6462
- BiLSTM	0.8143	0.6441
- MSD+BiLSTM	0.8065	0.6207

Table 5: The ablation study of our proposed method based on the test dataset in CASE 2023 shared task 4 across all subtasks. The result is reported in terms of primary evaluation measure macro-averaged f1 score. MSD stand for multi-sample dropout.

[5] https://codalab.lisn.upsaclay.fr/competitions/13087#results

of macro-averaged F1 score. We observed 2.2% performance decreases in subtask A and 3.7% performance decreases in subtask B based on macro-averaged F1 score when we remove both the BiLSTM module and multi-sample dropout strategy at a time which deduced the contribution of the multi-sample dropout training strategy and BiLSTM module components in our model.

5 Conclusion and Future Work

In this paper, we present an approach to automatically identify hate speech in multimodal settings using fine-tuned transformers models fusion architecture. We employ a BiLSTM module on top of the language model to handle the long-term dependencies present in the context. Moreover, we use the multi-sample dropout training strategy to speed up training and get better generalization ability. Experimental results demonstrated the efficacy of our proposed transformer-based method, where the hierarchical fusion of transformer variants with the BiLSTM module and multi-sample dropout prediction helped us to obtain competitive performance and ranked 5th in both subtasks in the CASE 2023 shared task 4: multimodal hate speech event detection.

Further research will be conducted on other large transformers models with a unified architecture of two or more. However, the classes of the dataset are imbalanced, so the weighted average fusion strategy of different models may be exploiting better context for hate speech from multimodal content effectively.

References

Pinkesh Badjatiya, Shashank Gupta, Manish Gupta, and Vasudeva Varma. 2017. Deep learning for hate speech detection in tweets. In *Proceedings of the 26th international conference on World Wide Web companion*, pages 759–760.

Aashish Bhandari, Siddhant Bikram Shah, Surendrabikram Thapa, Usman Naseem, and Mehwish Nasim. 2023. Crisishatemm: Multimodal analysis of directed and undirected hate speech in text-embedded images from russia-ukraine conflict. In *Proceedings of the IEEE/CVF Conference on Computer Vision and Pattern Recognition.*

Ekaba Bisong and Ekaba Bisong. 2019. Google colaboratory. *Building machine learning and deep learning models on google cloud platform: a comprehensive guide for beginners*, pages 59–64.

Raymond Brueckner and Björn Schulter. 2014. Social Signal Classification Using Deep BLSTM Recurrent Neural Networks. In *2014 IEEE International Conference on Coustics, Speech and Signal Processing (ICASSP)*, pages 4823–4827. IEEE.

Yitao Cai, Huiyu Cai, and Xiaojun Wan. 2019. Multimodal sarcasm detection in twitter with hierarchical fusion model. In *Proceedings of the 57th annual meeting of the association for computational linguistics*, pages 2506–2515.

Anusha Chhabra and Dinesh Kumar Vishwakarma. 2023. A literature survey on multimodal and multilingual automatic hate speech identification. *Multimedia Systems*, pages 1–28.

Jacob Devlin, Ming-Wei Chang, Kenton Lee, and Kristina Toutanova. 2018. Bert: Pre-training of deep bidirectional transformers for language understanding. *arXiv preprint arXiv:1810.04805.*

Nemanja Djuric, Jing Zhou, Robin Morris, Mihajlo Grbovic, Vladan Radosavljevic, and Narayan Bhamidipati. 2015. Hate speech detection with comment embeddings. In *Proceedings of the 24th international conference on world wide web*, pages 29–30.

Alexey Dosovitskiy, Lucas Beyer, Alexander Kolesnikov, Dirk Weissenborn, Xiaohua Zhai, Thomas Unterthiner, Mostafa Dehghani, Matthias Minderer, Georg Heigold, Sylvain Gelly, et al. 2020. An image is worth 16x16 words: Transformers for image recognition at scale. *arXiv preprint arXiv:2010.11929.*

Raul Gomez, Jaume Gibert, Lluis Gomez, and Dimosthenis Karatzas. 2020. Exploring hate speech detection in multimodal publications. In *Proceedings of the IEEE/CVF winter conference on applications of computer vision*, pages 1470–1478.

Hiroshi Inoue. 2019. Multi-sample dropout for accelerated training and better generalization. *arXiv preprint arXiv:1905.09788.*

Douwe Kiela, Hamed Firooz, Aravind Mohan, Vedanuj Goswami, Amanpreet Singh, Pratik Ringshia, and Davide Testuggine. 2020. The hateful memes challenge: Detecting hate speech in multimodal memes. *Advances in neural information processing systems*, 33:2611–2624.

Phillip Lippe, Nithin Holla, Shantanu Chandra, Santhosh Rajamanickam, Georgios Antoniou, Ekaterina Shutova, and Helen Yannakoudakis. 2020. A multimodal framework for the detection of hateful memes. *arXiv preprint arXiv:2012.12871.*

Anil Singh Parihar, Surendrabikram Thapa, and Sushruti Mishra. 2021. Hate speech detection using natural language processing: Applications and challenges. In *2021 5th International Conference on Trends in Electronics and Informatics (ICOEI)*, pages 1302–1308. IEEE.

Adam Paszke, Sam Gross, Francisco Massa, Adam Lerer, James Bradbury, Gregory Chanan, Trevor Killeen, Zeming Lin, Natalia Gimelshein, Luca Antiga, et al. 2019. Pytorch: An imperative style, high-performance deep learning library. *Advances in neural information processing systems*, 32.

Benet Oriol Sabat, Cristian Canton Ferrer, and Xavier Giro-i Nieto. 2019. Hate speech in pixels: Detection of offensive memes towards automatic moderation. *arXiv preprint arXiv:1910.02334*.

Umitcan Sahin, Izzet Emre Kucukkaya, Oguzhan Ozcelik, and Cagri Toraman. 2023. Arc-nlp at multimodal hate speech event detection 2023: Multimodal methods boosted by ensemble learning, syntactical and entity features. *arXiv preprint arXiv:2307.13829*.

Surendrabikram Thapa, Farhan Ahmad Jafri, Ali Hürriyetoğlu, Francielle Vargas, Roy Ka-Wei Lee, and Usman Naseem. 2023. Multimodal hate speech event detection - shared task 4, case 2023. In *Proceedings of the 6th Workshop on Challenges and Applications of Automated Extraction of Socio-political Events from Text (CASE)*.

Surendrabikram Thapa, Aditya Shah, Farhan Ahmad Jafri, Usman Naseem, and Imran Razzak. 2022. A multi-modal dataset for hate speech detection on social media: Case-study of russia-ukraine conflict. In *CASE 2022-5th Workshop on Challenges and Applications of Automated Extraction of Socio-Political Events from Text, Proceedings of the Workshop*. Association for Computational Linguistics.

Riza Velioglu and Jewgeni Rose. 2020. Detecting hate speech in memes using multimodal deep learning approaches: Prize-winning solution to hateful memes challenge. *arXiv preprint arXiv:2012.12975*.

Hajime Watanabe, Mondher Bouazizi, and Tomoaki Ohtsuki. 2018. Hate speech on twitter: A pragmatic approach to collect hateful and offensive expressions and perform hate speech detection. *IEEE access*, 6:13825–13835.

Thomas Wolf, Lysandre Debut, Victor Sanh, Julien Chaumond, Clement Delangue, Anthony Moi, Pierric Cistac, Tim Rault, Rémi Louf, Morgan Funtowicz, et al. 2019. HuggingFace's Transformers: State-of-the-art Natural Language Processing. *arXiv preprint arXiv:1910.03771*.

Chuanpeng Yang, Fuqing Zhu, Guihua Liu, Jizhong Han, and Songlin Hu. 2022. Multimodal hate speech detection via cross-domain knowledge transfer. In *Proceedings of the 30th ACM International Conference on Multimedia*, pages 4505–4514.

Jiawen Zhu, Roy Ka-Wei Lee, and Wen Haw Chong. 2022. Multimodal zero-shot hateful meme detection. In *Proceedings of the 14th ACM Web Science Conference 2022*, pages 382–389.

CSECU-DSG @ Causal News Corpus 2023: Leveraging RoBERTa and DeBERTa Transformer Model with Contrastive Learning for Causal Event Classification

Md. Akram Hossain, Abdul Aziz, and Abu Nowshed Chy
Department of Computer Science and Engineering
University of Chittagong, Chattogram-4331, Bangladesh
{akram.hossain.cse.cu, aziz.abdul.cu}@gmail.com,
and nowshed@cu.ac.bd

Abstract

Cause-effect relationships play a crucial role in human cognition, and distilling cause-effect relations from text helps in ameliorating causal networks for predictive tasks including natural language-based financial forecasting, text summarization, and question-answering. However, the lack of syntactic clues, the ambivalent semantic meaning of words, and complex sentence structures make it one of the challenging tasks in NLP. To address these challenges, CASE-2023 introduced a shared task 3 with two subtasks focusing on event causality identification with causal news corpus. In this paper, we demonstrate our participant systems for this task. We leverage two transformers models including DeBERTa and Twitter-RoBERTa along with the weighted average fusion technique to tackle the challenges of subtask 1 where we need to identify whether a text belongs to either causal or not. For subtask 2 where we need to identify the cause, effect, and signal tokens from the text, we proposed a unified neural network of DeBERTa and DistilRoBERTa transformer variants with contrastive learning techniques. The experimental results showed that our proposed method achieved competitive performance among the participants' systems and achieved 4th and 3rd rank in subtasks 1 and 2 respectively.

1 Introduction

A causal relation is a semantic relationship between two arguments known as cause and effect, where the occurrence of one (cause argument) incurs the occurrence of the other (effect argument). Causal relation extraction from text is also known as the study of causality extraction (CE) which gain attention in different domains including Biomedical, media, emergency management (Bui et al., 2010; Balashankar et al., 2019; Qiu et al., 2017), etc. Such causal relation plays an important role in various contemporary NLP tasks including question-answering (Q/A), product recommendation based on user comments, and other textual entailments (Yu et al., 2022; Yang et al., 2022). However, the implicit causal relationship between sentences, numerical connectives impact, and ambivalent semantic meaning of the text make CE one of the most challenging tasks in NLP.

Subtask 1	
Sentence	Label
He said he was about 100 metres away when he witnessed the attack.	0
It has organised a political convention to mobilise support to secular forces.	1
Subtask 2	
Text: In 2009, riots broke out in the capital, Urumqui, and in their wake, mass arrests were made and many Uyghurs were imprisoned.	
Label: O O B-C I-C I-C I-C I-C I-C O O B-S I-S I-S B-E I-E I-E I-E I-E I-E I-E I-E	

Table 1: Example of sub-task 1 and subtask 2 where subtask 2 labels are converted into BIO format, C = Cause, E = Effect, and S = Signal.

To address these challenges of event causality identification in texts, Tan et al. (2023) introduced a shared task 3 at the CASE-2023 workshop. The task is composed of two subtasks including a causal event classification task (subtask 1) and a cause-effect-signal span detection task (subtask 2). In subtask 1, participants ask to build an automatic system to classify a given text whether it contains a causal event meaning or not. Subtask 2 introduce different challenges for participant it aims to identify the cause, effect, and signal spans of that given text. To demonstrate a clear view of the task definition, we articulate a few examples from Subtask 1 and Subtask 2 in Table 1.

Prior work on event causality identification has

Proceedings of the 6th Workshop on Challenges and Applications of Automated Extraction of Socio-political Events from Text, pages 108–112, Varna, Bulgaria, Sep 7, 2023.
https://doi.org/10.26615/978-954-452-089-2_015

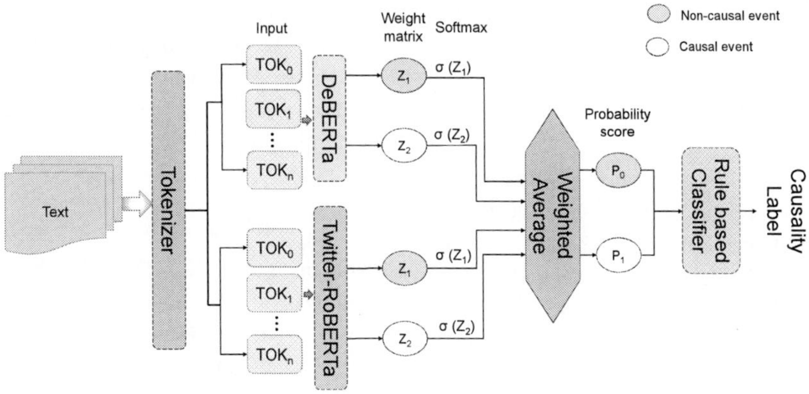

Figure 1: Our proposed model for subtask 1.

mostly employed semi-supervised methods (Mirza, 2014) based on features (e.g. psycho-linguistic, syntactic, etc.) or supervised methods (Gordeev et al., 2020; Ionescu et al., 2020) based on transformers model (e.g. BERT, RoBERTa, etc.). Though, transformer-based methods obtained more competitive results (Ionescu et al., 2020; Mariko et al., 2022), but those methods are either well performed for subtask 1 or subtask 2 problems but limited to well performed on both problems at the same time. In order to overcome this limitation, we proposed generalized architecture for both types of tasks. Where we fuse two different transformers models including DeBERTa and Twitter RoBERTa or DistilRoBERTa with different fusion techniques. We utilize the prediction level late fusion technique for subtask 1 whereas, for subtask 2 we use the feature level early fusion technique. Although these switching in place of transformers and fusion techniques help us to achieve competitive results in the competition. Moreover, we utilized unsupervised contrastive learning to address the spans section more precisely for subtask 2.

Accordingly, the remaining sections of the paper are organized as follows: Section 2 introduces our proposed system in CASE 2023 for automatically identifying causal events from given text, while Section 3 presents our system design, parameter settings, and primary evaluation measures. Additionally, in this section, we also discuss our results and performance analysis. Finally, we conclude with some future directions in Section 4.

2 Proposed Method

In this section, we describe our proposed approach for CASE 2023 task 3, subtask 1 and subtask 2.

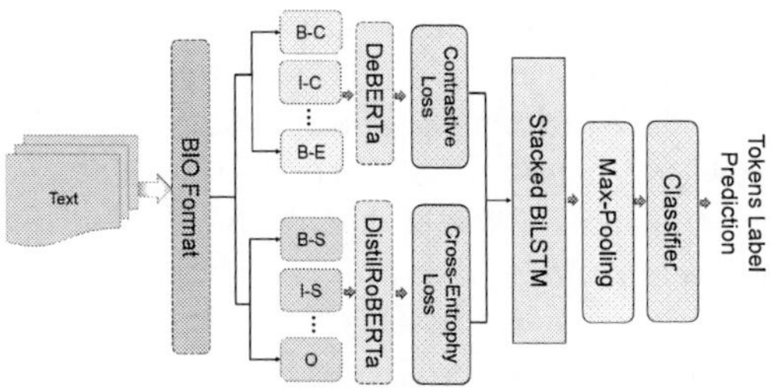

Figure 2: Our proposed model for subtask 2.

The overview of our proposed framework for subtask 1 is depicted in Figure 1. To extract the diverse contextual features from the text, we employ two transformer models including DeBERTa (He et al., 2021a) and one of RoBERTa variants Twitter_RoBERTa (Barbieri et al., 2020). Later, a linear feed-forward layer is utilized in each model to estimate the probability score of each class. Finally, for the effective fusion of the scores, we take the weighted arithmetic mean of the prediction scores of these models. A class that contains the highest probability scores is considered the final label.

On the other hand for subtask 2 we utilized two different transformer models DeBERTa and DistilRoBERTa independently to exploit cause-effect and signal span features respectively. Then we concatenate both transformers model features and feed to a stacked BiLSTM network to distill long-term relations among the tokens. Followed by the BiLSTM network we incorporate a max-pooling and classifier layer to predict tokens label. To improve system performance we calculate the contrastive loss for cause-effect token classification whereas we utilized cross-entropy loss for signal token classification since it may or may not contain in text.

However, Figure 2 illustrates our proposed method for subtask 2.

2.1 Transformer Model

DeBERTa[1] (He et al., 2021b) stands for decoding-enhanced BERT with disentangled attention. It improves the BERT and RoBERTa models using disentangled attention mechanism and enhanced mask decoder. We used the enhanced version of the DeBERTa model named DeBERTaV3 (He et al., 2021a). To improve the DeBERTa model, the DeBERTaV3 model used ELECTRA style pre-training where replacing mask language modeling (MLM) with the replaced token detection (RTD). It also used the gradient-disentangled embedding sharing (GDES) method to share the embeddings with the discriminator. These significantly improved the performance of the DeBERTa model in downstream tasks. Motivated by this, we employ Huggingfaces' (Wolf et al., 2019) implementation of *microsoft/deberta-v3-base* checkpoint to extract the feature representations of the sentence.

We also employ the Twitter_RoBERTa[2] (Barbieri et al., 2020), a RoBERTa-base model trained on 58M tweets, described and evaluated in the TweetEval benchmark. In our proposed framework, we use its to capture the diverse semantic features from short input text effectively. Moreover, in subtask 2 we used another transformer model DistilRoBERTa to extract word-based contextual representation to learn low-level features from the text. However, our experiments finds that DistilRoBERTa performed well in subtask 2 compare with Twitter RoBERTa. We utilize DistilRoBERTa base[3] (Sanh et al., 2019) model which is finetuned on conell-03 dataset.

2.2 BiLSTM

BiLSTM (Brueckner and Schulter, 2014) stands for bidirectional long short-term memory which is an extended version of recurrent neural network. BiLSTM employs two LSTM modules to distill inter and intra-relational structure from text using forward and backward feature learning strategy. In my proposed method, we employ the BiLSTM module with fused transformer features to overcome the shortfall of the transformer modules and extract the long-term causal relations from the text.

Unsupervised contrastive learning achieve excellent success on different nlp tasks in recent times (Wang and Liu, 2021). We average each cause or effect span logit's logarithmic probability score using $log(Softmax(x))$ to calculate the loss.

2.3 Fusion Techniques

To enhance the performance of individual models or address model limitations, fusion is an effective strategy. In our proposed framework, we also employ two different types of fusion strategies for the proposed method of subtask 1 and subtask 2. For subtask 1, we employ late fusion, i.e. prediction level fusion, whereas in subtask 2 we employ early fusion strategy, i.e. feature level fusion. We utilized a weighted average of DeBERTa and Twitter-RoBERTa model predictions for late fusion where weights were 0.6 and 0.4 respectively.

3 Experiment and Evaluation

In this section, we now describe the dataset and hyper-parameters settings with the finetuning strategy that we have employed to design our proposed system for the CASE 2023 shared task 3.

3.1 Dataset Description

The organizers used the Causal News Corpus(CNC) (Tan et al., 2022b), a benchmark dataset published in LREC-2022 to evaluate the performance of the participants' systems at the CASE 2023 event causality shared task. The dataset for subtask 1 is same as CASE 2022 (Tan et al., 2022a) but this time subtask 2 dataset is enlarged as compared to the previous version, the current version extended 160 to 1981 sentences, 183 to 2754 causal relations in total.

3.2 Experimental Setting

We now describe the details of our experimental settings and the hyper-parameter settings with the fine-tuning strategy that we have employed to design our proposed CSECU-DSG system for the CASE 2023 event causality identification shared task. In our CSECU-DSG system, we utilize three state-of-the-art Huggingface transformer models with fine-tuning, including DeBERTa, Twitter-RoBERTa,and DistilRoBERTa. We use simple-transformers API (Rajapakse, 2019) to implement our proposed system for subtask 1. We use the train and development data during the model training phase. We used the CUDA-enabled GPU and

[1]https://huggingface.co/microsoft/deberta-v3-base

[2]https://huggingface.co/cardiffnlp/twitter-roberta-base-sentiment

[3]https://huggingface.co/philschmid/distilroberta-base-ner-conll2003

Subtask 1				
Team Name	F1 Score	Accuracy	Recall	Preision
DeepBlueAI (1)	0.8466	0.8466	0.8613	0.8324
rpatel12 (2)	0.8436	0.8409	0.8728	0.8162
timos (3)	0.8375	0.8324	0.8786	0.8000
CSECU-DSG (4)	0.8268	0.8239	0.8555	0.8000
elhammohammadi (5)	0.8245	0.8125	0.8960	0.7635
Subtask 2				
timos (1)	0.7279	-	0.6398	0.8442
tanfiona (2)	0.5971	-	0.5918	0.6025
CSECU-DSG (3)	0.3796	-	0.3612	0.4000

Table 2: Comparative performance with other selected participants. For subtasks 1 and 2 F1 scores denote binary and macro F1 scores, respectively.

set the manual seed = 4 to generate reproducible results. We obtained the optimal parameter settings of our proposed model based on the performance of the development set and we used the default settings for the other parameters. In Subtask 2, we utilized augmented data provided by the organizer to train our model. The learning rate was 3e-05, batch size = 8, and we train the model for 10 epochs. The primary evaluation measure for both subtasks was the F1 score.

Method	F1 Score	Accuracy	Recall	Preision
CSECU-DSG	.8588	.8588	.8919	.8549
– Twitter-RoBERTa	.8470	.8470	.8756	.8481
– DeBERTa	.8538	.8538	.8972	.8469

Table 3: Individual component performance of our proposed method based on the development dataset of subtask 1.

3.3 Result and Analysis

The comparative results of our proposed CSECU-DSG system along with other top-performing systems (Tan et al., 2023) in subtasks 1 and 2 are presented in Table 2. Following the benchmark of CASE-2023 event causality identification subtask 1, participants' systems are ranked based on the primary evaluation metric F1 score where we see that our CSECU-DSG ranked 4th and 3rd in subtasks 1 and 2 respectively.

However, in subtask 1 our proposed system performance is relatively closer to top-performing systems which deduces the effectiveness of our system for causal event identification. On the other hand in subtask 2, though our system ranked well, still there are some limitations such that our model can predict only a single label for a single token whereas it may be a multi-labeled (cause or effect and signal) token which may hamper the system performance. In Table 3, we provide the individual component performance of our CSECU-DSG model of subtask 1. Where we can observe that the DeBERTa model is relatively well performed than the Twitter-RoBERTa which motivates us to employ a different transformer model in place of it for subtask 2.

4 Conclusion and Future Work

In this paper, we present two approaches to identifying causal events and extraction of causal relations from text. For the identification task, we proposed a unified neural network of two finetuned transformer models including DeBERTa and TwitterRoBERTa with a late-fusion technique. Similarly, for the extraction task, we utilize two transformers models but this time we incorporate the DistilRoBERTa model instead of the TwitterRoBERTa. Here, we design our model differently, we use DeBERTa with contrastive learning to train the cause-effect spans of text whereas DistilRoBERTa is used to train the signal span. Then we utilized an early fusion technique and pass the fused features to max-pooling and the final classifier label to get the predictions.

In the future, we intend to explore the challenges of nested causality extraction task where we will design a model to predict the multi-label of a single token at a time.

References

Ananth Balashankar, Sunandan Chakraborty, Samuel Fraiberger, and Lakshminarayanan Subramanian. 2019. Identifying predictive causal factors from news streams. In *Proceedings of the 2019 Conference on Empirical Methods in Natural Language Processing and the 9th International Joint Conference on Natural Language Processing (EMNLP-IJCNLP)*, pages 2338–2348.

Francesco Barbieri, Jose Camacho-Collados, Luis Espinosa Anke, and Leonardo Neves. 2020. Tweeteval: Unified benchmark and comparative evaluation for tweet classification. In *Findings of the Association for Computational Linguistics: EMNLP 2020*, pages 1644–1650.

Raymond Brueckner and Björn Schulter. 2014. Social signal classification using deep blstm recurrent neural networks. In *2014 IEEE international conference on acoustics, speech and signal processing (ICASSP)*, pages 4823–4827. IEEE.

Quoc-Chinh Bui, Breanndán Ó Nualláin, Charles A Boucher, and Peter Sloot. 2010. Extracting causal relations on hiv drug resistance from literature. *BMC bioinformatics*, 11(1):1–11.

Denis Gordeev, Adis Davletov, Alexey Rey, and Nikolay Arefyev. 2020. Liori at the fincausal 2020 shared task. In *Proceedings of the 1st Joint Workshop on Financial Narrative Processing and MultiLing Financial Summarisation*, pages 45–49.

Pengcheng He, Jianfeng Gao, and Weizhu Chen. 2021a. Debertav3: Improving deberta using electra-style pretraining with gradient-disentangled embedding sharing.

Pengcheng He, Xiaodong Liu, Jianfeng Gao, and Weizhu Chen. 2021b. Deberta: Decoding-enhanced bert with disentangled attention. In *International Conference on Learning Representations*.

Marius Ionescu, Andrei-Marius Avram, George-Andrei Dima, Dumitru-Clementin Cercel, and Mihai Dascalu. 2020. Upb at fincausal-2020, tasks 1 & 2: Causality analysis in financial documents using pretrained language models. In *Proceedings of the 1st Joint Workshop on Financial Narrative Processing and MultiLing Financial Summarisation*, pages 55–59.

Dominique Mariko, Hanna Abi Akl, Kim Trottier, and Mahmoud El-Haj. 2022. The financial causality extraction shared task (fincausal 2022). In *Proceedings of the 4th Financial Narrative Processing Workshop@ LREC2022*, pages 105–107.

Paramita Mirza. 2014. Extracting temporal and causal relations between events. In *Proceedings of the ACL 2014 Student Research Workshop*, pages 10–17.

Jiangnan Qiu, Liwei Xu, Jie Zhai, and Ling Luo. 2017. Extracting causal relations from emergency cases based on conditional random fields. *Procedia computer science*, 112:1623–1632.

TC Rajapakse. 2019. Simple transformers. *URL: https://simpletransformers. ai/[accessed 2022-08-25]*.

Victor Sanh, Lysandre Debut, Julien Chaumond, and Thomas Wolf. 2019. Distilbert, a distilled version of bert: smaller, faster, cheaper and lighter. *ArXiv*, abs/1910.01108.

Fiona Anting Tan, Hansi Hettiarachchi, Ali Hürriyetoğlu, Tommaso Caselli, Onur Uca, Farhana Ferdousi Liza, and Nelleke Oostdijk. 2022a. Event causality identification with causal news corpus - shared task 3, CASE 2022. In *Proceedings of the 5th Workshop on Challenges and Applications of Automated Extraction of Socio-political Events from Text (CASE)*, pages 195–208, Abu Dhabi, United Arab Emirates (Hybrid). Association for Computational Linguistics.

Fiona Anting Tan, Hansi Hettiarachchi, Ali Hürriyetoğlu, Onur Uca, Farhana Ferdousi Liza, and Nelleke Oostdijk. 2023. Event causality identification with causal news corpus - shared task 3, CASE 2023. In *Proceedings of the 6th Workshop on Challenges and Applications of Automated Extraction of Socio-political Events from Text (CASE)*. Association for Computational Linguistics.

Fiona Anting Tan, Ali Hürriyetoğlu, Tommaso Caselli, Nelleke Oostdijk, Tadashi Nomoto, Hansi Hettiarachchi, Iqra Ameer, Onur Uca, Farhana Ferdousi Liza, and Tiancheng Hu. 2022b. The causal news corpus: Annotating causal relations in event sentences from news. In *Proceedings of the Thirteenth Language Resources and Evaluation Conference*, pages 2298–2310, Marseille, France. European Language Resources Association.

Feng Wang and Huaping Liu. 2021. Understanding the behaviour of contrastive loss. In *Proceedings of the IEEE/CVF conference on computer vision and pattern recognition*, pages 2495–2504.

Thomas Wolf, Lysandre Debut, Victor Sanh, Julien Chaumond, Clement Delangue, Anthony Moi, Pierric Cistac, Tim Rault, Rémi Louf, Morgan Funtowicz, et al. 2019. HuggingFace's Transformers: State-of-the-art Natural Language Processing. *arXiv preprint arXiv:1910.03771*.

Jie Yang, Soyeon Caren Han, and Josiah Poon. 2022. A survey on extraction of causal relations from natural language text. *Knowledge and Information Systems*, pages 1–26.

Xiaoxiao Yu, Xinzhi Wang, Xiangfeng Luo, and Jianqi Gao. 2022. Multi-scale event causality extraction via simultaneous knowledge-attention and convolutional neural network. *Expert Systems*, 39(5):e12952.

NEXT: An Event Schema Extension Approach for Closed-Domain Event Extraction Models

Elena Tuparova[1,2], **Petar Ivanov**[1], **Andrey Tagarev**[1], **Svetla Boytcheva**[1,2], **Ivan Koychev**[2]
[1]*Ontotext AD, Bulgaria*
[2]*Faculty of Mathematics and Informatics, Sofia University, Bulgaria*
elena.tuparova@ontotext.com, petar.ivanov@ontotext.com,
andrey.tagarev@ontotext.com, svetla.boytcheva@ontotext.com,
koychev@fmi.uni-sofia.bg

Abstract

Event extraction from textual data is an NLP research task relevant to a plethora of domains. Most approaches aim to recognize events from a predefined event schema, consisting of event types and their corresponding arguments. For domains such as disinformation, where new topics frequently emerge, there is a need to adapt such a fixed schema of events to accommodate new types of events. We present NEXT (New Event eXTraction) - a resource-sparse approach to extend a close-domain model to novel event types, that requires a very small number of annotated samples for fine-tuning performed on a single GPU. Furthermore, our results suggest that this approach is suitable not only for the extraction of new event types but also for the recognition of existing event types, as the use of this approach on a new dataset leads to improved recall for all existing events while retaining precision.

1 Introduction

Event extraction from text is a research task with applications in a wide range of domains (Liu et al., 2021), including finance (Sheng et al., 2021a), social (Ritter et al., 2012; Kunneman and Van Den Bosch, 2016), biomedical (Wei et al., 2020) and security (Tanev et al., 2008).

The goal of the event extraction task is to determine the event type, extract the trigger - the most relevant word to the event, as well as any event arguments - other words and phrases relevant to the event (Liu et al., 2021). This is often approached as a closed-domain problem where the model aims to detect events from a predefined event schema consisting of a fixed set of event types and their corresponding argument types (Sheng et al., 2021b). In contrast, when the set of event types is not fixed or is not completely known at the onset, an open-domain approach is more suitable (Liu et al., 2019).

We explore the task of event extraction within the field of fake news and disinformation as a closed-domain problem. Nonetheless, the highly dynamic nature of the field implies that a methodology for easy extension of an existing closed domain event extraction approach to new event types is necessary. Ideally, such methodology would perform well with a small number of annotated samples, as producing a large annotated dataset for each newly emerging event type would be a very long and expensive process.

In this paper, we present a work-in-progress methodology which satisfies the requirements mentioned above. We select an existing model and extend it for a novel event type identified in fake news debunks with minimal resources when it comes to annotated data. We present how we define and annotate a new event, followed by how we fine-tune an existing model. Next, we provide a detailed analysis of how well the model learns the new event type, as well as how well it retains the ability to predict the event types for which it was previously trained.

2 Related Work

Event extraction is a widely studied topic and many different approaches towards it exist. Li et al. (2022) identify two main paradigms to solving the event extraction task - the pipeline paradigm, where event type, trigger and argument classification are done in sequence (Zhao et al., 2018; Chen et al., 2015; Li et al., 2020), and the joint paradigm, where event and arguments are classified simultaneously (Sheng et al., 2021b; Wadden et al., 2019; Yang et al., 2019). The latter paradigm prevents error propagation from one classification sub-task to the next. Other notable approaches to event extraction are as a classification task (Zhao et al., 2018; Chen et al., 2015), question answering task (or machine reading comprehension task) (Li et al., 2020; Zhou et al., 2021; Lu et al., 2023), sequence labelling task (Sheng et al., 2021b; Wadden et al., 2019) or sequence-to-structure generation task (Lu

Proceedings of the 6th Workshop on Challenges and Applications of Automated Extraction of Socio-political Events from Text, pages 113–123, Varna, Bulgaria, Sep 7, 2023.
https://doi.org/10.26615/978-954-452-089-2_016

et al., 2021). Another interesting approach to the event detection task is the presented in Peng et al. (2023) reinforcement learning one.

Lu et al. (2021) point out that most event extraction methods, among them pipeline and joint paradigm approaches, apply a decomposition strategy where event extraction sub-tasks are solved independently and their results are then combined to predict the whole event entity. This strategy has some drawbacks, such as the need for annotations for different sub-tasks and the difficulty of composing an optimal architecture for different sub-tasks. Lu et al. (2021) addresses both of these by modelling all sub-tasks in a uniform sequence-to-structure generative model called Text2Event, which extracts events from a text in an end-to-end manner. Another advantage of the model is being able to easily transfer to new event types.

In our study we aim to find a transferable low-resource solution to event extraction, such that it adapts well to new corpora and new event types with small amounts of annotated data and can be run on a single GPU. While there are other approaches to event extraction with little annotated data such as semi-supervised (Zhou et al., 2021; Huang and Ji, 2020), few-shot (Lai et al., 2020; Deng et al., 2020) and zero-shot (Huang et al., 2018; Lyu et al., 2021; Yue et al., 2023) learning, we chose the Text2Event model for its reported high performance in both supervised and transfer learning settings. For these purposes we extend the Text2Event model (Lu et al., 2021) with a novel event type by fine-tuning it on a small annotated sample set and then evaluate how well the model retains its performance on its original event types on a novel dataset of fake news debunks.

3 Data

3.1 Exploratory data analysis

For the purposes of the present research we work with a database of fake news debunks. We have extracted a total of 78,246 short documents in different languages, where each document is a fact-checked claim. Most claims are one to two sentences in length but can go up to a few paragraphs. We used SpaCy[1] to filter claims in other languages, resulting in 42,555 claims in English. Additionally, we split these claims into 54,280 individual sentences, using a sentence tokenizer from NLTK[2].

Table 1: Results from running the Text2Event dyiepp_ace2005_en_t_large pre-trained model on our datasets of whole claims and individual sentences

	Whole claims	**Sentences**
No event	32,967	43,259
At least one event	9,588	11,021
Single event	6,509	8,602
Multiple events	3,079	2,419
All documents	**42,555**	**54,280**

As a first step, we want to know what event types from widely used taxonomies can be recognized in this data, as it has no labels regarding events. To achieve this we ran the dyiepp_ace2005_en_t_large version of Text2Event[3] (which comes pre-trained on the ACE 2005 dataset[4]) on our dataset of claims and also on the dataset of individual sentences from claims. We aim to find out what events from the ACE 2005 taxonomy are present and in how many documents[5]. The number of documents with recognized events is presented in Table 1. In both settings in only around one-fifth of the documents, there is at least one recognized event.

Figure 1 shows the numbers of documents containing predictions for the top 10 most recognized event types, using whole claims and sentences as input respectively.

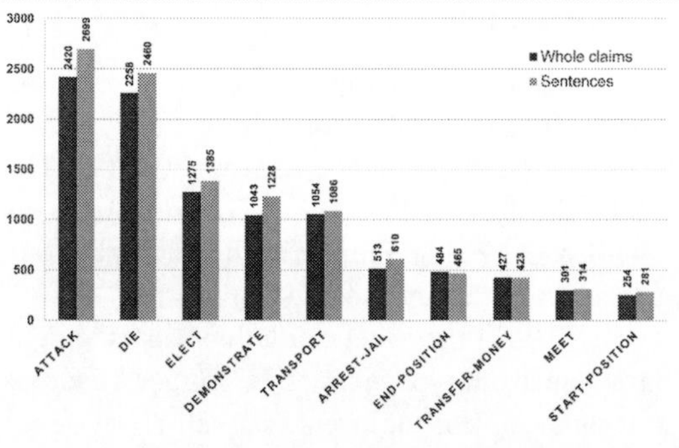

Figure 1: Number of documents containing predictions for the top 10 most recognized event types

[1] https://spacy.io/

[2] https://www.nltk.org/api/nltk.tokenize.html

[3] https://github.com/luyaojie/Text2Event

[4] https://catalog.ldc.upenn.edu/LDC2006T06

[5] When we write a document, we refer to an entity in the dataset, i.e. either a whole claim or a sentence, depending on the dataset.

3.2 New event type definition and annotated dataset creation

As the domain of our dataset is fake news and disinformation we define a new "Cure-Claim" event type which is of relevance to this particular area. A Cure-Claim event can be described as the act of stating whether something is a cure for a given medical condition or disease. We extracted 637 Cure-Claim candidate samples by selecting claims containing likely triggers (e.g. "cure", "treat", "heal"). Next, we defined the following seven arguments of the Cure-Claim event (step "Define new event annotation rules" on Figure 2):

- `Source` makes the claim;
- `Cure` is the remedy;
- `Condition` is what is treated by the cure;
- `Patient` is helped by the cure;
- `CureCreator` created the cure;
- `CureAdministrator` applies the cure.

An example of a document, mentioning the Cure-Claim event, is the following:

> "*Multiple posts shared repeatedly on Facebook* claim that *drinking tea made with pepper stems* is effective in preventing or ***curing*** *Covid-19*. The claim is false; the Association of Korean Medicine said there is no scientific evidence to support the claim."

Here, the first sentence is the event extent. ***Curing*** is the event trigger, and *"Multiple posts shared repeatedly on Facebook"*, *"drinking tea made with pepper stems"* and *"Covid-19"* are event arguments, respectively `Source`, `Cure` and `Condition`.

Due to the limited resources for annotation that we had, we selected 65 of these claims (around 10%) for manual annotation. Based on the official ACE event guidelines[6], we developed extensive annotator guidelines specifically for annotating Cure-Claim events. Following this, each document was annotated by three independent annotators, where the agreement between the majority was taken as final annotations. The resulting dataset contains 65 documents, of which 54 (83%) contain a Cure-Claim event. After performing sentence segmentation we obtain 74 sentences, of which again 54 (73%) contain a Cure-Claim event.

[6] `https://shorturl.at/DEFV4`

	ACE 2005	CCD
Documents	599	65
Sentences	16,372	74
Triggers	5,272	54
Arguments	9,612	147
Avg. no. triggers per event type	159.75	54
Med. no. triggers per event type	<100	54
Avg. no. sentences per document	27.33	1.14

Table 2: Comparison between ACE 2005 and novel Cure-Claim event dataset (CCD)

Comparison of statistics for the ACE 2005 dataset (as reported in Yang and Mitchell (2016)) and our annotated dataset for the Cure-Claim event are presented in Table 2.

3.3 Finding *k* for *k*-shot learning

We are interested in whether fewer than 74 annotated sentences would be sufficient to fine-tune the model for a new event type. To explore this, we use four different data splits of the type X/Y, where X is the percentage of training documents and Y is the percentage of test documents out of our annotated dataset. The data splits in question are 20/80, 40/60, 60/40 and 80/20.

4 Model

4.1 Text2Event overview

Text2Event (Lu et al., 2021) is a sequence-to-structure generative model that uses a transformer-based encoder-decoder architecture (Vaswani et al., 2017) to generate whole event structures from text in an end-to-end manner. The model is trained on the ACE 2005 and ERE datasets for English documents.

Text2Event is shown to perform well in transfer learning. The authors demonstrate fine-tuning on new event types on a separate subset of the same corpus. In contrast, we take the model pre-trained for the existing 33 event types on the whole ACE 2005 English dataset and fine-tune it for a new event type on a new corpus with different statistics from ACE 2005 (such as document length).

Text2Event can be trained or fine-tuned using substructure learning - the model learns separate substructures such as "(type, trigger words)" and "(role, argument words)", full structure learning - the whole event structure is learned at once, or curriculum learning, which combines the two.

4.2 Fine-tuning approach

We fine-tune the dyiepp_ace2005_en_t_large model which is pre-trained on the whole ACE 2005 English dataset on one NVIDIA RTX A5000 GPU.

We forgo substructure learning and use full structure learning only to fine-tune the model on the new event type. We use a learning rate of 1e-4 and a batch size of 16.

Given the small number of annotated training samples we use 5-fold cross-validation and compare the mean results of the models fine-tuned for different numbers of epochs (30, 100, 300 and 500) and on different train/test dataset splits (20/80, 40/60, 60/40 and 80/20).

Figure 2 illustrates our approach to annotated dataset creation and to using this dataset for fine-tuning the model.

5 Evaluation

5.1 Cross-validation experiments

We compare the performance of the fine-tuned models using precision, recall and F1-score on three subtasks: event type classification, trigger classification and argument classification. Definitions of true/false positives/negatives for trigger and argument classification are provided in the Appendix.

Table 3 contains the mean results from our cross-validation experiments. We first fine-tuned a model for 30 epochs which scored 0 on all metrics across all data splits. We then increased the number of fine-tuning epochs to 100 and more.

We first observe that when fine-tuned for larger number of epochs both event and trigger classification require as little as 12 samples to achieve the same level of precision as with four times as many samples. Recall, however, is poorer with fewer samples and improves significantly as the train set size increases. With 60 annotated samples the model learns to retrieve over 90% of the annotated Cure-Claim events.

Next, we examine the results for argument classification. We report separately scores for the cases when Cure-Claim events are predicted with the correct trigger (Correct-Trig-Arg-C columns) and when Cure-Claim events are predicted but with a wrong trigger (Wrong-Trig-Arg-C columns). Overall, both precision and recall tend to improve as the train set size increases, although drops in performance for the larger train set sizes are observed.

Compared to event type and trigger classification argument classification requires larger number of annotated training to achieve high precision, recall and F1 scores.

Standard deviations of the reported scores for Event-C, Trig-C and Correct-Trig-Arg-C range from 0.006 to 0.15 with only one outlier of 0.48. For Wrong-Trig-Arg-C the standard deviations range from 0.06 to 0.48, which could be due to this group being fairly smaller than the rest.

In addition to these results, in Figures 3 and 4 we also compare the number of additional argument classification mistakes from either false negative or false positive trigger classification cases. In the former case an event is annotated but not predicted, so all annotated arguments are counted as false negatives (Figure 3). In the latter case no event is annotated but one is predicted, so all predicted arguments are counted as false positives (Figure 4). We observe that as the train set size increases and the event classification precision and recall improve, the number of false positive or negative event predictions drops and so do consequently the corresponding false positive or negative argument predictions.

For all event classification subtasks the performance of the fine-tuned models increases with increase of the epoch count - the best results are generally reported for models fine-tuned for 500 epochs. Also, in most cases a bigger train set leads to better results. The biggest improvement in performance with increasing the training set size is observed for the models fine-tuned for 100 epochs. The models fine-tuned for 30 epochs output no significant results. All other models perform similarly when fine-tuned on the largest training set.

5.2 Cure-Claim prediction precision on broader dataset

We next fine-tuned the baseline model on the whole annotated dataset for the Cure-Claim event for 100 and 500 epochs. We evaluate the performance of the models on 2 broader datasets - the full dataset and a filtered subset with Cure-Claim candidate documents (10 times larger than our annotated dataset). For each dataset we manually evaluate 60 samples per model - half predicted only by that model and half predicted by both models. Comparing the two models by precision on those samples and by number of predictions made allows us to estimate whether performance worsens with more epochs (step "Estimate overfitting on new event type" in Figure 2).

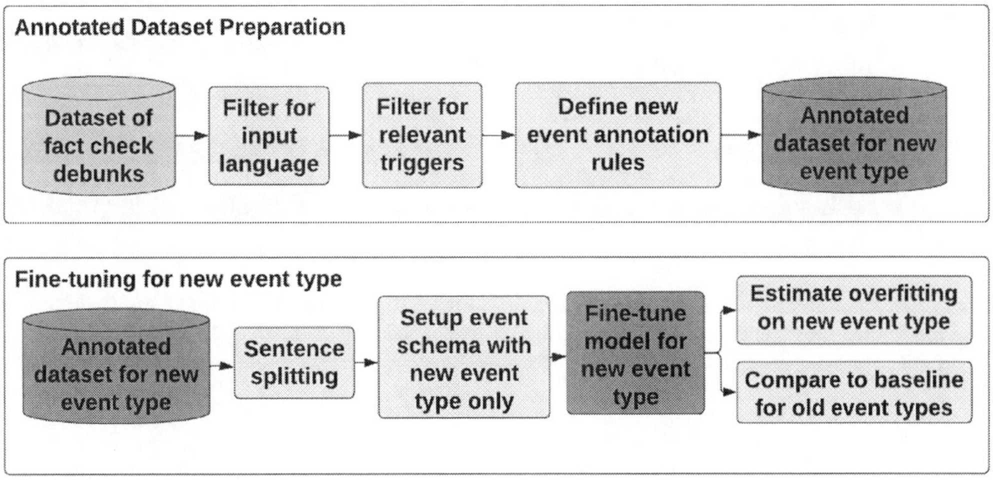

Figure 2: Steps towards building an annotated dataset and using it to fine-tune model on new event type

Model		Event-C			Trig-C			Correct-Trig-Arg-C			Wrong-Trig-Arg-C		
	split	P	R	F1	P	R	F1	P	R	F1	P	R	F1
100 epochs	20/80	0.00	0.00	0.00	0.00	0.00	0.00	0.00	0.00	0.00	0.00	0.00	0.00
	40/60	0.60	0.02	0.04	0.60	0.02	0.04	0.30	0.60	0.40	0.00	0.00	0.00
	60/40	0.83	0.84	0.82	0.76	0.83	0.78	0.54	0.75	0.63	0.75	0.83	0.79
	80/20	0.84	0.83	0.83	0.78	0.82	0.80	0.52	0.72	0.59	0.67	0.70	0.68
300 epochs	20/80	0.87	0.65	0.73	0.75	0.62	0.66	0.38	0.50	0.43	0.24	0.44	0.31
	40/60	0.80	0.78	0.79	0.71	0.76	0.73	**0.60**	0.74	**0.64**	0.43	0.76	0.55
	60/40	0.86	0.75	0.80	0.80	0.74	0.76	0.53	0.70	0.60	0.83	0.88	0.85
	80/20	0.84	0.83	0.84	0.80	0.82	0.81	0.53	0.73	0.61	0.60	0.60	0.60
500 epochs	20/80	0.85	0.69	0.75	0.72	0.66	0.68	0.48	0.60	0.53	0.32	0.54	0.40
	40/60	0.82	0.81	0.81	0.71	0.78	0.74	0.56	0.71	0.62	0.48	0.79	0.59
	60/40	**0.88**	0.83	0.85	**0.83**	0.82	0.82	0.55	0.74	0.63	**1.00**	**1.00**	**1.00**
	80/20	0.86	**0.92**	**0.89**	0.77	**0.92**	**0.84**	0.57	**0.76**	**0.64**	0.93	**1.00**	0.96

Table 3: Mean Precision (P), Recall (R) and F1-score for Cure-Claim event, trigger and argument classification (Event-C, Trig-C, Arg-C) for various train/test splits and number of fine-tuning epochs. Results for model fine-tuned for 30 epochs not shown as it scored 0 on all metrics across all train/test splits.

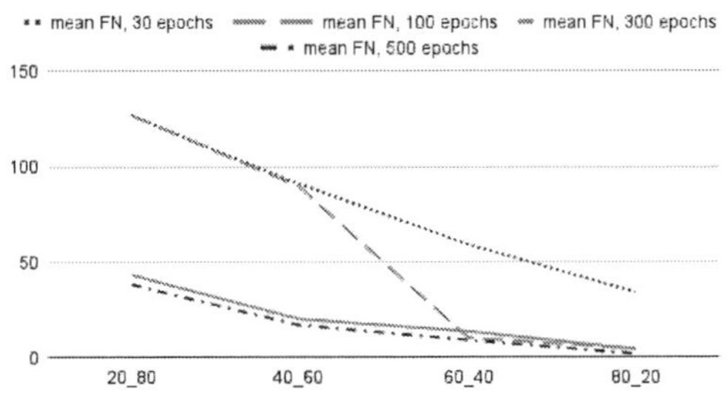

Figure 3: Number of false negative arguments for Cure-Claim event type across dataset splits and fine-tuning epochs

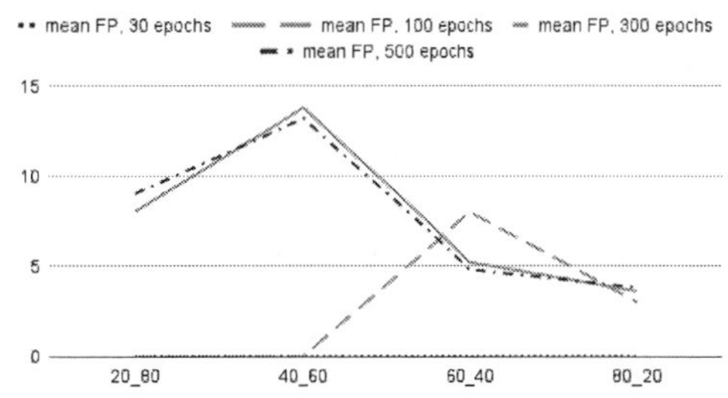

Figure 4: Number of false positive arguments for Cure-Claim event type across dataset splits and fine-tuning epochs

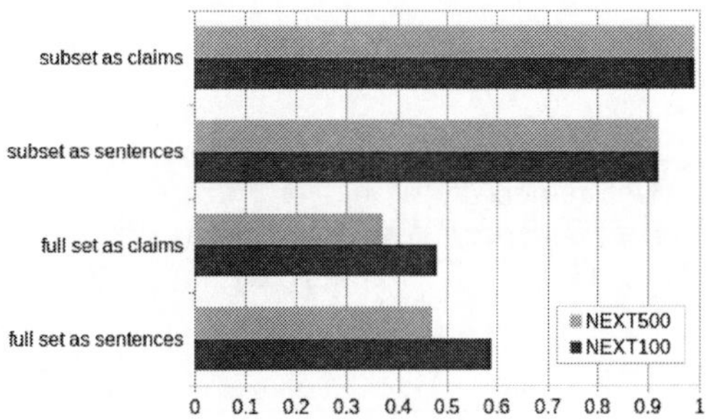

Figure 5: Estimated precision of event type classification on the filtered subset and the full dataset of fake news debunks for input provided as sentences and as claims.

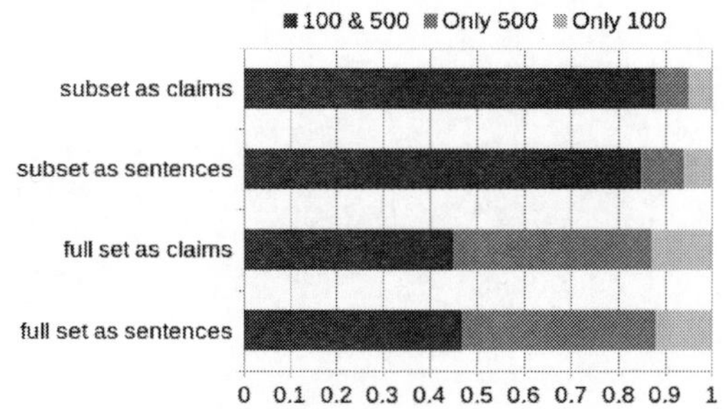

Figure 6: Fraction of predicted Cure-Claim events by each model on the filtered subset and the full dataset of fake news debunks for input provided as sentences and as claims.

Figure 5 shows the resulting estimates for precision of Cure-Claim event-type classification on the filtered subset and the full dataset. Both NEXT100 and NEXT500 achieve over 0.9 precision for the Cure-Claim event on the filtered subset samples, both when the sample is a whole claim and an individual sentence. These results surpass the models' precision in the earlier cross-validation experiments (Table 3) for all train/test splits on a larger evaluation set (60 samples per model).

On the other hand, precision drops significantly for both models on the samples from the whole dataset. For these more diverse samples we see that both fine-tuned models perform better when the input is provided as individual sentences. However, we also note that NEXT100 is more precise.

Figure 6 shows the fraction of predicted Cure-Claim events made by each fine-tuned model. We see that almost all predictions made on the filtered subset are made by both fine-tuned models. On the broader dataset, however, NEXT500 makes about 50% more predictions for Cure-Claim events than NEXT100. This, combined with the above-mentioned drop in precision of NEXT500 shown in Figure 5, suggests overfitting for NEXT500.

5.3 Overlap in original event types predictions between baseline and fine-tuned models

An essential part of the model fine-tuning is to assure that the model has not worsened its performance on the event types it was previously trained on. We don't have access to the annotated dataset with all event types that Text2Event was trained on, so to examine whether the fine-tuned model has retained the abilities of the original one, we compared their performance on the whole dataset of fake news debunks consisting of 42,555 claims and 54,280 sentences respectively. We compare the number of predictions per event type from the baseline model and the fine-tuned models, as well as the overlap of predicted events between any two or all three models.

Figure 7 shows that for the top 10 most common events the fine-tuned models predict many more event occurrences compared to the baseline model.

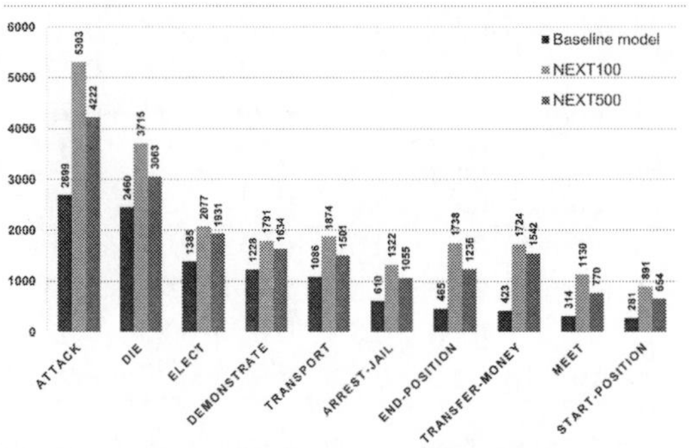

Figure 7: Number of documents containing predictions by baseline model, NEXT100 and NEXT500 (using sentence as input)

Figure 8 shows that for all event types almost all predictions by the baseline model are also predicted by the fine-tuned models, with NEXT100 having a higher overlap compared to NEXT500.

Another way to explore these overlaps is shown in Figure 9 where for each event type we can see what fraction of all predictions were made by all three models, by a particular pair of models, or by an individual model. We can observe that over half of all predictions either overlap between all three models or between the two fine-tuned models. Unlike the other two models, NEXT100 produces a significant number of predictions not matched by

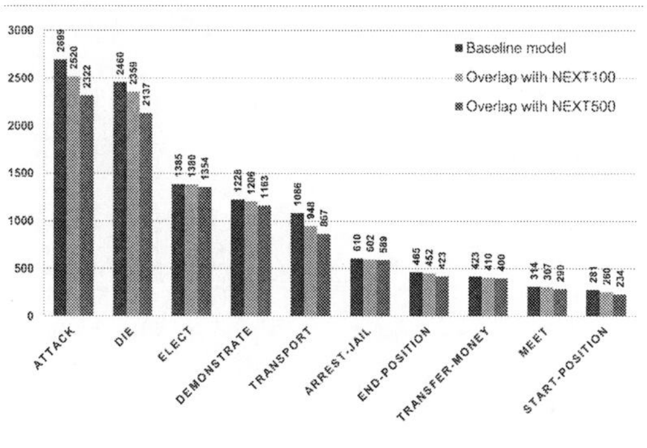

Figure 8: Number of documents containing predictions by baseline model and overlapped with NEXT100 and NEXT500 (using sentences as input)

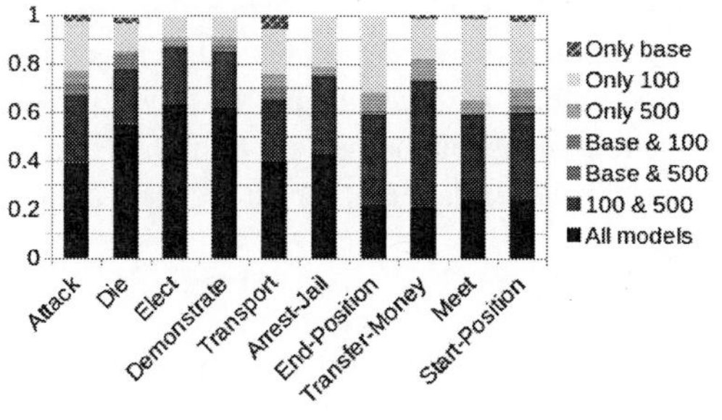

Figure 9: Overlap in event predictions between models (using sentences as input). For each event type the bar shows what fraction of predictions are made by all three models, by two of the models, or by a single one.

any of the other models. It is also worth noting that all predictions made by NEXT100, whether in agreement with other models or not, account for over 90% of all predictions.

Results of model evaluatuation on whole claims, rather than individual sentences, are very similar and figures and tables are included in the appendix.

5.4 Comparing precision of original event types predictions between baseline and fine-tuned models

For each event type we sample up to 20 predictions for each overlap subset (individual models, pairs of models, all models). For each prediction, we manually evaluated whether the corresponding document contains an event of such type, regardless of whether the trigger prediction is also correct. The resulting estimates for event type classification precision are given in Table 4. The estimated precision scores for individual models are obtained by combining the estimates over all relevant subsets (e.g. for the baseline model we add the number of correct predictions from only baseline, baseline & NEXT100, baseline & NEXT500 and all models) and are shown in Table 5.

5.5 Estimating recall of original event types predictions for baseline and fine-tuned models

We are unable to calculate recall and F1-score as those would require knowing the total number of positive samples for each event type for our fake news debunk dataset.

However, the precision of sampled predictions not made by the baseline model (i.e. made either by a single or by both fine-tuned models only) is on-par with the precision of sampled predictions made by the baseline model (usually also predicted by one or both of the fine-tuned models).

We can thus reason that the fine-tuned models not only retain the baseline model's recall but improve on it 2- to 4-fold, since for all event types the fine-tuned models generate two to four times as many predictions, as already shown in Figure 8.

6 Discussion

Our proposed approach NEXT to extend an existing event schema with new event types has a few advantages, but also limitations.

A notable advantage of this approach is that a dozen annotated samples are sufficient for achieving high precision given a sufficient number of fine-tuning epochs. Learning good recall, however, is a more challenging task and requires a larger number of samples - about 50.

Fine-tuning the model also does not require significant computational resources. All reported experiments were performed on a single CUDA-enabled GPU. Each fine-tuning of an individual model took a few minutes.

As expected, we observe that fine-tuning for many epochs leads to overfitting on the new event type. Namely, the precision of predictions for the new event type decreases with a larger number of epochs, while the number of predictions grows simultaneously. This problem can be mitigated by pre-filtering the sentences or claims on which the model is used, with a rule as simple as checking whether they contain likely triggers for the event type (e.g. "cure", "treat", "heal" for Cure-Claim events), as seen in Figure 5. Another solution would be to adopt a voting approach by considering only predictions made by both NEXT100 and

Event type	only base	only 100	only 500	base & 100	base & 500	100 & 500	all models
Attack	0.65	0.70	0.60	0.70	0.90	0.80	0.95
Die	0.95	1.00	1.00	1.00	1.00	1.00	1.00
Elect	1.00	0.85	0.83	1.00	1.00	1.00	1.00
Demonstrate	1.00	0.90	0.87	0.95	1.00	0.95	1.00
Transport	0.95	1.00	0.95	0.90	1.00	1.00	1.00
Arrest-Jail	0.83	0.85	0.80	1.00	0.50	0.90	1.00
End-Position	1.00	0.90	0.85	1.00	1.00	1.00	0.95
Transfer-Money	0.80	0.85	0.80	0.77	1.00	1.00	1.00
Meet	1.00	1.00	1.00	1.00	0.00	1.00	1.00
Start-Position	1.00	0.90	1.00	1.00	1.00	0.95	1.00

Table 4: Event type classification precision on subsets of sampled predictions made by individual models (baseline, NEXT100 or NEXT500) or by two or all models.

Event type	Base	NEXT100	NEXT500
Attack	0.91	0.84	0.87
Die	1.00	1.00	1.00
Elect	1.00	0.99	0.99
Demonstrate	1.00	0.98	0.98
Transport	0.99	0.99	1.00
Arrest-Jail	1.00	0.93	0.95
End-Position	0.95	0.95	0.97
Transfer-Money	0.99	0.97	0.98
Meet	1.00	1.00	1.00
Start-Position	1.00	0.95	0.97

Table 5: Event type classification precision on sampled predictions for baseline, NEXT100 and NEXT500 models.

NEXT500 models (or majority rule if a third fine-tuned model is used as well) as predictions shared between models tend to be more accurate compared to predictions made by individual models (Table with comparison is available in the Appendix).

Despite the large number of fine-tuning epochs for the new event type, this approach retains the model's capability of predicting existing event types. We showed that the majority of such predictions made by the baseline Text2Event model are also made by the fine-tuned models. Furthermore, the fine-tuned models generate two to four times as many predictions as the baseline model. This has only a minor effect on precision - a small drop in performance compared to the baseline model can be observed in Table 5. The largest drops in precision are by 0.07 for NEXT100 (Attack and Arrest-Jail) and 0.05 for NEXT500 (Arrest-Jail).

We attribute this rise in recall to the baseline model not having been trained or fine-tuned on samples from our claim debunks dataset. Though this dataset consists of texts from the same domain as ACE2005 (news media / publishing), the datasets differ on other parameters such as the average number of sentences per text. We observe that a few annotated samples for fine-tuning on one event type are sufficient to boost recall of all other event types.

7 Conclusion and further work

In this work we presented an approach to extend an existing event schema with new event types for closed-domain event extraction. Our approach uses a very small number of annotations containing full event structures (event type, trigger and arguments are all annotated).

The proposed approach also leads to improvement in the recall of existing event types, on which the model was pre-trained while retaining precision. It can thus be used not only to fine-tune the event extraction model for a new event type but to also simultaneously fine-tune the model for the existing event types on a new dataset without the need for annotation for all event types.

An interesting direction for future research would be evaluating whether this boost in performance would also be observed when the task is transferred to a dataset from a less related domain, e.g. biomedical, manufacturing, energy, etc. Further pre-training might also be of interest.

In terms of evaluation, it would be interesting to explore how our proposed approach compares to alternatives, such as open-domain approaches. Also, more documents from the initial dataset could be annotated for the original event types, in order to obtain a clearer picture of the baseline's model performance on them.

8 Acknowledgements

This research has received funding from the European Union's Horizon research and innovation programme under grant agreement No 101073921 (VIGILANT, `https://www.vigilantproject.eu/`).

References

Yubo Chen, Liheng Xu, Kang Liu, Daojian Zeng, and Jun Zhao. 2015. Event extraction via dynamic multi-pooling convolutional neural networks. In *Proceedings of the 53rd Annual Meeting of the Association for Computational Linguistics and the 7th International Joint Conference on Natural Language Processing (Volume 1: Long Papers)*, pages 167–176, Beijing, China. Association for Computational Linguistics.

Shumin Deng, Ningyu Zhang, Jiaojian Kang, Yichi Zhang, Wei Zhang, and Huajun Chen. 2020. Meta-learning with dynamic-memory-based prototypical network for few-shot event detection. In *Proceedings of the 13th International Conference on Web Search and Data Mining*. ACM.

Lifu Huang and Heng Ji. 2020. Semi-supervised new event type induction and event detection. In *Proceedings of the 2020 Conference on Empirical Methods in Natural Language Processing (EMNLP)*, pages 718–724, Online. Association for Computational Linguistics.

Lifu Huang, Heng Ji, Kyunghyun Cho, Ido Dagan, Sebastian Riedel, and Clare Voss. 2018. Zero-shot transfer learning for event extraction. In *Proceedings of the 56th Annual Meeting of the Association for Computational Linguistics (Volume 1: Long Papers)*, pages 2160–2170, Melbourne, Australia. Association for Computational Linguistics.

Florian Kunneman and Antal Van Den Bosch. 2016. Open-domain extraction of future events from twitter. *Natural Language Engineering*, 22(5):655–686.

Viet Dac Lai, Thien Huu Nguyen, and Franck Dernoncourt. 2020. Extensively matching for few-shot learning event detection. In *Proceedings of the First Joint Workshop on Narrative Understanding, Storylines, and Events*, pages 38–45, Online. Association for Computational Linguistics.

Fayuan Li, Weihua Peng, Yuguang Chen, Quan Wang, Lu Pan, Yajuan Lyu, and Yong Zhu. 2020. Event extraction as multi-turn question answering. In *Findings of the Association for Computational Linguistics: EMNLP 2020*, pages 829–838, Online. Association for Computational Linguistics.

Qian Li, Jianxin Li, Jiawei Sheng, Shiyao Cui, Jia Wu, Yiming Hei, Hao Peng, Shu Guo, Lihong Wang, Amin Beheshti, et al. 2022. A survey on deep learning event extraction: Approaches and applications. *IEEE Transactions on Neural Networks and Learning Systems*.

Jiangwei Liu, Liangyu Min, and Xiaohong Huang. 2021. An overview of event extraction and its applications. *arXiv preprint arXiv:2111.03212*.

Xiao Liu, Heyan Huang, and Yue Zhang. 2019. Open domain event extraction using neural latent variable models. In *Proceedings of the 57th Annual Meeting of the Association for Computational Linguistics*, pages 2860–2871, Florence, Italy. Association for Computational Linguistics.

Di Lu, Shihao Ran, Joel Tetreault, and Alejandro Jaimes. 2023. Event extraction as question generation and answering. In *Proceedings of the 61st Annual Meeting of the Association for Computational Linguistics (Volume 2: Short Papers)*, pages 1666–1688, Toronto, Canada. Association for Computational Linguistics.

Yaojie Lu, Hongyu Lin, Jin Xu, Xianpei Han, Jialong Tang, Annan Li, Le Sun, Meng Liao, and Shaoyi Chen. 2021. Text2Event: Controllable sequence-to-structure generation for end-to-end event extraction. In *Proceedings of the 59th Annual Meeting of the Association for Computational Linguistics and the 11th International Joint Conference on Natural Language Processing (Volume 1: Long Papers)*, pages 2795–2806, Online. Association for Computational Linguistics.

Qing Lyu, Hongming Zhang, Elior Sulem, and Dan Roth. 2021. Zero-shot event extraction via transfer learning: Challenges and insights. In *Proceedings of the 59th Annual Meeting of the Association for Computational Linguistics and the 11th International Joint Conference on Natural Language Processing (Volume 2: Short Papers)*, pages 322–332, Online. Association for Computational Linguistics.

Hao Peng, Ruitong Zhang, Shaoning Li, Yuwei Cao, Shirui Pan, and Philip S. Yu. 2023. Reinforced, incremental and cross-lingual event detection from social messages. *IEEE Transactions on Pattern Analysis and Machine Intelligence*, 45(1):980–998.

Alan Ritter, Mausam, Oren Etzioni, and Sam Clark. 2012. Open domain event extraction from twitter. In *Proceedings of the 18th ACM SIGKDD international conference on Knowledge discovery and data mining*, pages 1104–1112.

Jiawei Sheng, Shu Guo, Bowen Yu, Qian Li, Yiming Hei, Lihong Wang, Tingwen Liu, and Hongbo Xu. 2021a. Casee: A joint learning framework with cascade decoding for overlapping event extraction. *arXiv preprint arXiv:2107.01583*.

Jiawei Sheng, Shu Guo, Bowen Yu, Qian Li, Yiming Hei, Lihong Wang, Tingwen Liu, and Hongbo Xu. 2021b. CasEE: A joint learning framework with cascade decoding for overlapping event extraction. In *Findings of the Association for Computational Linguistics: ACL-IJCNLP 2021*, pages 164–174, Online. Association for Computational Linguistics.

Hristo Tanev, Jakub Piskorski, and Martin Atkinson. 2008. Real-time news event extraction for global crisis monitoring. In *Natural Language and Information Systems: 13th International Conference on Applications of Natural Language to Information Systems, NLDB 2008 London, UK, June 24-27, 2008 Proceedings 13*, pages 207–218. Springer.

Ashish Vaswani, Noam Shazeer, Niki Parmar, Jakob Uszkoreit, Llion Jones, Aidan N. Gomez, Lukasz Kaiser, and Illia Polosukhin. 2017. Attention is all you need.

David Wadden, Ulme Wennberg, Yi Luan, and Hannaneh Hajishirzi. 2019. Entity, relation, and event extraction with contextualized span representations. *arXiv preprint arXiv:1909.03546*.

Qiang Wei, Zongcheng Ji, Zhiheng Li, Jingcheng Du, Jingqi Wang, Jun Xu, Yang Xiang, Firat Tiryaki, Stephen Wu, Yaoyun Zhang, et al. 2020. A study of deep learning approaches for medication and adverse drug event extraction from clinical text. *Journal of the American Medical Informatics Association*, 27(1):13–21.

Bishan Yang and Tom M. Mitchell. 2016. Joint extraction of events and entities within a document context. In *Proceedings of the 2016 Conference of the North American Chapter of the Association for Computational Linguistics: Human Language Technologies*, pages 289–299, San Diego, California. Association for Computational Linguistics.

Sen Yang, Dawei Feng, Linbo Qiao, Zhigang Kan, and Dongsheng Li. 2019. Exploring pre-trained language models for event extraction and generation. In *Proceedings of the 57th Annual Meeting of the Association for Computational Linguistics*, pages 5284–5294, Florence, Italy. Association for Computational Linguistics.

Zhenrui Yue, Huimin Zeng, Mengfei Lan, Heng Ji, and Dong Wang. 2023. Zero- and few-shot event detection via prompt-based meta learning.

Yue Zhao, Xiaolong Jin, Yuanzhuo Wang, and Xueqi Cheng. 2018. Document embedding enhanced event detection with hierarchical and supervised attention. In *Proceedings of the 56th Annual Meeting of the Association for Computational Linguistics (Volume 2: Short Papers)*, pages 414–419, Melbourne, Australia. Association for Computational Linguistics.

Yang Zhou, Yubo Chen, Jun Zhao, Yin Wu, Jiexin Xu, and Jinlong Li. 2021. What the role is vs. what plays the role: Semi-supervised event argument extraction via dual question answering. *Proceedings of the AAAI Conference on Artificial Intelligence*, 35(16):14638–14646.

A Appendix

A.1 Keywords

For the building of the Cure-Claim event type dataset, we have used the following keywords:

- cure, cures, cured, curing
- heal, heals, healed, healing
- treat, treats, treated, treating, treatment, treatments
- remedy, remedies
- relieve, relieves, relieved, relieving
- boost, boosts, boosted, boosting

In addition to the listed above keywords, the following ones were identified as triggers during the annotation process: stop, kill, prevent, regular.

A.2 Trigger classification evaluation

We classify trigger prediction as follows:

- TP (true positive) - event is annotated and prediction matches its type and trigger;
- TN (true negative) - no event is annotated and no event is predicted;
- FP (false positive) - no event is annotated but one is predicted OR event is annotated but predicted trigger does not match;
- FN (false negative) - event is annotated but none is predicted.

A.3 Argument classification evaluation

We consider the following four different scenarios:

1. An annotated event is predicted with the correct trigger.
2. An annotated event is predicted, but with a wrong trigger.
3. There is an annotated Cure-Claim event, but none is predicted. In this case we count the event and all its annotated arguments as false negatives.
4. There is no annotated Cure-Claim event, but one is predicted. In this case we count the event and all its predicted Cure-Claim arguments as false positives.

For the first two scenarios we report mean precision, recall and F1-score. In both cases we classify the argument prediction as follows:

- TP (true positive) - the argument prediction matches an annotated argument's type and span;
- FP (false positive) - the argument prediction matches an annotated argument's type but not span OR the argument prediction does not match any annotated argument's type;
- FN (false negative) - there is no argument prediction that matches an annotated argument's type and/or span.

We don't report true negative predictions for argument classification.

When event is annotated, but not predicted, we count all annotated arguments as false negative predictions. When event is not annotated, but is predicted, we count all predicted arguments as false positive predictions.

A.4 Additional results of baseline and fine-tuned models comparison

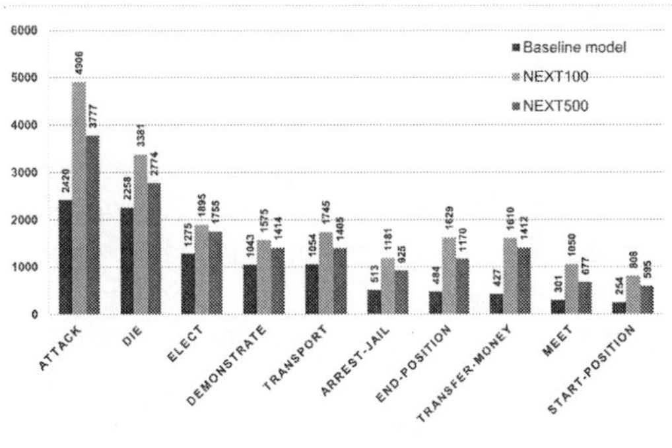

Figure 10: Number of documents containing predictions by baseline model, NEXT100 and NEXT500 (using claims as input)

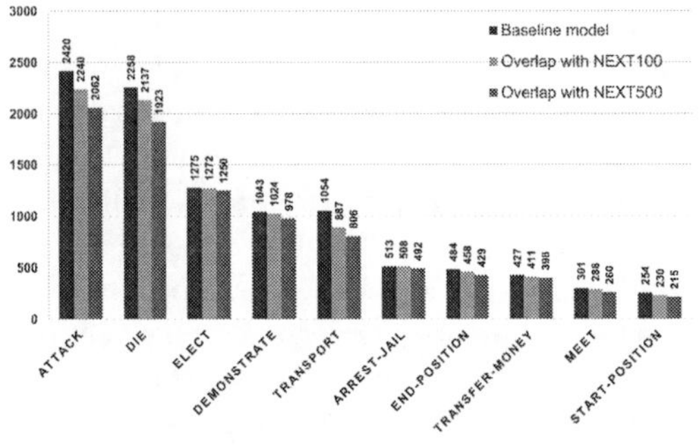

Figure 11: Number of documents containing predictions by baseline model and overlapped with NEXT100 and NEXT500 (using claims as input)

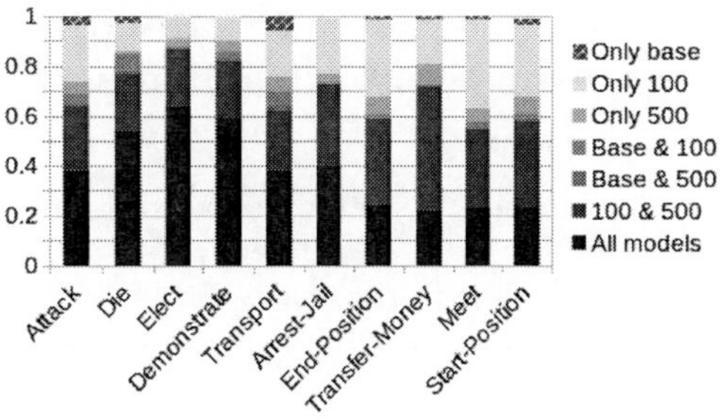

Figure 12: Overlap in event predictions between models (using whole claims as input). For each event type the bar shows what fraction of predictions is made by all three models, by two of the models, or by a single one.

Input	NEXT100 only	NEXT500 only	both
full set as sentences	0.53	0.33	0.60
full set as claims	0.50	0.27	0.47
subset as sentences	0.83	0.87	0.93
subset as claims	0.88	0.83	1.00

Table 6: Event type classification precision for CureClaim predictions made by NEXT100 only, NEXT500 only, or both models.

Negative documents are positive: Improving event extraction performance using overlooked negative data

Osman Mutlu
Koç University
Rumelifeneri Yolu 34450
Sarıyer, İstanbul/Turkey
omutlu@ku.edu.tr

Ali Hürriyetoğlu
KNAW Humanities Cluster DHLab
Oudezijds Achterburgwal 185, 1012DK
Amsterdam, the Netherlands
ali.hurriyetoglu@dh.huc.knaw.nl

Abstract

The scarcity of data poses a significant challenge in closed-domain event extraction, as is common in complex NLP tasks. This limitation primarily arises from the intricate nature of the annotation process. To address this issue, we present a multi-task model structure and training approach that leverages the additional data, which is found as not having any event information at document and sentence levels, generated during the event annotation process. By incorporating this supplementary data, our proposed framework demonstrates enhanced robustness and, in some scenarios, improved performance. A particularly noteworthy observation is that including only negative documents in addition to the original data contributes to performance enhancement. When training the model with only 80% of the original data alongside negative documents, the outcome closely paralleled employing the entire original data set without any negative documents. Our findings offer promising insights into leveraging extra data to mitigate data scarcity challenges in closed-domain event extraction.

1 Introduction

Closed-domain event extraction is a specialized task in Natural Language Processing (NLP) that focuses on automatically identifying and extracting specific events or occurrences from text within a restricted domain, such as biomedical research, financial markets, political events, or sports (Xiang and Wang, 2019; Parolin et al., 2021). It plays a crucial role in capturing and categorizing relevant events, their attributes, and relationships, enabling applications such as information retrieval (Abuleil and Evens, 2004), trend analysis (Cheng et al., 2022; Wang et al., 2012), and knowledge base construction (Schrodt and Idris, 2014; Hürriyetoğlu et al., 2021; Jenkins et al., 2023). However, despite the advancements in NLP models, the scarcity of annotated data poses a persistent bottleneck in achieving accurate and reliable event extraction models. The limited availability of annotated data, crucial for training and evaluating such models, hinders their performance and generalizability (Caselli et al., 2021; Hu et al., 2022).

The annotation process plays a vital role in event extraction, requiring domain experts to meticulously label relevant events and their associated attributes. However, this process is often labor-intensive, time-consuming, and expensive (Pustejovsky and Stubbs, 2012). The complexity and diversity of event types further complicate the task, as events can vary in structure, context, and representation. Moreover, the need for inter-annotator agreement adds to the complexity, requiring multiple annotators to reach a consensus on the event labels. These challenges contribute to the limited availability of annotated data, restricting the performance and generalizability of event extraction models.

To overcome the data scarcity challenge, we propose a model structure and training schema that harnesses the additional data generated as a natural by-product of the annotation process. Specifically, we utilize coarse-grained data that classifies documents or sentences as containing an event or not, as shown in Table 1. The first example shows the inherent document and sentence labels in a token-annotated document, while the second example is a document with no event information. This data can be easily generated from already annotated documents for event extraction, and one could easily gather more samples without token-level annotations. Labeling such data is relatively painless, effectively circumventing most of the aforementioned issues with annotating event extraction documents. Thus, achieving a higher data quality is considerably cheaper and easier. We analyze the trade-off between using token annotations and

Proceedings of the 6th Workshop on Challenges and Applications of Automated Extraction of Socio-political Events from Text, pages 124–135, Varna, Bulgaria, Sep 7, 2023.
https://doi.org/10.26615/978-954-452-089-2_017

Document No	Sentence No	Sentence	Sentence label	Document label
1	1	He said the union had already send a statutory letter to the Uber office here in connection with the strike.	Negative	Positive
	2	The leaders of the union also said the local taxi drivers had launched an **attack** against the online taxi drivers at the airport.	Positive	
	3	The online taxi drivers have been having a tough time for the last one year.	Negative	
	4	Uber and Ola are two prominent online taxi service providers in Kochi.	Negative	
	5	Earlier, some trade unions representing local taxi operators had come out in **protest** against the online taxi networks such as Uber and Ola.	Positive	
2	1	Tributes paid to Field Marshal Cariappa, students sing prayers at his 'samadi'	Negative	Negative
	2	Madikeri: Rich tributes were paid to the late Field Marshal K.M.Cariappa at "Roshanara" here, where his "samadhi" is located, to observe the birth anniversary of one of the great soldiers of the country.	Negative	
	3	Prayers in different languages were rendered by students of the Bharatiya Vidya Bhavan-Kodagu Vidyalaya (BVB-KV) and family members of the late Field Marshal.	Negative	

Table 1: A table that consists of 2 sample documents from ACL CASE 2021 shared task. The first document is positive and token-annotated. The second document has no event information, therefore negative. The event triggers are shown in bold, and event arguments are underlined.

coarse-grained labels, evaluating performance variations with different ratios of these data types.

In our training schema, we incorporate the extra coarse data as two auxiliary tasks alongside the main event extraction task: document binary classification and sentence binary classification. By utilizing this supplementary data, our approach aims to augment the training set and enhance the performance and robustness of the event extraction model. The integration of this additional data has yielded promising results, effectively addressing the limitations caused by the lack of annotated data in closed-domain event extraction.

This study contributes to the field by providing a practical solution to the data scarcity problem in closed-domain event extraction. By leveraging the extra data generated during the annotation process, we strive to advance the state-of-the-art in event extraction, paving the way for more accurate and efficient systems across various domains. The outcomes of our research have potential implications for numerous downstream applications, ultimately benefiting various sectors that rely on event extraction for knowledge extraction and decision-making processes (Hogenboom et al., 2016).

The following section provide a brief overview on studies related to our study. Next we provide details of the multi-task model and the data we utilize for our experiments in Sections 3 and 4 respectively. The experimental setting is described in Section 5 in terms of a baseline and three experiment sets. We report results of our experiments in Section 6 and summarize our findings in Section 7.

2 Related Work

The performance of event extraction has been significantly depended on the amount of relevant data utilized for creating an event extraction system (Chen and Ji, 2009; Hsu et al., 2022). The variety of the data contributes to the performance and generalizability of an event extraction system as well (Yörük et al., 2022).

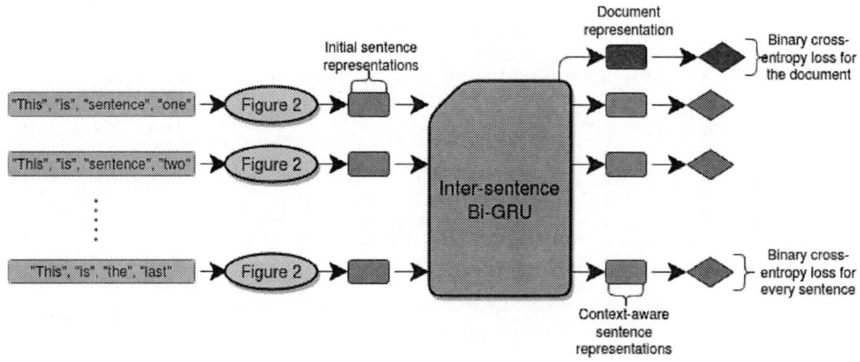

Figure 1: The main structure of the multi-task model. After creating embeddings for each sentence in the document (see Figure 2), these are sent through a bi-GRU to get a context-aware representation for each sentence and a single representation for the whole document. The losses for the document and the sentences are obtained by passing these embeddings through their respective classification layers.

The design of an event extraction system is another major determiner of the performance (Pei et al., 2023). The design should be able to utilize and encode as much as information available in the data for the target task. Consequently, syntax-oriented rule creation (Fleissner and Fang, 2012; Oostdijk et al., 2016), joint learning (Chen et al., 2018), multi-task learning (drissiya El-allaly et al., 2021), and pre-trained architectures (Yang et al., 2019) have been developed and successfully applied in many event extraction scenarios.

We follow these approaches both for data by increasing the size and variety of the data and benefiting from multi-task learning that is based on pre-trained architectures. Although in different domains, both Rei and Søgaard (2019) and Tong et al. (2021) are highly similar to our approach. They both adopt a multi-task structure within a joint learning framework, leveraging data at multiple levels of granularity. However, our approach diverges from theirs primarily in terms of incorporating document-level information, alongside sentence-level. An innovative aspect of our study is the revelation that integrating negative documents substantially augments performance and robustness, particularly in scenarios with limited data availability.

3 Model Structure

To solve event extraction tasks using deep learning techniques, they are commonly approached as token classification problems. In token classification, each word or token in the input text is assigned a label indicating its role in the event extraction process. One popular labeling scheme is the BIO format (Ramshaw and Marcus, 1995), which stands for "Beginning, Inside, and Outside." In this format, each token is labeled as either B-event, I-event, or O. The B-event label denotes the beginning of an event mention, the I-event label indicates that the token is inside the event mention, and the O label signifies that the token is outside any event mention. By converting the event annotations into the BIO format, deep learning models can be trained to recognize and classify tokens based on their involvement in events, facilitating the automated extraction of important information from text.

The model structure is designed to effectively leverage document and sentence-level information, alongside the main task of token classification, in a coherent manner. To achieve this, our model[1] predicts labels and trains on all three levels simultaneously, enabling comprehensive learning. Inspired by ScopeIt (Patra et al., 2020), our multi-task architecture, illustrated in Figure 1, enables the creation of representations for tokens, sentences, and documents to then put these through the respective classification layers for each task. We build on their model structure by adding the facilities for the token classification task. So, our model trains on the two auxiliary tasks, document and sentence classification tasks, in addition to the primary token classification task.

The model processes each sentence, with its split tokens, using a transformers-based encoder[2] to ob-

[1] https://github.com/OsmanMutlu/ms_thesis

[2] https://huggingface.co/

tain representations for individual tokens. To address the limited input problem of the encoder, each sentence is processed independently. Within each sentence, a bidirectional Gated Recurrent Unit (bi-GRU) (Cho et al., 2014), dubbed intra-sentence bi-GRU, is employed to further enhance token representations and generate a representation for the entire sentence by concatenating the last hidden states from both directions of the bi-GRU. These sentence embeddings are further enriched with contextual information by passing them through a second bi-GRU, named inter-sentence bi-GRU. Additionally, a single representation for the entire document is obtained by concatenating the last hidden states from the inter-sentence bi-GRU in both directions. Each representation, whether for tokens, sentences, or documents, is then passed through their respective classification layers to calculate the corresponding losses. The document and sentence tasks employ binary cross-entropy loss, while the token task utilizes categorical cross-entropy loss. The losses from each task are combined, yielding a final loss value for backpropagation (Rumelhart et al., 1986).

It is important to note that we maintain a consistent model structure across all our experiments, even if document or sentence loss is not calculated in certain scenarios. This ensures a standardized approach and facilitates fair comparisons across different variations of the model.

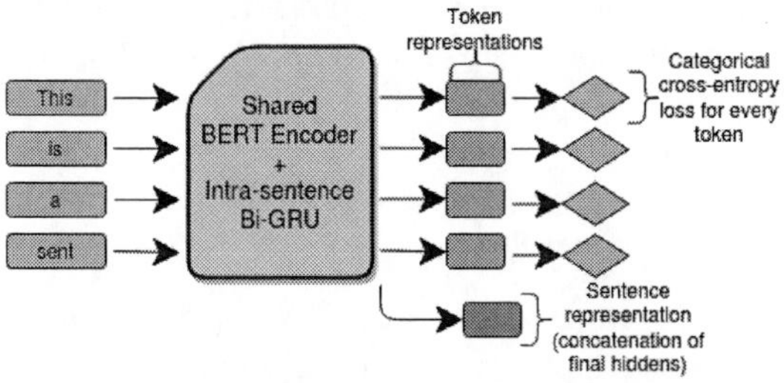

Figure 2: Each sentence of the document goes through a shared transformers-based encoder and a bi-GRU to produce embeddings for each token and the sentence. A categorical cross-entropy loss is calculated for each token after passing their embeddings through a classification layer.

4 Data

We leverage the data provided by the ACL CASE 2021 shared task (Hürriyetoğlu et al., 2021), which focuses on detecting protest events in the languages English, Portuguese, Spanish, and Hindi. The shared task encompasses four sequential steps, representing different stages of a real-world event extraction pipeline (Duruşan et al., 2022). For our experiments, we specifically utilize a subset of the English training data from subtask four, along with the corresponding English test data.

The training data consists of 717 token-annotated documents. These annotations were distributed in BIO format, meaning there are no overlapping labels for any individual token, effectively turning this task into token classification. The test set, which remains the same across all experiments since token classification serves as the primary task, includes 179 token-annotated documents. The distribution of token labels for the training and test sets is outlined in Table 2.

4.1 Inherent coarse-grained data

As mentioned earlier, our training schema takes advantage of the additional data inherent in the token-annotated documents. From a document classification perspective, the training set contains 717 positive documents, as all documents have at least one token annotation. Conversely, there are no negative documents. Regarding sentence classification, out of 14.06 sentences on average per document, 29% are positively labeled as they contain at least one token annotation. This translates to 2,893 positive and 7,191 negative sentences. It's worth noting that the statistics for the test set are irrelevant for coarse-grained data, given that token classification is the primary task.

4.2 Negative documents

Some of our experiments (explained in section 5) uses extra data that is not any part of the original 717 token-annotated documents. This extra data is sourced from subtask 1 of the same shared task and consists of 717 negatively labeled documents, indicating the absence of token annotations. These negative documents emerge as a by-product of the annotation process. When selecting documents for token-level annotation, the non-selected ones inadvertently contribute to the creation of negative documents. This set of 717 negative documents were randomly selected out of 7,412 negative documents in training set of subtask 1.

	etime	fname	organizer	participant	place	target	trigger
Train	1,071	1,089	1,187	2,435	1,436	1,334	4,096
Test	260	224	223	542	313	286	929

Table 2: The distribution of token labels for the training and test sets of subtask 4 of ACL CASE 2021 shared task.

5 Experimental Setup

Aside from the baseline, we conducted three main sets of experiments to address three key research questions, with each subsequent set incorporating additional data. In the first set, we utilized the inherent coarse-grained data available in token-annotated documents. In the second set, we introduced negative documents to balance the positive ones and further explored the effects of the document classification task. In the third set, we removed some of the 717 documents to be used as extra coarse-grained data without token annotations.

For each experiment set, we conducted three experiments based on different combinations of losses in addition to the token classification loss: only sentence classification loss (variation 1), only document classification loss (variation 2), and both sentence and document classification losses (variation 3). This approach allowed us to assess the individual effects of each auxiliary task introduced. Although some weights of the model may not update in certain cases due to the architecture, we maintained the same model for all experiments to ensure fair comparisons. Each experiment was run three times to calculate average performance and standard deviation scores. Additionally, we gradually decreased the amount of data in each experiment to measure the influence of data size on model performance.

Listed below are the parameters employed for our model. It's important to note that no parameter-specific experiments were conducted to fine-tune these values. They remain consistent throughout all experiments, thereby minimizing the potential impact of parameter variations. The selection of these parameters was driven by pragmatic considerations, encompassing factors such as data size, GPU capacity, and practical feasibility. The parameter settings are as follows:

- *Number of training epochs*: 30
- *Pretrained transformers model*: sentence-transformers/paraphrase-xlm-r-multilingual-v1
- *Learning rate for the encoder*: 2e-5
- *Learning rate for the general model*: 1e-4 (same as ScopeIt)
- *Batch size of documents*: 16
- *Maximum num of sentences in a document*: 200
- *Maximum token length of a sentence*: 128
- *Number of GRU layers*: 2
- *Size of GRU hidden layer*: 512
- *Development data*: random selection of 10% from the training data

Baseline:

As for the baseline, our model was trained using the 717 span-annotated documents. It's important to note that for the baseline model, the inter-sentence bi-GRU and MLPs for document and sentence classification did not train, as we solely utilized the loss for the primary task. However, the same model structure was retained to facilitate a fair comparison. To evaluate our experiments, we use a Python implementation [3] of the original [4] conlleval evaluation script, which we simply refer to as the F1 score.

Experiment Set 1:

In Experiment Set 1, we focused on the inherent information present in token annotations, aforementioned in Section 4.1, without incorporating any additional coarse-grained data. This allowed us to measure the impact of introducing auxiliary tasks to the baseline model without modifying the existing data. This reference point was important for comparing loss variations in the other two experiment sets and determining whether the fine-grained task of token classification inherently encompasses the coarser tasks during training.

[3] `https://github.com/sighsmile/conlleval`, accessed on July 6, 2023.

[4] `www.cnts.ua.ac.be/conll2000/chunking/conlleval.txt`, accessed on July 6, 2023.

Experiment Set 2:

Experiment Set 2 addressed the limitation of introducing the document classification task in the baseline model, where all 717 token-annotated documents were positive. To balance out the positive documents and mitigate the training challenges, we introduced negative documents obtained from another subtask of the same shared task as mentioned in Section 4.2. As this change only affected the calculation of document classification loss, there was no need to repeat this experiment for loss variation 1 (only sentence classification loss).

Experiment Set 3:

Finally, in Experiment Set 3, we investigated the effects of including extra coarse-grained data. To simulate a real-world scenario where researchers decide how many documents to annotate, we modified the data size reduction scenario. Instead of completely discarding a certain percentage of the data, we utilized that percentage of documents as extra training data for the sentence and document classification tasks. This experiment set aims to answer the following question; in a scenario where token-annotated data is small, and the training curve does not indicate data saturation for token classification, would easy-to-label coarse-grained data improve the model performance?

6 Results and Discussion

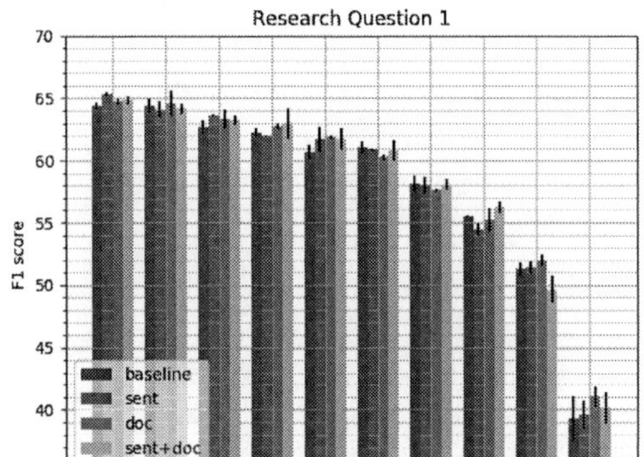

Figure 3: Results from experiment set 1. The black line in each bar indicates the standard deviation. "sent", "doc," and "sent+doc" is for variation 1, 2, and 3 for loss calculation, respectively.

Experiment Set 1:

The results obtained from the initial experiment set, depicted in Figure 3, closely align with our baseline performance, with minor fluctuations attributable to the standard deviation from three runs. Notably, we observe that incorporating document and sentence classification tasks alone does not yield any improvement in the absence of new data introduced to our model. This suggests that during training for the token classification task, the internal representations of our model already encompass the essential information for coarser tasks.

Experiment Set 2:

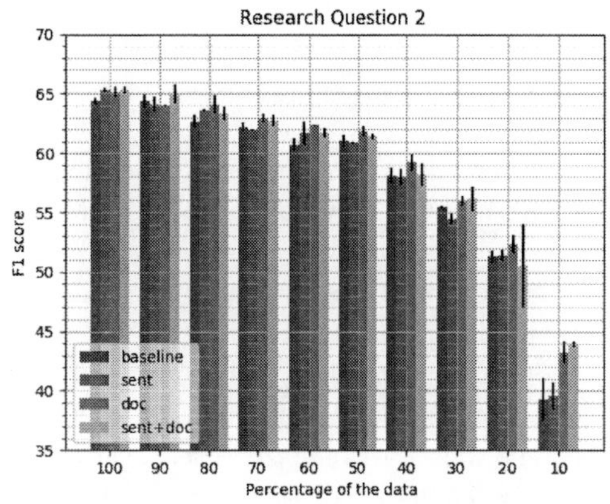

Figure 4: Results from experiment set 2. The black line in each bar indicates the standard deviation. "sent", "doc," and "sent+doc" is for variation 1, 2, and 3 for loss calculation, respectively.

Figure 4 illustrates a clear improvement in results, particularly evident when the data size is reduced to at least 80%. The introduction of negative documents to balance the positive ones is responsible for enhancing the model's performance. Since acquiring negative documents is relatively straightforward – they naturally arise during the document selection process for token-level annotations – this method offers a quick and effective way to boost existing event extraction models. This outcome represents a significant finding from our experiments; even in documents with no information related to events, the model can still exhibit improvements.

Experiment Set 3:

Figure 5 demonstrates a substantial overall gain. Notably, we observe that with only 60% of the

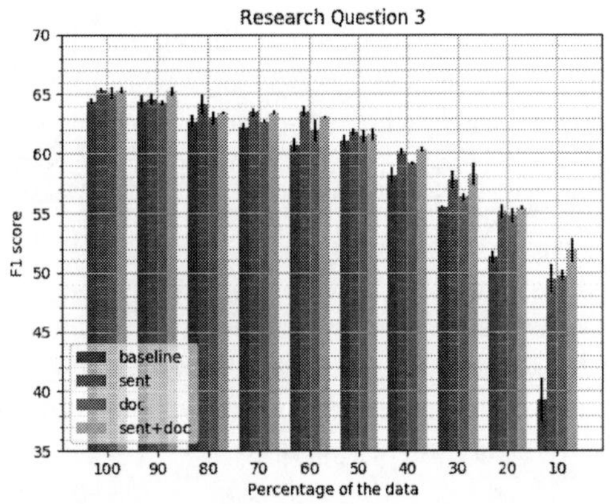

Figure 5: Results from experiment set 3. The black line in each bar indicates the standard deviation. "sent", "doc," and "sent+doc" is for variation 1, 2, and 3 for loss calculation, respectively.

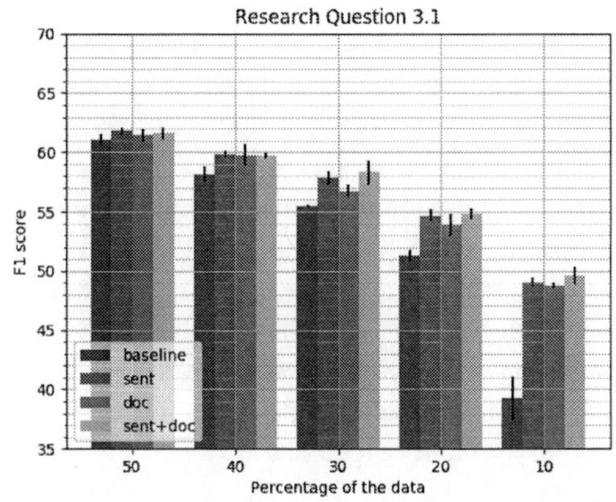

Figure 6: Results from experiment set 3.1. The black line in each bar indicates the standard deviation. "sent", "doc," and "sent+doc" is for variation 1, 2, and 3 for loss calculation, respectively.

717 documents token-annotated, and the remaining 40% having only document and sentence labels, we still achieve results comparable to having all documents token-annotated. Additionally, a general trend emerges, indicating that as token-annotated data decreases and extra coarse-grained data increases, the improvements from the baseline become more pronounced. This trend is further investigated in the experiment set 3.2. Experiment Set 3 involves two variables: token-annotated data size and extra coarse-grained data size. To clarify the impact of each, we conduct experiment set 3.1, where we fix the extra coarse-grained data size and focus solely on changes in token-annotated data size.

Experiment Set 3.1:

Starting with 50% of the data, we fix the discarded 50% as extra coarse-grained data and use it in all subsequent runs. By doing so, we can analyze performance changes between experiments without confusion as to whether the change originated from alterations in extra data size or token data size. As shown in Figure 6, the results align with the original experiment set 3, confirming that the improvement increases as the token data size decreases. Comparing the yellow line representing 10% of the data from this experiment with the same data size in the experiment set 3 reveals that having even more extra coarse-grained data than 50% could lead to further performance gains.

Experiment Set 3.2:

Designed to measure the impact of utilizing coarse-grained data in scenarios akin to few-shot learning settings, this experiment set presents noteworthy results, as depicted in Figure 7. The model exhibits significant improvement over the baseline, suggesting that leveraging coarse-grained data enhances the model's robustness, even with minimal data sizes.

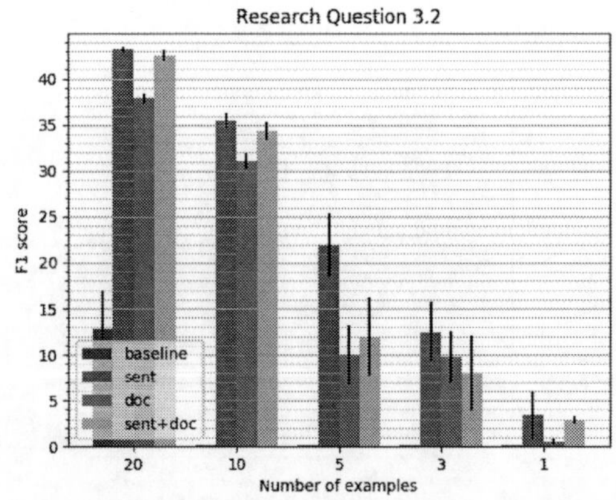

Figure 7: Results from experiment set 3.2. The black line in each bar indicates the standard deviation. "sent", "doc", and "sent+doc" is for variation 1, 2, and 3 for loss calculation, respectively.

7 Conclusion and Future Work

In this study, we addressed the challenge of data scarcity in closed-domain event extraction, a common hurdle in complex NLP tasks. Through our proposed multi-task model structure and training approach, we successfully leveraged additional data generated during the token annotation process. The inclusion of this supplementary data, particularly negative documents without event information, proved to be crucial in enhancing the performance and robustness of our event extraction model.

Our experiments demonstrated that introducing extra coarse-grained data, which identifies documents and sentences without events, significantly contributed to performance improvements. The integration of document and sentence classification tasks alongside token classification did not yield noticeable benefits on their own, reaffirming that the internal representations of our model already encompassed essential information for coarser tasks. Remarkably, even in scenarios where only a portion of the data was token-annotated, the model's performance remained comparable to situations with complete token annotations. We observed a clear trend of increasing performance gains as the token-annotated data size decreased and the extra coarse-grained data size increased. This trend was further reinforced when examining few-shot learning settings, where leveraging coarse-grained data notably enhanced the model's robustness even with minimal data sizes.

In conclusion, our findings offer promising insights into mitigating data scarcity challenges in closed-domain event extraction by effectively utilizing extra data obtained during the annotation process. This practical solution opens the door to more robust and efficient event extraction systems across various domains, with implications for knowledge extraction and decision-making processes. We utilized gold-standard data throughout all our experiments. We will be investigating the possible usage of silver coarse-grained data, which does not even require the considerable ease of labeling documents or sentences. We also plan to include more event information extraction data sets to test our hypothesis further.

References

Saleem Abuleil and Martha Evens. 2004. Events extraction and classification for arabic information retrieval systems. In *16th IEEE International Conference on Tools with Artificial Intelligence*, pages 769–773.

Tommaso Caselli, Osman Mutlu, Angelo Basile, and Ali Hürriyetoğlu. 2021. PROTEST-ER: Retraining BERT for protest event extraction. In *Proceedings of the 4th Workshop on Challenges and Applications of Automated Extraction of Socio-political Events from Text (CASE 2021)*, pages 12–19, Online. Association for Computational Linguistics.

Guandan Chen, Wenji Mao, Qingchao Kong, and Han Han. 2018. Joint learning with keyword extraction for event detection in social media. In *2018 IEEE International Conference on Intelligence and Security Informatics (ISI)*, page 214–219. IEEE Press.

Zheng Chen and Heng Ji. 2009. Can one language bootstrap the other: A case study on event extraction. In *Proceedings of the NAACL HLT 2009 Workshop on Semi-supervised Learning for Natural Language Processing*, pages 66–74, Boulder, Colorado. Association for Computational Linguistics.

Wai Khuen Cheng, Khean Thye Bea, Steven Mun Hong Leow, Jireh Yi-Le Chan, Zeng-Wei Hong, and Yen-Lin Chen. 2022. A review of sentiment, semantic and event-extraction-based approaches in stock forecasting. *Mathematics*, 10(14).

Kyunghyun Cho, Bart van Merriënboer, Dzmitry Bahdanau, and Yoshua Bengio. 2014. On the properties of neural machine translation: Encoder–decoder approaches. In *Proceedings of SSST-8, Eighth Workshop on Syntax, Semantics and Structure in Statistical Translation*, pages 103–111, Doha, Qatar. Association for Computational Linguistics.

Fırat Duruşan, Ali Hürriyetoğlu, Erdem Yörük, Osman Mutlu, Çağrı Yoltar, Burak Gürel, and Alvaro Comin. 2022. Global contentious politics database (glocon) annotation manuals.

Ed drissiya El-allaly, Mourad Sarrouti, Noureddine En-Nahnahi, and Said Ouatik El Alaoui. 2021. Mttlade: A multi-task transfer learning-based method for adverse drug events extraction. *Information Processing & Management*, 58(3):102473.

Sebastian Fleissner and Alex Chengyu Fang. 2012. A syntax-oriented event extraction approach. In *KDIR 2012 - Proceedings of the International Conference on Knowledge Discovery and Information Retrieval*, pages 336–339. 4th International Conference on Knowledge Discovery and Information Retrieval, KDIR 2012 ; Conference date: 04-10-2012 Through 07-10-2012.

Frederik Hogenboom, Flavius Frasincar, Uzay Kaymak, Franciska de Jong, and Emiel Caron. 2016. A survey of event extraction methods from text for decision support systems. *Decision Support Systems*, 85:12–22.

I-Hung Hsu, Kuan-Hao Huang, Elizabeth Boschee, Scott Miller, Prem Natarajan, Kai-Wei Chang, and Nanyun Peng. 2022. DEGREE: A data-efficient generation-based event extraction model. In *Proceedings of the 2022 Conference of the North American Chapter of the Association for Computational Linguistics: Human Language Technologies*, pages 1890–1908, Seattle, United States. Association for Computational Linguistics.

Yibo Hu, MohammadSaleh Hosseini, Erick Skorupa Parolin, Javier Osorio, Latifur Khan, Patrick Brandt, and Vito D'Orazio. 2022. ConfliBERT: A pre-trained language model for political conflict and violence. In *Proceedings of the 2022 Conference of the North American Chapter of the Association for Computational Linguistics: Human Language Technologies*, pages 5469–5482, Seattle, United States. Association for Computational Linguistics.

Ali Hürriyetoğlu, Osman Mutlu, Erdem Yörük, Farhana Ferdousi Liza, Ritesh Kumar, and Shyam Ratan. 2021. Multilingual protest news detection - shared task 1, CASE 2021. In *Proceedings of the 4th Workshop on Challenges and Applications of Automated Extraction of Socio-political Events from Text (CASE 2021)*, pages 79–91, Online. Association for Computational Linguistics.

Ali Hürriyetoğlu, Erdem Yörük, Osman Mutlu, Fırat Duruşan, Çağrı Yoltar, Deniz Yüret, and Burak Gürel. 2021. Cross-Context News Corpus for Protest Event-Related Knowledge Base Construction. *Data Intelligence*, 3(2):308–335.

Chris Jenkins, Shantanu Agarwal, Joel Barry, Steven Fincke, and Elizabeth Boschee. 2023. Massively multi-lingual event understanding: Extraction, visualization, and search.

Nelleke Oostdijk, Ali Hürriyetoglu, Marco Puts, Piet Daas, and Antal van den Bosch. 2016. Information extraction from social media : A linguistically motivated approach. In *Actes de la conférence conjointe JEP-TALN-RECITAL 2016. Volume 10 : RisqueTAL*, pages 23–33, Paris, France. Association pour le Traitement Automatique des Langues. Extraction d'information des réseaux sociaux : une approche motivée linguistiquement.

Erick Skorupa Parolin, Latifur Khan, Javier Osorio, Patrick T. Brandt, Vito D'Orazio, and Jennifer Holmes. 2021. 3m-transformers for event coding on organized crime domain. In *2021 IEEE 8th International Conference on Data Science and Advanced Analytics (DSAA)*, pages 1–10.

Barun Patra, Vishwas Suryanarayanan, Chala Fufa, Pamela Bhattacharya, and Charles Lee. 2020. ScopeIt: Scoping task relevant sentences in documents. In *Proceedings of the 28th International Conference on Computational Linguistics: Industry Track*, pages 214–227, Online. International Committee on Computational Linguistics.

Kevin Pei, Ishan Jindal, Kevin Chen-Chuan Chang, ChengXiang Zhai, and Yunyao Li. 2023. When to use what: An in-depth comparative empirical analysis of OpenIE systems for downstream applications. In *Proceedings of the 61st Annual Meeting of the Association for Computational Linguistics (Volume 1: Long Papers)*, pages 929–949, Toronto, Canada. Association for Computational Linguistics.

James Pustejovsky and Amber Stubbs. 2012. *Natural Language Annotation for Machine Learning: A guide to corpus-building for applications.* " O'Reilly Media, Inc.".

Lance Ramshaw and Mitch Marcus. 1995. Text chunking using transformation-based learning. In *Third Workshop on Very Large Corpora*.

Marek Rei and Anders Søgaard. 2019. Jointly learning to label sentences and tokens. *Proceedings of the AAAI Conference on Artificial Intelligence*, 33(01):6916–6923.

David E Rumelhart, Geoffrey E Hinton, and Ronald J Williams. 1986. Learning representations by back-propagating errors. *nature*, 323(6088):533–536.

Philip A. Schrodt and Muhammed Yassin Idris. 2014. Three's a charm?: Open event data coding with el:diablo, petrarch, and the open event data alliance.

Yiqi Tong, Yidong Chen, and Xiaodong Shi. 2021. A multi-task approach for improving biomedical named entity recognition by incorporating multi-granularity information. In *Findings of the Association for Computational Linguistics: ACL-IJCNLP 2021*, pages 4804–4813.

Xiaofeng Wang, Matthew S. Gerber, and Donald E. Brown. 2012. Automatic crime prediction using events extracted from twitter posts. In *Social Computing, Behavioral - Cultural Modeling and Prediction*, pages 231–238, Berlin, Heidelberg. Springer Berlin Heidelberg.

Wei Xiang and Bang Wang. 2019. A survey of event extraction from text. *IEEE Access*, 7:173111–173137.

Sen Yang, Dawei Feng, Linbo Qiao, Zhigang Kan, and Dongsheng Li. 2019. Exploring pre-trained language models for event extraction and generation. In *Proceedings of the 57th Annual Meeting of the Association for Computational Linguistics*, pages 5284–5294, Florence, Italy. Association for Computational Linguistics.

Erdem Yörük, Ali Hürriyetoğlu, Fırat Duruşan, and Çağrı Yoltar. 2022. Random sampling in corpus design: Cross-context generalizability in automated multicountry protest event collection. *American Behavioral Scientist*, 66(5):578–602.

A Detailed Results

In this chapter of the appendices, tables with detailed results for all the experiments is listed. Each table contains a column named "exp_base" referring to the same baseline results for reference. "sent", "doc" and "sent+doc" columns represent the usage of only sentence classification loss (variation 1), only document classification loss (variation 2), and both sentence and document classification loss (variation 3) in addition to token classification loss when training, respectively.

Acknowledgments

We acknowledge the funding of this study by the European Research Council (ERC) Starting Grant 714868 awarded to Dr. Erdem Yörük for his project Emerging Welfare. Additionally, this research has been supported by the European Union's Horizon 2020 program project ODEUROPA under grant agreement number 101004469.

#num of documents	exp_base	sent	doc	sent+doc
717	64.3420 ± 0.2921	65.3298 ± 0.1894	64.7353 ± 0.2444	64.8228 ± 0.3512
645	64.3836 ± 0.5550	64.0928 ± 0.6175	64.5901 ± 1.0282	64.1613 ± 0.4205
573	62.7110 ± 0.5453	63.6060 ± 0.0960	63.3323 ± 0.7521	63.2426 ± 0.3936
501	62.1977 ± 0.3972	61.9715 ± 0.0423	62.7257 ± 0.2095	62.9463 ± 1.2105
430	60.6711 ± 0.5854	61.6818 ± 1.0062	61.8722 ± 0.1173	61.7387 ± 0.8262
358	61.0600 ± 0.4680	60.8886 ± 0.0812	60.2817 ± 0.2523	60.8147 ± 0.8071
286	58.1234 ± 0.6325	58.0093 ± 0.6460	57.6096 ± 0.1267	58.0629 ± 0.4495
215	55.4766 ± 0.1252	54.4221 ± 0.4860	55.2202 ± 0.9379	56.1987 ± 0.4816
143	51.2678 ± 0.5567	51.4187 ± 0.4740	51.9452 ± 0.4664	49.6417 ± 1.0795
71	39.2988 ± 1.8238	39.5794 ± 1.1141	41.0561 ± 0.8125	40.1392 ± 1.2548

Table 3: Detailed results for experiment set 1, which focuses on the effects of our auxiliary tasks without any data addition.

#num of documents	exp_base	sent	doc	sent+doc
717	64.3420 ± 0.2921	65.3298 ± 0.1894	65.1503 ± 0.4439	65.3221 ± 0.2928
645	64.3836 ± 0.5550	64.0928 ± 0.6175	64.0194 ± 0.0571	65.0234 ± 0.8096
573	62.7110 ± 0.5453	63.6060 ± 0.0960	64.1297 ± 0.7640	63.3397 ± 0.5576
501	62.1977 ± 0.3972	61.9715 ± 0.0423	63.0002 ± 0.3124	62.7757 ± 0.5070
430	60.6711 ± 0.5854	61.6818 ± 1.0062	62.3406 ± 0.0275	61.7372 ± 0.3482
358	61.0600 ± 0.4680	60.8886 ± 0.0812	61.8366 ± 0.4351	61.4128 ± 0.2562
286	58.1234 ± 0.6325	58.0093 ± 0.6460	59.2479 ± 0.7000	58.2156 ± 0.9521
215	55.4766 ± 0.1252	54.4221 ± 0.4860	55.9617 ± 0.4265	56.1648 ± 1.0320
143	51.2678 ± 0.5567	51.4187 ± 0.4740	52.3773 ± 0.7498	50.5637 ± 3.4775
71	39.2988 ± 1.8238	39.5794 ± 1.1141	43.2710 ± 0.8947	43.9792 ± 0.2619

Table 4: Detailed results for experiment set 2, which focuses on the effect of adding negatively labeled documents with no event information.

#num of token annotated documents	#num of extra auxiliary data	exp_base	sent	doc	sent+doc
717	0	64.3420 ± 0.2921	65.3298 ± 0.1894	65.1503 ± 0.4439	65.3221 ± 0.2928
645	72	64.3836 ± 0.5550	64.5663 ± 0.5121	64.2650 ± 0.1842	65.2259 ± 0.3991
573	144	62.7110 ± 0.5453	64.1659 ± 0.8118	63.0057 ± 0.4911	63.4717 ± 0.0919
501	216	62.1977 ± 0.3972	63.4803 ± 0.3426	62.7125 ± 0.1686	63.4292 ± 0.1548
430	287	60.6711 ± 0.5854	63.5683 ± 0.4099	61.9322 ± 0.9456	63.0599 ± 0.0922
358	359	61.0600 ± 0.4680	61.7831 ± 0.3405	61.4165 ± 0.5701	61.5980 ± 0.4963
286	431	58.1234 ± 0.6325	60.1496 ± 0.2897	59.1478 ± 0.1192	60.2890 ± 0.2159
215	502	55.4766 ± 0.1252	57.7715 ± 0.7474	56.2983 ± 0.3384	58.2433 ± 0.9674
143	574	51.2678 ± 0.5567	55.0612 ± 0.6047	54.7686 ± 0.6523	55.4178 ± 0.1332
71	646	39.2988 ± 1.8238	49.4441 ± 1.1924	49.7398 ± 0.4377	51.8297 ± 0.9912

Table 5: Detailed results for experiment set 3, which focuses on the effects of adding extra coarse-grained data.

#num of token annotated documents	#num of extra auxiliary data	exp_base	sent	doc	sent+doc
358	359	61.0600 ± 0.4680	61.7831 ± 0.3405	61.4165 ± 0.5701	61.5980 ± 0.4963
286	359	58.1234 ± 0.6325	59.8364 ± 0.2759	59.7761 ± 0.8661	59.7066 ± 0.2504
215	359	55.4766 ± 0.1252	57.8553 ± 0.5770	56.6985 ± 0.5273	58.2742 ± 0.9637
143	359	51.2678 ± 0.5567	54.6631 ± 0.5420	53.9005 ± 0.9373	54.7954 ± 0.4511
71	359	39.2988 ± 1.8238	49.0730 ± 0.3271	48.7882 ± 0.2006	49.6189 ± 0.7479

Table 6: Detailed results for experiment set 3.1, which is variation of experiment set 3 where extra data size is fixed.

#num of token annotated documents	exp_base	sent	doc	sent+doc
20	12.8237 ± 4.0776	43.2263 ± 0.3178	37.8599 ± 0.5719	42.5216 ± 0.5838
10	0.0000 ± 0.0000	35.4900 ± 0.7729	31.1247 ± 0.8497	34.3691 ± 1.0103
5	0.0000 ± 0.0000	21.9365 ± 3.4075	9.9743 ± 3.1956	11.9494 ± 4.2202
3	0.0000 ± 0.0000	12.4881 ± 3.2203	9.7442 ± 2.7849	7.9693 ± 4.0605
1	0.0000 ± 0.0000	3.3871 ± 2.5824	0.5398 ± 0.3380	2.8559 ± 0.4523

Table 7: Detailed results for experiment set 3.2, which is variation of experiment set 3 with tiny data sizes.

IIC_Team@Multimodal Hate Speech Event Detection 2023: Detection of Hate Speech and Targets using Xlm-Roberta-base

Karanpreet Singh
Institute of Informatics and Communication
University of Delhi
Delhi, India
karanpreet.singh@iic.ac.in

Vajratiya Vajrobol
Institute of Informatics and Communication
University of Delhi
Delhi, India
tiya101@south.du.ac.in

Nitisha Aggarwal
Institute of Informatics and Communication
University of Delhi
Delhi, India
nitisha@south.du.ac.in

Abstract

Hate speech has emerged as a pressing issue on social media platforms, fueled by the increasing availability of multimodal data and easy internet access. Addressing this problem requires collaborative efforts from researchers, policymakers, and online platforms. In this study, we investigate the detection of hate speech in multimodal data, comprising text-embedded images, by employing advanced deep learning models. The main objective is to identify effective strategies for hate speech detection and content moderation. We conducted experiments using four state-of-the-art classifiers: XLM-Roberta-base, BiLSTM, XLNet base cased, and ALBERT, on the CrisisHateMM dataset, consisting of over 4700 text-embedded images related to the Russia-Ukraine conflict. The best findings reveal that XLM-Roberta-base exhibits superior performance, outperforming other classifiers across all evaluation metrics, including an impressive F1 score of 84.62 for sub-task 1 and 69.73 for sub-task 2. Additionally, it is worth highlighting that our study achieved the remarkable feat of securing the 3rd position in both sub-tasks. The future scope of this study lies in exploring multimodal approaches to enhance hate speech detection accuracy, integrating ethical considerations to address potential biases, promoting fairness, and safeguarding user rights. Additionally, leveraging larger and more diverse datasets will contribute to developing more robust and generalised hate speech detection solutions.

1 Introduction

Hate speech on social media has become a major issue, with online platforms being used to denigrate and degrade people or entire groups based on their colour, religion, ethnicity, or handicap (Parihar et al., 2021). In the virtual world, the concept of hate speech can be complex and nuanced, making it difficult to address effectively (Mathew et al., 2019; Banks, 2010; Das, 2023). To address the issue, international conventions, and multilateral initiatives have been developed, however, implementing laws in the virtual sphere remains a difficult undertaking. Despite social media firms' efforts, suppressing hate speech is an ongoing process. The increasing amount of multimedia content, powered by quicker and more accessible mobile internet, has altered the social media environment. Instagram, Snapchat, Vine, and TikTok have championed multimedia, prompting established behemoths like Facebook and Twitter to follow suit. This transition has shifted social media from a predominantly text-based environment to one in which video, audio, and photographs take center stage, allowing users to express themselves in more interesting and diverse ways (Castaño-Pulgarín et al., 2021).

The detection of hate speech during political events is especially important for preserving democracy, reducing violence, protecting vulnerable communities, and fostering civil dialogue. Effective detection ensures fair elections, platform integrity, national cohesion, and informed decision-making while balancing free speech protection with actions to eliminate harmful content. Traditional moderation procedures, such as manual text and multimedia inspection, confront substantial restrictions as a result of the massive volume of data created on social media platforms. Human moderators are unable to keep up with the exponential increase in content, resulting in delays in recognizing and correcting hate speech, allowing harmful content to propagate unchallenged. Furthermore, human moderators' biases and subjective interpretations can lead to inconsistent results. To handle the size and pace of data growth, automated hate speech identification systems are crucial.

Automated hate speech detection systems utilise artificial intelligence (AI) techniques to analyse large volumes of data and identify content that con-

Proceedings of the 6th Workshop on Challenges and Applications of Automated Extraction of Socio-political Events from Text, pages 136–143, Varna, Bulgaria, Sep 7, 2023.
https://doi.org/10.26615/978-954-452-089-2_018

tains hate speech or offensive language these systems rely on Natural Language Processing (NLP) algorithms to preprocess and transform the text data into numerical representations, such as word embeddings. AI models, like recurrent neural networks (RNNs), long short-term memory (LSTM) networks, or transformers, are then employed to extract contextual and semantic features from the text. The model is trained on labeled datasets, learning to recognize patterns and characteristics indicative of hate speech (Smitha et al., 2018; Beskow et al., 2020; De la Pena Sarracén et al., 2018).

To address the need for large datasets to train AI models, the CrisisHateMM Dataset (Bhandari et al., 2023) is introduced, aiding the Shared task on Multimodal Hate Detection at CASE 2023 (Thapa et al., 2023). This dataset includes two primary tasks, with sub-task 1 focusing on classifying text-embedded images into two categories: hate speech and non-hate speech. sub-task 2 involves the classification of targets in the text-embedded images into three categories: individual, organisation, and community. Within the datasets, predominantly comprised of images linked to the Russia-Ukraine conflict, this widespread political event has been the subject of significant hateful language and has been thoroughly examined by researchers (Thapa et al., 2022). By employing a subtask-based methodology, this research approach allows for detailed analysis and interpretability, providing valuable insights into hate speech characteristics and target identification in social media content. The dataset's multimodal and contextually relevant annotations facilitate benchmarking and advancements in combating hate speech on social media platforms.

The paper proposes a novel approach for hate speech identification utilising the textual model Xlm-Roberta-base, achieving impressive results. In sub-task 1, the approach achieves an accuracy of 84.65% and an F1 score of 84.63%. In sub-task 2, it demonstrates solid performance with an accuracy of 72.31% and an F1 score of 69.73%. The method effectively detects hate speech in text-embedded images, showcasing its strong performance in this aspect. Additionally, the study shows significant improvement in target recognition in images with objectionable text, showcasing the efficacy of the proposed approach in enhancing hate speech detection and target identification. Notably, the paper secured the 3rd position in both tasks, signifying its competitive standing within the competition. The accomplishments of this study make a substantial contribution to the field of hate speech identification and further highlight its rank and achievements in the competition.

The paper begins with a concise introduction to the problem of hate speech on social media. It then provides a comprehensive review of previous research on the topic and the technological advancements in recent years, including various approaches, methodologies, datasets, and experimental findings. The dataset is described in detail, statistical analysis is used to gain insights, and preprocessing procedures are covered. The article introduces the approach using NLP models (XLM-Roberta-base, BiLSTM, XLNet base cased, and ALBERT) and reports on how well they perform in identifying hate speech. Results demonstrate the models' efficacy and the discussion analyses the results and discusses constraints. The conclusion highlights the importance of the research in preventing hate speech while summarising the major contributions. References list the sources used to conduct the study.

2 Literature survey

Hate speech on social media is a worrying issue when people utilise online venues to disseminate harmful or discriminatory content, fostering animosity and division. The pervasive effects it has on social cohesiveness, mental health, and actual violence highlight the urgent need for effective content moderation measures to address and reduce this problem.

A study (Gitari et al., 2015) explored the development of a classifier to detect hate speech in web discourses, specifically focusing on race, nationality, and religion themes. They employed sentiment analysis techniques, including subjectivity detection, to identify and rate the polarity of sentiment expressions. By creating a hate speech lexicon based on subjectivity and semantic features, the model effectively classified hate speech. Experimental results with a hate corpus demonstrated the practical applicability of the approach in real-world web discourse scenarios. Researchers (Djuric et al., 2015) also tackled the challenge of hate speech detection in online user comments. Hate speech, defined as abusive speech targeting specific group characteristics like ethnicity, religion, or gender, poses a significant problem for websites that allow user feedback, leading to negative consequences for their online business and user experience. To address this issue, the paper proposed a novel approach using neural language models to learn distributed low-dimensional representations of comments. These representations are then utilised as inputs to a classification algorithm, effectively addressing the issues of high dimensionality and sparsity that had previously hindered the state-of-the-art hate speech detection methods. As a result, their approach demonstrated high efficiency and effectiveness in detecting hate speech in online comments. The study (MacAvaney et al., 2019) addressed the escalating problem of hate speech dissemination in online content and the difficulties confronted by automatic approaches in detecting such content in text. These challenges encompassed the intricacies of language, divergent definitions of hate speech, and limited availability of data for training and testing these systems. Additionally, the lack of interpretability in many recent approaches posed a significant hurdle, making it arduous to comprehend the rationale behind the system's decisions. To overcome these obstacles, the paper proposed a multi-view Support Vector Machine (SVM) approach, which achieved nearly state-of-the-art performance in hate speech detection while maintaining simplicity and providing more easily interpretable decisions compared to neural methods. The paper concluded by discussing both technical and practical challenges that still persist in this area, emphasising the need for further research to enhance hate speech detection systems for online content.

In 2022, Alkomah et al conducted a comprehensive study on hate speech detection systems, reviewing textual features, machine learning models, and datasets (Alkomah and Ma, 2022). The analysis of 138 relevant papers revealed that many approaches lack consistency in detecting various hate speech categories. The dominant methods often involve combining multiple deep learning models, while several hate speech datasets were found to be small and unreliable for detection tasks. The study provides valuable insights into the complexities of hate speech and highlights the need for improved approaches and larger, more reliable datasets to effectively combat hate speech and foster healthier online communities. Another research in the same year (Rana and Jha, 2022) addressed the pressing need to monitor hate speech on social media platforms, particularly in multimedia content. While text-based filtering has been extensively studied, detecting hate speech in multimedia presents unique challenges. A preliminary study revealed that the speaker's emotional state significantly influences hateful content, prompting the paper to focus on auditory and semantic features. Introducing the first multimodal deep learning framework, the study combines emotional auditory features with semantics to detect hate speech effectively. Results demonstrate improved detection compared to text-based models. Additionally, a new Hate Speech Detection Video Dataset (HS-DVD) is introduced, filling the gap in available datasets for this purpose. This research contributes to advancing hate speech detection in multimedia, providing a valuable resource to combat hateful content on social media platforms. (Mazari et al., 2023) conducted a study dedicated to multi-aspect hate speech detection on social media. The overwhelming amount of unfiltered toxic content, including cyberbullying, cyberstalking, and hate speech, has become a significant challenge and a focus of active research. The proposed approach utilises a pre-trained Bidirectional Encoder Representations from Transformers (BERT) model combined with Deep Learning (DL) models to create ensemble learning architectures. The DL models incorporate Bidirectional Long-Short Term Memory (Bi-LSTM) and/or Bidirectional Gated Recurrent Unit (Bi-GRU) on FastText and GloVe word embeddings. Individual training of these models on multi-label hateful datasets and their combination with BERT results in highly effective hate speech detection on social media. By leveraging recent word embedding techniques and DL architectures in conjunction with BERT, the study achieves an impressive ROC-AUC score of 98.63%, significantly enhancing hate speech detection capabilities in multi-aspect scenarios. Recently, one more research by Liam Hebert et al. (2023) introduced the Multi-Modal Discussion Transformer (mDT), a groundbreaking multi-modal graph-based transformer model designed for hate speech detection in online social networks. Unlike traditional text-only methods, mDT takes a holistic approach by considering both text and images when labelling a comment as hate speech. The model leverages graph transformers to capture contextual relationships within the entire discussion surrounding a comment and utilises interwoven fusion layers to combine text and image embeddings, rather than processing different modalities separately. Comparative evaluations against text-only baselines and extensive ablation studies showcase the superior performance of mDT. The paper concludes by emphasising the significance of multimodal solutions in delivering social value in online contexts and highlights that capturing a holistic view of conversations significantly advances the detection of anti-social behaviour like hate speech. This research presents a promising step towards more effective hate speech detection methods by considering both textual and visual cues in social media discussions (Hebert et al., 2023).

3 Methodology

The study utilised Figure 1 to split the training data into 80% training sets and 20% validation sets. Before model input, a preprocessing step was performed to prepare the textual data. The Xlm-RoBERTa-base, BiLSTM, XLNet base cased, and ALBERT models were fine-tuned on the training sets to enhance hate speech identification. Testing predictions were then generated using the fine-tuned models, demonstrating the effectiveness of the proposed approach in hate speech detection and target identification.

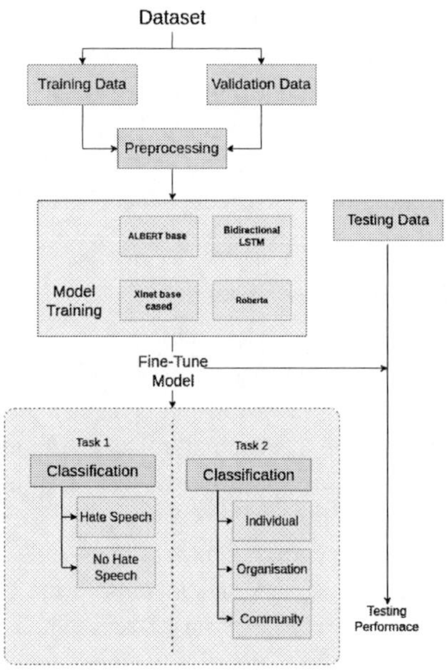

Figure 1: Process Flow of Hate Speech Detection and Target Identification Processes.

Class Name	Number of Words	Number of Unique Words	Maximum Text length (character)	Average Words (per post)
No Hate	82532	14974	1673	49
Hate	63721	12224	1297	32

Table 1: Distribution of extracted text length for 'Hate Speech' and 'Non-Hate speech.

3.1 Dataset

The CrisisHateMM dataset contains over 4700 text-embedded images related to the Russia-Ukraine conflict. It includes 2665 instances of hate speech and 2058 instances of non-hate speech. The dataset is further categorised into directed hate speech (2428 instances) and undirected hate speech (237 instances), with annotations for targets classified into individual (1027), community (417), and organisational (984) categories.

Table 1 indicates regarding sub-task 1 that the "No Hate" class has more posts and a higher number of words compared to the "Hate" class. However, further analysis is necessary to fully understand the significance of these differences. For sub-task 2, target detection is valuable for comprehending the distribution of textual content, post lengths, and word usage across different categories (Individual, Community, and Organisation) in the dataset (Table 2).

Class Name	Number of Words	Number of Unique Words	Max Text Length	Avg Words (per post)
Individual	25.9k	6.4k	1082	31.42
Community	12.9k	4.0k	1297	38.70
Organisation	24.9k	6.7k	382	31.74

Table 2: Text Length Distribution for 'Individual', 'Organisation', and 'Community' Classes.

In the preprocessing step, the initial transformation involves extracting text from images using the Google Vision API. Subsequently, various techniques are applied to clean and refine the text data before inputting it into the model. The process begins by eliminating any HTML tags present in the text, followed by the normalization of accent characters to their ASCII equivalents. Punctuation marks and special characters are eliminated, and the entire text is converted to lowercase for uniformity. The text is subsequently tokenized into individual words and any unnecessary spaces are stripped. This preprocessing step aims to prepare the text data in a standardised and meaningful format, enhancing the model's performance. For subtask 1, Table 3 presents a comparison between the unprocessed text in column 1 and the processed text in column 2, along with their respective labels in column 3. For subtask 2, a similar comparison is shown in Table 4, where column 1 contains the unprocessed text, column 2 displays the processed text, and column 3 indicates the corresponding labels. The preprocessing step plays a vital role in optimising the input data for the hate speech detection models, ensuring that the models can effectively capture the relevant patterns and features from the text-embedded images.

Extracted Text From Images	Preprocessed text	Label
BREAKING NEWS: PRESIDENT ZELENSKYY TRIPPED AND FELL HERE THIS MORNING imglip.com	breaking news president zelenskyy tripped and fell here this morning imglipcom	Hate Speech
PROTESTORS AROUND THE WORLD RALLY IN SUPPORT OF UKRAINE STORYFUL/AP	protestors around the world rally in support of ukraine storyfulap	No Hate Speech

Table 3: Example of text extracted from CrisisHateMM dataset for sub-task 1

Extracted Text From Images	Preprocessed text	Label
HEY JOE, RUSSIA HAS INVADED UKRAINE WITH HEAVY ARSENAL! WHAT YOU GONNA DO?	hey joe russia has invaded ukraine with heavy arsenal what you gonna do im holding a climate denialism roundtable imgflipcom	Individual
58 13 CCM All saver 'WISHING THEM DEATH' Russian NHL players face horrible anger	58 13 ccm all saver wishing them death russian nhl players face horrible anger	Community
THE WEST HAS GIVEN THE BEST SONG AWARD TO NATO NATO imgflip.com	the west has given the best song award to nato nato imgflipcom	organisation

Table 4: Example of text extracted from CrisisHateMM dataset for sub-task 2

3.2 Model training and evaluation

At the classification stage, four deep learning models, namely Xlm-RoBERTa-base, BiLSTM, XLNet base cased, and ALBERT—are used to categorise posts containing hate speech based on the pre-processed text. The ability of these models to extract complex patterns and contextual information from the textual data is a commonality shared by them. To do this, they employ advanced language representation techniques and attention mechanisms. A thorough evaluation of their capacity to correctly identify hate speech within the text-embedded images is provided by the use of critical metrics to measure each participant's performance, including accuracy, F1 score, precision, and recall. To ensure their dependability and suitability for the crucial task of identifying hate speech, these models go through extensive testing and analysis against the established metrics.

3.2.1 Bidirectional LSTM

Bidirectional Long Short-Term Memory (BiLSTM) is based on LSTM architecture that processes input data in both forward and backward directions. The hidden state in typical LSTM is updated based on previous information in the input sequence (i.e., from left to right). Bidirectional LSTM, on the other hand, processes the input sequence in two passes: one from left to right (ahead direction) and one from right to left (reverse way). The capacity of Bidirectional LSTM to capture information from both past and future contexts is a critical advantage for comprehending the context and dependencies in a sequence. Because the model is bidirectional, it can capture long-term dependencies and context that traditional unidirectional LSTMs may miss.

3.2.2 Xlnet base cased

'xlnet-base-cased' is a variation of the XLNet language model that is part of Google Research's Transformer-based family. It enhances the BERT model by using a permutation-based training strategy to overcome some shortcomings. It is suited for a variety of natural language processing tasks such as text categorization, sentiment analysis, language synthesis, and question answering after being trained on a large corpus. Because it is 'cased,' it keeps casing information in input text, which is useful for some jobs. Researchers and developers can fine-tune the 'xlnet-base-cased' model for specific tasks by using its rich language representation capabilities, which capture complex linguistic patterns and context for a wide range of natural language processing applications.

3.2.3 ALBERT-base-v2

ALBERT-base-v2 is a language model variant of ALBERT (A Lite BERT), aiming to be a more efficient and parameter-reduced version of BERT. The suffix "base" denotes that it is smaller than larger variants such as 'ALBERT-large' or 'ALBERT-xlarge'. ALBERT achieves efficiency by utilising parameter-sharing techniques such as factorised embeddings and cross-layer parameter sharing, which results in quicker training times without sacrificing performance. It is trained using masked language modelling (MLM) on a huge corpus and may be fine-tuned for various NLP tasks. ALBERT has grown in prominence due to its competitive performance, particularly in resource-constrained circumstances, and is now a common choice in NLP applications.

3.2.4 Xlm-RoBERTa-base

Xlm-RoBERTa-base' is a variant of the XLM-R (Cross-lingual Language Model - Roberta) language model. It is a multilingual version of the RoBERTa model, based on the transformer architecture, designed for cross-lingual language understanding. The model is trained on a large corpus of text data from multiple languages using masked language modeling (MLM) and translation language modeling (TLM) objectives. This allows it to effectively process and understand text from various languages. The "cased" in the name indicates that it retains case information during training and inference, treating uppercase and lowercase characters as distinct tokens. XLM-Roberta-base is widely used in multilingual NLP tasks (Conneau et al., 2020), transferring knowledge across languages and performing well on tasks involving different languages.

4 Results and discussion

Classification results of Sub-task 1 are reported in Table 5 for all four classifiers. XLM-Roberta-base has outperformed all other classifiers in terms of all four metrics. XLM-Roberta-base has been trained on large corpses of text data hence it can understand the context of text more effectively as compared to the other classical NLP models. From the values of the F1-score, it can be concluded that the models have learned the context of both classes and performed well to identify each class.

	BiLSTM	ALBERT	XLnet	XLM-Roberta
Acc.	68.62	81.71	82.84	84.65
F1	68.62	81.56	82.78	84.62
Recall	69.00	81.60	83.03	85.07
Prec.	68.86	81.53	82.74	84.76

Table 5: Model Performance for Hate Speech Detection (sub-task 1).

The classification results for sub-task 2 are summarised in Table-6, utilising the same four classifiers as in sub-task 1. Once again, XLM-Roberta-base stands out as the best performer, surpassing the other classifiers in all four evaluation metrics. This exceptional performance can be credited to its extensive training on text data, which enables it to comprehend the context of textual content more effectively than traditional NLP models. The Precision values further validate that the models have successfully achieved accurate target classification for individual, community, and organisational categories. These results reaffirm the significance of XLM-Roberta-base in hate speech detection and target classification within text-embedded images, underlining its potential for advancing research in this field. XLM-Roberta-base's superior performance in hate speech detection for both sub-tasks, outperforming other classifiers. Its extensive pretraining on vast text corpora, bidirectional context comprehension, large capacity, multilingual proficiency, and fine-tuning on CrisisHateMM dataset contribute to its exceptional understanding of hate speech content. Ethical considerations and challenges in detecting hate speech were acknowledged. The CrisisHateMM dataset's value for research, providing insights into hate speech complexities, was emphasised. Leveraging advanced NLP models like XLM-Roberta-base holds significant potential for effective hate speech detection and content moderation, fostering a safer online environment.

	BiLSTM	Albert	XLnet	XLM-Roberta
Acc.	56.19	67.35	66.52	72.23
F1	54.84	65.35	62.32	69.73
Recall	58.99	65.35	61.56	68.94
Prec.	59.99	65.36	64.47	71.01

Table 6: Performance Comparison of NLP Models for Target Identification (sub-task 2).

Furthermore, our achievement of the 3rd rank in both sub-tasks using solely textual models, as evident in Table 7 and Table 8, not only underscores the efficiency of the XLM-Roberta-base model but

Team Name	Recall	Precision	F1	Accuracy
ARC-NLP	85.67	85.63	85.65	85.78
bayesiano98	85.61	85.28	85.28	85.33
IIC Team	**85.08**	**84.76**	**84.63**	**84.65**
DeepBlueAI	83.56	83.35	83.42	83.52

Table 7: In Subtask A: Hate Speech Detection leaderboard, our team, IIC Team, ranks third based on the F1 score, demonstrating competitive performance across all classification metrics.

Team Name	Recall	Precision	F1	Accuracy
ARC-NLP	76.36	76.37	76.34	79.34
bayesiano98	73.30	75.54	74.10	77.27
IIC Team	**68.94**	**71.05**	**69.73**	**72.31**
Sarika22	67.77	68.41	68.05	71.49

Table 8: In Subtask B: Target Detection, our team, IIC Team, secured the third position on the leaderboard, leading in all classification metrics based on the F1 score.

also highlights the prudent management of computational resources. This approach aptly aligns with resource-conscious strategies, demonstrating a commitment to optimizing performance while maintaining a responsible balance.

5 Conclusion

This research focuses on text-embedded images used in social media to express opinions and emotions, which unfortunately also serve as platforms for spreading hate speech, propaganda, and extremist ideologies. Notably, during the Russia-Ukraine war, both sides extensively utilised text-embedded images for propaganda and hate speech dissemination. The growing abundance of offensive content on social media poses challenges in effectively detecting and moderating such material. To address this issue, we utilise the CrisisHateMM dataset, an innovative multimodal dataset containing over 4,700 text-embedded images from the Russia-Ukraine conflict. The dataset is meticulously annotated for hate and non-hate speech, further categorising hate speech into directed and undirected forms and providing annotations for individual, community, and organisational targets. Our research involves two subtasks: Sub-task 1 focuses on hate speech detection in text-embedded images, while Sub-task 2 aims to identify the targets of hate speech. To achieve accurate results, we employ advanced feature extraction techniques and utilise deep learning models for both subtasks, yielding promising outcomes. In Sub-task 1, our textual model, XLM-Roberta-base, demonstrated superior performance, achieving the highest accuracy on test(unseen) data with a recall of 85.08%, precision of 84.76%, F1 score of 84.63%, and accuracy of 84.65%. Additionally, in Sub-task 2, the Xlm-Roberta-base model outperformed other approaches, achieving a recall of 68.94%, precision of 71.05%, F1 score of 69.73%, and accuracy of 72.31% These results highlight the effectiveness of our approach in hate speech detection and target identification in text-embedded images during the Russia-Ukraine conflict. Exploring multimodal approaches, accessing larger and more diverse datasets, fine-tuning strategies, addressing biases, integrating automated systems with social media platforms, extending detection to multiple languages, and improving interpretability and contextual understanding are all part of the future of hate speech detection and content moderation. Exploring zero-shot and few-shot learning methodologies, as well as addressing ethical concerns, are also essential. In summary, future research promises effective and responsible ways for combating hate speech on social media through the use of AI developments.

References

Fatimah Alkomah and Xiaogang Ma. 2022. A literature review of textual hate speech detection methods and datasets. *Information*, 13(6):273.

James Banks. 2010. Regulating hate speech online. *International Review of Law, Computers & Technology*, 24(3):233–239.

David M Beskow, Sumeet Kumar, and Kathleen M Carley. 2020. The evolution of political memes: Detecting and characterizing internet memes with multi-modal deep learning. *Information Processing & Management*, 57(2):102170.

Aashish Bhandari, Siddhant B Shah, Surendrabikram Thapa, Usman Naseem, and Mehwish Nasim. 2023. Crisishatemm: Multimodal analysis of directed and undirected hate speech in text-embedded images from russia-ukraine conflict. In *Proceedings of the IEEE/CVF Conference on Computer Vision and Pattern Recognition*, pages 1993–2002.

Sergio Andrés Castaño-Pulgarín, Natalia Suárez-Betancur, Luz Magnolia Tilano Vega, and Harvey Mauricio Herrera López. 2021. Internet, social media and online hate speech. systematic review. *Aggression and Violent Behavior*, 58:101608.

Alexis Conneau, Kartikay Khandelwal, Naman Goyal, Vishrav Chaudhary, Guillaume Wenzek, Francisco

Guzmán, Edouard Grave, Myle Ott, Luke Zettlemoyer, and Veselin Stoyanov. 2020. Unsupervised cross-lingual representation learning at scale.

Mithun Das. 2023. Classification of different participating entities in the rise of hateful content in social media. In *Proceedings of the Sixteenth ACM International Conference on Web Search and Data Mining*, pages 1212–1213.

Nemanja Djuric, Jing Zhou, Robin Morris, Mihajlo Grbovic, Vladan Radosavljevic, and Narayan Bhamidipati. 2015. Hate speech detection with comment embeddings. In *Proceedings of the 24th international conference on world wide web*, pages 29–30.

Njagi Dennis Gitari, Zhang Zuping, Hanyurwimfura Damien, and Jun Long. 2015. A lexicon-based approach for hate speech detection. *International Journal of Multimedia and Ubiquitous Engineering*, 10(4):215–230.

Liam Hebert, Gaurav Sahu, Nanda Kishore Sreenivas, Lukasz Golab, and Robin Cohen. 2023. Multi-modal discussion transformer: Integrating text, images and graph transformers to detect hate speech on social media. *arXiv preprint arXiv:2307.09312*.

Sean MacAvaney, Hao-Ren Yao, Eugene Yang, Katina Russell, Nazli Goharian, and Ophir Frieder. 2019. Hate speech detection: Challenges and solutions. *PloS one*, 14(8):e0221152.

B Mathew, R Dutt, P Goyal, and A Mukherjee. 2019. Spread of hate speech in online social media. In *Proceedings of the 10th ACM Conference on Web Science*. Anais.

Ahmed Cherif Mazari, Nesrine Boudoukhani, and Abdelhamid Djeffal. 2023. Bert-based ensemble learning for multi-aspect hate speech detection. *Cluster Computing*, pages 1–15.

Anil Singh Parihar, Surendrabikram Thapa, and Sushruti Mishra. 2021. Hate speech detection using natural language processing: Applications and challenges. In *2021 5th International Conference on Trends in Electronics and Informatics (ICOEI)*, pages 1302–1308.

Gretel Liz De la Pena Sarracén, Reynaldo Gil Pons, Carlos Enrique Muniz Cuza, and Paolo Rosso. 2018. Hate speech detection using attention-based lstm. *EVALITA evaluation of NLP and speech tools for Italian*, 12:235.

Aneri Rana and Sonali Jha. 2022. Emotion based hate speech detection using multimodal learning. *arXiv preprint arXiv:2202.06218*.

ES Smitha, Selvaraju Sendhilkumar, and GS Mahalaksmi. 2018. Meme classification using textual and visual features. In *Computational Vision and Bio Inspired Computing*, pages 1015–1031. Springer.

Surendrabikram Thapa, Farhan Ahmad Jafri, Ali Hürriyetoğlu, Francielle Vargas, Roy Ka-Wei Lee, and Usman Naseem. 2023. Multimodal hate speech event detection - shared task 4, case 2023. In *Proceedings of the 6th Workshop on Challenges and Applications of Automated Extraction of Socio-political Events from Text (CASE)*.

Surendrabikram Thapa, Aditya Shah, Farhan Ahmad Jafri, Usman Naseem, and Imran Razzak. 2022. A multi-modal dataset for hate speech detection on social media: Case-study of russia-ukraine conflict. In *CASE 2022-5th Workshop on Challenges and Applications of Automated Extraction of Socio-Political Events from Text, Proceedings of the Workshop*. Association for Computational Linguistics.

Event Causality Identification - Shared Task 3, CASE 2023

Fiona Anting Tan
Institute of Data Science, National University of Singapore, Singapore
tan.f@u.nus.edu

Hansi Hettiarachchi
School of Computing and Digital Technology, Birmingham City University, United Kingdom
hansi.hettiarachchi@mail.bcu.ac.uk

Ali Hürriyetoğlu
KNAW Humanities Cluster DHLab, The Netherlands
ali.hurriyetoglu@dh.huc.knaw.nl

Nelleke Oostdijk
Centre for Language Studies, Radboud University, The Netherlands
nelleke.oostdijk@ru.nl

Onur Uca
Department of Sociology, Mersin University, Turkey
onuruca@mersin.edu.tr

Surendrabikram Thapa
Department of Computer Science, Virginia Tech, United States of America
surendrabikram@vt.edu

Farhana Ferdousi Liza
School of Computing Sciences University of East Anglia, United Kingdom
f.liza@uea.ac.uk

Abstract

The Event Causality Identification Shared Task of CASE 2023 is the second iteration of a shared task centered around the Causal News Corpus. Two subtasks were involved: In Subtask 1, participants were challenged to predict if a sentence contains a causal relation or not. In Subtask 2, participants were challenged to identify the Cause, Effect, and Signal spans given an input causal sentence. For both subtasks, participants uploaded their predictions for a held-out test set, and ranking was done based on binary F1 and macro F1 scores for Subtask 1 and 2, respectively. This paper includes an overview of the work of the ten teams that submitted their results to our competition and the six system description papers that were received. The highest F1 scores achieved for Subtask 1 and 2 were 84.66% and 72.79%, respectively.

Keywords: Causal News Corpus, Causal event classification, Cause-Effect-Signal span detection

1 Introduction

A causal relation represents a semantic relationship between a Cause argument and an Effect argument, where the occurrence of the Cause triggers the occurrence of the Effect (Barik et al., 2016). The extraction of causal information from text holds significant implications for downstream applications in natural language processing (NLP), like for summarization and prediction (Radinsky et al., 2012; Radinsky and Horvitz, 2013; Izumi et al., 2021; Hashimoto et al., 2014), question answering (Dalal et al., 2021; Hassanzadeh et al., 2019; Stasaski et al., 2021), inference and understanding (Jo et al., 2021; Dunietz et al., 2020).

Given the limited availability of data for causal text mining (Asghar, 2016; Xu et al., 2020; Yang et al., 2022; Tan et al., 2022b), in 2022, the Causal News Corpus (CNC) was created (Tan et al., 2022b).[1] We also introduced a shared task to promote modelling for two causal text mining tasks: (1) Causal Event Classification and (2) Cause-Effect-Signal Span Detection (Tan et al., 2022a). This paper describes the second iteration of this shared task. In this iteration, some parts of our data have updated labels and for Subtask 2, much more annotated data is provided.

The remainder of the paper is organized as follows: Section 2 describes the dataset and its annotations. Section 3 formally introduces the two subtasks for the shared task. Section 4 describes the evaluation metrics and competition set-up. Next, Section 5 summarizes the methods used by par-

[1] The CNC was created by a similar group of authors, some of which did not work on this shared task.

Proceedings of the 6th Workshop on Challenges and Applications of Automated Extraction of Socio-political Events from Text, pages 144–150, Varna, Bulgaria, Sep 7, 2023.
https://doi.org/10.26615/978-954-452-089-2_019

Stat.	Label	Train	Dev	Test	Total
#	*Causal*	1624	185	173	1982
Sent-	*Non-causal*	1451	155	179	1785
ences	Total	3075	340	352	3767
Avg.	*Causal*	33.44	34.41	35.93	33.75
#	*Non-causal*	26.69	26.85	28.67	26.90
words	Total	30.25	30.96	32.24	30.50

Table 1: Subtask 1 Data Summary Statistics.

Statistic	Train	Dev	Test	Total
# Sentences	1624	185	173	1982
# Relations	2257	249	248	2754
Avg. rels/sent	1.39	1.35	1.43	1.39
Avg. # words	33.44	34.41	35.93	33.75
Cause	11.56	12.20	12.96	11.74
Effect	10.71	10.18	11.54	10.74
Signal	1.45	1.53	1.46	1.46
Avg # *Sig.*/rel	0.70	0.64	0.79	0.70
Prop. of rels w/ *Sig.*	0.68	0.63	0.76	0.69

Table 2: Subtask 2 Data Summary Statistics.

ticipants in the competition. Finally, Section 6 concludes this paper.

2 Dataset

Our shared task uses Version 2 (V2) of the Causal News Corpus (Tan et al., 2022b), which is based on the corpora released in the scope of Hürriyetoğlu et al. (2021).[2] V2 incorporates additional span annotations for Subtask 2. As compared to the previous version of 160 sentences and 183 relations, the current version contains 1981 sentences and 2754 causal relations. Annotations were also revised for some examples across both Subtasks. The summary statistics for Subtask 1 and 2 are available in Tables 1 and 2 respectively.

3 Shared Task Description

The task is comprised of two subtasks related to Event Causality Identification: (1) Causal Event Classification and (2) Cause-Effect-Signal Span Detection. The objective of each subtask is described below in Sections 3.1 and 3.2. The 2023 edition is the second iteration of this shared task which was first introduced in 2022 (Tan et al., 2022a). The shared task is re-launched to work on the larger and revised CNC-V2 discussed in the earlier Section. Additionally, for Subtask 2, the traditional evaluation metrics (P, R and F1) were updated to use fairer evaluation calculations, discussed in Section 4.1.

3.1 Subtask 1: Causal Event Classification

The aim of this task is to classify whether an event sentence contains any cause-effect meaning. Systems had to predict *Causal* or *Non-causal* labels per test sentence. An event sentence was defined to be *Causal* if it contains at least one causal relation.

3.2 Subtask 2: Cause-Effect-Signal Span Detection

The objective of this task is to detect the consecutive spans relevant to a *Causal* relation. There are three types of spans involved in a *Causal* relation: The *Cause* span refers to words that describe the event that triggers another *Effect* event. The *Effect* span refers to words that describe the resulting event arising from a *Cause* event. *Signals* are optionally present, and are words that explicitly indicate a *Causal* relation is present. In our dataset, multiple *Causal* relations can exist in a sentence, and participants have to identify all of them.

4 Evaluation & Competition

4.1 Evaluation Metrics

Evaluation metrics were the same as the shared task launched last year (Tan et al., 2022a). For Subtask 1, Precision (P), Recall (R), F1, Accuracy (Acc) and Matthews Correlation Coefficient (MCC) metrics were used. For Subtask 2, Macro P, R and F1 were used. Evaluation was conducted at the relation level. In other words, examples with multiple causal relations were unpacked and each relation contributed equally to the final score. We designed an evaluation algorithm that allows participants to submit multiple Cause-Effect-Signal span predictions per input sequence in any order. One change from the previous years' evaluation is that we use the FairEval implementation[3] of `seqeval` (Nakayama, 2018; Ramshaw and Marcus, 1995) in Subtask 2 to prevents double penalties of close-to-correct predictions (Ortmann, 2022).

4.2 Baseline

For Subtask 1, we replicate last year's BERT benchmark (Tan et al., 2022b,a). The model fine-tunes the pre-trained (PTM) Bidirectional Encoder Representations from Transformers (BERT) model

[2] https://github.com/tanfiona/CausalNewsCorpus

[3] https://huggingface.co/spaces/hpi-dhc/FairEval

Rank	Team Name	Codalab Username	R	P	F1	Acc	MCC
1	-	DeepBlueAI	86.13	83.24	**84.66**	**84.66**	**69.37**
2	InterosML (Patel, 2023)	rpatel12	87.28	81.62	84.36	84.09	68.37
3	BoschAI (Schrader et al., 2023)	timos	87.86	80.00	83.75	83.24	66.83
4	CSECU-DSG (Hossain et al., 2023)	csecudsg	85.55	80.00	82.68	82.39	64.95
5	-	elhammohammadi	**89.60**	76.35	82.45	81.25	63.52
6	BERT Baseline	tanfiona	89.02	75.86	81.91	80.68	62.37
7	Anonymous	sgopala4	86.13	78.01	81.87	81.25	62.88
8	MLModeler5 (Bhatia et al., 2023)	nitanshjain	87.28	65.37	74.75	71.02	44.83
9	VISU	kunwarv4	52.60	**85.85**	65.23	72.44	48.19
10	-	pakapro	47.40	44.09	45.68	44.60	-10.72

Table 3: Subtask 1 Leaderboard. Ranked by Binary F1. All scores are reported in percentages (%). Highest score per column is in bold.

Rank	Team Name	Codalab Username	Overall			Cause (n=119)			Effect (n=119)			Signal (n=98)		
			R	P	F1	R	P	F1	R	P	F1	R	P	F1
1	BoschAI (Schrader et al., 2023)	timos	**63.98**	**84.42**	**72.79**	**59.66**	**85.28**	**70.20**	**62.88**	**82.76**	**71.46**	**70.44**	**85.36**	**77.18**
2	1Cademy Baseline	tanfiona	59.18	60.25	59.71	54.20	60.92	57.36	59.04	65.98	62.32	64.75	54.75	59.33
3	CSECU-DSG (Hossain et al., 2023)	csecudsg	36.12	40.00	37.96	40.00	42.86	41.38	31.44	33.43	32.40	36.72	44.22	40.12
4	-	pakapro	0.00	0.00	0.00	0.00	0.00	0.00	0.00	0.00	0.00	0.00	0.00	0.00

Table 4: Subtask 2 Leaderboard. Ranked by Overall Macro F1. All scores are reported in percentages (%). Highest score per column is in bold.

(Devlin et al., 2019) for sequence classification. After BERT encodes sentences into word embeddings, the hidden state corresponding to the `[CLS]` token is fed through a binary classification head to obtain the predicted logits. We used the `bert-base-cased` pre-trained model.

For Subtask 2, we replicate the top submission from last year's shared task. Team 1Cademy (Chen et al., 2022)[4] framed the challenge as a reading comprehension task that aims to predict the start and end token positions of each Cause, Effect, and Signal span. We used the `albert-xxlarge-v2` (Lan et al., 2019) pre-trained model.

4.3 Competition Set-up

We used the Codalab website to host our competition.[5]

Registration 29 participants requested to participate on the Codalab page. However, we required participants to email us some personal details (Name, Institution and Email) to avoid teams from creating multiple accounts to cheat. Eventually, only 23 participants were successfully registered, out of which, only 10 accounts participated by uploading predictions.

Trial and Test Periods The trial period started on May 01, 2023, where the training and validation data were released. Participants could upload any number of submissions against the validation set, and they could also submit results for the validation set at any point in time. The main purpose of this setting is for participants to familiarise themselves with the Codalab platform.

The test period started on June 15, 2023 and ended on July 7, 2023. Each participant was allowed only 5 submissions to prevent participants from over-fitting to the test set. After the competition ended, an additional scoring page was created,[6] where participants could upload one result a day to generate more scores for their description papers. None of the scores from this additional scoring page were included into the final leaderboard.

For both Subtasks, the performance was ranked by F1 score: the binary F1 score for Subtask 1, and the Macro F1 score for Subtask 2.

5 Participant Systems

5.1 Overview

Nine participants successfully submitted scores to Subtask 1 while only three successfully submitted scores to Subtask 2 during test period. Table 3 and

[4]https://github.com/Gzhang-umich/1CademyTeamOfCASE

[5]The competition page is at https://codalab.lisn.upsaclay.fr/competitions/11784.

[6]The additional scoring page is at https://codalab.lisn.upsaclay.fr/competitions/14265.

Ra-	Team Name	Codalab	Overall			Cause (n=119)			Effect (n=119)			Signal (n=98)		
nk		Username	R	P	F1	R	P	F1	R	P	F1	R	P	F1
1	BoschAI (Schrader et al., 2023)	timos	**53.47**	**82.59**	**64.91**	**47.39**	**82.52**	**60.20**	**50.41**	**80.26**	**61.93**	**64.68**	**84.97**	**73.45**
2	1Cademy Baseline	tanfiona	38.68	41.98	40.26	33.64	40.45	36.73	36.04	43.96	39.60	47.00	41.59	44.13
3	CSECU-DSG (Hossain et al., 2023)	csecudsg	21.16	24.80	22.84	24.63	26.46	25.51	14.66	16.97	15.73	23.96	31.51	27.22
4	-	pakapro	0.00	0.00	0.00	0.00	0.00	0.00	0.00	0.00	0.00	0.00	0.00	0.00

Table 5: Subtask 2 Leaderboard for Examples with Multiple Causal Relations. This leaderboard was not used in the competition ranking but provided here for discussion purposes. All scores are reported in percentages (%). Highest score per column is in bold.

4 reflects the leaderboard for Subtask 1 and 2 respectively for evaluation metrics described earlier in Section 4.1. For Subtask 2, we further provided the performance for each span type (i.e., Cause, Effect and Signal). We also provide a separate leaderboard for examples with multiple causal relations in Table 5.

For Subtask 1, the top performing team was DeepBlueAI, scoring 84.66% for F1. DeepBlueAI also topped the charts for Acc and MCC scores. Team InterosML (Patel, 2023) followed closely after, with an F1 score of 84.36%. Unfortunately, DeepBlueAI did not submit a paper, so we do not know the method they used. InterosML's (Patel, 2023) employed a two-phased approach to finetune the model first using RoBERTa embeddings and with contrastive loss.

For Subtask 2, the top performing team was BoschAI (Schrader et al., 2023) with an F1 score of 72.79%, far higher than the 1Cademy baseline that we provided. A key modelling decision that they had was to stack multiple token labels into one target label, thereby allowing their model to detect multiple causal relations per sequence. This key feature sets them ahead of the model design of the 1Cademy baseline. This can be observed by the large improvements in overall F1 score of 24.65% for examples with multiple causal relations in Table 5 (40.26% vs 64.91.%).

All participants used pre-trained models in their frameworks. For Subtask 1, although multiple teams described a similar sequence classification framework using BERT and RoBERTa, different F1 scores were reported. This suggests the importance of carefully designing and implementing suitable hyperparamters in training a model.

5.2 Methods

We summarize the systems of the six teams that submitted description papers below, sorted according to their leaderboard ranking. Only four papers were accepted to be included in the proceedings of the CASE workshop.

5.2.1 Subtask 1

InterosML (Patel, 2023)'s methodology involved two phases: (1) pre-training a baseline RoBERTa model with supervised contrastive loss (SuperCon), and (2) Fine-tuning the pre-trained model on Subtask 1 itself. For Phase 1, the positive instances refer to sequences containing causal relations, while negative instances refer to sequences without causal relations. The authors demonstrate the usefulness of using contrastive loss, achieving high F1 score of 84.36%, clinching 2nd place, and only slightly below the first place's score. In their paper, they present T-SNE visualizations to investigate the effectiveness of their model on the classification task.

BoschAI (Schrader et al., 2023) used a sequence classification framework that outputs a prediction based on the [CLS] embedding. They experimented with two pre-trained models, BERT-large and RoBERTa-large. A weighted cross-entropy loss was applied to up-weight positive samples.

CSECU-DSG (Hossain et al., 2023) used two transformer models, DeBERTa and RoBERTa to extract contextualized embeddings, which are then combined through a linear feed-forward layer to estimate the probability score of each class. A weighted average of the scores from the two modules is used to obtain the final probability of the scores for each label.

Anonymous they experimented with two models: (1) BERT-base sequence classifier and (2) few-shot prompting of GPT-4 using 0, 2, 4, 6, 14 prompts. In their experiments, they showed that a fine-tuned BERT classifier obtains an F1 score of 81.8%, exceeding the best score possible with GPT-4 of 70.7%. They also did not find a correlation between increasing the number of prompts shown to GPT-4 with any improvements in F1.

MLModeler5 (Bhatia et al., 2023) used a RoBERTa sequence classification model to classify input sequences with a binary label indicating if causal relations exists in the sequence or not. Their main contribution is the exploration of four datasets, created by processing the original data with four different heuristics-based method. According to their experiments, their model performed best when trained on a dataset that had stop words removed and abbreviations were replaced in the input sequences.

VISU used multiple embedding methods (static, stacked, and contextualized) for this task. For non-contextualized embeddings, a BiLSTM was applied onto various embeddings from GloVe, fastText or frozen-BERT. For contextualized embeddings, a linear layer was applied onto various embeddings like ERT-base, BART, DistilBERT or RoBERTa. In their experiments, they demonstrate that contextualized embeddings obtain the highest F1 scores, the best being RoBERTa which scored an F1 of 65.23%.

5.2.2 Subtask 2

BoschAI (Schrader et al., 2023) approached the task as a sequence tagging task using the BILOU (Alex et al., 2007) labeling scheme. This scheme extends the BIO scheme by adding markers for the end of a multi-token sequence (L) and a single-token entity (U). They experimented with two pre-trained models, BERT-large and RoBERTa-large, that generate embeddings fed to a linear layer to obtain logits per token, then the logits were parsed through a CRF output layer to compute the most likely consistent tag sequence. However, this approach can only predict a single output sequence per sample, which is not suitable for sentences with multiple causal chains. To address this, the BILOU labels are stacked using a pipe (|) operator similar to Straková et al. (2019), allowing the model to consider multiple causal relations within a single instance. Three layers are used to keep the label space manageable. Stacked labels occurring in the training and validation data are added, resulting in approximately 300 three-layer BILOU labels. During evaluation, these stacked labels are split into three distinct layers, allowing the model to predict up to three different causal relations per sentence. Data augmentation was also used to increase the number of training samples. This approach was able to rank first in the subtask with an F1-score of 72.79%.

CSECU-DSG (Hossain et al., 2023) employed two different transformer models, namely DeBERTa and DistilRoBERTa, independently for capturing cause-effect and signal span features, respectively. Subsequently, they combined both sets of features and fed them into a stacked BiLSTM network to capture long-term relationships among the tokens. After the BiLSTM network, a max-pooling layer and classifier were incorporated to predict token labels. To enhance system performance, the authors introduced a contrastive loss for cause-effect token classification, whereas, for signal token classification, they utilized cross-entropy loss, considering that signal tokens may or may not be present in the text. The R, P, and F1 achieved by the approach were 36.12%, 40.00%, and 37.96% respectively.

6 Conclusion

In conclusion, our shared task investigated two important tasks in causal text mining, namely: (1) Causal Event Classification, and (2) Cause-Effect-Signal Span Detection. Our shared task attracted 23 registered participants and 10 active participants. Based on the six description papers received, some novel methods that exceeded our initial baseline were proposed. The best F1 scores achieved for Subtask 1 and 2 were 84.66% and 72.79% respectively.

References

Beatrice Alex, Barry Haddow, and Claire Grover. 2007. Recognising nested named entities in biomedical text. In *Biological, translational, and clinical language processing*, pages 65–72.

Nabiha Asghar. 2016. Automatic extraction of causal relations from natural language texts: a comprehensive survey. *arXiv preprint arXiv:1605.07895*.

Biswanath Barik, Erwin Marsi, and Pinar Öztürk. 2016. Event causality extraction from natural science literature. *Res. Comput. Sci.*, 117:97–107.

Amrita Bhatia, Ananya Thomas, Nitansh Jain, and Jatin Bedi. 2023. MLModeler5 @ Causal News Corpus 2023: Using roberta for casual event classification. In *Proceedings of the 6th Workshop on Challenges and Applications of Automated Extraction of Socio-political Events from Text (CASE)*, Varna, Bulgaria (Hybrid). Association for Computational Linguistics.

Xingran Chen, Ge Zhang, Adam Nik, Mingyu Li, and Jie Fu. 2022. 1Cademy @ causal news corpus 2022: Enhance causal span detection via beam-search-based position selector. In *Proceedings of the 5th Workshop on Challenges and Applications of*

Automated Extraction of Socio-political Events from Text (CASE), pages 100–105, Abu Dhabi, United Arab Emirates (Hybrid). Association for Computational Linguistics.

Dhairya Dalal, Mihael Arcan, and Paul Buitelaar. 2021. Enhancing multiple-choice question answering with causal knowledge. In *Proceedings of Deep Learning Inside Out (DeeLIO): The 2nd Workshop on Knowledge Extraction and Integration for Deep Learning Architectures*, pages 70–80, Online. Association for Computational Linguistics.

Jacob Devlin, Ming-Wei Chang, Kenton Lee, and Kristina Toutanova. 2019. BERT: Pre-training of deep bidirectional transformers for language understanding. In *Proceedings of the 2019 Conference of the North American Chapter of the Association for Computational Linguistics: Human Language Technologies, Volume 1 (Long and Short Papers)*, pages 4171–4186, Minneapolis, Minnesota. Association for Computational Linguistics.

Jesse Dunietz, Greg Burnham, Akash Bharadwaj, Owen Rambow, Jennifer Chu-Carroll, and Dave Ferrucci. 2020. To test machine comprehension, start by defining comprehension. In *Proceedings of the 58th Annual Meeting of the Association for Computational Linguistics*, pages 7839–7859, Online. Association for Computational Linguistics.

Chikara Hashimoto, Kentaro Torisawa, Julien Kloetzer, Motoki Sano, István Varga, Jong-Hoon Oh, and Yutaka Kidawara. 2014. Toward future scenario generation: Extracting event causality exploiting semantic relation, context, and association features. In *Proceedings of the 52nd Annual Meeting of the Association for Computational Linguistics (Volume 1: Long Papers)*, pages 987–997, Baltimore, Maryland. Association for Computational Linguistics.

Oktie Hassanzadeh, Debarun Bhattacharjya, Mark Feblowitz, Kavitha Srinivas, Michael Perrone, Shirin Sohrabi, and Michael Katz. 2019. Answering binary causal questions through large-scale text mining: An evaluation using cause-effect pairs from human experts. In *Proceedings of the Twenty-Eighth International Joint Conference on Artificial Intelligence, IJCAI-19*, pages 5003–5009. International Joint Conferences on Artificial Intelligence Organization.

MD. Akram Hossain, Abdul Aziz, and Abu Nowshed Chy. 2023. CSECU-DSG @ Causal News Corpus 2023: Leveraging roberta and deberta transformer model with contrastive learning for causal event classification. In *Proceedings of the 6th Workshop on Challenges and Applications of Automated Extraction of Socio-political Events from Text (CASE)*, Varna, Bulgaria (Hybrid). Association for Computational Linguistics.

Ali Hürriyetoğlu, Osman Mutlu, Erdem Yörük, Farhana Ferdousi Liza, Ritesh Kumar, and Shyam Ratan. 2021. Multilingual protest news detection - shared task 1, CASE 2021. In *Proceedings of the 4th Workshop on Challenges and Applications of Automated Extraction of Socio-political Events from Text (CASE 2021)*, pages 79–91, Online. Association for Computational Linguistics.

Kiyoshi Izumi, Hitomi Sano, and Hiroki Sakaji. 2021. Economic causal-chain search and economic indicator prediction using textual data. In *Proceedings of the 3rd Financial Narrative Processing Workshop*, pages 19–25, Lancaster, United Kingdom. Association for Computational Linguistics.

Yohan Jo, Seojin Bang, Chris Reed, and Eduard H. Hovy. 2021. Classifying argumentative relations using logical mechanisms and argumentation schemes. *Trans. Assoc. Comput. Linguistics*, 9:721–739.

Zhenzhong Lan, Mingda Chen, Sebastian Goodman, Kevin Gimpel, Piyush Sharma, and Radu Soricut. 2019. ALBERT: A lite BERT for self-supervised learning of language representations. *CoRR*, abs/1909.11942.

Hiroki Nakayama. 2018. seqeval: A python framework for sequence labeling evaluation. Software available from https://github.com/chakki-works/seqeval.

Katrin Ortmann. 2022. Fine-grained error analysis and fair evaluation of labeled spans. In *Proceedings of the Thirteenth Language Resources and Evaluation Conference*, pages 1400–1407, Marseille, France. European Language Resources Association.

Rajat Patel. 2023. InterosML @ Causal News Corpus 2023: Understanding causal relationships. In *Proceedings of the 6th Workshop on Challenges and Applications of Automated Extraction of Socio-political Events from Text (CASE)*, Varna, Bulgaria (Hybrid). Association for Computational Linguistics.

Kira Radinsky, Sagie Davidovich, and Shaul Markovitch. 2012. Learning causality for news events prediction. In *Proceedings of the 21st World Wide Web Conference 2012, WWW 2012, Lyon, France, April 16-20, 2012*, pages 909–918. ACM.

Kira Radinsky and Eric Horvitz. 2013. Mining the web to predict future events. In *Sixth ACM International Conference on Web Search and Data Mining, WSDM 2013, Rome, Italy, February 4-8, 2013*, pages 255–264. ACM.

Lance Ramshaw and Mitch Marcus. 1995. Text chunking using transformation-based learning. In *Third Workshop on Very Large Corpora*.

Timo Pierre Schrader, Simon Razniewski, Lukas Lange, and Annemarie Friedrich. 2023. BoschAI @ Causal News Corpus 2023: Robust cause-effect span extraction using multi-layer sequence tagging and data augmentation. In *Proceedings of the 6th Workshop on Challenges and Applications of Automated Extraction of Socio-political Events from Text (CASE)*, Varna, Bulgaria (Hybrid). Association for Computational Linguistics.

Katherine Stasaski, Manav Rathod, Tony Tu, Yunfang Xiao, and Marti A. Hearst. 2021. Automatically generating cause-and-effect questions from passages. In *Proceedings of the 16th Workshop on Innovative Use of NLP for Building Educational Applications*, pages 158–170, Online. Association for Computational Linguistics.

Jana Straková, Milan Straka, and Jan Hajic. 2019. Neural architectures for nested ner through linearization. In *Proceedings of the 57th Annual Meeting of the Association for Computational Linguistics*. Association for Computational Linguistics.

Fiona Anting Tan, Hansi Hettiarachchi, Ali Hürriyetoğlu, Tommaso Caselli, Onur Uca, Farhana Ferdousi Liza, and Nelleke Oostdijk. 2022a. Event causality identification with causal news corpus - shared task 3, CASE 2022. In *Proceedings of the 5th Workshop on Challenges and Applications of Automated Extraction of Socio-political Events from Text (CASE)*, pages 195–208, Abu Dhabi, United Arab Emirates (Hybrid). Association for Computational Linguistics.

Fiona Anting Tan, Ali Hürriyetoğlu, Tommaso Caselli, Nelleke Oostdijk, Tadashi Nomoto, Hansi Hettiarachchi, Iqra Ameer, Onur Uca, Farhana Ferdousi Liza, and Tiancheng Hu. 2022b. The causal news corpus: Annotating causal relations in event sentences from news. In *Proceedings of the Thirteenth Language Resources and Evaluation Conference*, pages 2298–2310, Marseille, France. European Language Resources Association.

Jinghang Xu, Wanli Zuo, Shining Liang, and Xianglin Zuo. 2020. A review of dataset and labeling methods for causality extraction. In *Proceedings of the 28th International Conference on Computational Linguistics*, pages 1519–1531, Barcelona, Spain (Online). International Committee on Computational Linguistics.

Jie Yang, Soyeon Caren Han, and Josiah Poon. 2022. A survey on extraction of causal relations from natural language text. *Knowl. Inf. Syst.*, 64(5):1161–1186.

Multimodal Hate Speech Event Detection - Shared Task 4, CASE 2023

Surendrabikram Thapa
Department of Computer Science, Virginia Polytechnic Institute and State University, United States of America
sbt@vt.edu

Farhan Ahmad Jafri
Department of Computer Science, Jamia Millia Islamia, India
farhanjafri88888@gmail.com

Ali Hürriyetoğlu
KNAW Humanities Cluster DHLab, The Netherlands
ali.hurriyetoglu@dh.huc.knaw.nl

Francielle Vargas
Institute of Mathematical and Computer Sciences, University of São Paulo, Brazil
francielleavargas@usp.br

Roy Ka-Wei Lee
Singapore University of Technology and Design Singapore, Singapore
roy_lee@sutd.edu.sg

Usman Naseem
College of Science and Engineering, James Cook University, Australia
usman.naseem@jcu.edu.au

Abstract

Ensuring the moderation of hate speech and its targets emerges as a critical imperative within contemporary digital discourse. To facilitate this imperative, the shared task **Multimodal Hate Speech Event Detection** was organized in the sixth CASE workshop co-located at RANLP 2023. The shared task has two subtasks. The sub-task A required participants to pose hate speech detection as a binary problem i.e. they had to detect if the given text-embedded image had hate or not. Similarly, sub-task B required participants to identify the targets of the hate speech namely individual, community, and organization targets in text-embedded images. For both sub-tasks, the participants were ranked on the basis of the F1-score. The best F1-score in sub-task A and sub-task B were 85.65 and 76.34 respectively. This paper provides a comprehensive overview of the performance of 13 teams that submitted the results in Subtask A and 10 teams in Subtask B.

1 Introduction

The rise of social media has altered the global communication and information landscape, allowing people from all walks of life to share their opinions and perspectives on a wide range of topics, including heated geopolitical events (Overbey et al., 2017; Chen and Zimbra, 2010). This free-flowing exchange of ideas, however, has not been without difficulties. The rapid proliferation of hate speech, which includes harsh language, disrespectful statements, and discriminatory rhetoric directed at individuals or groups based on their ethnicity, nationality, or beliefs, is one of the most alarming concerns afflicting online platforms (Parihar et al., 2021). In times of political crisis, such as the Russia-Ukraine Crisis, the prevalence of hate speech becomes even more pronounced (Thapa et al., 2022). Its impact goes beyond dividing communities; it also brings about considerable concerns for sustaining peace and stability in regions facing conflict-related issues.

Text-embedded images have gained popularity due to their easy sharability and the combination of visual and textual elements, making them a common mode for information sharing (Chen et al., 2022; Bhandari et al., 2023; Lee et al., 2021). However, this convenience also has a downside – it amplifies the prevalence of hate speech in social media. To combat the propagation of hate content through text-embedded images, the identification of hate speech within such media holds significant importance (Cao et al., 2022; Pramanick et al., 2021b; Sharma et al., 2022). By detecting and curbing hate speech within these images, we can work towards maintaining a healthier digital environment. In an attempt to curb hate speech in the context of the Russia-Ukraine crisis, Bhandari et al. (2023) proposed a multimodal dataset of 4,723 text-embedded images annotated for presence of hate speech, direction of hate speech (targeted vs untargeted) and targets of hate speech. Building on this groundwork and to attract greater attention toward the issue of hate speech in text-embedded images, we introduced a shared task at the CASE 2023 workshop (co-located with RANLP 2023) utilizing the dataset. The shared task has two subtasks: subtask

Proceedings of the 6th Workshop on Challenges and Applications of Automated Extraction of Socio-political Events from Text, pages 151–159, Varna, Bulgaria, Sep 7, 2023.
https://doi.org/10.26615/978-954-452-089-2_020

A which deals with the identification of hate speech and subtask B which deals with the identification of targets in hate speech. Through this shared task, we intend to stimulate active engagement and collaboration in addressing this critical challenge of identifying and mitigating hate speech within the digital landscape, specifically in the context of text-embedded images.

The rest of the paper is organized as follows: Section 2 gives a brief outlook of the related works in multimodal hate speech classification. In section 3, the subtasks of the shared task are presented. Similarly, section 4 describes the CrisisHateMM dataset in brief. Section 5 describes the system that we used in the competition along with the evaluation metrics. Similarly, section 6 sheds light on the methodologies used by the teams that submitted the system description papers. Section 7 gives a brief analysis of the system descriptions, and section 8 finally concludes the paper.

2 Related Work

The task of detecting hate speech in social media has gained significant traction, primarily focusing on text-based content (Alam et al., 2022; Chhabra and Vishwakarma, 2023). However, there has been lesser efforts in classification of text-embedded images for hate speech in social media (Gomez et al., 2020; Bhandari et al., 2023). In recent times, there has been a notable surge in scholarly interest towards identifying hate speech in memes or images containing text (Ji et al., 2023; Hermida and Santos, 2023; Karim et al., 2022; Yang et al., 2022, 2019a; Perifanos and Goutsos, 2021). Memes often combine images and text with the intention of humor. On the other hand, text-embedded images are essentially images that incorporate text within them. This category encompasses not only memes but also other forms of textual-visual content, such as screenshots taken from TV headlines. In these cases, the image itself serves to provide context, while the accompanying text conveys the information within that context. While meme analysis has been a focal point for researchers, the examination of hate speech in these text-embedded images deserves equal attention. The introduction of this shared task stems from the recognition of this research gap.

Similarly, the exploration of memes or multimodal textual-visual data has predominantly concentrated on the broader scope of general social media platforms. The efforts to create dedicated datasets and conduct research within specific contexts have been quite limited. Recently, some research have shown efforts to understand such multimodal textual-visual data for specific contexts and applications. For instance, Pramanick et al. (2021a) investigated harmful memes and their targets in the context of the COVID-19 pandemic. They labeled COVID-19-related memes to indicate harmfulness and the targets of these harmful memes. Expanding on this work, Pramanick et al. (2021b) also studied memes related to the US election using the same labeling approach. Additionally, Naseem et al. (2023) introduced a dataset containing 10,244 memes critical of vaccines. These initiatives are gradually paving the way for future research that aligns with specific contexts. This shared task is also an attempt to attract the attention of the research community, encouraging their involvement in context-oriented investigations.

3 Task Description

According to Warner and Hirschberg (2012), hate speech is a particular form of offensive language that considers stereotypes to express an ideology of hate. Here, we assume that offensive language is a type of opinion-based information that is highly confrontational, rude, or aggressive (Zampieri et al., 2019), which may be led explicitly or implicitly (Vargas et al., 2021; Poletto et al., 2021). In the same settings, hate speech is a particular form of offensive language used against target groups, mostly based on their social identities.

3.1 Subtask 1: Hate Speech Detection

The goal of this task is to identify whether the given text-embedded image contains hate speech or not. The dataset used for this subtask consists of text-embedded images, and these images are annotated to indicate the presence or absence of hate speech. More precisely, the dataset for this sub-task comprises two labels: "Hate Speech" and "No Hate Speech".

3.2 Subtask 2: Identification of Targets of Hate Speech

The goal of this subtask is to identify the targets of hate speech in a given hateful text-embedded image. Although hate speech text-embedded images may contain various potential targets falling into numerous categories, our subtask focuses solely on identifying three predetermined targets outlined within the dataset used in our shared task. The text-embedded images in the dataset are annotated for "community", "individual" and "organization" targets. Consequently, our objective centers on the identification of these particular targets within text-embedded images featuring hate speech.

4 Dataset

In our shared task, we used the CrisisHateMM dataset (Bhandari et al., 2023). This dataset consists of a total of 4,723 text-embedded images centered around the Russia-Ukraine Crisis (Thapa et al., 2022). Within these 4,723 text-embedded images, 2,058 did not have any instances of hate speech, while the remaining 2,665 contained elements of hate speech. Among these 2,665 images with hate speech, a subset of 2,428 text-embedded images exhibited instances of targeted or directed hate speech. In our shared task, we used only text-embedded images that exhibited directed hate speech and those that did not have any hate speech. Thus, a total of 4,486 text-embedded images were used in our shared task. We split the dataset into train, evaluation, and test stages for both subtasks A and B in a stratified manner, maintaining a proportionate split ratio of approximately 80-10-10.

Subtask	Classes	Train	Eval	Test
Subtask A	Hate	1942	243	243
	No Hate	1658	200	200
Subtask B	Individual	823	102	102
	Community	335	40	42
	Organization	784	102	98

Table 1: Statistics of the dataset at train, evaluation, and test phase of our shared task

5 Evaluation and Competition

This section describes our competition environment including ranking methods and other details regarding the competition.

5.1 Evaluation Metrics

In order to assess the performance of participants' submissions, we used accuracy, precision, recall, and macro F1-score. The rank of the participants was determined by sorting based on the macro F1-score.

5.2 Competition Setup

We hosted our competition using the Codalab[1]. The competition had two phases: an evaluation phase, which introduced participants to the Codalab system, and a testing phase which determined the final leaderboard ranking based on performance.

Registration: A total of 51 participants registered for our competition. The diverse range of email domains used indicated that the competition successfully attracted individuals from various geographical regions. Among all the registered participants, a total of 13 teams submitted their predictions.

Competition Timelines: The competition started on May 1, 2023, with the release of training and evaluation data. The first phase was the evaluation phase. As the purpose of the evaluation phase was to make participants familiarize with codalab, the evaluation data labels were also provided to participants. Subsequently, the test phase started on June 15, 2023, with the release of test data that didn't have any ground truth labels. Originally planned to conclude on June 30, 2023, the test phase was extended to July 7, 2023, in response to multiple participant requests. Finally, the deadline for submitting the system description paper was set for July 24, 2023.

6 Participants' Methods

6.1 Overview

A total of 13 participants submitted scores for subtask A, while subtask B received 10 successful submissions. The leaderboards for subtasks A and B are presented in Table 2 and 3 respectively. Notably, in both subtasks, ARC-NLP (Sahin et al., 2023) achieved the highest performance in terms of the F1-score, with scores of 85.65 for subtask A and 76.34 for subtask B. Our next step involves an in-depth discussion of each team's approaches to gain a thorough understanding of the technical intricacies involved.

6.2 Methods

Below, we provide a summary of the systems from the eight teams that submitted description papers, organized based on their leaderboard ranking. Among these submissions, seven papers have

[1]The competition page can be found here: `https://codalab.lisn.upsaclay.fr/competitions/13087`.

Rank	Team Name	Codalab Username	Accuracy	Precision	Recall	F1-score
1	ARC-NLP (Sahin et al., 2023)	arc-nlp	**85.78**	**85.63**	**85.67**	**85.65**
2	-	bayesiano98	85.33	85.28	85.61	85.28
3	IIC_Team (Singh et al., 2023)	karanpreet_singh	84.65	84.76	85.08	84.63
4	-	DeepBlueAI	83.52	83.35	83.56	83.42
5	CSECU-DSG (Aziz et al., 2023)	csecudsg	82.62	82.44	82.52	82.48
6	Ometeotl (Armenta-Segura et al., 2023)	Jesus_Armenta	81.04	80.94	81.21	80.97
7	SSN-NLP-ACE (K et al., 2023)	Avanthika	79.01	78.81	78.78	78.80
8	VerbaVisor (Esackimuthu and Balasundaram, 2023)	Sarika22	78.56	78.49	78.06	78.21
9	-	rabindra.nath	78.33	78.42	77.68	77.88
10	Lexical Squad (Kashif et al., 2023)	md_kashif_20	73.59	73.72	72.7.	72.87
11	GT	lueluelue	52.60	52.19	52.19	52.19
12	Team + 1	pakapro	49.66	49.39	49.38	49.36
13	ML_Ensemblers	Sathvika.V.S	57.79	72.40	53.34	42.94

Table 2: Sub-task A (Hate Speech Classification) Leaderboard, Ranked by Macro F1-Score. All scores are presented as percentages (%). The highest score in each column is highlighted in bold.

been accepted for inclusion in the proceedings of the CASE workshop.

6.2.1 Subtask A

ARC-NLP (Sahin et al., 2023) leveraged syntactic features from the text extracted from the dataset along with ensemble learning in order to predict the presence of hate speech. The information from textual and visual encoders is used to train the multi-layer perception (MLP) (Murtagh, 1991). Similarly, XGBoost (Chen and Guestrin, 2016), Light Gradient Boosting Machine (LGBM) (Alzamzami et al., 2020), and Gradient Boosting Machine (GBM) (Natekin and Knoll, 2013; Ayyadevara and Ayyadevara, 2018) are trained on syntactical and Bag of Words-based features (Zhang et al., 2010). A weighted ensemble (Hürriyetoğlu et al., 2022; Sahin et al., 2022) is used to make the final decision. This method stands as the first method with an F1-score of 85.65.

IIC_Team (Singh et al., 2023) implemented XLM-Roberta-base, BiLSTM, XLNet base cased, and ALBERT on the CrisisHateMM (Bhandari et al., 2023) dataset, consisting of over text-embedded images related to the Russia-Ukraine conflict. The models were fine-tuned on the training sets to enhance hate speech identification, in which they slit the dataset in 80% for training and 20% for validation. Lastly, a robust preprocessing step was performed to prepare the textual data. The authors obtained a high performance presenting an impressive F1 score of 84.62 for sub-task 1 using XLM-Roberta-base. Finally, even though in this proposal the authors did not provide any evaluation related to potential social bias in hate speech technologies (Davani et al., 2023; Vargas et al., 2023), for future works, they aim to tackle strategies towards social bias mitigation, as well as improve the amount of data and its diversity in order to obtain more generalized and accurate results.

CSECU-DSG (Aziz et al., 2023) used a multimodal approach by contextualizing text characteristics using the BERT transformers model. The Bi-LSTM was used to understand long-term contextual relationships and facilitate the extraction of hate speech from the text recovered from images. The ViT transformers model was used to extract visual information from photographs. They used a multi-sample dropout method after combining the outputs of the multimodal and BiLSTM modules to arrive at the final prediction. By achieving an F1-score of 82.48 and an accuracy of 82.62, this technique ranked fifth in subtask A.

Ometeotl (Armenta-Segura et al., 2023) used the pre-trained transformer approach BertForSequenceClassification model with the bert-base-uncased architecture from huggingface[2]. They didn't utilize any preprocessing for subtask A and achieved an F1 score of 80.97. The authors secured the 6th rank in subtask A.

SSN-NLP-ACE (K et al., 2023) extracted the text from text-embedded images using Google Vision API and extracted the features using the TF-IDF (Adhikari et al., 2021) approach. They used the traditional machine learning approach i.e. support vector machine (SVM). In the SVM, the closest data points are the support vectors in finding the optimal plane. The kernel applied in SVM is RBF (Radial Basis Function). The authors tuned the parameters to maximize F1-score to 78.80 and an accuracy of 79.01 in subtask A.

[2] https://huggingface.co/

Rank	Team Name	Codalab Username	Accuracy	Precision	Recall	F1-score
1	ARC-NLP (Sahin et al., 2023)	arc-nlp	**79.34**	**76.37**	**76.36**	**76.34**
2	-	bayesiano98	77.27	73.30	75.54	74.10
3	IIC_Team (Singh et al., 2023)	karanpreet_singh	72.31	71.05	68.94	69.73
4	VerbaVisor (Esackimuthu and Balasundaram, 2023)	Sarika22	71.49	68.41	67.77	68.05
5	CSECU-DSG (Aziz et al., 2023)	csecudsg	69.01	65.75	65.25	65.30
6	-	DeepBlueAI	69.83	66.48	64.62	65.25
7	Ometeotl (Armenta-Segura et al., 2023)	Jesus_Armenta	64.05	67.93	56.48	56.77
8	SSN-NLP-ACE (K et al., 2023)	Avanthika	64.05	70.13	53.84	52.58
9	ML_Ensemblers	Sathvika.V.S	52.89	48.88	44.44	43.32
10	pakapro	Team + 1	35.12	35.59	34.42	33.42

Table 3: Sub-task B (Targets of Hate Speech Classification) Leaderboard, Ranked by Macro F1-Score. All scores are presented as percentages (%). The highest score in each column is highlighted in bold.

VerbaVisor (Esackimuthu and Balasundaram, 2023) implemented Artificial Neural Networks (ANN) (Mishra and Srivastava, 2014) model along with the ALBERT (Lan et al., 2019) model for this subtask. Out of these two ALBERT performed the best with a F1-score of 78.21. The ANN model performed poorly as compared to ALBERT.

Lexical Squad (Kashif et al., 2023) used an approach to combine both textual and visual information from the text-embedded images. They used a combined representation from different unimodal models: XLNet (Yang et al., 2019b) and BERT (Kenton and Toutanova, 2019) for textual features and Inception-V3 (Szegedy et al., 2016) for visual features. Stacking was used to generate a combined representation. This approach gave them a F1-score of 74.96 which is above 3 points improvement when using XLNet alone and above 5 points improvement when using BERT alone. When solely utilizing Inception-V3, they achieved an F1-score of 48.11. The empirical evaluations by the authors showed that the approach yielded poor performances when a model had to leverage a lot of visual information to make decisions.

ML_Ensemblers used a variety of algorithms, which includes Naive Bayes (Rish et al., 2001), k-Nearest Neighbors (KNN) (Jiang et al., 2007), Random Forest (Breiman, 2001), Decision Trees (Kotsiantis, 2013), and Support Vector Machine (SVM) (Cortes and Vapnik, 1995; Pisner and Schnyer, 2020). Among these algorithms, Naive Bayes displayed the highest performance with an F1-score of 42.94. It's important to note that the mentioned approach is not an ensemble, as each algorithm was assessed separately rather than being combined into a unified model. The approach ranked 13th in subtask A.

6.2.2 Subtask B

ARC-NLP (Sahin et al., 2023) made use of entity features along with CLIP (Radford et al., 2021) embeddings to create a feature that was leveraged to classify targets of hate speech. Similar to the approach for subtask A, the ensemble methods were then used to make the final decision. The method was ranked first in the competition with an F1-score of 76.34. The importance of NER in hate speech and target classification has been an interest of the academic community and this method reaffirms that the NER characteristics are very important.

IIC_Team (Singh et al., 2023) implemented XLM-Roberta-base, BiLSTM, XLNet base cased, and ALBERT on the CrisisHateMM (Bhandari et al., 2023) dataset related to the Russia-Ukraine conflict. The authors obtained an F1 score of 69.73 for sub-task 2 using XLM-Roberta-base.

VerbaVisor (Esackimuthu and Balasundaram, 2023) applied ALBERT to approach the problem of target detection in our shared task. They were able to get the fourth rank with an F1-score of 68.05.

CSECU-DSG (Aziz et al., 2023) used the multimodal technique in which they adjusted the BERT (Kenton and Toutanova, 2019) transformers model to extract the text's contextualized properties. The Vision Transformers (ViT) (Dosovitskiy et al., 2020) model was used to extract the visual information from the given image, and the Bi-LSTM was used to learn the long-term contextual dependency that enables the model to extract the hate information present in the context. On top of the outputs from the multimodal and BiLSTM modules, the multi-sample dropout strategy is then applied to obtain the final prediction. This approach gave them an F1-score of 65.30 and an accuracy of 69.01.

Ometeotl (Armenta-Segura et al., 2023) employed the huggingface bert-base-uncased architecture with the pre-trained transformer method BertForSequenceClassification model. Unlike subtask A, for subtask B, they used preprocessing outside of BERT processing of the text, such as eliminating special letters or stopwords, and they received an F1 score of 56.77. The authors placed the seventh rank in subtask B. The case study of different examples led them to hypothesize that image features are more important in target identification than hate speech classification.

SSN-NLP-ACE (K et al., 2023) employed the TF-IDF technique to extract the features from the text of text-embedded images. They approached subtask B using the conventional machine-learning method of Logistic Regression (Nick and Campbell, 2007). It is a technique for statistical analysis that makes use of probability estimates. The hyperparameters were optimized by the authors and an F1-score of 52.58 was achieved.

ML_Ensemblers employed multiple algorithms for target detection. They utilized various algorithms namely Naive Bayes algorithm (Rish et al., 2001; Thapa et al., 2020), k-Nearest Neighbors (kNN) (Jiang et al., 2007), Random Forest (Breiman, 2001), Decision Tree (Kotsiantis, 2013), and Support Vector Machine (SVM) (Cortes and Vapnik, 1995; Pisner and Schnyer, 2020). Among these, the multinomial Naive Bayes algorithm performed the best with an F1-score of 43.32.

7 Discussion

The methods from different participants gave interesting insights into various methods. Particularly, transformer-based methods were seen to be more effective. Most participants utilized BERT-based variations to extract textual features from the dataset. For the extraction of visual features, participants turned to vision transformers, CLIP (Radford et al., 2021), and established methods like Inception-V3. The methodology proposed by Sahin et al. (2023) suggested that syntactical and entity features are equally important to leverage textual information from the dataset, particularly from instances that were related to the identification of targets of hate speech. While it is important to comprehend the utility of transformer-based models, K et al. (2023) suggested that traditional machine learning algorithms can also give a satisfactory performance in hate speech classification. While their algorithm excelled in subtask A, addressing target identification remained challenging for such traditional machine learning approaches. The promising direction for future research is to explore the applications of vision-language models specifically pretrained for the classification of hate speech in text-embedded images of memes.

8 Conclusion

In conclusion, through our shared task at CASE 2024, we were able to contribute to promoting the research and interest in hate speech and target classification in text-embedded images. The shared task was successful in attracting over 50 participants. The participants altogether made over 250 submissions on the test set. The highest performance of F1-score 85.65 was achieved in subtask A and F1-score 76.34 in subtask B. This shows that there is still scope for improvement in the tasks proposed in our shared task. Building on the momentum of this successful shared task, we intend to continue the shared task in the future with more subtasks in languages other than English. This expansion will aim to foster a more inclusive understanding of hate speech detection that goes beyond linguistic and cultural boundaries.

Acknowledgments

The organizers would like to thank Fiona Anting Tan (National University of Singapore) for her technical assistance in setting up the codalab. Additionally, we express our sincere appreciation to the reviewers who provided important feedback on the system description papers.

References

Surabhi Adhikari, Surendrabikram Thapa, Priyanka Singh, Huan Huo, Gnana Bharathy, and Mukesh Prasad. 2021. A comparative study of machine learning and nlp techniques for uses of stop words by patients in diagnosis of alzheimer's disease. In *2021 International Joint Conference on Neural Networks (IJCNN)*, pages 1–8. IEEE.

Firoj Alam, Stefano Cresci, Tanmoy Chakraborty, Fabrizio Silvestri, Dimiter Dimitrov, Giovanni Da San Martino, Shaden Shaar, Hamed Firooz, and Preslav Nakov. 2022. A survey on multimodal disinformation detection. In *Proceedings of the 29th International Conference on Computational Linguistics*, pages 6625–6643.

Fatimah Alzamzami, Mohamad Hoda, and Abdulmotaleb El Saddik. 2020. Light gradient boosting machine for general sentiment classification on short texts: a comparative evaluation. *IEEE access*, 8:101840–101858.

Jesus Armenta-Segura, César Jesús Núñez-Prado, Grigori Olegovich Sidorov, Alexander Gelbukh, and Rodrigo Francisco Román-Godínez. 2023. Ometeotl@Multimodal Hate Speech Event Detection 2023: Hate speech and text-image correlation detection in real life memes using pre-trained bert models over text. In *Proceedings of the 6th Workshop on Challenges and Applications of Automated Extraction of Socio-political Events from Text (CASE)*, Varna, Bulgaria (Hybrid). Association for Computational Linguistics.

V Kishore Ayyadevara and V Kishore Ayyadevara. 2018. Gradient boosting machine. *Pro machine learning algorithms: A hands-on approach to implementing algorithms in python and R*, pages 117–134.

Abdul Aziz, MD. Akram Hossain, and Abu Nowshed Chy. 2023. CSECU-DSG@Multimodal Hate Speech Event Detection 2023: Transformer-based multimodal hierarchical fusion model for multimodal hate speech detection. In *Proceedings of the 6th Workshop on Challenges and Applications of Automated Extraction of Socio-political Events from Text (CASE)*, Varna, Bulgaria (Hybrid). Association for Computational Linguistics.

Aashish Bhandari, Siddhant B Shah, Surendrabikram Thapa, Usman Naseem, and Mehwish Nasim. 2023. Crisishatemm: Multimodal analysis of directed and undirected hate speech in text-embedded images from russia-ukraine conflict. In *Proceedings of the IEEE/CVF Conference on Computer Vision and Pattern Recognition*, pages 1993–2002.

Leo Breiman. 2001. Random forests. *Machine learning*, 45:5–32.

Rui Cao, Roy Ka-Wei Lee, Wen-Haw Chong, and Jing Jiang. 2022. Prompting for multimodal hateful meme classification. In *Proceedings of the 2022 Conference on Empirical Methods in Natural Language Processing*, pages 321–332.

Hsinchun Chen and David Zimbra. 2010. Ai and opinion mining. *IEEE Intelligent Systems*, 25(3):74–80.

Keyu Chen, Ashley Feng, Rohan Aanegola, Koustuv Saha, Allie Wong, Zach Schwitzky, Roy Ka-Wei Lee, Robin O'Hanlon, Munmun De Choudhury, Frederick L Altice, et al. 2022. Categorizing memes about the ukraine conflict. In *International Conference on Computational Data and Social Networks*, pages 27–38. Springer.

Tianqi Chen and Carlos Guestrin. 2016. Xgboost: A scalable tree boosting system. In *Proceedings of the 22nd acm sigkdd international conference on knowledge discovery and data mining*, pages 785–794.

Anusha Chhabra and Dinesh Kumar Vishwakarma. 2023. A literature survey on multimodal and multilingual automatic hate speech identification. *Multimedia Systems*, pages 1–28.

Corinna Cortes and Vladimir Vapnik. 1995. Support-vector networks. *Machine learning*, 20:273–297.

Aida Mostafazadeh Davani, Mohammad Atari, Brendan Kennedy, and Morteza Dehghani. 2023. Hate speech classifiers learn normative social stereotypes. *Transactions of the Association for Computational Linguistics*, 11:300–319.

Alexey Dosovitskiy, Lucas Beyer, Alexander Kolesnikov, Dirk Weissenborn, Xiaohua Zhai, Thomas Unterthiner, Mostafa Dehghani, Matthias Minderer, Georg Heigold, Sylvain Gelly, et al. 2020. An image is worth 16x16 words: Transformers for image recognition at scale. In *International Conference on Learning Representations*.

Sarika Esackimuthu and Prabavathy Balasundaram. 2023. VerbaVisor@Multimodal Hate Speech Event Detection 2023: Hate speech detection using transformer model. In *Proceedings of the 6th Workshop on Challenges and Applications of Automated Extraction of Socio-political Events from Text (CASE)*, Varna, Bulgaria (Hybrid). Association for Computational Linguistics.

Raul Gomez, Jaume Gibert, Lluis Gomez, and Dimosthenis Karatzas. 2020. Exploring hate speech detection in multimodal publications. In *Proceedings of the IEEE/CVF winter conference on applications of computer vision*, pages 1470–1478.

Paulo Cezar de Q Hermida and Eulanda M dos Santos. 2023. Detecting hate speech in memes: a review. *Artificial Intelligence Review*, pages 1–19.

Ali Hürriyetoğlu, Hristo Tanev, Vanni Zavarella, Reyyan Yeniterzi, Osman Mutlu, and Erdem Yörük. 2022. Challenges and applications of automated extraction of socio-political events from text (case 2022): Workshop and shared task report. In *Proceedings of the 5th Workshop on Challenges and Applications of Automated Extraction of Socio-political Events from Text (CASE)*, pages 217–222.

Junhui Ji, Wei Ren, and Usman Naseem. 2023. Identifying creative harmful memes via prompt based approach. In *Proceedings of the ACM Web Conference 2023*, pages 3868–3872.

Liangxiao Jiang, Zhihua Cai, Dianhong Wang, and Siwei Jiang. 2007. Survey of improving k-nearest-neighbor for classification. In *Fourth international conference on fuzzy systems and knowledge discovery (FSKD 2007)*, volume 1, pages 679–683. IEEE.

Avanthika K, Mrithula KL, and Thenmozhi D. 2023. SSN-NLP-ACE@Multimodal Hate Speech Event Detection 2023: Detection of hate speech and targets using logistic regression and svm. In *Proceedings of the 6th Workshop on Challenges and Applications of*

Automated Extraction of Socio-political Events from Text (CASE), Varna, Bulgaria (Hybrid). Association for Computational Linguistics.

Md Rezaul Karim, Sumon Kanti Dey, Tanhim Islam, Md Shajalal, and Bharathi Raja Chakravarthi. 2022. Multimodal hate speech detection from bengali memes and texts. In *International Conference on Speech and Language Technologies for Low-resource Languages*, pages 293–308. Springer.

Mohammad Kashif, Mohammad Zohair, and Saquib Ali. 2023. Lexical Squad@Multimodal Hate Speech Event Detection 2023: Multimodal hate speech detection using fused ensemble approach. In *Proceedings of the 6th Workshop on Challenges and Applications of Automated Extraction of Socio-political Events from Text (CASE)*, Varna, Bulgaria (Hybrid). Association for Computational Linguistics.

Jacob Devlin Ming-Wei Chang Kenton and Lee Kristina Toutanova. 2019. Bert: Pre-training of deep bidirectional transformers for language understanding. In *Proceedings of NAACL-HLT*, pages 4171–4186.

Sotiris B Kotsiantis. 2013. Decision trees: a recent overview. *Artificial Intelligence Review*, 39:261–283.

Zhenzhong Lan, Mingda Chen, Sebastian Goodman, Kevin Gimpel, Piyush Sharma, and Radu Soricut. 2019. Albert: A lite bert for self-supervised learning of language representations. In *International Conference on Learning Representations*.

Roy Ka-Wei Lee, Rui Cao, Ziqing Fan, Jing Jiang, and Wen-Haw Chong. 2021. Disentangling hate in online memes. In *Proceedings of the 29th ACM international conference on multimedia*, pages 5138–5147.

Manish Mishra and Monika Srivastava. 2014. A view of artificial neural network. In *2014 international conference on advances in engineering & technology research (ICAETR-2014)*, pages 1–3. IEEE.

Fionn Murtagh. 1991. Multilayer perceptrons for classification and regression. *Neurocomputing*, 2(5-6):183–197.

Usman Naseem, Jinman Kim, Matloob Khushi, and Adam G Dunn. 2023. A multimodal framework for the identification of vaccine critical memes on twitter. In *Proceedings of the Sixteenth ACM International Conference on Web Search and Data Mining*, pages 706–714.

Alexey Natekin and Alois Knoll. 2013. Gradient boosting machines, a tutorial. *Frontiers in neurorobotics*, 7:21.

Todd G Nick and Kathleen M Campbell. 2007. Logistic regression. *Topics in biostatistics*, pages 273–301.

Lucas A Overbey, Scott C Batson, Jamie Lyle, Christopher Williams, Robert Regal, and Lakeisha Williams. 2017. Linking twitter sentiment and event data to monitor public opinion of geopolitical developments and trends. In *Social, Cultural, and Behavioral Modeling: 10th International Conference, SBP-BRiMS 2017, Washington, DC, USA, July 5-8, 2017, Proceedings 10*, pages 223–229. Springer.

Anil Singh Parihar, Surendrabikram Thapa, and Sushruti Mishra. 2021. Hate speech detection using natural language processing: Applications and challenges. In *2021 5th International Conference on Trends in Electronics and Informatics (ICOEI)*, pages 1302–1308. IEEE.

Konstantinos Perifanos and Dionysis Goutsos. 2021. Multimodal hate speech detection in greek social media. *Multimodal Technologies and Interaction*, 5(7):34.

Derek A Pisner and David M Schnyer. 2020. Support vector machine. In *Machine learning*, pages 101–121. Elsevier.

Fabio Poletto, Valerio Basile, Manuela Sanguinetti, Cristina Bosco, and Viviana Patti. 2021. Resources and benchmark corpora for hate speech detection: a systematic review. *Language Resources and Evaluation*, 55(3):477–523.

Shraman Pramanick, Dimitar Dimitrov, Rituparna Mukherjee, Shivam Sharma, Md Shad Akhtar, Preslav Nakov, and Tanmoy Chakraborty. 2021a. Detecting harmful memes and their targets. In *Findings of the Association for Computational Linguistics: ACL-IJCNLP 2021*, pages 2783–2796.

Shraman Pramanick, Shivam Sharma, Dimitar Dimitrov, Md Shad Akhtar, Preslav Nakov, and Tanmoy Chakraborty. 2021b. Momenta: A multimodal framework for detecting harmful memes and their targets. In *Findings of the Association for Computational Linguistics: EMNLP 2021*, pages 4439–4455.

Alec Radford, Jong Wook Kim, Chris Hallacy, Aditya Ramesh, Gabriel Goh, Sandhini Agarwal, Girish Sastry, Amanda Askell, Pamela Mishkin, Jack Clark, et al. 2021. Learning transferable visual models from natural language supervision. In *International conference on machine learning*, pages 8748–8763. PMLR.

Irina Rish et al. 2001. An empirical study of the naive bayes classifier. In *IJCAI 2001 workshop on empirical methods in artificial intelligence*, volume 3, pages 41–46.

Umitcan Sahin, Izzet Emre Kucukkaya, Oguzhan Ozcelik, and Cagri Toraman. 2023. ARC-NLP at Multimodal Hate Speech Event Detection 2023: Multimodal methods boosted by ensemble learning, syntactical and entity features. In *Proceedings of the 6th Workshop on Challenges and Applications of Automated Extraction of Socio-political Events from Text (CASE)*, Varna, Bulgaria (Hybrid). Association for Computational Linguistics.

Umitcan Sahin, Oguzhan Ozcelik, Izzet Emre Kucukkaya, and Cagri Toraman. 2022. Arc-nlp at case 2022 task 1: Ensemble learning for multilingual protest event detection. In *Proceedings of the 5th Workshop on Challenges and Applications of Automated Extraction of Socio-political Events from Text (CASE)*, pages 175–183.

Shivam Sharma, Firoj Alam, Md Shad Akhtar, Dimitar Dimitrov, Giovanni Da San Martino, Hamed Firooz, Alon Halevy, Fabrizio Silvestri, Preslav Nakov, Tanmoy Chakraborty, et al. 2022. Detecting and understanding harmful memes: A survey. In *Proceedings of the Thirty-First International Joint Conference on Artificial Intelligence*, pages 5597–5606.

Karanpreet Singh, Vajratiya Vajrobol, and Nitisha Aggarwal. 2023. IIC_Team@Multimodal Hate Speech Event Detection 2023: Detection of hate speech and targets using xlm-roberta-base. In *Proceedings of the 6th Workshop on Challenges and Applications of Automated Extraction of Socio-political Events from Text (CASE)*, Varna, Bulgaria (Hybrid). Association for Computational Linguistics.

Christian Szegedy, Vincent Vanhoucke, Sergey Ioffe, Jon Shlens, and Zbigniew Wojna. 2016. Rethinking the inception architecture for computer vision. In *Proceedings of the IEEE conference on computer vision and pattern recognition*, pages 2818–2826.

Surendrabikram Thapa, Aditya Shah, Farhan Ahmad Jafri, Usman Naseem, and Imran Razzak. 2022. A multi-modal dataset for hate speech detection on social media: Case-study of russia-ukraine conflict. In *CASE 2022-5th Workshop on Challenges and Applications of Automated Extraction of Socio-Political Events from Text, Proceedings of the Workshop*. Association for Computational Linguistics.

Surendrabikram Thapa, Priyanka Singh, Deepak Kumar Jain, Neha Bharill, Akshansh Gupta, and Mukesh Prasad. 2020. Data-driven approach based on feature selection technique for early diagnosis of alzheimer's disease. In *2020 international joint conference on neural networks (IJCNN)*, pages 1–8. IEEE.

Francielle Vargas, Isabelle Carvalho, Ali Hürriyetoğlu, Thiago A. S. Pardo, and Fabrício Benevenuto. 2023. Socially responsible hate speech detection: Can classifiers reflect social stereotypes? In *Proceedings of the International Conference on Recent Advances in Natural Language Processing*, Varna, Bulgaria.

Francielle Vargas, Fabiana Goes, Isabelle Carvalho, Fabrício Benevenuto, and Thiago Pardo. 2021. Contextual-lexicon approach for abusive language detection. In *Proceedings of the Recent Advances in Natural Language Processing*, pages 1438–1447, Held Online.

William Warner and Julia Hirschberg. 2012. Detecting hate speech on the world wide web. In *Proceedings of the Second Workshop on Language in Social Media*, pages 19–26, Montréal, Canada.

Chuanpeng Yang, Fuqing Zhu, Guihua Liu, Jizhong Han, and Songlin Hu. 2022. Multimodal hate speech detection via cross-domain knowledge transfer. In *Proceedings of the 30th ACM International Conference on Multimedia*, pages 4505–4514.

Fan Yang, Xiaochang Peng, Gargi Ghosh, Reshef Shilon, Hao Ma, Eider Moore, and Goran Predovic. 2019a. Exploring deep multimodal fusion of text and photo for hate speech classification. In *Proceedings of the third workshop on abusive language online*, pages 11–18.

Zhilin Yang, Zihang Dai, Yiming Yang, Jaime Carbonell, Russ R Salakhutdinov, and Quoc V Le. 2019b. Xlnet: Generalized autoregressive pretraining for language understanding. *Advances in neural information processing systems*, 32.

Marcos Zampieri, Shervin Malmasi, Preslav Nakov, Sara Rosenthal, Noura Farra, and Ritesh Kumar. 2019. Predicting the type and target of offensive posts in social media. In *Proceedings of the 17th Annual Conference of the North American Chapter of the Association for Computational Linguistics: Human Language Technologies*, pages 1415–1420, Minnesota, United States.

Yin Zhang, Rong Jin, and Zhi-Hua Zhou. 2010. Understanding bag-of-words model: a statistical framework. *International journal of machine learning and cybernetics*, 1:43–52.

Detecting and Geocoding Battle Events from Social Media Messages on the Russo-Ukrainian War: Shared Task 2, CASE 2023

Hristo Tanev
Joint Research Centre
European Commission
Ispra, Italy
hristo.tanev@ec.europa.eu

Nicolas Stefanovitch
Joint Research Centre
European Commission
Ispra, Italy
nicolas.stefanovitch@ec.europa.eu

Andrew Halterman
Michigan State University
Department of Political Science
Michigan, USA
ahalterman0@gmail.com

Onur Uca
Sociology Department
Mersin University
Mersin, Turkey
onuruca@mersin.edu.tr

Vanni Zavarella
University of Cagliari
Cagliari, Italy
v.zavarella@unica.it

Ali Hürriyetoğlu
KNAW Humanities
Cluster DHLab
Netherlands
ali.hurriyetoglu@dh.huc.knaw.nl

Bertrand De Longueville
Joint Research Centre
European Commission
Ispra, Italy
bertrand.de-longueville@ec.europa.eu

Leonida Della Rocca
Engineering S.p.A.
Rome, Italy
leonida.della-rocca@ext.jrc.ec.europa.eu

Abstract

The purpose of the shared task 2 at the Challenges and Applications of Automated Extraction of Socio-political Events from Text (CASE) 2023 workshop was to test the abilities of the participating models and systems to detect and geocode armed conflicts events in social media messages from Telegram channels reporting on the Russo Ukrainian war. The evaluation followed an approach which was introduced in CASE 2021 (Giorgi et al., 2021): For each system we consider the correlation of the spatio-temporal distribution of its detected events and the events identified for the same period in the ACLED (Armed Conflict Location and Event Data Project) database (Raleigh et al., 2010). We use ACLED for the ground truth, since it is a well established standard in the field of event extraction and political trend analysis, which relies on human annotators for the encoding of security events using a fine grained taxonomy. Two systems participated in this shared task, we report in this paper on both the shared task and the participating systems.

1 Introduction

Automatic discovery of an event's location is an important sub-task of event extraction: most events occur at a defined location, reported in text. Usually the event time can be guessed by the time of the publication of the news article or the social media post and the presence of temporal adverbs. However, it is far more difficult to detect the location: multiple events can be reported in the same story, each with potentially no, one, or multiple locations mentioned in the text (Halterman, 2019; Radford, 2021; Akdemir et al., 2018).

Event geoparsing, as distinguished from simple geoparsing, is an important part of the event extraction process (Halterman, 2019; Dewandaru et al., 2020; Halterman, 2023). The purpose of this shared task was to provide a real-world evaluation of event geoparsing and challenge the researchers, working on event detection, to propose solutions for event geocoding. Another critical aspect of this evaluation is the comparison between automated and manually curated datasets in line with Giorgi

Proceedings of the 6th Workshop on Challenges and Applications of Automated Extraction of Socio-political Events from Text, pages 160–166, Varna, Bulgaria, Sep 7, 2023.
https://doi.org/10.26615/978-954-452-089-2_021

et al. (2021) and Zavarella et al. (2022).

Our evaluation methodology is based on spatio-temporal correlation, using the PRIO GRID geographical cells (Tollefsen et al., 2012): We measured the correlation between the geographical cells in which armed clashes were detected by the participating systems and the cells containing events from the gold standard data. Details about the evaluation methodology are given in the section *Data set and evaluation methodology*.

In the previous two years the shared task has featured protest events with complex geographical patterns. This year data, referring to Russo Ukrainian conflict, features battles situated along the Russian Ukrainian border.

Conflict has a different structure than protest. Protests are followed instantly by journalists, there is a civilian population, you can get information about the same protest from different news sources. In a military conflict it is difficult to access information as there is much less reporting from open source. And the information is often unreliable and imprecise. Conflict or their shape and size can be hidden or difficult to assess. All these are the main reasons why this work is both valuable and difficult.

This year we had two submissions, which used two different paradigms to event detection, exhibiting different behaviour: The TMA system, a combination of transformer-based classification model and a geoparser, which achieved better correlation and NEXUS, a rule based system also combined with a geoparser.

2 Related work

Socio-political event extraction (SPE) has long been a challenge for the natural language processing (NLP) community, as reflected in previous editions of the Challenges and Applications of Automated Extraction of Socio-political Events from Text (CASE) workshops (Hürriyetoğlu et al., 2022). Specifically, event extraction in the security domain has been identified as an important application area in the automatic information retrieval domain (Best et al., 2008). Similarly, deriving geolocated information from social networks has been seen early identified as an application-rich discipline (Intagorn et al., 2010; De Longueville et al., 2010). Despite the fact that detection and geocoding of events from social media sources have been studied for more than a decade, the field is still vibrant and innovative as advances in Artificial Intelligence make new approaches possible, and as the evolution of the Web and its social media services constitute a "moving target" for automatic information extraction efforts.

3 Data

The goal of this task is to evaluate the performance of automatic discovery of event locations systems on modeling the spatial and temporal patterns of violence in the Russo-Ukrainian War. The data consists of Telegram messages from channels reporting about developments in the Russo-Ukrainian war. We evaluate the capability of participant systems to reproduce the manually curated Russo-Ukrainian War-related dataset.

3.1 Input Data

We provided one collection of English-language messages from Telegram channels with a large number of followers and constant broadcasts about the Russo-Ukraine war. The data was scraped using the official API from Telegram.

Telegram Telegram is the most important social media of data for this topic as it is very popular in the belligerant countries: Russia ranks second in the world in terms of Telegram users (24.15 million) and Ukraine ranks eighth (7.02 million). Data was scraped from Russian and Ukrainian Telegram accounts with a large number of followers who posted messages in English using the official Telegram API. We gathered nearly 326K original English Telegram Massages from Telegram Channels. Table 1 shows the Telegram Channels used and the number of followers.

Intel Slava Z	418 374 subscribers
MoD Russia	95 788 subscribers
Ukraine NOW	157 719 subscribers
Pravda_Gerashchenko_en	24 003 subscribers
UKR LEAKS_eng	52 226 subscribers
Ukraine Today	21 545 subscribers

Figure 1: Telegram Channels (verified channels) - (English Language)

The date ranges of the Telegram data and the date ranges of the gold standard are the same. The date range of Telegram data is February 24, 2022 / August 24, 2022

3.2 Gold Standard Data

The Armed Conflict Location and Event Data Project (ACLED) collects real-time data on the locations, dates, actors, fatalities, and types of all reported political violence and protest events around the world. The data ACLED collects is detailed and manually curated. For this study, we have used ACLED data from the date range: February 24, 2022 / August 24, 2022, and considered as events only the events located in Ukraine with the `Battle` event type. After the specified edits, we have an ACLED data set of 18K rows. This dataset was used as the gold standard data for the study.

We challenged the participant systems to reproduce the Gold Standard data set from ACLED's Curated Data comprising curated disorder events directly related to the Russo-Ukrainian War.

4 Evaluation

The performance of event geolocation is evaluated by computing correlation coefficients on event counts aggregated on cell-days, using uniform grid cells of approximately 55 kilometers sides from the PRIO-GRID data set (Tollefsen et al., 2012). We use these analytical measures as a proxy to the spatio-temporal pattern of violence in the Russo-Ukrainian War.

4.1 Metrics

We use the cell-days counts for two different analysis: the correlation with the total daily "Battle cell" counts (i.e., time trends alone) and the event counts for each cell-day (i.e., spatial and temporal trends together).

Temporal Trends The first analysis only considers the total number of "activated" cells (i.e., for which at least one Battle typed event was recorded), in the system output and Gold Standard data set. This time series analysis is sufficient to estimate how well the automatic systems capture the time trends of the conflict. However, it does not compute accuracy of system data in estimating the spatial variation of the target process.

Spatial and Temporal Trends We also measure the correlation coefficients on the absolute event counts with respect to Gold Standard, over each single cell-day.

For both analyses, we use two types of correlation coefficients to assess variable's relationship: Pearson coefficient r and Spearman's rank correlation coefficient ρ. Moreover, we used Root Mean Squared Error (RMSE) to measure the absolute value of the error on estimating cell/event counts from the Gold Standard.

5 Participating systems

5.1 XLM-RoBERTa and NEROne

The **TMA** system was composed of two modules: event classification and geolocation. The classifier was a `xml-roberta-small` (Liu et al., 2019) transformer model fine tuned using data from the ACLED dataset on all the 26 fine-grained classes using a batch size of 32 and 3 epochs. The training data was sampled over several years over 800k availlable data point in such a way to avoid highly skewed distribution: a maximum of 1k data points for each category, which resulted in a relatively small dataset of 23.6k datapoints and also lead to using the small version of the model instead of the large one.

The geolocation was performed using the NEROne system (Steinberger and Pouliquen, 2007) which is mulitlingual system based on the geonames dataset[1] with flexible matching and linking capacities, and which is able to provide the 3-levels of geographical information as expected by the scorer. Moreover, NEROne is able to guess the most likely place name among all the different geographical entities mentioned in a text.

An event was reported for a given text only if the ACLED type matched any label under `Battle` event type, and if a most likely place name was identified and it was located in Ukraine, moreover only entities for which the 3 levels of geolocation were predicted were considered. NEROne has the possibility to detect time expressions in a text, whenever that was the case, the date reported by NEROne was used, otherwise the publication date was considered.

5.2 NEXUS and Mordecai3

NEXUS is a multilingual event extraction system (Tanev et al., 2008) in the domain of conflict and disasters. It exploits language resources which are learned semi-automatically (Tanev et al., 2009). NEXUS is running as a module inside the Europe Media Monitor (EMM) (Best et al., 2005). In this shared task, however, we have run NEXUS as a standalone system, in order to discovers armed conflicts, reported in these posts. Regarding the spatio-temporal components of the detected events, NEXUS uses as event time, the time when the post

[1] http://www.geonames.org/

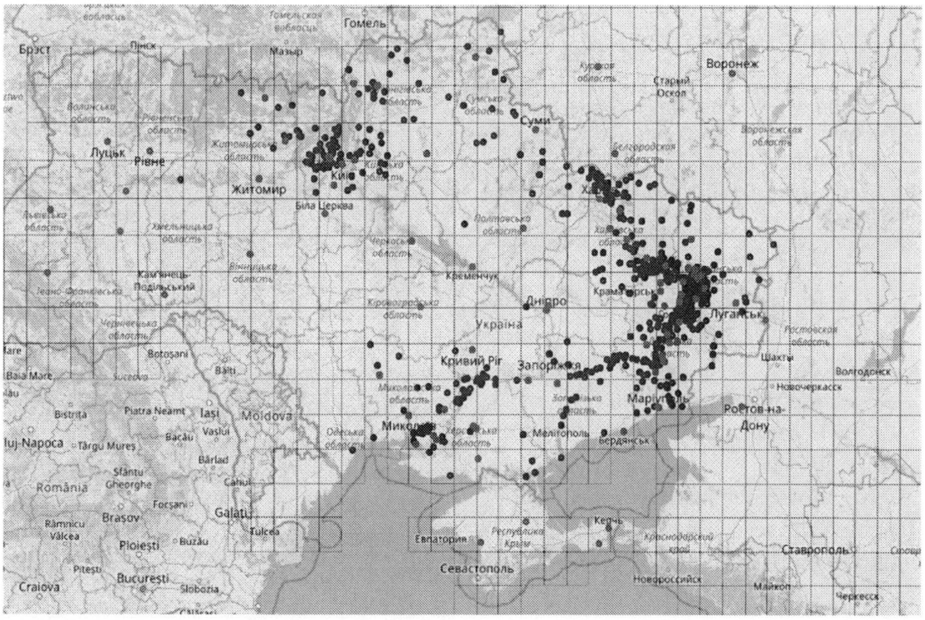

Figure 2: The geo-referenced Ukraine-Russo conflict records from Gold Standard (small blue dots) overlaid with the PRIO-GRID cells over the Ukraine.The red dots represent events recognized by the XLM-RoBERTa classification model and NERone system from Telegram.

was published, while the location is detected with the Mordecai3 geoparser (Halterman, 2023).

NEXUS classifies news articles and social media posts into a taxonomy of security related events, disasters, and humanitarian crises. Among the security related event classes, the system is capable of detecting military events, such as *battles*, *air attacks* and *shelling*, *criminal events*, such as robbery, kidnapping, murder, rape, assault, cyberattacks, as well as legal events such as trial and arrest.

Apart from the event type, location and time, NEXUS also detects other event metadata, such as conflict and crime perpetrators, dead and injured victims, kidnapped people, arrested, and displaced during war and disaster. Figure 3 shows an overview of the NEXUS event template.

Event classification is performed through AND/OR combinations of keywords, learned through weakly supervised multilingual terminology learning (Tanev, 2022). For the English language NEXUS uses a statistical SVM classifier, whose output is combined with the keyword classification, using empirically derived heuristics.

For our shared task run we filtered only the news which contain events of type *Armed conflict*, which is the NEXUS equivalent of the ACLED *Battle*.

Mordecai3 (Halterman, 2023) is an event geoparser that employs a two-step process for identifying an event's locations and resolving them to their geographic coordinates. First, it identifies all place names in the input text using named entity recognition and attempts to resolve each to their entry in the Geonames gazetteer (Wick and Boutreux, 2011). As features, it uses string and vector similarity between the extracted placenames and candidate geolocations from the Geonames gazetteer, along with contextual information from the other placenames present in the text. It uses these features in a neural networked trained on several thousand labeled events to select the best entry from Geonames. To conduct the second step of linking events and

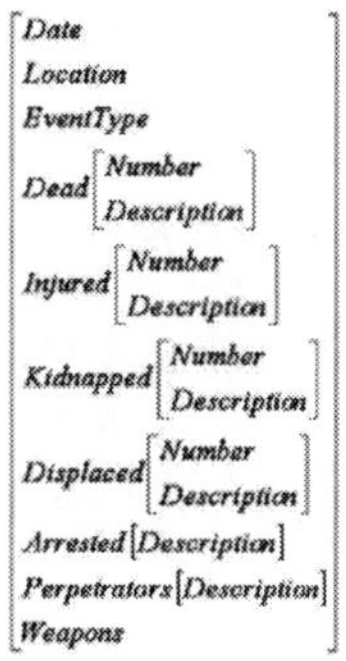

Figure 3: Event template generated by the NEXUS event extraction system

	r	ρ	RMSE
NexMor3	0.127	0.155	98.70
TMA	0.338	0.295	73.40

Table 1: Correlation coefficients and error rates for daily Battle cell counts: r represents Pearson correlation coefficient, ρ is Spearman's rank correlation coefficient, and RMSE is the Root Mean Squared Error computed on day-cell units.

locations, it uses a fine-tuned question answering model (Halterman et al., 2023) that asks variations of "Where did [event] take place?" and identifies the location names that overlap with the answer span. Mordecai3 can identify multiple locations for a single event if they are present.

Only Telegram documents with ArmedConflict events (the NEXUS' counterpart of ACLED's Battle) identified with NEXUS were processed with Mordecai3.

6 Results

Table 1 shows the Pearson r, Spearman correlation coefficient ρ and Root Mean Squared Error (RMSE) of the total daily "Battle cell" counts of the two participant systems with respect to the Gold Standard, over the 6 months target time range. Here, the correlations are between the total number of cells per day where the system found an event vs. the number of cells where an event happened according to the Gold Standard (i.e., temporal patterns and not spatial patterns). These correlation measures are tolerant to errors in geocoding (as long as the events are located in Ukraine) and estimate the capability of the systems to detect from the source texts the evolution over time of the military clash events, independent of their location. We see that TMA system largely outperforms the Nexus-Mordecai3 system (*NexMor3* in the table) in both Pearson r and Spearman ρ coefficients.

Table 2 reports Pearson r, Spearman correlation coefficient ρ, and Root Mean Squared Error (RMSE) over cell-day event counts of the two participant systems with respect to Gold Standard, for the 6 months time range. Here the variables range over the whole set of PRIO-GRID cells included in the Ukraine territory and, thus, shows the correlation of event numbers across geo-cells, thus evaluating the systems' geolocation capabilities. The correlation scores for this metrics are in the lower to insignificant range as well for both systems, with a noticeable prevalence of TMA over Nexus-Mordecai3.

	r	ρ	RMSE
NexMor3	0.083	0.088	0.002
TMA	0.180	0.196	0.002

Table 2: Correlation coefficients and error rates for *cell-day* event counts of the Baseline and participant systems with respect to Gold Standard.

In Figure 4 and 5 we plot the time series of total daily Battle cells for the Gold Standard and TMA and Nexus-Mordecai3 systems, respectively. Only the TMA system seems to slightly capture the variation in the temporal pattern (i.e., an initial large number of Battle events which gradually declines, with recurrent escalations), but both system systems detect only a fraction of the events: While the average number of event per day is ca 10, the average number of event detected by the TMA system is around 2.5.

A more lenient representation of the agreement with Gold Standard is shown in Table 3. Here we report the confusion matrix between grid cells that Gold Standard and system runs code as experiencing at least a Battle event. It can be observed that only few of the cells classified as Battle by Gold Standard are detected by the automatic systems, which on the other hand incorrectly classified as Battle several additional cells.

6.1 Discusion

The correlations with the Gold standard obtained by both systems in this year shared tasks were much lower than the performance of the systems in the 2021 issue of same task, when data from the Black Lives Matter protests (Giorgi et al., 2021) were used as a Gold standard. Moreover, the Nexus system was also used in this 2021 shared task issue, achieving six times higher temporal correlation with the Gold standard than on the data from Russo Ukrainian conflict. This clearly shows that detecting and geolocating battles from the Russo Ukrainian war was far more challenging than replicating the data from Black Lives Matter protests. Table 3 shows that both systems have very low recall 2% and 9.3% and overall poor performances. There are several potential reasons for could lead to these results outside the intrinsic performance of each system: a) it could be that the data sample from Telegram channel did not contain the actual information allowing to recover the information present in the ACLED dataset; b) it could be that the data is unverified or biased, as such the systems are penalized even if the correctly detect the event

		Gold Standard		Precision	Recall	F1
		true	false			
TMA	true	157	220	0.416	0.093	0.152
	false	1530	2435255			
NexMor3	true	39	75	0.34	0.02	0.04
	false	1648	2435400			

Table 3: Confusion matrix of grid cells experiencing at least one Battle event (true) versus inactive cells (false), for the Gold Standard and the participant systems.

and the location contained in a message. Properly assessing these will require further research.

The TMA system performs better at event classification, this could be due to the fact that it is a state of the art transformer-based model, but also the fact that it was trained on ACLED data, therefore having trained to detect the very types in the ground trurth could also play a role. It is not possible to assess properly which geoparser was the most efficient as the correlation as reported location depend on detected events.

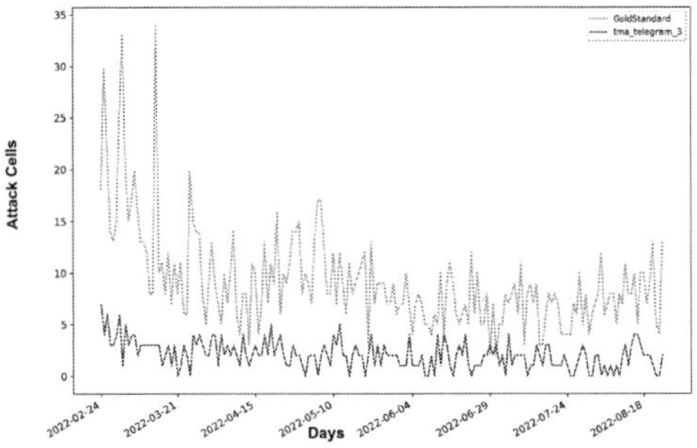

Figure 4: Time series of total daily Battle cells from the Gold Standard (in yellow) against TMA XLM RoBERTa/NERone runs on Telegram input data (in green).

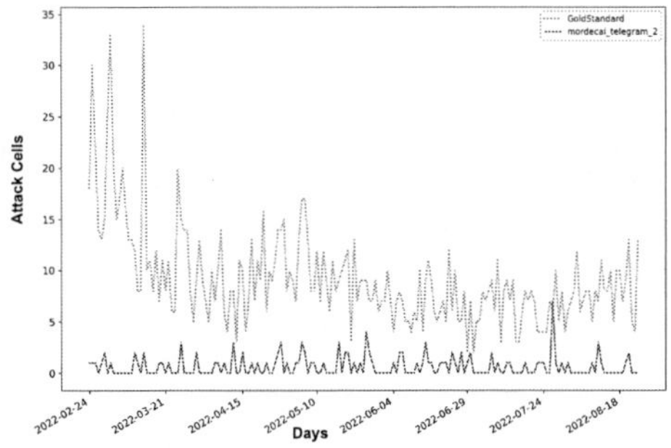

Figure 5: Time series of total daily Battle cells from the Gold Standard (in yellow) against NEXUS-Mordecai3 system runs on Telegram input data (in green).

7 Conclusions

The purpose of the database replication shared task is to provide a flexible benchmark for evaluation and comparison between event geocoding systems without annotated corpus of events and locations.

This year we tested the capabilities of the event detection systems to detect and geolocate battles event type in the Russo-Ukrainian war from Telegram messages in English, comparing the extracted events against a subset of the ACLED database, dedicated to the war in Ukraine. Two systems participated this year: Each system was an aggregation of two subsystems - event detection and classification and a geoparser, based on different paradigms.

The first system was a combination of Nexus and the Mordecai3 geoparser and the second consisted of event classifier based on XLM-RoBERTa combined with NERone geoparser. XLM RoBERTa and NERone obtained much better correlation in both evaluation scenarios: temporal and spacio-temporal.

A conclusion from this year shared task is that tracking armed conflicts is a challenging task, due to the incompleteness of the information: biased because of political consideration or unavailable because of security reasons, and in most case difficult to verify. Nevertheless, one of the participating systems achieved a medium level of correlation, which is a satisfactory result, given the difficulty of this year task.

References

Arda Akdemir, Ali Hürriyetoğlu, Erdem Yörük, Burak Gürel, Çağri Yoltar, and Deniz Yüret. 2018. Towards generalizable place name recognition systems: Analysis and enhancement of ner systems on english news from india. In *Proceedings of the 12th Workshop on Geographic Information Retrieval*, GIR'18, New York, NY, USA. Association for Computing Machinery.

Clive Best, Jakub Piskorski, Bruno Pouliquen, Ralf Steinberger, and Hristo Tanev. 2008. Automating event extraction for the security domain. In *Intelligence and Security Informatics*.

Clive Best, Erik van der Goot, Ken Blackler, Teófilo Garcia, and David Horby. 2005. Europe media monitor. *Technical Report EUR221 73 EN, European Commission*.

Bertrand De Longueville, Gianluca Luraschi, Paul Smits, Stephen Peedell, and Tom De Groeve. 2010. Citizens as sensors for natural hazards: A vgi integration workflow. *Geomatica*, 64(1):41–59.

Agung Dewandaru, Dwi Hendratmo Widyantoro, and Saiful Akbar. 2020. Event geoparser with pseudo-location entity identification and numerical argument extraction implementation and evaluation in indonesian news domain. *ISPRS International Journal of Geo-Information*, 9(12):712.

Salvatore Giorgi, Vanni Zavarella, Hristo Tanev, Nicolas Stefanovitch, Sy Hwang, Hansi Hettiarachchi, Tharindu Ranasinghe, Vivek Kalyan, Paul Tan, Shaun Tan, Martin Andrews, Tiancheng Hu, Niklas Stoehr, Francesco Ignazio Re, Daniel Vegh, Dennis Atzenhofer, Brenda Curtis, and Ali Hürriyetoğlu. 2021. Discovering black lives matter events in the United States: Shared task 3, CASE 2021. In *Proceedings of the 4th Workshop on Challenges and Applications of Automated Extraction of Socio-political Events from Text (CASE 2021)*, pages 218–227, Online. Association for Computational Linguistics.

Andrew Halterman. 2019. Geolocating political events in text. In *Proceedings of the Third Workshop on Natural Language Processing and Computational Social Science, 17th Annual Conference of the North American Chapter of the Association for Computational Linguistics (NAACL)*, pages 29–39.

Andrew Halterman. 2023. Mordecai3: A neural geoparser and event geolocator. *working paper*.

Andrew Halterman, Philip A Schrodt, Andreas Beger, Benjamin E Bagozzi, and Grace Scarborough. 2023. Creating custom event data without dictionaries: A bag-of-tricks. *International Studies Association Conference Paper*.

Ali Hürriyetoğlu, Hristo Tanev, Vanni Zavarella, Reyyan Yeniterzi, Osman Mutlu, and Erdem Yörük. 2022. Challenges and applications of automated extraction of socio-political events from text (case 2022): Workshop and shared task report.

Suradej Intagorn, Anon Plangprasopchok, and Kristina Lerman. 2010. Harvesting geospatial knowledge from social metadata. In *ISCRAM*.

Yinhan Liu, Myle Ott, Naman Goyal, Jingfei Du, Mandar Joshi, Danqi Chen, Omer Levy, Mike Lewis, Luke Zettlemoyer, and Veselin Stoyanov. 2019. RoBERTa: A robustly optimized bert pretraining approach. *arXiv:1907.11692*.

Benjamin J. Radford. 2021. Regressing location on text for probabilistic geocoding. In *Proceedings of the 4th Workshop on Challenges and Applications of Automated Extraction of Socio-political Events from Text (CASE 2021)*, pages 53–57, Online. Association for Computational Linguistics.

Clionadh Raleigh, rew Linke, Håvard Hegre, and Joakim Karlsen. 2010. Introducing acled: An armed conflict location and event dataset. *Journal of peace research*, 47(5):651–660.

Ralf Steinberger and Bruno Pouliquen. 2007. Cross-lingual named entity recognition. *Lingvisticæ Investigationes*, 30(1):135–162.

Hristo Tanev. 2022. Ontopopulis, a system for learning semantic classes. In *Proceedings of the 5th International Conference on Computational Linguistics in Bulgaria (CLIB 2022)*, pages 8–12.

Hristo Tanev, Jakub Piskorski, and Martin Atkinson. 2008. Real-time news event extraction for global crisis monitoring. In *Natural Language and Information Systems: 13th International Conference on Applications of Natural Language to Information Systems, NLDB 2008 London, UK, June 24-27, 2008 Proceedings 13*, pages 207–218. Springer.

Hristo Tanev, Vanni Zavarella, Jens Linge, Mijail Kabadjov, Jakub Piskorski, Martin Atkinson, and Ralf Steinberger. 2009. Exploiting machine learning techniques to build an event extraction system for portuguese and spanish. *Linguamática*, 1(2):55–66.

Andreas Forø Tollefsen, Håvard Strand, and Halvard Buhaug. 2012. Prio-grid: A unified spatial data structure. *Journal of Peace Research*, 49(2):363–374.

Marc Wick and C Boutreux. 2011. Geonames. *GeoNames Geographical Database*.

Vanni Zavarella, Hristo Tanev, Ali Hürriyetoğlu, Peratham Wiriyathammabhum, and Bertrand De Longueville. 2022. Tracking COVID-19 protest events in the United States. shared task 2: Event database replication, CASE 2022. In *Proceedings of the 5th Workshop on Challenges and Applications of Automated Extraction of Socio-political Events from Text (CASE)*, pages 209–216, Abu Dhabi, United Arab Emirates (Hybrid). Association for Computational Linguistics.

Challenges and Applications of Automated Extraction of Socio-political Events from Text (CASE 2023): Workshop and Shared Task Report

Ali Hürriyetoğlu
KNAW Humanities Cluster DHLab
name.surname@dh.huc.knaw.nl

Hristo Tanev
European Commission
hristo.tanev@ec.europa.eu

Osman Mutlu
Koc University
omutlu@ku.edu.tr

Surendrabikram Thapa
Virginia Tech
surendrabikram@vt.edu

Fiona Anting Tan
National University of Singapore
tan.f@u.nus.edu

Erdem Yörük
Koc University
eryoruk@ku.edu.tr

Abstract

We provide a summary of the sixth edition of the CASE workshop that is held in the scope of RANLP 2023. The workshop consists of regular papers, three keynotes, working papers of shared task participants, and shared task overview papers. This workshop series has been bringing together all aspects of event information collection across technical and social science fields. In addition to contributing to the progress in text based event extraction, the workshop provides a space for the organization of a multimodal event information collection task.

1 Introduction

Nowadays, the unprecedented quantity of easily accessible data on social, political, and economic processes offers ground-breaking potential in guiding data-driven analysis in social and human sciences and in driving informed policy-making processes. Governments, multilateral organizations, and local and global NGOs present an increasing demand for high-quality information about a wide variety of events ranging from political violence, environmental catastrophes, and conflict, to international economic and health crises (Coleman et al., 2014; Della Porta and Diani, 2015) to prevent or resolve conflicts, provide relief for those that are afflicted, or improve the lives of and protect citizens in a variety of ways. The citizen actions against the COVID measures in the period 2020-2022 and the war between Russia and Ukraine are only two examples where we must understand, analyze, and improve the real-life situations using such data. Finally, these efforts respond to "growing public interest in up-to-date information on crowds" as well. [1]

The workshop Challenges and Applications of Automated Extraction of Socio-political Events from Text (CASE 2023) is held in the scope of the conference Recent Advances in Natural Language Processing (RANLP). CASE 2023 is the sixth edition of a workshop series (Hürriyetoğlu et al., 2022b, 2021b; Hürriyetoğlu et al., 2020).

We provide brief notes about the accepted papers, shared tasks, and keynote speeches in the following sections.

2 Accepted papers

This year, all seven submissions were accepted by the program committee. A quick summary of these papers are provided below.

- Osorio and Vásquez (2023) collect and annotate a dataset in 3 different granularity: whether a document is related to criminal activities, whether each sentence is related to lethal behaviors, and each sentence's membership to 11 predefined categories of events. Following these granularities, the authors design three binary classification tasks and apply numerous non-neural and neural models to the annotated dataset; they observe good performance and provide analysis for data slices with lower performance.

- Tanev and Longueville (2023) discern "main" location, where the event in question occurred, versus "secondary" locations, that provide extra context such as the origin of the protestors and the first event location in a series of protests. They accomplish this by training a BERT model on news articles annotated with the main event location (CASE 2021 shared task news dataset). The secondary locations are all other mentioned locations. They compared their results to that of two SVM models and a baseline that assumes only the first sentence contains the main location. Their model

[1] https://sites.google.com/view/crowdcountingconsortium/faqs

Proceedings of the 6th Workshop on Challenges and Applications of Automated Extraction of Socio-political Events from Text, pages 167–175, Varna, Bulgaria, Sep 7, 2023.
https://doi.org/10.26615/978-954-452-089-2_022

outperformed all other systems with an F1 of 0.8 and accuracy 0.73.

- Delucia et al. (2023) proposes an extension of the Multiple-instance learning (MIL) framework to better handle a common problem in computational social science: given noisy reports from text sources, how can researchers identify if a bag of reports (here, tweets within a country-day) report a true event. The authors show that MIL improves civil unrest detection over methods based on simple aggregation. The experiments conducted on hyperparameters (key instance ratio n and instance supervision b) show an improvement from MIL-n compared to vanilla MIL and other variants by model selection.

- Mbouadeu et al. (2023) This paper studies the news headlines event linking task that given a title of news (typically a sentence), maps it to an event concept from a knowledge graph. The challenge is how to compare different (zero-shot) models' performance. They propose a benchmark for the evaluation and compare multiple models. By comparing three families of approaches (a) similarity based on rule or embeddings, (b) off-the-shelf entity linking tools, and (c) prompting Large Language Models, the authors show that the approach (c) has the best performance even though different approaches could be complementary to each other.

- Slavcheva et al. (2023) presents a semantic model to structure protest event ontology, and provides some general description of the practical work with the Bulgarian data. The paper presents both the modelling framework and the implementation. The model is a practical application of the Unified Eventity Representation (UER) formalism, which is based on the Unified Modeling Language (UML), whose four-layer architecture (i.e., user objects, model, metamodel, and metametamodel) provides flexible means for building the semantic representations of the language units along a scale of generality and specificity.

- Tuparova et al. (2023) proposes a method that extends the detection capability of existing event detection models to new event types. The authors have an experimental setup for few-shot learning when there is a limited training sources. Moreover, they provide several analyses on the experimental results. The main strength is in using low resource (single GPU) in order to fine tune the model in a reasonable time by providing a small set of samples by leveraging the transfer learning feature of the pre-trained model. The performance on the detection of the already known events tends to improve as well.

- Mutlu and Hürriyetoğlu (2023) The paper propose a solution to address the issue of data scarcity in closed-domain event extraction. The proposed solution leverages on the use of a side-product of data annotation campaigns that are the data containing no annotation, by considering this information as a discriminant that improves the extraction performance. The authors propose a multi-task model where they leverage additional data present after the token annotation process. Experiments are well conducted, by showing the efficacy of the method using different gradually decreasing dataset dimensions.

3 Shared tasks

3.1 Task 1: Multilingual Protest News Detection

The performance of an automated system depends on the target event type as it may be broad or potentially the event trigger(s) can be ambiguous. The context of the trigger occurrence needs to be considered as well. For instance, depending on the context, the 'protest' event type may or may not be synonymous with 'demonstration'. Moreover, the hypothetical cases such as future protest plans may need to be excluded from the results. Finally, the relevance of a protest depends on the actors, since only citizen-led events are in the scope of contentious political events. This challenge becomes even harder in a cross-lingual and zero-shot setting where training data are not available in new languages. We tackle the task in four steps and hope state-of-the-art approaches will yield optimal results.

This shared task was announced as a re-run of the same tasks from CASE 2021 (Hürriyetoğlu et al., 2021a) and CASE 2022 (Hürriyetoğlu et al., 2022a). Although it attracted some interest, we did not receive any task description papers for this edition.

3.2 Task 2: Automatically Replicating Manually Created Event Datasets

The purpose of Task 2 is to test the abilities of the event extraction systems to map events on the World map, by finding the locations where they have taken place. This year the subtitle of the task was "Detecting and Geocoding Battle Events from Social Media Messages on the Russo-Ukrainian War": The purpose of the task was to detect armed clash events in Russian and Ukrainian Telegram messages and to geocode them, i.e., find the location of the battles at the level of a populated place (Tanev et al., 2023a).

Until recently, event geocoding has been considered a topic, covered by the works in the area of Geoinformation systems. Only in the last years the NLP community started to consider ML algorithms for geocoding (Halterman, 2023), also in the context of event detection (Tanev et al., 2023b). In this context, we can consider our shared task as an evaluation exercise for such event geocoding systems.

The evaluation of the systems participating at shared task 2 relies on an original evaluation methodology which compares the battle coordinates, found by the systems with the locations of such events from a Gold standard data set.

As a Gold standard this year we used a selected subset of the ACLED event database (Raleigh et al., 2010), covering the first six months start of the Russo - Ukrainian conflict, namely 24 February 2022 - 24 August 2022 and considering only the events of type *battle*.

We provided the participants with English language text messages from Telegram channels originating from Russia and Ukraine. We gathered nearly 326K original English Telegram Massages from six Telegram channels.

The Telegarm data is available from a public Github repository [2].

Two systems participated in this year's evaluation: The top ranked system relied on a combination of a XLMRoberta (Liu et al., 2019) classifier, trained on ACLED, and a rule based geocoder using the JRC NEROne named entity recognition system (Jacquet et al., 2019). The second ranked system used the NEXUS (Tanev et al., 2008) keyword based event classifier and Mordecai3 geoparser (Halterman, 2023).

The first system, based on XLMRoberta, achieved a moderate level of correlation with the ACLED dataset, which is a good result, considering the possibly low coverage of this year Telegram dataset, regarding Russo Ukrainian war.

We hypothesize that there is a low coverage of the Telegram dataset this year, since in the 2021 issue of this task (Giorgi et al., 2021), participating systems achieved much higher correlation with the ACLED Gold standard, including the NEXUS system. The low correlation can be explained with the low coverage of the war, where battles are not always reported in the media, especially in Telegram. There is a lot of imprecise information on the social media and in contrast ACLED gold standard relies on a wide range of verified sources, including radio and TV, and manually curates the data.

Our conclusion from this year database replication task was that social media is not the best source of information about armed conflicts.

3.3 Task 3: Event Causality Identification

Causality is a core cognitive concept and appears in many natural language processing (NLP) works that aim to tackle inference and understanding. We are interested in studying event causality in the news and, therefore, introduce the Causal News Corpus (Tan et al., 2022b). The dataset comprises of 3,767 event sentences extracted from protest event news, that have been annotated with sequence labels on whether it contains causal relations or not. Subsequently, causal sentences are also annotated with Cause, Effect and Signal spans. Two corresponding subtasks were involved in our shared task: In Subtask 1, participants were challenged to predict if a sentence contains a causal relation or not. In Subtask 2, participants were challenged to identify the Cause, Effect, and Signal spans given an input causal sentence. We hope that our shared task promotes research on the topic of detection and extraction of causal events in news.

This year's competition is the second iteration of the shared task, first introduced in 2022 (Tan et al., 2022a), and uses the latest version of the Causal News Corpus (CNC-V2), also known as RECESS (Tan et al., 2023a). As compared to V1 comprising of 160 sentences and 183 relations, the V2 contains 1,981 sentences and 2,754 causal relations for

[2] https://github.com/htanev/RussoUkrainianWarTelegram

Subtask 2. Annotations were also revised for some examples across both subtasks.

Tan et al. (2023b) provides an overview of the work of the ten teams that submitted their results to our competition and the six system description papers that were received. The top F1 score for Subtask 1 was 84.66% by Team DeepBlueAI, who did not submit a description paper. Team InterosML (Patel, 2023) scored a similar high score of 84.36%, and used a two step approach: first pre-training a baseline RoBERTa model with supervised contrastive loss, then fine-tuning the model on Subtask 1 itself. The top F1 score for Subtask 2 was 72.79% by Team BoschAI (Schrader et al., 2023), who used a sequence tagging approach to fine-tune BERT-large and RoBERTa-large, and adapted the target labels to allow prediction of up to three different causal relations per sentence.

3.4 Task 4: Multimodal Hate Speech Event Detection

Hate speech detection is one of the most important aspects of event identification during political events like invasions (Thapa et al., 2022). In the case of hate speech event detection, the event is the occurrence of hate speech, the entity is the target of the hate speech, and the relationship is the connection between the two. Since multimodal content is widely prevalent across the internet, the detection of hate speech in text-embedded images is very important.

Given a text-embedded image, task 4 aims to automatically identify the hate speech and its targets[3]. This task had two subtasks (Thapa et al., 2023). In subtask 1, participants were given a dataset of text-embedded images and the participants had to classify whether the given image contained hate speech or not. It was tasked as a binary classification problem of classifying hate speech and non-hate speech. Similarly, in subtask 2, the participants were given a dataset of hateful text-embedded images where they had to classify what the targets of hate speech were. This subtask was posed as a multi-class classification problem where targets were individual, community, and organization. The dataset curated by Bhandari et al. (2023) was used in this task. More than 50 participants registered for the competition.

Thapa et al. (2023) presents the overview of the performance of 13 teams who submitted their scores in subtask 1 and 10 teams who submitted their scores in subtask 2. The ranking was done on the basis of the macro F1-score. The competition saw a wide range of methodologies ranging from traditional machine learning models to powerful transformer architectures. The first team ARC-NLP (Sahin et al., 2023) proposed an ensemble of multilayer perceptions (for representations from textual and visual encoders) and various boosting algorithms (using syntactical and Bag-of-words representations) for subtask 1. The team was able to score an F1-score of 85.65%. Similarly, for subtask 2, they used Named Entity Recognition (NER) features along with CLIP representations. An ensemble approach similar to subtask 1 was able to give them the first position with an F1-score of 76.34%.

Similarly, many teams used transformer-based approaches. Out of the submitted papers for subtask 1, IIC_Team (Singh et al., 2023) ranked at rank 3 (F1-score 84.63%), Ometeotl (Armenta-Segura et al., 2023) at rank 6 (F1-score of 80.97%), and VerbaVisor (Esackimuthu and Balasundaram, 2023) at rank 8 (F1-score of 78.21%) were able to get the best performances with XLM-Roberta-base, BertForSequence classification, and ALBERT models respectively. All of them used the text extracted from the given dataset of text-embedded images using Google Vision API. In subtask 2, IIC_Team, VerbaVisor, and Ometeotl were able to get the rank of 3 with an F1-score of 69.73%, rank 4 with an F1-score of 68.05% and rank 7 with F1-score of 56.88% respectively with same models used in subtask 1.

Often, the visual information is also necessary. The first team utilized both textual and visual information effectively to get a high F1-score. Two teams viz. CSECU-DSG and LexicalSquad leveraged both textual and visual information. CSECU-DSG (Aziz et al., 2023) used a combination of BERT and vision transformers (ViT) (Dosovitskiy et al., 2020) to leverage textual and visual information respectively. They were able to get an F1-score of 82.48% and 65.30% in subtask 1 and subtask 2 respectively. They were placed at the fifth rank in both subtasks. Similarly, LexicalSquad (Kashif et al., 2023) participated only in subtask 1 where they used XLNet and BERT for textual features and Inception-V3 for visual features. With this combined representation, they were able to get an

[3] https://codalab.lisn.upsaclay.fr/competitions/13087

F1-score of 74.96%. This ranked them at the tenth position in the leaderboard.

Traditional machine learning algorithms were also used by some teams where they performed decently well. SSN-NLP-ACE and ML_Ensemblers used various traditional machine learning approaches. SSN-NLP-ACE (K et al., 2023) used TF-IDF features with SVM (with RBF kernel) to get an F1-score of 78.80% in subtask 1 ranking them in the seventh position in the leaderboard. They used TF-IDF features with logistic regression for subtask 2 which ranked them at eighth position with an F1-score of 52.58%. Similarly, ML_Ensemblers used a variety of algorithms like Naive Bayes, KNN, SVM, and Decision Trees out of which Naive Bayes performed the best in both subtasks with an F1-score of 42.94% and 43.32% in subtask 1 and subtask 2 respectively. They were able to secure the rank of 13 and 9 in subtask 1 and subtask 2 respectively.

4 Keynotes

Three scholars delivered three keynote speeches that are summarized below.

4.1 Using Automated Text Processing to Understand Social Movements and Human Behaviour

Erdem Yörük's keynote will describe two large-scale ERC-funded projects that employs computational social science methods to extract data on protests and public opinion. The first is the Global Contentious Politics Dataset (GLOCON) Project. [4] is the first automated comparative protest event database on emerging markets using local news sources (Duruşan et al., 2022). The countries included in the GLOCON dataset are India, South Africa, Argentina, Brazil and Turkey. Glocon has been created by using natural language processing, and machine learning in order to extract protest data from online news sources. The project develops fully automated tools for document classification, sentence classification, and detailed protest event information extraction that performs in a multi-source, multi-context protest event setting with consistent performances of recall and precision for each country context. GLOCON counts the number of events such as strikes, rallies, boycotts, protests, riots, and demonstrations, i.e. the "repertoire of contention," and operationalizes protest events by various social groups. The project has developed a novel bottom-up methodology that is based on a random sampling of news archives, as opposed to keyword filtering. The high-quality Gold standard corpus is designed in a way that can accommodate context variability from the outset as it is compiled randomly from a variety of news sources from different countries (Hürriyetoğlu et al., 2021; Yörük et al., 2021). The second one, Politus Project, aims at scaling up traditional survey polls for public opinion research with AI-based social data analytics. Politus develops an AI-based innovation that combines quantitative and computational methods to create a data platform that delivers representative, valid, instant, real-time, multi-country, and multi-language panel data on key political and social trends. The project will collect content information from Twitter and process it with AI tools to generate a large set of indicators on political and social trends through its data platform. The deep learning models and NLP tools will be designed from the ground up as language-independent and generalizable systems. The platform will deliver geolocated hourly panel data on demography, ideology, topics, values, and beliefs, behavior, sentiment, emotion, attitudes, and stance of users aggregated at the district level. In this keynote, Dr. Yörük will describe the general methodology of the projects, including data collection, data analysis, and their approach for representativeness, which is based on multilevel regression with post-stratification.

4.2 Bulgarian Event Corpus for the Construction of a Bulgaria-centric Knowledge Graph

The Bulgarian Event Corpus is being constructed within the CLaDA-BG (Bulgarian National Interdisciplinary Research E-Infrastructure for Bulgarian Language and Cultural Heritage Resources and Technologies. In the spirit of European CLARIN and DARIAH) we aim to support researchers in Humanities and Social Sciences (H&SS) to access the necessary datasets for their research. The different types of objects of study, representation and search are integrated on the basis of common metadata and content categories. The approach for interlinking of the datasets is called contextualization. The implementation of contextualization in CLaDA-BG will utilize a common Bulgaria-centered knowl-

[4] https://glocon.ku.edu.tr/

edge graph - BGKG. The knowledge facts within BGKG are constructed around events of different types. Thus, construction of BGKG requires a set of appropriate language resources for training of Bulgarian language pipeline for extraction of events from text documents. A key element within these language resources is the Bulgarian Event Corpus. In the talk I will present the design of the annotation schema, the annotation process, relation to ontologies and RDF representation. We have started with the CIDOC-CRM ontology for the construction of the annotation schema. This ontology provides a good conceptualization of events motivated by the domain of museums which is appropriate for our goals. During the design of the annotation schema, we extended the ontology with new events depending on the content of the corpus. The documents to be annotated were selected from scientific and popular publications of the partners within CLaDA-BG and articles from Bulgarian Wikipedia. The annotation is done on several layers: Named Entities, Events, Roles, Linking, terms and keywords.

4.3 With a little help from NLP: My Language Technology applications with impact on society

Ruslan Mitkov will present original methodologies developed by the speaker, underpinning implemented Language Technology tools which are already having an impact on the following areas of society: e-learning, translation and interpreting and care for people with language disabilities.

The first part of the presentation will introduce an original methodology and a tool for generating multiple-choice tests from electronic textbooks. The application draws on a variety of Natural Language Processing (NLP) techniques which include term extraction, semantic computing and sentence transformation. The presentation will include an evaluation of the tool which demonstrates that generation of multiple-choice tests items with the help of this tool is almost four times faster than manual construction and the quality of the test items is not compromised. This application benefits e-learning users (both teachers and students) and is an example of how NLP can have a positive societal impact, in which the speaker passionately believes. The latest version of the system based on deep learning techniques will also be briefly introduced.

The talk will go on to discuss two other original recent projects which are also related to the application of NLP beyond academia. First, a project, whose objective is to develop next-generation translation memory tools for translators and, in the near future, for interpreters, will be briefly presented. Finally, a project will be outlined which focuses on helping users with autism to read and better understand texts. The speaker will put forward ideas as to what we can do next.

The presentation will finish with a brief outline of the latest (and forthcoming) research topics (to be) which the speaker plans to pursue and his vision on the future NLP applications. In particular, he will share his views as to how NLP will develop and what should be done for NLP to be more successful, more inclusive and more ethical.

5 Conclusion

Many aspects of event information modeling and collection are reported in the scope of CASE 2023. Hosting a shared task that is on multimodal problem and having submissions about languages other than English (e.g., Bulgarian) are distinguishing aspects of this edition.

References

Jesus Armenta-Segura, César Jesús Núñez-Prado, Grigori Olegovich Sidorov, Alexander Gelbukh, and Rodrigo Francisco Román-Godínez. 2023. Ometeotl@multimodal hate speech event detection 2023: Hate speech and text-image correlation detection in real life memes using pre-trained bert models over text. In *Proceedings of the 6th Workshop on Challenges and Applications of Automated Extraction of Socio-political Events from Text (CASE)*, Varna, Bulgaria (Hybrid). Association for Computational Linguistics.

Abdul Aziz, Md. Akram Hossain, and Abu Nowshed Chy. 2023. Csecu-dsg@multimodal hate speech event detection 2023: Transformer-based multimodal hierarchical fusion model for multimodal hate speech detection. In *Proceedings of the 6th Workshop on Challenges and Applications of Automated Extraction of Socio-political Events from Text (CASE)*, Varna, Bulgaria (Hybrid). Association for Computational Linguistics.

Aashish Bhandari, Siddhant B Shah, Surendrabikram Thapa, Usman Naseem, and Mehwish Nasim. 2023. Crisishatemm: Multimodal analysis of directed and undirected hate speech in text-embedded images from russia-ukraine conflict. In *Proceedings of the IEEE/CVF Conference on Computer Vision and Pattern Recognition Workshops*, pages 1993–2002.

Peter T Coleman, Morton Deutsch, and Eric C Marcus. 2014. *The handbook of conflict resolution: Theory and practice*. John Wiley & Sons.

Donatella Della Porta and Mario Diani. 2015. *The Oxford handbook of social movements*. Oxford University Press.

Alexandra Delucia, Mark Dredze, and Anna L. Buczak. 2023. A multi-instance learning approach to civil unrest event detection on twitter. In *Proceedings of the 6th Workshop on Challenges and Applications of Automated Extraction of Socio-political Events from Text (CASE)*, Varna, Bulgaria (Hybrid). Association for Computational Linguistics.

Alexey Dosovitskiy, Lucas Beyer, Alexander Kolesnikov, Dirk Weissenborn, Xiaohua Zhai, Thomas Unterthiner, Mostafa Dehghani, Matthias Minderer, Georg Heigold, Sylvain Gelly, et al. 2020. An image is worth 16x16 words: Transformers for image recognition at scale. In *International Conference on Learning Representations*.

Fırat Duruşan, Ali Hürriyetoğlu, Erdem Yörük, Osman Mutlu, Çağrı Yoltar, Burak Gürel, and Alvaro Comin. 2022. Global contentious politics database (glocon) annotation manuals.

Sarika Esackimuthu and Prabavathy Balasundaram. 2023. Verbavisor@multimodal hate speech event detection 2023: Hate speech detection using transformer model. In *Proceedings of the 6th Workshop on Challenges and Applications of Automated Extraction of Socio-political Events from Text (CASE)*, Varna, Bulgaria (Hybrid). Association for Computational Linguistics.

Salvatore Giorgi, Vanni Zavarella, Hristo Tanev, Nicolas Stefanovitch, Sy Hwang, Hansi Hettiarachchi, Tharindu Ranasinghe, Vivek Kalyan, Paul Tan, Shaun Tan, et al. 2021. Discovering black lives matter events in the united states: Shared task 3, case 2021. In *Proceedings of the 4th Workshop on Challenges and Applications of Automated Extraction of Socio-political Events from Text (CASE 2021)*, pages 218–227.

Andrew Halterman. 2023. Mordecai3: A neural geoparser and event geolocator. *working paper*.

Ali Hürriyetoğlu, Osman Mutlu, Fırat Duruşan, Onur Uca, Alaeddin Gürel, Benjamin J. Radford, Yaoyao Dai, Hansi Hettiarachchi, Niklas Stoehr, Tadashi Nomoto, Milena Slavcheva, Francielle Vargas, Aaqib Javid, Fatih Beyhan, and Erdem Yörük. 2022a. Extended multilingual protest news detection - shared task 1, CASE 2021 and 2022. In *Proceedings of the 5th Workshop on Challenges and Applications of Automated Extraction of Socio-political Events from Text (CASE)*, pages 223–228, Abu Dhabi, United Arab Emirates (Hybrid). Association for Computational Linguistics.

Ali Hürriyetoğlu, Osman Mutlu, Erdem Yörük, Farhana Ferdousi Liza, Ritesh Kumar, and Shyam Ratan. 2021a. Multilingual protest news detection - shared task 1, CASE 2021. In *Proceedings of the 4th Workshop on Challenges and Applications of Automated Extraction of Socio-political Events from Text (CASE 2021)*, pages 79–91, Online. Association for Computational Linguistics.

Ali Hürriyetoğlu, Hristo Tanev, Vanni Zavarella, Jakub Piskorski, Reyyan Yeniterzi, Osman Mutlu, Deniz Yuret, and Aline Villavicencio. 2021b. Challenges and applications of automated extraction of socio-political events from text (CASE 2021): Workshop and shared task report. In *Proceedings of the 4th Workshop on Challenges and Applications of Automated Extraction of Socio-political Events from Text (CASE 2021)*, pages 1–9, Online. Association for Computational Linguistics.

Ali Hürriyetoğlu, Hristo Tanev, Vanni Zavarella, Reyyan Yeniterzi, Osman Mutlu, and Erdem Yörük. 2022b. Challenges and applications of automated extraction of socio-political events from text (CASE 2022): Workshop and shared task report. In *Proceedings of the 5th Workshop on Challenges and Applications of Automated Extraction of Socio-political Events from Text (CASE)*, pages 217–222, Abu Dhabi, United Arab Emirates (Hybrid). Association for Computational Linguistics.

Ali Hürriyetoğlu, Erdem Yörük, Osman Mutlu, Fırat Duruşan, Çağrı Yoltar, Deniz Yüret, and Burak Gürel. 2021. Cross-Context News Corpus for Protest Event-Related Knowledge Base Construction. *Data Intelligence*, 3(2):308–335.

Ali Hürriyetoğlu, Vanni Zavarella, Hristo Tanev, Erdem Yörük, Ali Safaya, and Osman Mutlu. 2020. Automated extraction of socio-political events from news (AESPEN): Workshop and shared task report. In *Proceedings of the Workshop on Automated Extraction of Socio-political Events from News 2020*, pages 1–6, Marseille, France. European Language Resources Association (ELRA).

Guillaume Jacquet, Jakub Piskorski, Hristo Tanev, and Ralf Steinberger. 2019. Jrc tma-cc: Slavic named entity recognition and linking. participation in the bsnlp-2019 shared task. In *Proceedings of the 7th Workshop on Balto-Slavic Natural Language Processing*, pages 100–104.

Avanthika K, Mrithula Kl, and Thenmozhi D. 2023. Ssn-nlp-ace@multimodal hate speech event detection 2023: Detection of hate speech and targets using logistic regression and svm. In *Proceedings of the 6th Workshop on Challenges and Applications of Automated Extraction of Socio-political Events from Text (CASE)*, Varna, Bulgaria (Hybrid). Association for Computational Linguistics.

Mohammad Kashif, Mohammad Zohair, and Saquib Ali. 2023. Lexical squad@multimodal hate speech event detection 2023: Multimodal hate speech detection using fused ensemble approach. In *Proceedings of the 6th Workshop on Challenges and Applications of Automated Extraction of Socio-political Events from Text (CASE)*, Varna, Bulgaria (Hybrid). Association for Computational Linguistics.

Yinhan Liu, Myle Ott, Naman Goyal, Jingfei Du, Mandar Joshi, Danqi Chen, Omer Levy, Mike Lewis, Luke Zettlemoyer, and Veselin Stoyanov. 2019. RoBERTa: A robustly optimized bert pretraining approach. *arXiv:1907.11692*.

Steve Fonin Mbouadeu, Martin Lorenzo, Ken Barker, and Oktie Hassanzadeh. 2023. An evaluation framework for mapping news headlines to event classes in a knowledge graph. In *Proceedings of the 6th Workshop on Challenges and Applications of Automated Extraction of Socio-political Events from Text (CASE)*, Varna, Bulgaria (Hybrid). Association for Computational Linguistics.

Osman Mutlu and Ali Hürriyetoğlu. 2023. Negative documents are positive: Improving event extraction performance using overlooked negative data. In *Proceedings of the 6th Workshop on Challenges and Applications of Automated Extraction of Socio-political Events from Text (CASE)*, Varna, Bulgaria (Hybrid). Association for Computational Linguistics.

Javier Osorio and Juan Vásquez. 2023. Classifying organized criminal violence in mexico using ml and llms. In *Proceedings of the 6th Workshop on Challenges and Applications of Automated Extraction of Socio-political Events from Text (CASE)*, Varna, Bulgaria (Hybrid). Association for Computational Linguistics.

Rajat Patel. 2023. Interosml @ causal news corpus 2023: Understanding causal relationships: Supervised contrastive learning for event classification. In *Proceedings of the 6th Workshop on Challenges and Applications of Automated Extraction of Socio-political Events from Text (CASE)*, Varna, Bulgaria (Hybrid). Association for Computational Linguistics.

Clionadh Raleigh, rew Linke, Håvard Hegre, and Joakim Karlsen. 2010. Introducing acled: An armed conflict location and event dataset. *Journal of peace research*, 47(5):651–660.

Umitcan Sahin, Izzet Emre Kucukkaya, Oguzhan Ozcelik, and Cagri Toraman. 2023. Arc-nlp at multimodal hate speech event detection 2023: Multimodal methods boosted by ensemble learning, syntactical and entity features. In *Proceedings of the 6th Workshop on Challenges and Applications of Automated Extraction of Socio-political Events from Text (CASE)*, Varna, Bulgaria (Hybrid). Association for Computational Linguistics.

Timo Pierre Schrader, Simon Razniewski, Lukas Lange, and Annemarie Friedrich. 2023. Boschai @ causal news corpus 2023: Robust cause-effect span extraction using multi-layer sequence tagging and data augmentation. In *Proceedings of the 6th Workshop on Challenges and Applications of Automated Extraction of Socio-political Events from Text (CASE)*, Varna, Bulgaria (Hybrid). Association for Computational Linguistics.

Karanpreet Singh, Vajratiya Vajrobol, and Nitisha Aggarwal. 2023. IIC_Team@multimodal hate speech event detection 2023: Detection of hate speech and targets using xlm-roberta-base. In *Proceedings of the 6th Workshop on Challenges and Applications of Automated Extraction of Socio-political Events from Text (CASE)*, Varna, Bulgaria (Hybrid). Association for Computational Linguistics.

Milena Slavcheva, Hristo Tanev, and Onur Uca. 2023. On the road to a protest event ontology for bulgarian: Conceptual structures and representation design. In *Proceedings of the 6th Workshop on Challenges and Applications of Automated Extraction of Socio-political Events from Text (CASE)*, Varna, Bulgaria (Hybrid). Association for Computational Linguistics.

Fiona Anting Tan, Hansi Hettiarachchi, Ali Hürriyetoğlu, Tommaso Caselli, Onur Uca, Farhana Ferdousi Liza, and Nelleke Oostdijk. 2022a. Event causality identification with causal news corpus - shared task 3, CASE 2022. In *Proceedings of the 5th Workshop on Challenges and Applications of Automated Extraction of Socio-political Events from Text (CASE)*, pages 195–208, Abu Dhabi, United Arab Emirates (Hybrid). Association for Computational Linguistics.

Fiona Anting Tan, Hansi Hettiarachchi, Ali Hürriyetoğlu, Nelleke Oostdijk, Tommaso Caselli, Tadashi Nomoto, Onur Uca, Farhana Ferdousi Liza, and See-Kiong Ng. 2023a. RECESS: Resource for extracting cause, effect, and signal spans. In *Proceedings of the 13th International Joint Conference on Natural Language Processing and the 3rd Conference of the Asia-Pacific Chapter of the Association for Computational Linguistics*, Bali, Indonesia. Association for Computational Linguistics.

Fiona Anting Tan, Hansi Hettiarachchi, Ali Hürriyetoğlu, Nelleke Oostdijk, Onur Uca, Surendrabikram Thapa, and Farhana Ferdousi Liza. 2023b. Event causality identification - shared task 3, case 2023. In *Proceedings of the 6th Workshop on Challenges and Applications of Automated Extraction of Socio-political Events from Text (CASE)*, Varna, Bulgaria (Hybrid). Association for Computational Linguistics.

Fiona Anting Tan, Ali Hürriyetoğlu, Tommaso Caselli, Nelleke Oostdijk, Tadashi Nomoto, Hansi Hettiarachchi, Iqra Ameer, Onur Uca, Farhana Ferdousi Liza, and Tiancheng Hu. 2022b. The causal news corpus: Annotating causal relations in event sentences from news. In *Proceedings of the Thirteenth Language Resources and Evaluation Conference*, pages 2298–2310, Marseille, France. European Language Resources Association.

Hristo Tanev and Bertrand De Longueville. 2023. Where "where" matters : Event location disambiguation with a bert language model. In *Proceedings of the 6th Workshop on Challenges and Applications of Automated Extraction of Socio-political Events from Text (CASE)*, Varna, Bulgaria (Hybrid). Association for Computational Linguistics.

Hristo Tanev, Jakub Piskorski, and Martin Atkinson. 2008. Real-time news event extraction for global crisis monitoring. In *Natural Language and Information Systems: 13th International Conference on Applications of Natural Language to Information Systems, NLDB 2008 London, UK, June 24-27, 2008 Proceedings 13*, pages 207–218. Springer.

Hristo Tanev, Nicolas Stefanovitch, Andrew Halterman, Onur Uca, Vanni Zavarella, Ali Hürriyetoğlu, Bertrand De Longueville, and Leonida Della Rocca. 2023a. Detecting and geocoding battle events from social media messages on the russo-ukrainian war: Shared task 2, case 2023. In *Proceedings of the 6th Workshop on Challenges and Applications of Automated Extraction of Socio-political Events from Text (CASE)*. Association for Computational Linguistics (ACL).

Hristo Tanev, Nicolas Stefanovitch, Andrew Halterman, Onur Uca, Vanni Zavarella, Ali Hürriyetoğlu, Bertrand De Longueville, and Leonida Della Rocca. 2023b. Where "where"' matters : Event location identification with a BERT language model. In *Proceedings of the 6th Workshop on Challenges and Applications of Automated Extraction of Socio-political Events from Text (CASE)*. Association for Computational Linguistics (ACL).

Surendrabikram Thapa, Farhan Jafri, Ali Hürriyetoğlu, Francielle Vargas, Roy Ka-Wei Lee, and Usman Naseem. 2023. Multimodal hate speech event detection - shared task 4, case 2023. In *Proceedings of the 6th Workshop on Challenges and Applications of Automated Extraction of Socio-political Events from Text (CASE)*, Varna, Bulgaria (Hybrid). Association for Computational Linguistics.

Surendrabikram Thapa, Aditya Shah, Farhan Ahmad Jafri, Usman Naseem, and Imran Razzak. 2022. A multi-modal dataset for hate speech detection on social media: Case-study of russia-ukraine conflict. In *CASE 2022-5th Workshop on Challenges and Applications of Automated Extraction of Socio-Political Events from Text, Proceedings of the Workshop*. Association for Computational Linguistics.

Elena Tuparova, Petar Ivanov, Andrey Tagarev, Svetla Boytcheva, and Ivan Koychev. 2023. Next: An event schema extension approach for closed-domain event extraction models. In *Proceedings of the 6th Workshop on Challenges and Applications of Automated Extraction of Socio-political Events from Text (CASE)*, Varna, Bulgaria (Hybrid). Association for Computational Linguistics.

Erdem Yörük, Ali Hürriyetoğlu, Fırat Duruşan, and Çağrı Yoltar. 2021. Random sampling in corpus design: Cross-context generalizability in automated multicountry protest event collection. *American Behavioral Scientist*, 0(0):00027642211021630.

Author Index

Association for Computational Linguistics
209 N. Eighth Street
Stroudsburg, Pennsylvania 18360

ISBN 978-1-7138-9047-8

CURRAN ASSOCIATES INC.
proceedings
.com